Nothing Absolute

Series Board

James Bernauer

Drucilla Cornell

Thomas R. Flynn

Kevin Hart

Richard Kearney

Jean-Luc Marion

Adriaan Peperzak

Thomas Sheehan

Hent de Vries

Merold Westphal

Michael Zimmerman

John D. Caputo, *series editor*

PERSPECTIVES IN
CONTINENTAL
PHILOSOPHY

KIRILL CHEPURIN AND
ALEX DUBILET, EDITORS

Nothing Absolute
*German Idealism and the
Question of Political Theology*

FORDHAM UNIVERSITY PRESS
New York ■ *2021*

Copyright © 2021 Fordham University Press

All rights reserved. No part of this publication may be reproduced, stored in a retrieval system, or transmitted in any form or by any means—electronic, mechanical, photocopy, recording, or any other—except for brief quotations in printed reviews, without the prior permission of the publisher.

Fordham University Press has no responsibility for the persistence or accuracy of URLs for external or third-party Internet websites referred to in this publication and does not guarantee that any content on such websites is, or will remain, accurate or appropriate.

Fordham University Press also publishes its books in a variety of electronic formats. Some content that appears in print may not be available in electronic books.

Visit us online at www.fordhampress.com.

Library of Congress Cataloging-in-Publication Data available online at https://catalog.loc.gov.

Printed in the United States of America

23 22 21   5 4 3 2 1

First edition

Contents

    Introduction: Immanence, Genealogy, Delegitimation   *1*
    Kirill Chepurin and Alex Dubilet

1. Knot of the World: German Idealism between Annihilation and Construction   *35*
    Kirill Chepurin

2. Utopia and Political Theology in the "Oldest Systematic Program of German Idealism"   *54*
    S. D. Chrostowska

3. Relational Division   *73*
    Daniel Colucciello Barber

4. Otherwise Than Terror: Ten Theses on the Modernist Secular   *87*
    Daniel Whistler

5. Kant's Unexpected Materialism: How the Object Saves Kant (and Us) from the Moral Law   *104*
    James Martel

6. Earth Unbounded: Division and Inseparability in Hölderlin and Günderrode   *124*
    Joseph Albernaz

7. Kant with Sade with Hegel: The Death of God and the Joy of Reason   *144*
    Oxana Timofeeva

8	A Political Theology of Tolerance: Universalism and the Tragic Position of the Religious Minority *Thomas Lynch*	*160*
9	Hegel, Blackness, Sovereignty *Vincent Lloyd*	*174*
10	Political Theology of the Death of God: Hegel and Derrida *Agata Bielik-Robson*	*188*
11	Exception without Sovereignty: The Kenotic Eschatology of Schelling *Saitya Brata Das*	*207*
12	Once More, from Below: The Concept of Reduplication and the Immanence of Political Theology *Steven Shakespeare*	*223*
13	On the General Secular Contradiction: Secularization, Christianity, and Political Theology *Alex Dubilet*	*240*
	List of Contributors	*257*
	Index	*261*

Nothing Absolute

Introduction
Immanence, Genealogy, Delegitimation

KIRILL CHEPURIN AND ALEX DUBILET

Across its recent renaissance, political theology has remained a notoriously multivalent term, a contested terrain defined by wide-ranging political and theological commitments. What political theology brings conceptually into play, what is theoretically at stake in this interdisciplinary site of inquiry, and what genealogical resources are pertinent to it—all of this is decided on anew with each political-theological investigation. New theoretical engagements repeatedly redraw the entire problematic: the debate is as much within a constituted field named political theology, as it is about the very existence and coherence of the field as such, as well as the status, scope, and significance of its fundamental concepts. There seemingly is no neutral space one could term political theology, concepts being always polemical and neutral space being always only a neutralized one. This instability of definition has made the field at once fecund and elusive, generative and highly contested. Why is the invocation of the name *political theology* significant today? And why invoke it alongside the post-Enlightenment—and also highly generative and debated—movement of thought known as German Idealism?

Political Theology and the Contemporary Moment

Within modern theoretical space, the term *political theology* came into prominence with Carl Schmitt's *Political Theology: Four Chapters on the Concept of Sovereignty* (1922). There we find Schmitt's famous dictum: "All significant concepts of the modern theory of the state are secularized theological concepts not only because of their historical development—in which they were transferred [*übertragen*] from theology to the theory of the state, whereby, for example, the omnipotent God became the omnipotent lawgiver—but also because of their systematic structure."[1] Already at this juncture, a number of key elements cluster around political theology as a problematic: the structural systematic analogy and historical transfer of concepts and operations between the theological and the political realms; the focus on problematizing the supposedly secular character of modernity; and the centrality of transcendence and sovereignty. Of course, the question of secularization, so central to political theology, was not exhausted by the Schmittian frame—it was a *topos* richly debated by such figures as Walter Benjamin, Karl Löwith, Jacob Taubes, and Hans Blumenberg.[2]

Aligning his project explicitly with the Enlightenment tradition, Blumenberg resisted the idea that modernity is the continuation of Christianity by other means, seeing in the idea of secularization an attempt to delegitimate the world of modernity, to reduce it to a cover-up operation of seizing the contents and structures that were originally Christian without acknowledging it. Instead, as the charged title of his groundbreaking study of modernity indicates, Blumenberg sought to legitimate the modern world as a distinct epoch, that of the "immanent self-assertion of reason." In this, he also rejected the term *political theology*, associated by him with Schmitt's delegitimation of modernity in the service of transcendence. And yet, from a broader standpoint, Blumenberg's study itself engages with what may be seen as the central problematic of political theology: the interrogation of the continuities and discontinuities between theological pasts and the secular-modern world.

At one point in the book, polemicizing against Löwith's thesis on the secularization of Christian eschatology in modernity, Blumenberg identifies the beginning of what Löwith sees as the specifically modern secularization process already in early Christianity's neutralization of Jewish apocalypticism. Against the latter's apocalyptic urgency and demand for the immediate end of the world, Christianity made, per Blumenberg, the move of *postponing* the end indefinitely, transforming apocalypticism into eschatology and granting new value to the world itself, precisely as the space between creation and redemption, as the not-yet in which we must live. At another point, Blumenberg traces in detail the emergence of the basic metaphysical structures of the world of modernity—alienation, contingency, self-assertion, the possibility of "immanently" mastering and altering reality—out of and in response to late-medieval nominalism. And, no less importantly, he sees the main task of modernity as the overcoming of

Gnosticism—a characteristic modernity shares, for him, with Christianity. In other words, the structural continuities between the Christian and the modern world are there for Blumenberg as well, even if their implications are distinctly different.[3] The assessment of these structures and implications is precisely at the core of political theology, which continues to this day to interrogate the interactions and interchanges between the Christian and the secular—against any simplistic theories of overcoming, against any easy disburdenment.

The term *political theology* has also elicited fully countervailing understandings. For example, more explicitly theological—predominantly, though not exclusively, Christian—formulations of the problematic have arisen. Here, political theology begins to mean something different: it asks after the politics that form or should form within specific theological traditions, in other words, after the political dimension of the theological— explored under theological rubrics such as natural law, eschatology, justice, or faith. Such positions may disregard the previous debates, or be situated against them, pointing out how Schmitt and others have failed, in their political theology, to be properly theological in one way or another— and offering robustly theological constructions as a corrective and the supposedly more proper way of doing political theology. The politics that emerge as a result vary, but the fundamental questions of these investigations are different from the previously mentioned debates: What are the proper politics of a given theological tradition? What is a suitably theological vision of politics? And yet, these debates often remain provincially and dogmatically theological, failing to problematize the standing and standpoint of theology itself—and hence overlooking Christianity's own imbrications, political and metaphysical, with secular modernity.

In opposition to both, a liberal and secular position has recently come into prominence. From its less sophisticated (Mark Lilla) to its more sophisticated (Victoria Kahn) variants, such a position sees political theology predominantly as the cunning deployment of theological supplements within the realm of the political—rendering political theology a question of transcendent authority and mystification, a question of legitimation, sanctification, and grounding.[4] Equating political theology with the theological legitimation of political authority, as for example Kahn does, produces as its corollary the necessity of its critique: it is produced as a concept against which to polemicize. Kahn rejects wholesale the diagnosis of the political-theological underpinnings of modernity and sees this suggestion as entirely a retrograde "return" that must be resisted.

In positions such as Kahn's, the secular is defended against theological supplements, but the critical purchase of political theology as a discourse is lost. This critical dimension has always sought to reassess modernity, secularity, and politics: not in order to mystify them but in order to prevent them from all-too quickly disburdening themselves of their theological pasts and declaring themselves to be free from theology, enacting a sort of self-mystification through which they appear absolutely novel and free. Broadly liberal positions, whatever their scholarly merits, fail to register that the significance of political theology as a problematic and a discourse lies less in the way it transcendently legitimates power or authority—thereby requiring a self-righteous secular critique that stages a reenactment of the Enlightenment critique of religion—and more in the way it undercuts the triumphalist narratives that secularized modernity produces of itself, shedding critical light on the claims of secular self-legitimation that occur through polemical dissociations from Christianity.

In other words, the task is never as easy as affirming a theological tradition to generate a politics or, by contrast, purifying the political of all theology—this is precisely what political theology as a discourse, at its best, disallows. This dominant binary—which in a way reproduces the Schmitt-Blumenberg opposition between conservative or Christian delegitimations of secular modernity and the quasi-Enlightenment legitimation of its specifically secular character—is not all that political theology offers. Over the last two decades, the field of political theology has reemerged as a fundamentally critical field for exploring the religious entanglements of secular modernity and for uncovering the theological underpinnings of philosophical and political concepts. Rather than a conservative project that seeks the reassertion of transcendent sovereignty, political theology, in this articulation, has entailed new ways of theorizing the status of modernity and secularity and also thereby of rethinking the very nature of the religious-secular binary.[5] At stake is neither a theological grounding of political concepts nor a working out of the politics of specific theological traditions, but a calling into question of modernity's own secularist presuppositions.

What this means in practice is varied. The Italian trajectory offers one important version of such a practice: it carries out a theoretical diagnosis of the apparatus of political theology in order to better trace an exit out of it, but without thereby mistakenly defending a phantasmatic secular politics. On one side of this trajectory, we encounter Giorgio Agamben's retheorization of the relation of sovereign power, the state of exception, and bare life and an outlining of the providential machine of the West.[6] On the other side, we see Roberto Esposito articulate such an exit through a critical reconstruction of the *dispositif* of the person, a theorization of the exteriority of thought to the subject, and a novel rearticulation of the questions of community, life, and immanence vis-à-vis the political-theological paradigm.⁷ Broadly aligned with this theoretical trajectory is a general formation of political theology that includes Alain Badiou's and Slavoj Žižek's recuperation of St. Paul, Antonio Negri's investigation of Job, Catherine Malabou's work on Spinoza and the sacred and, earlier, Michel Foucault's elaboration of pastoral power.⁸ Whatever their difference, for all of these thinkers—across their various projects—the fundamental question is neither a theological legitimation of politics, nor the formation of a purely secular politics, nor a reactivation of a Christian paradigm, but the tracing of complex conceptual morphologies that counteract any easy separation between theology and secular thought.⁹ These projects inquire into some of the fundamental categories of modernity and its forms of self-relation in expansive assemblages and narratives that are not afraid of the powers of the theological and its archives.

Within this general critical orientation, there is a particularly compelling trajectory, one that pursues the delegitimation and ungrounding of the world of modernity without the saving grace of theological recuperation. It endeavors to diagnose the co-imbrication between—and to jointly subvert—the logics of transcendence in their secular as well as their religious forms. It seeks to unground the legitimacy of the world and all salvific and sovereign transcendences—thereby refusing the absolutization of either side of the duality. This kind of political theology from below had its twentieth-century precursors in Benjamin's explorations of divine violence, no less than in Taubes's apocalyptic questioning of the world and its legitimacy. Benjamin's messianism and Taubes's apocalypticism—precisely the kind of apocalypticism that, on Blumenberg's account, both Christianity and modernity foreclose—are irreducible to the Schmitt-Blumenberg opposition, broadly conceived, and delineate positions that remain crucial for ongoing articulations of political theology. Here, political theology amounts to a struggle against the combined interplay of secular and theological transcendences and legitimations, rather than merely the choice of one against the other in perpetual polemical oscillation. We are no longer talking about crises of legitimation, as though the world of which we were a part is coming undone, but rather about a discourse that acknowledges that perhaps this world never should have been granted any legitimacy at all. Or, as Taubes famously declared, in opposition to Schmitt: "Let it go down. I have no spiritual investment in the world as it is."¹⁰

Rather than taking the secular world and what is transcendent to it as the central theoretical opposition, the dividing line must be located elsewhere: between immanence and the entire bipartite apparatus that unites the world and sovereign transcendence. Whatever exactly immanence indicates—and that is, as we will show shortly, a contested terrain—it is, significantly, decoupled from any easy adequation with secularity or the modern world and, as such, no longer serves as an index of its legitimacy. It becomes, instead, a fulcrum for the delegitimation of the world-whole and the subversion of all transcendence—with the remaining theoretical task being the novel articulation of this kind of immanence. To many, this attempt to think immanence as separate and separated from the world, in all of its entanglements with secularity and modernity, will undoubtedly sound foreign and paradoxical. After all, immanence has indexed and named the condition of the modern world, in various ways, for a variety of conflicting positions, from Schmitt to Blumenberg, from Charles Taylor to Radical Orthodoxy, and many others. It is one of the most common tropes in theorizing modernity. And yet, the morphology and thus the force of immanence is more complex than it might appear in the customary identifications of the framework of modernity with immanence and immanentization.

There are different approaches that make clear why, despite being commonly figured as such, immanence cannot be simply equated with secular modernity. First, we should recall the fact that modern secularity is indelibly tied with the rise of the modern nation-state. It was no lesser a figure than Thomas Hobbes that at the origin of political modernity established the conjunction of secular state power with sovereignty and transcendence. Perhaps, if we focus exclusively on the secular, as a domain of sensibilities, behaviors, and ways of knowing, we might think we live in an immanent age; but political modernity, with its ineluctable centrality of the state and sovereign power, has always been deeply imbricated with transcendence. As Hussein Ali Agrama, among others, has taught us to see, secularism—as a political doctrine and mode of statecraft that stresses the state's sovereign and transcendent power to continually produce and reproduce the charged boundary that separates the political from the religious—has been intimately entangled with and even productive of the lived reality of modern secularity.[11] One could not have the latter without the former. Nor is the transcendence of secularism only figured in its sovereign power. As Talal Asad has argued, the production of the citizen-subject—at the expense of other forms of attachment and identity—is based on transcendent mediation, and "in an important sense, this transcendent mediation *is* secularism."[12] Modern secularity, necessarily entailing modern secularism, remains in its core entangled with transcendence—not only through the operations of sovereignty, but also through operations of political mediation.

It is important as well to recall the ways the modern world remains linked with transcendence in its temporalized form, under the rubric of progress. In modernity, the world becomes a (supposedly immanent) field of projects and possibilities that the subject can make use of, actualize, master—and reality thereby becomes *producible*.[13] The modern idea of progress, accordingly, sees the world as the process of such actualization, production, and mastery. This process functions within the horizon of an ideal end point where reality is supposed to be mastered and human life is supposed to be fulfilled or reconciled. Regardless of whether we take it to be attainable or merely regulative, this goal is at once immanent and transcendent, driving it from within toward an external telos. The entire process thereby turns into a process of constant self-transcending—of fixing humanity's gaze on a phantasmic telos of complete mastery, freedom, or fulfillment that is constitutively not-yet. The proliferation of images of utopian futurity in modernity are indicative of such a telos. Modernity structures its immanence with a view to a transcendent future and installs the figure of the subject as the one who masters this future; but the subject thereby is also subjected to and by that transcendent futurity, indeed, only becoming subject (and not a mere object on the path of progress) by means of striving toward the telos of absolute mastery and efficiency, an operation through which the world-process reproduces itself. In this "horizontal transcendence,"[14] the subject is always in the process of self-transcending.[15]

State sovereignty and the not-yet of a transcendent futurity are hardly the only ways to expose the modern world as a transcendent structure. In its explorations of the way the modern world is constituted through coloniality and slavery—and the attendant logics of separation, otherness, enclosure, hierarchization, and exclusion—contemporary work in black studies and decolonial studies offers another. As Sylvia Wynter argues, the birth of the modern world coincides structurally with that of the (transcendent) figure of Man as the new model of being human, with its constitutive exclusion of the non- or sub-human (colonized and racialized) other—a model of the human that reoccupies, politically and theologically, the earlier figure of the Christian. Racialized otherness functions, from the onset of modernity, as the condition of possibility of the modern subject's seemingly immanent self-assertion and universalist self-description, forming "the non-supernatural but no less extrahuman ground," the transcendent beyond to the properly human, "on which the world of modernity was to institute itself." This excluded ground is thereby inscribed into the "new grounds of legitimacy" of the modern world, and the "new notion of the world," as at once the assumption and the production of separation, domination, colonial difference, and other forms of transcendence through which the world of Man goes on to reproduce and legitimate itself. In this, the earth becomes an immanent-transcendent racialized globe—a globality imposed, as it were, from above upon the degraded earth as well as upon the enslaved as the bare earth's inhabitants and structural correlate.[16]

The logic of modern racialized transcendence is further explored in contemporary radical black studies, in the latter's interrogation of the modern world as built on and perpetuating itself through the constitutive exclusion of blackness. Here, blackness indexes what is foreclosed from the modern (human) subject and its concomitant values and logics, including those of coherence, freedom, futurity, and possibility. In the overall distribution of race and the extra-human in modernity, blackness occupies the structural (non-)position of nothingness. As such, blackness becomes the zero point that remains beneath the binaries in and through which the world operates, as that over and against which, by way of obliterating its being, the modern subject and the modern world can assume their transcendent sovereign function.[17] To affirm this nothing or zero point, as some of the central work in radical black studies suggests,[18] is to refuse the regime of being of and in the world that is shown to be intrinsically violent, and to do so without any call for the world's redemption or justification—without and against all attempts (whether religious or secular) to legitimate the world, a legitimacy that is violently imposed upon the excluded, the obliterated, and the enslaved.

Thus, while the modern world may appear as equatable with immanence when narrated by and from various perspective engaged in polemics about theology and secularization, it is exposed, across the spectrum of contemporary critical theory, as a violent transcendent apparatus. In a more abstract register (which should, however, be thought together with the explorations of the modern world's transcendence considered so far), François Laruelle and those inspired by his thought have likewise worked to diagnose the world as a transcendent structure. For Laruelle, the world names the horizon of reality as coherent, rationally cognizable, and supposedly self-sufficient. The world, this transcendental illusion, as Laruelle terms it in a nod to Kant, operates by way of doubling and separation, by way of *dividing* the Real, creating the binaries that structure our thinking, such as light and dark, good and evil, human and nonhuman, which are then (to be) mediated into a coherent whole. This reality is not only divisive but also hierarchical, insofar as one of the binary terms is considered to be higher than the other—and thus a structure of authority and domination, no matter the (philosophical, Christian, or secular) guise it takes. The Real, which is for Laruelle an ante-ontological reality that is prior to the imposition of a world thus understood, is thereby completely foreclosed: the world is, in fact, nothing but a complex apparatus of authorities and decisions that, as it were, colonize and impose themselves upon the Real—an apparatus of desire, exploitation, and conquest. The world is, significantly, a transcendent structure; by contrast, it is the Real, as preceding all division, that Laruelle associates with radical immanence. The philosophical and ethical task becomes, accordingly, to expose the world as an illusion: an imposed construction, an inherently violent demand for coherence and sufficiency, which obscures and excludes the radical immanence of the Real while feeding off of it.[19]

These lines of political-theological reflection put into question the legitimacy and beneficence of the world and its authorities—whether secular or religious—and, by insisting on the unredeemable perspective and role of (the world's) victims, reject the justifications found in theodicy and its secular counterparts. As such, this reactivates what may be termed a Gnostic perspective within the political-theological debate, one that refuses the world and its modalities of justification.[20] This refusal is, in fact, what Gnosticism indexes already in twentieth-century philosophy and political theology, including Blumenberg's characterization of Christianity as the first and modernity as the second overcoming of Gnosticism.[21] In this sense, Gnosticism operates as a generic and transhistorical concept beyond its initial function as an umbrella term for early heresies that variously conceive the creator of the world (known as the demiurge) as malevolent and the world as illegitimate. It names an apocalyptic orientation that radically disinvests from the world and strips it of all legitimacy—an orientation in which all purposefulness of this world's reality, and all sense of this world as worthy of being upheld and invested in, disappears. It was Taubes who most unapologetically claimed the position of antiworldly Gnosticism, and by doing so disclosed an overlooked moment of coincidence between the two seemingly opposite sides structuring the political-theological debates: Schmitt and Blumenberg may have disagreed on everything, but they each display a strong anti-Gnostic tendency. This coincidence suggests that whatever their oppositional and polemical self-situating, sovereignty and the world form a single bipartite mechanism of legitimation.

No less significantly, even though Gnosticism, at least since the classic study by Adolf von Harnack,[22] has been associated with radical transcendence, as soon as the (Christian-modern) world is exposed as an apparatus of transcendence, it becomes possible instead to associate Gnosticism with that which simultaneously opposes the transcendence of the world and of God the creator, and thus with radical immanence. Such is, indeed, an important move performed in contemporary thought from Laruelle onward. In response to the bipartite mechanism of transcendence, the new Gnostic tendency is to immanently refuse the world and to insist instead on a dispossessed and dispossessive immanence, indexing not the way of the world or the subject in the world, but what refuses to take part in what the world declares to be the only possible existence: existence in the service of transcendence, be it God, the sovereign, or the world itself.

This Gnostic immanence may amount to "an eternally alien immanence" (to use Fred Moten's turn of phrase)—a dispossessed nothingness, underneath and prior to any absolutes, that permanently opposes enlightenment and Western regimes of domination from the position of "a radical materiality whose *anima*tion . . . has been overlooked by masterful looking."[23] For Moten, this immanence aligns not with the (secular, colonial) world of the self-possessed subject, but with the earth and the impersonal flesh, for it is "the flesh's dislocative immanence" that contains the capacity to undo the modern imposition of property and the proper.[24] Moten's discourse makes us attuned to "an irreducibly material immanence, of that which lies below"[25]—and to the fact that this immanence not only ungrounds the world-whole, but is the underground, the improper, the underneath of the world, an "anoriginal dispossession . . . the undercommons."[26]

Moten's thought suggests one avenue of exploration for what happens when immanence does not merely designate the secular world of modernity and the self-transcending, self-possessed subject acting in that world—but, freed from this adequation, immanence opens in a number of diverse directions. One could think here of Denise Ferreira da Silva, who theorizes a Deleuzian-Leibnizian immanence of "plenum" as a way of thinking the ultimate destitution of the world of subjugation, indeed its apocalyptic end, for the sake of a total reconstruction or the restitution of all value.[27] In a different vein, Daniel Whistler theorizes a Schellingian immanent indifference to the (Hegelian-modern) world of negativity and incessant differentiation.[28] Alex Dubilet articulates an immanence decoupled from the subject, a dispossessed life without a why, through a reconstruction of Meister Eckhart's speculative experimentalism.[29] None of these configurations of immanence can easily be designated as merely religious or secular; they are critical and constructive tools that index what is foreclosed and violated by transcendence (be it divine or worldly) and explore novel theoretical pathways of thinking otherwise than through the religious-secular binary.

At stake is not only ungrounding modern forms of sovereignty and decoupling immanence from its equation with the secular world, but also the subversion of modernity's self-legitimating conceptual narratives. This involves precisely a rejection of theoretically playing off the Christian and the secular against each other, a playing off that tends to yield a legitimation of the secular modern or a call for a return to the Christian against the secular. Instead, we must take seriously the insights of those scholars who have argued that, in important ways, secularism is another name for Christianity, that the fundamental operations of secularism and Christianity are not as opposed as they claim.[30] We should insist on the insight that the logic of conversion and universality, no less than the logics of possibility and mediation, fundamentally persist across the Christian-secular divide.[31] We might also consider the way both the Christian and the secular are apparatuses of deferral and futurity, of distension and reproduction, generating subjection as their lot and foreclosing the radical utopian immanence of the Real.[32] It is a question of rejecting the frame of secularity, but doing so without affirming Christianity as its supposed proper other—something that theological critiques of modernity have too often presumed. In this formulation, political theology is no longer a space for a reactivation of Christianity or theology against the secular, but a theoretical site for the speculative incubation of concepts that critically insists that the Christian and the secular form a unitary conjuncture essential to the ideological self-description of the world of modernity.

Cutting across and putting into question the religious-secular binary, this volume works political-theologically with concepts other than sovereignty—concepts such as immanence, nothingness, the world, the earth, utopia, indifference, justification, *tsimtsum*, or *kenosis*—in and through German Idealism. As such, this volume partakes in the kind of genealogical explorations that have always played a central role in the field of political theology. One only needs to recall the contestation over the role of premodern figures (e.g., Paul or the Gnostics) or early modern figures (e.g., Hobbes or Spinoza) to detect the importance that genealogy has played for the articulation of central elements of political theology. From Schmitt, Blumenberg, and Taubes onward, the genealogical dimension has always had a complex function: it has redrawn historical origins and recovered historical materials in unexpected ways in order to transform the structuring concepts of present-day political theology. Indeed, each significant genealogical investigation contains the capacity to transfigure the entire political-theological problematic, determining it anew for the contemporary moment and generating novel theoretical trajectories for its future.

Whereas the early modern moment grappled with the question of the political constitution of the state in the aftermath of the Reformation and the Wars of Religion, German Idealism was the first speculative attempt to think the entanglement of modernity and religion in the philosophical register in the wake of the Enlightenment and the French Revolution. Put this way, it is clear that German Idealism should be no less important for the contemporary political-theological imaginary than its early modern counterpart—but this has hardly been the case.[33] By staging an encounter between German thought from Kant to Marx and contemporary reformulations of the political-theological problematic, this volume seeks to remedy this theoretical lacuna.

German Idealism and the Political-Theological Diagnosis of Modernity

Without much exaggeration, German Idealism may be called the first philosophical articulation of the political-theological problematic in the aftermath of the Enlightenment and the advent of secularity. The philosophies of history, philosophies of religion, and histories of philosophy in German Idealism were all sites for the historical and conceptual tracing of continuities and inheritances, of dislocations and transformations, connecting Christianity and modernity. Indeed, one might say that German Idealism advanced, for the first time, a comprehensive political-theological *genealogy* of modernity—of the modern subject, the modern world, the modern state or community, and even the modern colonial project[34]—in its conjunction with Christianity and its various inflections. In German Idealism, we encounter a political-theological diagnosis of modernity as coimplicated and coimbricated with Christianity—a diagnosis guided by a set of questions: How does the project of *Neuzeit* relate historically and conceptually to Christianity, from its early to its late-medieval and modern forms? In what ways did Christianity lead to and remain constitutively at the heart of modernity? What makes modernity's structures of rationality, subjectivity, freedom, community, and universality Christian or non-Christian—an inheritance and transformation of Christianity or a deviation from it? What sort of Christianity was it that modernity inherited? In these lines of questioning, German idealist engagement with Christianity ceases to be a project of either secularization or resacralization—frameworks through which Hegel's philosophy in particular has often been interpreted—and becomes genealogical and conceptual.

Hegel, Fichte, and Schelling are all exemplary in the genealogical nature of their speculative investigations. In turning to them, we can make visible some of the ways German Idealism elaborates entanglement with Christianity as the fundamental condition of modernity and modern thought. For Hegel, modern freedom and subjectivity—as well as the very tripartite structure of thinking—are inextricable from Christianity and its structures of individuality, its ideas of hierarchy and universality, its eschatology and its justification of the world and of suffering, and the figure of Christ as the mediator and the notion of *kenosis*, with the result that Hegel's own historical moment constitutes for him the culmination of this Christian trajectory. More generally, Hegel's basic approach to philosophy of history may be seen as genealogical: in his analysis of how history has led up rationally to the present moment, Hegel begins from the actual in order to trace its origins, structures, and presuppositions. Of course, in the same gesture, Hegel also *idealizes* the actual and justifies the current point of world-history, but the genealogical aspect should not be obscured by this. The Owl of Minerva only begins its flight once the movement has been completed—flying back so as to trace how this movement came about and developed.

Theologically, it is the Lutheran line of Christianity—understood in a heterodox way that unites it with the eschatological tradition exemplified by the likes of Joachim of Fiore—that stands at the heart of Hegel's engagement with modernity as the culmination of the fundamentally Christian tradition.[35] From the standpoint of political theology, it is significant, however, that this line is reconfigured by Hegel not via the concept of faith but via a *critique* of religious sentiment and religious faith—concepts given theoretical weight at the time most prominently by Friedrich Schleiermacher. To faith, Hegel opposes the concepts of revelation and mediation: the revelation of the divine in and as the world, leading dialectically to the universal actualization of freedom. This results in understanding modernity as sublating or remediating traditional Christianity, conceptually (in philosophy) and practically (in modern ethical life and the state). For Hegel, modernity self-consciously becomes *the* epoch of mediation, actualization, and universality, but the origin of these operations always remains Christian. In this regard, Hegel himself may be seen as representing the high point of European-Christian modernity—a judgment that many essays in this volume share.

In Fichte's philosophy of history, modernity—as the epoch of alienation, individuation, religious wars, globalization, and colonialism—is shot through by the opposition of what he initially configures as two types of

Christianity, the Johannine and the Pauline, that structurally define subsequent religious and philosophical conflicts and positions. The Pauline trajectory determines, for Fichte, the mainstream of medieval and modern thought; while the Johannine names what the Pauline, with its investment in worldly power and sovereignty, forecloses. What is initially defined as Johannine Christianity turns out, however, to be not Christianity per se, but the ante-historical persistence of an originary religion that must be thought of as preceding the world and ungrounding the primacy of history—as the nondialectical, nonmediatable core of the dialectic of the implicit and the explicit; of past, present, and future; of immanence and transcendence; of the modern state and the true ethical community. Fichte attempts at once to critique and justify modernity—as a specific moment of this dialectic, an epoch of alienation and domination that is, nonetheless, necessary within the movement of history—but also, significantly, to diagnose modernity and trace the genealogy of its conceptual structures without falling into the modern myth of self-legitimation or orthodox religious critique. This is done, in other words, not as a defense of Christian faith but in order to manifest a certain systematic structure that undermines (and functions otherwise than through) the clear demarcation separating the religious and the secular.

Even Schelling—who in his late, so-called positive philosophy offered a "theistic" critique of Hegel's thought as too immanentist and rationalist, instead embracing (at least according to the standard account) the transcendent God of Pauline Christianity—may be seen as wrestling, throughout his thinking, with the world of modernity and its genealogy. Already in his early metaphysics, it is the not-yet of the modern world—its negativity and alienation, its freedom as infinite striving for freedom in the future, its character of expansion and domination (over what is considered to constitute mere possibility for the subject of modernity), and the work of actualization it demands—that leads Schelling to think the absolute not as an absolutization of the world, but as an immanence that precedes the movement of negation and actualization as well as cuts through the world of mediation. For Schelling at his most subversive, the logic of the absolute and the logic of that which is *nothing* vis-à-vis the world, and which ungrounds the not-yet of the world, crucially coincide.[36] What Schelling diagnoses is the constitutive neediness and negativity of the modern world and modern rationality, the way modernity is permeated by both a nostalgic longing and the striving for a future of reconciliation, fulfillment, and bliss—and how it is precisely its most secular forms (e.g., modern morality, subjectivity, domination over nature) that are infused with this longing and striving. The secular world is defined constitutively as the structure of lack and as the transition from an inaccessible past to a wished-for future that is, however, never *now*, but only endlessly deferred and foreclosed. In all this, modernity for Schelling at once inherits Platonic and Christian forms of temporality and intensifies them by making this negativity and lack, and not God, into the first, ultimate reality—an intensification by way of inversion.[37]

The novelty of this line of questioning, which stands at the origin of nineteenth- and twentieth-century genealogical inquiry—including political theology and secularization theory—must not go unnoticed. This is not merely a return of religion: after all, it was thinkers such as Friedrich Jacobi and Friedrich Schleiermacher who represented, in the post-Kantian climate, the side of religiosity. Jacobi in particular consistently opposed the German idealists (first Kant, then Fichte, then Schelling), accusing them, and modern thought more generally, of pantheism and atheism. Lamenting what he saw as the loss of faith and transcendence resulting from philosophy's illegitimate use of religious archives, Jacobi sought to expose German Idealism's nihilistic perversion of true religiosity. In this, his position prefigured contemporary Christian critiques of modernity—and indeed proleptically contributed to the contemporary fixation of (and on) the religious-secular binary. By contrast, German Idealism sought neither to critique modernity from the standpoint of Christianity (although some, especially the late Schelling, participated in this as well) nor to defend secular philosophy or secular modernity against its religious opponents. Both positions merely reproduce the religious-secular binary, which German Idealism, across its array of speculative explorations, sought to question and undermine. Nor should German Idealism be seen as merely a post-Enlightenment synthesis of modernity and Christianity; instead, it is precisely the *original* interwovenness of the two that here, for the first time, becomes the subject of an all-encompassing genealogical analysis. In this, German Idealism contributes directly to the field of political theology, whose critical and analytical power has come in large part precisely from its recognition of this interwovenness and the resulting challenge it has posed to the self-congratulatory narratives, secularist no less than religious.

This is the constitutive reason why German Idealism has been the subject of both irritation and praise, in religious and secular camps alike. Obviously, German idealist critique of modernity *can* be used for explicitly religious or explicitly secularist goals, as has often been done, not least by German idealists themselves. However, significantly for this volume, it is its appreciation of the entanglements of modernity with Christianity, its attempts to trace these entanglements genealogically, and its grappling with what came to be known as the secularization thesis—that marks German Idealism as a crucial political-theological archive and resource.

The decisive question is, *what is to be done* with this resource? If the intention here is not to draw on the archive of German Idealism for the sake of recuperating Christianity or shoring up secularist narratives, then what kind of use remains for this archive? We see two distinct trajectories of response, both proceeding from the fact of the originary political-theological entanglement of Christianity and modernity. Whereas one seeks to uncover, within German Idealism, resources for articulating conceptual paradigms that contribute to contemporary political theology by challenging the religious-secular binary, the other focuses on German Idealism as itself a high point of this entanglement—as itself a high point of modernity—in order to critique it. From both of these perspectives, it remains necessary that political theology revisits, and continues revisiting, the German idealist archive.

German Idealism between Nothingness and the World

In a post-Enlightenment and postrevolutionary moment, German Idealism proves to be important not only for its genealogical and diagnostic investigations but also for its capacity to speculatively articulate immanence as preceding (and thus putting into question) all transcendence. German Idealism creates varied conceptual frameworks of immanence that are irreducible to the (Christian-modern) world—this world of division, domination, and the incessant not-yet of universality and progress, a world that entices the subject with its seemingly endless possibilities and promises of the way it could be, thereby reproducing the way it is. Indeed, these frameworks, while being foreclosed by the Christian-modern apparatus of the world, index what has the power to delegitimate and subvert it. This is an unorthodox portrait of German Idealism, to be sure, one that resists reducing it to a philosophy of the subject alienated from the world, determined by structures of division and diremption that, in turn, necessitate the (conservative) logics of synthesis, reconciliation, and wholeness, characteristic of the Christian-modern paradigm. More orthodox readings miss the way that German Idealism attempts to think not only the overcoming of division into unity (an overcoming that is premised on the very fact of division and strives to subsume everything into the universal) but also, and more decisively, the various ways of questioning and undermining the very structure of division as the ultimate horizon of reality. At its most radical, German Idealism theorizes what is prior to and cannot be inscribed into the Christian-modern world—indexed by such concepts as nothingness, chaos, bliss, indifference, and the earth. As shown by the contributions to this volume, these are all names for what is neither transcendent nor immanent to the world, but for a radical immanence that subverts the very amalgamation of immanence and transcendence. The resulting portrait of post-Kantian thought is one of *a series of experiments with immanence* in opposition to the logics that structure the Christian-modern world: division and unity, particularity and universality, futurity and transcendence.

To provide an example, Joseph Albernaz's contribution to the volume explores this ante-worldly immanence under the name of the earth, as thought by Friedrich Hölderlin and Karoline von Günderrode.[38] The earth is the first common, the Real-in-common which is then enclosed, divided, and segregated by the colonial regime of the world. The sovereign, transcendent character of this regime is evident already in what Hölderlin, Schelling, Hegel, and later Carl Schmitt consider to be its inaugurating act: judgment (*Ur-teil*), which combines the operation of division (into particular kinds, properties, and territories) with that of unification (where the divided particulars are subsumed under universals). The resulting process of possession, division, and appropriation is foundational for the modern colonial project and Christian in its origin and significance. The earth as the common, by contrast, allows us to think that which refuses and ungrounds division and exploitation (in particular, the exploitation of the earth by the Christian-modern apparatus of transcendence). As a result, the earth becomes a political-theological ruin—and yet, to inhabit this ruin (of the common) is to think the *ruination* of the universalizing, dominating order of reality. What results from this, is a movement of local and alien immanence that destitutes and collapses the world, revealing it to be imposed and exploitative, feeding on the immanence of the earth and the common while foreclosing it.

In a convergent fashion, James Martel's contribution exposes in Kant, the originator of the problematics found in German Idealism and Romanticism, a materiality that persists in priority to the transcendental order (of subject and object), revealing the latter to be secondary and imposed, to be promising salvation in the future by foreclosing material immanence in the now. By remaining with and within the ordinary and material, we can, for Martel, *an-archically* resist such an imposition—a resistance that carries with it a messianic aspect, a messianism of the ordinary in the Benjaminian vein. This messianicity saves us, immediately, from the transcendental structure of salvation itself—from the way the transcendental philosopher imagines the world is or ought to be.

This kind of immanence carries with it not just a refusal of the ways of the world but also a "nihilistic" threat of undoing the very structures that uphold religious and secular authority or sovereignty. The absolute is, throughout German Idealism, intimately related to an affirmation of (the) nothing that seeks to escape any logic of the world's givenness or any absolutization of the world and its powers. This conjunction of immanence and the refusal to be subjected to the world did not go undetected by German Idealism's contemporaries. Jacobi, with his investment in transcendence, correctly sensed the German idealist threat (to transcendence) in his double identification of German Idealism with Spinozism and nihilism. Failing to grasp its metaphysical and political-theological innovation, he sought to reduce German Idealism to the simplistic fantasy of an "egotistic," merely subjective I, to a "will that wills nothing" and thus reduces all to nothing.[39] To this, Jacobi contrasted "the true" or God as "the outside," the transcendent reality sustained by faith—as, ultimately, a faith *in* the outside and thus in the world and its ontological priority over nothingness, ruin, and discontinuity. Relatedly, Jean Paul saw Idealism and Romanticism as "the lawless, capricious spirit of the present age, which would egotistically annihilate the world and the universe in order to clear a space merely for free *play* in the void."[40] Or, as Jacobi succinctly put it, "Man has this choice, however, and this alone: Nothingness or a God."[41]

German Idealism, indeed, often chose (the) nothing. That did not, however, necessarily entail choosing the *subjective* or making the capricious subject into an omnipotent God, as Jacobi tendentiously proclaimed. Not even early Romanticism, at the height of what is often taken to be its subjectivism, considered the logic of artistic creation to be subjective in this narrow sense.[42] The conjunction of nihilism with Spinozism—the philosophy of impersonal immanence—remained not fully thought through by Jacobi, even if he was the one to accuse German Idealism of both.

The example of Schelling is crucial here. Already in 1795, several years before Jacobi's open letter on Fichte's nihilism, Schelling proclaimed the will that wills nothing—the non-will, without mediation or striving, without expansion or want, the will that is prior to and refuses all demands of the world—as the absolutely Real from which all thought must begin.[43] This non-will was for him not the subjective I but the full dissolution or annihilation of the subject *and* the object, in their inextricable relation—a relation in which the subject is opposed to the object, a *not-I*, and wants (mastery over) it. Without such relation, premised on the subject-object opposition, the subject cannot exist as the subject of (the possibility of) mastery, production, and freedom. The philosophy of Kant and the early Fichte were for Schelling representative of this logic—the logic of divisive relationality, the inside/outside, and the endless striving to overcome this originary division, as the logic through which the world is produced and reproduced by the subject through synthesis, ultimately through the expansionism of finite reason. (Finitude marking here precisely the gap between subject and reality, proclaimed to be primary and ineliminable.) Schelling's radical move was to refuse this gap through which the subject and the world was produced and to think instead the absolute as immanent groundlessness, the void of the Real that is absolutely nonproductive and even annihilative of any possibility of division and relation—to think the absolute as what he would later call absolute indifference (*Indifferenz*), in which the very logic of difference, negativity, and care is voided.[44]

The absolute, as absolutely groundless (*grundlos*),[45] was affirmed by Schelling as the only unconditioned point of beginning for any thought that seeks to not absolutize the world—the world as always not yet perfect, not yet moral, postponing fulfillment into an indefinite, transcendent future which only leads to reproducing the divisions and negativities of the way things are. Understood in this way, the world must be annihilated, if there is to be a way of thinking in terms other than those this regime of reality demands or proclaims to be the only terms possible. As Kirill Chepurin's essay in this volume points out, this *No* to the world was the atopic starting point not only for Schelling but also for (the later) Fichte and for Friedrich Schlegel—for whom this was an explicitly revolutionary operation, a decreation of the world toward chaos or nothingness, an immanent materiality from which indifferently to construct any world and any binary opposition without justifying the world under construction as the best possible. There was for them, furthermore, *bliss* to be found in this atopic operation—not a happiness *in* the world, but a joy at the annihilation of the world, at exposing the world as imposed and unfree. The world is ungrounded in order to inhabit a void without relation to or care for the world, a freedom from the world in which no world is possible or needed.

As Oxana Timofeeva argues in this volume, even Hegel, the idealist thinker most invested in the world as it is, knew the joy—and enjoyment—found at the end of the world. Reason joyfully inhabits this end as the ruin from which philosophy, in the figure of the Owl of Minerva, begins its constitutively belated flight. In this postapocalyptic political-theological situation of a world that has always already ended and a God that is always already dead—which must, however, be thought of as the *beginning* of thought—Hegel is joined by Kant and Sade. Together they form a transition through the catastrophic situation of solitude and death, ultimately rejoicing in this situation as at once apocalyptic, rational, and utopian, one in which a new collectivity, a new "we," may be seen to emerge.

Thus, in German Idealism, Jacobi's pronouncement of nihilism is at once endorsed and reversed. As Schelling puts it in his 1806 *Aphorisms*, polemically endorsing Jacobi's charge, "the doctrine of the absolute [is] a doctrine of the absolutely nothing." "Indeed," Schelling continues, deploying nothingness against the Jacobian outside but also against the Kantian-Fichtean logic of synthesis premised on the separation of subject and object, "[it is] a doctrine of the absolute nothingness of things," ungrounding what dogmatically "appeared to him [i.e., Jacobi] as the quintessential reality."[46] The structure of transcendence in which the Jacobian subject of faith (in God and in the world) exists is here dismantled in order to reveal an immanence that does not operate through the divisions that the world declares ineliminable. In this, Idealism becomes a Spinozism, not of the world, but of what, from the point of view of the world, appears as the void—the immanently Real that thought must inhabit. This absolutely Real is indexed by the collapse of all worldly structures and mediations. Starting from 1795, Schelling repeatedly insists that the absolute cannot be mediated (and so cannot be synthesized), and can only be a nothingness (*Nichts*), a "nothing at all (= 0)," from the perspective of the world. At the standpoint of this immanent nothingness, the finite world is completely *vernichtet*.[47]

At moments like these, rather than fearing the nothing, as Jean Paul did in reaction to its perceived lawlessness, German Idealism embraces it in order to proceed immanently *from* the nothing, absolute bliss, or absolute indifference. As a result, the starting operation of Idealism is a total suspension and even annihilation of the world, its affirmative reduction to a nothingness or chaos, the a-position, the atopic standpoint that the speculative thinker must occupy. At this standpoint, any givenness of the world, any binary opposition through the lens of which we are accustomed to seeing the world (such as subject and object, but also higher and lower, possible and actual, particular and universal, finite and infinite), is refused. This standpoint needs to be affirmed as first in order to expose the world as secondary, imposed, and derivative, instead of taking the world dogmatically as a necessary and unsurpassable horizon. If to affirm the absolute is to reduce the world to nothing, then, one might say, *nothing is absolute*.

Even the figure of the finite subject, as alienated from the objective world which the subject seeks to master (and which in turn threatens to overpower the subject), only appears as foundational as the result of the constitution of objectivity as a realm severed from subjectivity. To think otherwise than through finitude does not therefore necessarily mean falling into the arrogance of subjectivity or supposedly overstepping the subject's limits. At issue is the refusal of the whole discourse of finitude, entrenched as it is in the constitution of reality that divides the subject from the object and encloses them in a circle in which they must endlessly struggle. Rather than remaining within this circle by envisaging a universal whole which would sublate into itself all divisions—one can, instead, refuse (the legitimacy and inevitability of) the very act of setting up such a regime of reality in the first place. Doing so uncovers the beginning of speculative thought—as well as of bliss and joy—in the annihilation of the world.

The stakes of this annihilation, but also the paradoxes arising from it, are traced in Chepurin's contribution, which reconfigures the German idealist trajectory through the tension between two basic operations: annihilation and construction. These operations are central to German Idealism, from the early Schelling to Schlegel to Fichte, Hegel and even Marx, insofar as they attempt to think the conditions of possibility of the finite world—to narrate or construct a world (or *this* world)—without absolutizing the way it is, instead proceeding from the Real that must be thought of as preceding and irreducible to the world. To think the Real, therefore, requires annihilating the world. To think this annihilation, this inhabitation of the void without the world, however, is not enough. For what is to be done about the fact that the world, with its divisions and mediations, *is* there and the subject is always already in the world? The world must therefore be confronted and constructed, so as not to be made a ghost—but if to think the world is to think its conditions of possibility, then can the world be thought without justifying it as necessarily the way it is? This is what Chepurin calls "the transcendental knot," a problem faced by German Idealism no less than by contemporary thought. Even in thinking the end of the world, there remains the danger of absolutizing the way the world is; to find ways of not doing so is a crucial task that German Idealism bequeaths to political theology.

One of the fundamental logics upholding the world is the logic of mediation, familiar to us from (the late) Hegel.[48] The way mediation joins with sovereignty is analyzed in Daniel Colucciello Barber's and Alex Dubilet's contributions to this volume. For Barber, the true function of Schmittian sovereignty is to uphold the world defined through divisive relationality and mediation, Christian (and Christocentric) in origin. In introducing the figure of Christ as the mediator, Christianity makes mediation itself into the horizon that is at once divine and worldly, directed toward the universal future (of salvation), the possibility of which is established by the mechanism of mediation. This structure persists into modernity. What is usually taken to be the immanence of the world, the way it remediates all positions into one universalizing world process and discards, suppresses, or sublates all that might remain outside of it (the way it happens, for example, in Hegel's philosophy of history), reveals transcendence as its condition of possibility. It reveals, that is, the sovereign act, the decision that institutes it, to which Barber opposes Taubesian apocalypticism, while radicalizing it further toward a refusal of sovereignty without reliance on the world, a *nihil* without a care for worldly possibilities or the possibility of the world. In affirming this completely baseless negativity as the *now-here* of world-annihilation, coinciding with God understood as a term that is absolutely incommensurable with the logic of the world, Barber's paper joins others in the volume that bring together German Idealism, apocalypticism, and the atopic nowhere—positioning it, however, not with but against German Idealism, or, more precisely, against its trajectory that bears the name Hegel. What emerges from this analysis is the structural coincidence of the Christian mechanism of mediation that holds the world together and defers its apocalyptic end, on the one hand, and the modern primacy of mediation as the field of worldly possibility held together by the law (of the world) instituted by the sovereign act, on the other.

Dubilet's contribution turns to Marx's "On the Jewish Question" in order to diagnose the collusive interplay between mediation and sovereignty as modes of transcendence that, together, prevent real immanence from irrupting. It does so by recovering the logic of "the general secular contradiction"—the division between the state and civil society that materializes and secularizes the structure of diremption originally articulated in theological form, as the opposition between heaven and earth. In this analysis, the logic of Christianity is shown to be imbricated with the political form of secular modernity itself. Moreover, this account reveals that the modern secular state does not inaugurate the political theology of immanence; rather it constitutes a mechanism of transcendent mediation. The exception that mediates across the two realms renders transcendence livable, but it also reproduces the dirempted life, establishing it as the unsurpassable horizon and foreclosing all operations of dissolution or abolition that could collapse the structure of civil society and the state that governs "the order of the world." Although immediate transcendence (sovereignty) may be positioned, as it is in the Schmittian paradigm, as radically distinct from its mediational counterpart, in relation to real immanence the two operate as a collusive ensemble.

The topic of the secular state and its production of citizenship is picked up by Thomas Lynch in connection with the liberal doctrine of religious toleration. Lynch's essay traces the way the modern state relies on the Christian logic of universality as mediation in order to legitimate itself and its sorting out of religion into legitimate and illegitimate forms—into forms that support the universal (i.e., the state itself) and forms that potentially endanger it. For Lynch, this universalist logic underlies both Hegel and liberal theorists of toleration: only that difference can be tolerated which promotes and upholds the universal. "Which religions are compatible with secularism?" This becomes the guiding question, and any failure to disentangle religion from politics is turned into the demand that we secularize better—which serves to obscure the way the very binary of the religious and the political is produced and reproduced from within the Christian-modern logic of the universal. Against this regime of difference to be mediated and transcended toward universality, Lynch positions the idea of indifference as refusing to negotiate between differences—as "negating those regimes by which difference is organized and rendered consistent."

In this way, we circle back to the theorization of an indifference that refuses mediation—but which also, as Dubilet suggests in his essay's conclusion, may refuse the universal name "human." The work of Daniel Whistler is crucial here, insofar as it attempts to think a non-Hegelian trajectory within German Idealism, one that would refuse the primacy of mediation and human (transcendental) subjectivity in thinking the world. In a recent essay, Whistler has shown how Schelling seeks to exhibit reality indifferently from a utopic standpoint prior to all difference and particularity (which always already exist *within* the regime of mediation)—a standpoint that can only be grasped as nonhuman or even inhuman.[49] In his essay in this volume, Whistler shows indifference to be a way of rethinking the secular modern without being beholden to the understandings of secularization as the negation of particularity or its remediation into a universal. If one can think an immanence (here equated with indifference) that refuses the logics of mediation and universality—Christian in their origins and inherited by modernity—then perhaps this immanence can provide a different way of thinking the secular itself? To that end, Whistler theorizes abstraction as indifference, which results in a complete destitution of the transcendental, collapsing the subject-object dichotomy and refusing to mediate between particular possibilities. Instead of sublating them into a universality, this abstraction neutralizes and remains absolutely indifferent to them. In its indifference and nullity, it may also be said to be universal, but in a completely nonstandard sense—as an immediate imposition of a plane of immanence that operates, one could say, without relation to particulars. This imposition may carry with it a kind of violence, too, but this violence—and this logic of the secular—although modern, is no longer the Christian-Hegelian modern; as such, it offers a different conceptual apparatus for the political-theological understanding of modernity.

Saitya Brata Das continues the Schellingian polemics with Hegel in his essay, which instead of theorizing immanence anew articulates the late Schelling's radical transcendence as the counter to the Hegelian theodicy of worldly immanence. In Hegel, the world is understood as potentiality, as the world-historical possibility actualized by spirit as the subject of history. In this theodicy of history, the world is justified by its own movement, that of actualizing possibility. Indeed—to complement Das's analysis—to see the movement of the world as one of progressive actualization of possibility, the way Hegel does, is itself quintessentially modern. As Hans Blumenberg has shown, the inaugurating move of modernity, the move that inaugurates the program of the subject's self-assertion, is to make the world (and not God) into the totality of possibility. Faced with reality as possibility yet to be actualized, the task of the modern subject becomes that of producing reality, of mastering it by making use of it, exploring the possibilities inherent in it, and exploiting them to the fullest.[50] The subject becomes the subject of this process of actualization—the figure of possibility itself. This is, one could say, the way the modern world legitimates itself: by thinking of itself as open and producible, as making room for and enacting all the possibility. For Das, the significance of late-Schellingian political theology is, by contrast, to delegitimate worldly sovereignty by eschatologically emptying it out, by freely letting it pass away. In this Schellingian *kenosis*, the very logic of theodicy is refused, dissolved in the beatitude of an actuality without telos.

Agata Bielik-Robson's contribution offers a different move against Hegelian *kenosis*. She opposes Hegel's teleological-sacrificial logic of the death of God with the idea of God's free self-withdrawal (*tsimtsum*) found in the Jewish tradition, from Luria to Derrida. Both concepts, *kenosis* and *tsimtsum*, may be said to lie at the foundation of modernity—an optic in which the death of God ceases to be a Christian monopoly. *Kenosis* and *tsimtsum* both open up the space of finitude in which the world can be affirmed, but in radically different ways. In Hegel, God may freely consent to die, yet his self-sacrificial death lays an infinite burden upon the world—a debt and guilt that can only be repaid at the end of history. History is thereby turned into a space of divine sovereignty even in God's death. By contrast, what *tsimtsum* allows us to think is a gift *without* sacrifice, a self-contraction of God that simply lets finitude be, without reason or telos. The "religion of flowers" that Hegel criticized as not serious enough, here aligned with *tsimtsum*, turns out to be an immanently anti-Hegelian moment opening up onto a non-Christian, also future-oriented yet nonsacrificial, logic of modernity.

If the Hegelian dialectic is complicit with the Christian-modern world, then one move is to think the nondialectical as that which refuses this world immanently, as multiple essays in this volume do. Another move, however, which lies broadly within the Hegelian trajectory itself, would be to open up the dialectical movement, to un-resolve it—perhaps transforming it into a spiral. This is suggested by S. D. Chrostowska in her contribution, which focuses on the so-called "Oldest Systematic Program of German Idealism." The basic gesture of the "Oldest Systematic Program" is messianic and revolutionary, forgoing the religious-secular binary in order to think an openness to the utopic that resists closure and mastery. As Chrostowska argues, an entire tradition of dialectical utopianism follows this gesture. The openness of the spiral resists the Schmittian closure of political theology—disclosing its alternative forms and perspectives, siding not with authority, but with the emancipation of the suffering and the oppressed. In this, Chrostowska endorses not the dialectic in its late-Hegelian form, but the earlier, Romantic-Hegelian revolutionary impulse and the liberatory political theologies to which it helped give rise.

The figure of an opening or gap is analyzed critically in Steven Shakespeare's contribution. Shakespeare diagnoses the ambivalence of German Idealism as at once pointing toward an immanence that subverts the subject and its world *and* as foreclosing this immanence by way of the gap between the self and its reflected counterpart, the *I* and the *not-I*. Interrogating the constitution and failure of the subject and its world through Kant, Schelling, and Kierkegaard, Shakespeare traces in these thinkers three different attempts to think the gap without resolving or dialectically unifying it, without appealing to any sort of transcendent authority that would serve to close the gap. Instead, these thinkers reduplicate and intensify this gap of subjectivity as a way of signaling the immanently fractured, nonunitary character of reality. Reduplication points thereby to the inevitable problem of expression inherent in theories of immanence, insofar as expression requires a minimal difference to be possible. In these thinkers, this minimal difference is transformed into the dialectical motor of life, which remains however (despite—or indeed precisely because of—its proclamations of universality) a fundamentally Christian logic, transforming others, most directly Judaism, into the embodiment of the unlife. It is through this investment in life, with the hierarchical and supersessionist logics it engenders, that Idealism ultimately forecloses immanence and reproduces transcendence. The resulting theoretical question, which Shakespeare leaves open, is whether reduplication, and thus the expression of immanence without appeal to models of truth from above, can be divorced from this structure of supersession.

The move of recuperation and subjugation is, of course, likewise at the heart of the Hegelian world history. In his contribution, Vincent Lloyd seeks to think that which is occluded by this recuperation—namely, Africa as, for Hegel, the continent *prior* to history—and to find in this ante-historical origin resources for refusing the moves of dialectical recuperation, for pushing back against Hegel's methodical ambition to mediate everything from the normative world-historical standpoint. Africa and blackness index in Hegel that which is unspeakable and without recognition, whose functioning in and against Hegel's narrative Lloyd proceeds to trace—as the exteriority that *persists*, unassimilable to the dialectic. Africa can only be articulated by way of the complete dismantling of the apparatus of history, the absolute stripping-away of spirit or subjectivity. What results from this is a pure contingency of raw events and objects without a binding force, a life of immediacy without any sense of totality. In this, a different kind of sovereignty emerges, embodied for Hegel in the figure of the Congo queen, whose agency is despotic and immediate, secular in the sense of being driven wholly by materialistic concerns. In a different way than Barber and Dubilet, Lloyd also diagnoses the presence of sovereignty at the basis of the supposedly immanent movement of history. At the same time, to think immanent exteriority as embodied in the Congo queen is to complicate any celebratory idealizations of the figure of the non-sovereign—to see in it the obverse side of the same conjunction of sovereignty and mediation.

Two tendencies within German Idealism emerge across the volume's oftentimes diverging contributions. On the one hand, as a series of experiments in de-absolutizing and even annihilating the (modern, Christian-European) world—in affirmatively reducing it to nothingness, chaos, the earth, or indifference—German Idealism may be mobilized to think that which ungrounds and cannot be inscribed into dominant Christian-secular logics. On the other hand, even when German Idealism seeks to think the zero point that precedes the construction of the world, its next move is, all too often, to reconstruct the world as it is starting from this zero point, thereby justifying the (modern, Christian-European) world. In German idealist philosophy of history especially, the path of the absolute goes through world history, justifying it as an image of (and a necessary point of transition on the way to) the absolute. This trajectory points to the ways in which post-Kantian thought not only opens up a thinking of immanence but also, ultimately, forecloses it by realigning it with the modern world in the idealist philosophies of subjectivity, history, and the state.

Thus, in Fichte, the standpoint of the *Wissenschaftslehre* displaces the world totally, appearing as "the doctrine of nothing" to the dogmatist who would absolutize the way the world is—a standpoint that culminates, in the ethical register, in the idea of blessedness or bliss as refusing the logics of domination and the not-yet. At the same time, however, and from the same standpoint, Fichte proceeds to think the *necessity* of the progress of history and its culmination in Christian-European modernity as the actualization of the divine in and as the world. The world, and with it the state, strives to dissolve in the life of the divine—and yet this striving necessarily traverses Christianity and modern European history as its contemporary culmination and the closest that humanity has come to its end goal. This is, one could say, the tension between Fichte's 1806 *The Way Towards the Blessed Life* and his *Characteristics of the Present Age*, published in the same year. The former thinks bliss, nonproductivity, non-sovereignty—just as the latter uses them to *justify* the evils of history (including colonial and state violence), as mere stages toward the final epoch in which bliss would be realized and all domination would cease.

This tension, and this overwriting of immanence by way of its inscription into a theodical project of justifying the world, is generally characteristic of the way German Idealism repeatedly forecloses the utopic immanence of nothingness or bliss by positioning it as the end goal of the world process, thereby, one could say, idealizing the world as it is. Schelling is guilty of this as well. One of his last works, *Exhibition of the Purely Rational Philosophy* (1847–1852), is particularly explicit in this regard. What the world is meant to do, for Schelling, is to actualize the totality of possibility until its full exhaustion—and what the philosopher is supposed to do is to trace the logic of this actualization in and as world history. The latter follows the natural logic of the *Stufenfolge* (succession of steps), in which the higher subsumes and builds on the lower, gradually getting closer to the all-encompassing "organic" unity. This naturalization of hierarchy and progress is extended by Schelling to European colonial history and thus becomes indicative of the modern logic of racialization, with Schelling speaking about "lower" races serving as mere possibility for the "higher"—a racialized logic endorsed by him as the way things simply and necessarily are. The lower is, according to this conception, destined to die out naturally as soon as it comes into contact with the higher (as illustrated by Schelling appealing to the disappearance of "the American natives")—or to be put to use by the higher (as in the transportation of African slaves to America) thereby saving the lower from world-historical abandonment and giving it the possibility of becoming part of something higher—of becoming part of the logic of possibility itself.[51] Not unlike in Fichte, the philosopher must refuse all divisions and think their all-dissolution in bliss, as refusing sovereignty and domination—and yet, in order to think this as the end goal of history, the philosopher must think the path *to* this nondomination as going by necessity *through* domination—and, furthermore, through domination in its historical forms, culminating in Christian-European modernity.

These two moves—thinking an immanence that refuses domination, sovereignty, or the not-yet, and positioning this immanence as the telos of the world that is not yet ethical, not yet free, not yet fully divine—need at once to be kept separate and grasped in their conjunction within German Idealism. This is, one could say, what happens when nothingness, bliss, and immanence are inscribed into the world's logic of possibility, into the path of historical development, actualization, and progress: a folding back of immanence into the world of modernity. German Idealism is torn between wanting not to absolutize the world, by affirming that which refuses and even annihilates it—and to think the way the world is, identifying the logic of the world with the logic of ideality and thereby justifying the world. This tension is indicative of the post-Enlightenment, postrevolutionary moment as one in which modernity at once culminates and its cracks begin to show: the Christian-modern paradigm here at once reaches its peak and ceases to be self-evident, becoming a (theoretical and genealogical) problem for thought. This allows an unprecedented series of experiments in deconstructing or ungrounding the modern world, but it also leads to German Idealism's holding on to the world of modernity that it inherited. In making the first grand attempt to self-reflectively think through the genealogical foundations of modernity, German Idealism ultimately ends up justifying them—and thereby justifying the project of modernity itself.

Can one ever think the world without justifying it? Is it possible to think an immanence that would immanently refuse the world, on the one hand, *and* the world as the regime of reality through which the subjects of modernity inevitably are required to pass, even as they assert an antagonism toward it, on the other? How is what is foreclosed by the Christian-modern to be thought? How does one think the enactment—the operativity or inoperativity—of this otherwise that would not fall back into the logics of restoration, fulfillment, actualization, or universality? How does one proceed from or out of the zero point of radical immanence—or how does one persist in it while also doing justice to the victims and exclusions of the world? The questions that German Idealism, in all its tensions and ambivalences, bequeaths to political theology are numerous—and remain absolutely central to its future.

Notes

1. Carl Schmitt, *Political Theology: Four Chapters on the Concept of Sovereignty*, trans. George Schwab (Cambridge, MA: MIT Press, 1988), 36. Hobbes's *Leviathan* is particularly important for Schmitt's understanding of both how the concept of sovereignty was *historically* transferred from theology to politics and how modern sovereignty was *structurally* the same as divine sovereignty. See

Carl Schmitt, *The Leviathan in the State Theory of Thomas Hobbes* (Chicago: University of Chicago Press, 2008). More generally, Hobbes may be said to be determinate for Schmitt's entire project of political theology insofar as he defines for Schmitt the paradigm of modernity and modern sovereignty.

2. See Walter Benjamin, "On Violence," in *Selected Writings*, vol. 1, *1913–1926*, ed. Marcus Bullock and Michael W. Jennings (Cambridge, MA: Belknap Press of Harvard University Press, 1996), 236–252; Walter Benjamin, "On the Concept of History," in *Selected Writings*, vol. 4, *1938–1940*, ed. Howard Eiland and Michael W. Jennings (Cambridge, MA: Belknap Press of Harvard University Press, 2006), 389–400; Karl Löwith, *Meaning in History: The Theological Implications of the Philosophy of History* (Chicago: Chicago University Press, 1949); Jacob Taubes, *Occidental Eschatology*, trans. David Ratmoko (Stanford, CA: Stanford University Press, 2009); Jacob Taubes, *The Political Theology of Paul*, trans. Dana Hollander (Stanford, CA: Stanford University Press, 2004); and Hans Blumenberg, *The Legitimacy of the Modern Age*, trans. Robert M. Wallace (Cambridge, MA: MIT Press, 1983).

3. For Blumenberg's discussion of immanent self-assertion of reason and the overcoming of Gnosticism, see *Legitimacy*, esp. 125–226. For more on these implications for and in Blumenberg from a political-theological perspective, see Joseph Albernaz and Kirill Chepurin, "The Sovereignty of the World: Towards a Political Theology of Modernity (after Blumenberg)," in *Interrogating Modernity: Debates with Hans Blumenberg*, ed. Agata Bielik-Robson and Daniel Whistler (New York, NY: Palgrave Macmillan, 2020).

4. Mark Lilla, *The Stillborn God: Religion, Politics, and the Modern West* (New York: Vintage, 2008); Victoria Kahn, *The Future of Illusion: Political Theology and Early Modern Texts* (Chicago: University of Chicago Press, 2014).

5. For a useful critical genealogy of political theology, see Yannik Thiem, "Political Theology," in *The Encyclopedia of Political Thought*, ed. Michael T Gibbons (Malden, MA: Wiley Blackwell, 2015), 2807–2822.

6. Giorgio Agamben, *Homo Sacer: Sovereign Power and Bare Life*, trans. Daniel Heller-Roazen (Stanford, CA: Stanford University Press, 1998); *State of Exception*, trans. Kevin Attell (Chicago: University of Chicago Press, 2005); *The Kingdom and the Glory: For a Theological Genealogy of Economy and Government*, trans. Lorenzo Chiesa (Stanford, CA: Stanford University Press, 2011).

7. Roberto Esposito, *Two: The Machine of Political Theology and the Place of Thought*, trans. Zakiya Hanafi (New York: Fordham University Press, 2015).

8. Alain Badiou, *Saint Paul: The Foundation of Universalism*, trans. Ray Brassier (Stanford, CA: Stanford University Press, 2003); Slavoj Žižek, *The Ticklish Subject: The Absent Centre of Political Ontology* (London: Verso, 1997); Antonio Negri, *The Labor of Job: The Biblical Text as a Parable of Human Labor*, trans. Matteo Mandarini (Durham, NC: Duke University Press, 2009); Catherine Malabou, "Before and Above: Spinoza and Symbolic Necessity," *Critical Inquiry* 43, no. 1 (Autumn 2016): 84–109; Michel Foucault, *Security,*

Territory, Population: Lectures at the Collège de France 1977–1978, trans. Graham Burchell (London: Picador, 2009).

9. Another inventive example of this line of thinking is Adam Kotsko, *Neoliberalism's Demons: On the Political Theology of Late Capital* (Stanford, CA: Stanford University Press, 2018).

10. Taubes, *Political Theology of Paul*, 103.

11. Hussein Ali Agrama, *Questioning Secularism: Islam, Sovereignty, and the Rule of Law in Modern Egypt* (Chicago: University of Chicago Press, 2012).

12. Talal Asad, *Formations of the Secular: Christianity, Islam, Modernity* (Stanford, CA: Stanford University Press, 2003), 5.

13. See Albernaz and Chepurin, "Sovereignty of the World."

14. For Jean Hyppolite's description of the Hegelian movement of spirit in these terms, see his *Genesis and Structure of Hegel's* Phenomenology of Spirit, trans. Samuel Cherniak and John Heckman (Evanston, IL: Northwestern University Press, 1974), 544 and 557. For an account of the transcendent telos of the modern world, see also Albernaz and Chepurin, "Sovereignty of the World."

15. One detects something similar—a structure of transcendence persisting in modernity under the guise of immanence—in the logics of self-organization that arise across the Enlightenment. Although in a sense breaking with theologies of salvation, discourses of self-organization generate knowledges that justify a faith not in God but in history and the world—thereby underwriting a secular form of providence and legitimating modernity. See Alex Dubilet, review of Jonathan Sheehan and Dror Wahrman, *Invisible Hands: Self-Organization and the Eighteenth Century* (Chicago: Chicago University Press, 2015), *Immanent Frame*, May 26, 2016, https://tif.ssrc.org/2016/05/26/invisible-hands/.

16. Sylvia Wynter, "Unsettling the Coloniality of Being/Power/Truth/Freedom: Towards the Human, After Man, Its Overrepresentation—An Argument," *CR: The New Centennial Review* 3, no. 3 (2003): 264, 260, 296, 319. Relatedly, Nelson Maldonado-Torres writes, "It is as if the production of the 'less than human' functioned as the anchor of a process of autonomy and self-assertion." Maldonado-Torres, *Against War: Views from the Underside of Modernity* (Durham, NC: Duke University Press, 2008), 238. For a discussion of the way the modern logics of separation, otherness, and exclusion lead to hierarchical arrangements of the human, the less-than-human, and the non-human through a theory of racializing assemblages, see Alexander G. Weheliye, *Habeas Viscus: Racializing Assemblages, Biopolitics, and Black Feminist Theories of the Human* (Durham, NC: Duke University Press, 2014). On the production of "colonial difference" in and as modernity, and on the conjunction of colonialism and the exploitation of nature/the earth, see Walter D. Mignolo and Catherine E. Walsh, *On Decoloniality: Concepts, Analytics, Praxis* (Durham, NC: Duke University Press, 2018), esp. chaps. 7 and 8. For an important analysis of the conjunction of globalization and racialization in modernity, see also Jared Hickman, *Black Prometheus: Race and Radicalism in the Age of Atlantic Slavery* (Oxford: Oxford University Press, 2017). What

Hickman, inspired in many ways by Blumenberg's association of modernity with immanence, calls the new "planetary" or "global immanence" of modernity is, however, what we analyze as fundamentally an immanent-*transcendent* structure.

17. On blackness as the nothingness that allows the modern world and the modern subject to emerge and affirm themselves as the universal being, see Calvin L. Warren, *Ontological Terror: Blackness, Nihilism, and Emancipation* (Durham, NC: Duke University Press, 2018). On the relation between the human, the world, and the slave, see Frank B. Wilderson III, *Red, White and Black: Cinema and the Structure of U.S. Antagonism* (Durham, NC: Duke University Press, 2010).

18. See, for example, Jared Sexton, "The Social Life of Social Death: On Afro-Pessimism and Black Optimism," *InTensions*, no. 5 (2011): 1–47; Jared Sexton Interviewed by Daniel Colucciello Barber, "On Black Negativity, or the Affirmation of Nothing," *Society and Space*, September 18, 2017, https://www.societyandspace.org/articles/on-black-negativity-or-the-affirmation-of-nothing/.

19. For an encapsulation of Laruelle's thinking of the world and the Real, see "A Summary of Non-Philosophy," trans. Ray Brassier, *Pli* 8 (1999): 138–148. For the ethico-political dimension of this conceptual dyad, see François Laruelle, *General Theory of Victims*, trans. Jessie Hock and Alex Dubilet (Cambridge: Polity, 2015).

20. See Anthony Paul Smith, "Against Tradition to Liberate Tradition," *Angelaki: Journal of the Theoretical Humanities* 19, no. 2 (2014): 145–159; Anthony Paul Smith, *Laruelle: A Stranger Thought* (Cambridge: Cambridge University Press, 2016), esp. 153–160; and Laruelle, *General Theory of Victims*.

21. For a useful intellectual-historical overview of the role of Gnosticism as an appellation and position, see Willem Styfhals, *No Spiritual Investment in the World: Gnosticism and Postwar German Philosophy* (Ithaca, NY: Cornell University Press, 2019).

22. Adolf von Harnack, *Marcion: The Gospel of the Alien God*, trans. J. E. Steeley and L. D. Bierma (Jamestown, NY: Labyrinth Press, 1990; German original: 1923).

23. Fred Moten, *Black and Blur* (Durham, NC: Duke University Press, 2017), 67.

24. Fred Moten, *Stolen Life* (Durham, NC: Duke University Press, 2018), 181. Of course, all discussion of the flesh, Moten's included, returns to the *locus classicus*: Hortense Spillers, "Mama's Baby, Papa's Maybe: An American Grammar Book," in *Black, White, and in Color: Essays on American Literature and Culture* (Chicago: University of Chicago Press, 2003), 203–229.

25. Moten, *Stolen Life*, 113.

26. Moten, 27. For the full articulation of the undercommons, see Stefano Harney and Fred Moten, *The Undercommons: Fugitive Planning and Black Study* (Brooklyn, NY: Autonomedia, 2013).

27. Denise Ferreira da Silva, "Toward a Black Feminist Poethics: The Quest(ion) of Blackness Toward the End of the World," *Black Scholar* 44, no. 2 (2014): 81–97.

28. Daniel Whistler, "Abstraction and Utopia in Early German Idealism," *Russian Journal of Philosophy and Humanities* 2, no. 1 (2017): 3–22. See also Whistler's essay in this volume.

29. Alex Dubilet, *The Self-Emptying Subject: Kenosis and Immanence, Medieval to Modern* (New York: Fordham University Press, 2018). Dubilet further elaborates immanence as decoupled from the logic of the subject and the world, in dialogue with Harney and Moten's undercommons and Laruelle's non-philosophy, in "An Immanence without the World: On Dispossession, Nothingness, and Secularity," *Qui Parle* (forthcoming).

30. See Gil Anidjar, "Secularism," *Critical Inquiry* 33, no. 1 (2006): 52–77; Webb Keane, *Christian Moderns: Freedom and Fetish in the Mission Encounter* (Berkeley: University of California Press, 2007). As Anidjar notes, secularism should be seen as "the means by which Christianity *forgot and forgave* itself" (63).

31. Daniel Colucciello Barber, "World-Making and Grammatical Impasse," *Qui Parle* 25 (2016): 179–206; Daniel Colucciello Barber, *On Diaspora: Christianity, Religion, and Secularity* (Eugene: Cascade Books, 2011). On the articulation of immanence decoupled from the secular, see also: Daniel Colucciello Barber, *Deleuze and the Naming of God: Post-Secularism and the Future of Immanence* (Edinburgh: Edinburgh University Press, 2014).

32. Alex Dubilet, "The Catastrophic Joy of Abandoning Salvation: Thinking the Postsecular with Georges Bataille," *Journal of Critical Religious Theory* 16, no. 2 (2017): 163–178, and Dubilet, *Self-Emptying Subject*, esp. 173–178. On the figure of utopian immanence, see Kirill Chepurin, "Beginning with Kant: Utopia, Immanence, and the Origin of German Idealism," *Russian Journal of Philosophy and Humanities* 2, no. 1 (2017): 71–90; for this question, in a different intellectual context, see Kirill Chepurin and Alex Dubilet, "Russia's Atopic Nothingness: Ungrounding the World-Historical Whole with Pyotr Chaadaev," *Angelaki* 24, no. 6 (2019): 135–151.

33. One might recall that Slavoj Žižek has offered innovative political-theological reinterpretations of Hegel through a Lacanian lens. Within Žižek's Hegelian reading, the true radicality of Christianity lies in its uncompromising affirmation of the death of God as the loss of all transcendent guarantees. Ultimately, Žižek's reading connects Christianity with radical atheism in a way that affirms the unity and singular trajectory of the West. See Slavoj Žižek and John Milbank, *The Monstrosity of Christ: Paradox or Dialectic?*, ed. Creston Davis (Cambridge, MA: MIT Press, 2009), 234–303. The present volume points to a different set of theoretical directions. Neither ascribing primacy to psychoanalytic paradigms nor invested in recuperative gestures in relation to Christianity, it moves beyond the Žižek-Milbank polemics, as significant as those polemics may have been for political theology in the first decade of this

century. For a useful synthetic but critical account of Žižek's trajectory in relation to theology, see Marika Rose, "Slavoj Žižek," in *The Palgrave Handbook of Radical Theology*, ed. Christopher D. Rodkey and Jordan E. Miller (New York: Palgrave Macmillan, 2018), 479–495.

34. Hegel's philosophy of history, Fichte's *Characteristics of the Present Age*, and Schelling's *Exhibition of the Purely Rational Philosophy* all variously inscribed colonialism into the project of modern universalism grounded in Christianity.

35. See especially Cyril O'Regan, *The Heterodox Hegel* (Albany: State University of New York Press, 1994).

36. On the figures of refusing and even annihilating the world of mediation and history in Schelling, see Kirill Chepurin, "Indifference and the World: Schelling's Pantheism of Bliss," *Sophia* 58, no. 4 (2019): 613–630; "To Break All Finite Spheres: Bliss, the Absolute I, and the End of the World in Schelling's 1795 Metaphysics," *Kabiri: The Official Journal of the North American Schelling Society* 2 (2020): 40–67; and Chepurin's paper in this volume.

37. On the inversion characteristic of modernity—which makes the finite world (rather than God) into the exemplification of reality—and the theoretical implications thereof, see, for example, Schelling, *Aphorismen über die Naturphilosophie* (Hamburg: Felix Meiner Verlag, 2018), 61.

38. We should recall that German Romanticism is frequently read today within the broader post-Kantian ambit of German Idealism (and rightly so). Recent examples include Frederick C. Beiser, *German Idealism: The Struggle against Subjectivism, 1781–1801* (Cambridge, MA: Harvard University Press, 2008), and Dalia Nassar, *The Romantic Absolute: Being and Knowing in Early German Romantic Philosophy, 1795–1804* (Chicago: Chicago University Press, 2013).

39. F. H. Jacobi, *The Main Philosophical Writings and the Novel* Allwill, trans. George di Giovanni (Montreal-Kingston: McGill-Queen's University Press, 1994), 515.

40. Jean Paul, "School for Aesthetics," trans. Margaret R. Hale, in *German Romantic Criticism*, ed. A. Leslie Willson (New York: Continuum, 1982), 32.

41. Jacobi, *Main Philosophical Writings*, 524.

42. For nonsubjectivist readings of early Romanticism, see, for example, Walter Benjamin, "The Concept of Criticism in German Romanticism," in *Selected Writings*, vol. 1, ed. Marcus Bullock and Michael W. Jennings (Cambridge: Belknap Press, 1996), 116–200; Maurice Blanchot, "The Athenaeum," in *The Infinite Conversation*, trans. Susan Hanson (Minneapolis: University of Minnesota Press, 1993), 351–359; Philippe Lacoue-Labarthe and Jean-Luc Nancy, *The Literary Absolute*, trans. Philip Barnard and Cheryl Lester (Albany: State University of New York Press, 1988).

43. F. W. J. Schelling, "Vom Ich als Princip der Philosophie," in *Werke: Historisch-kritische Ausgabe* (Stuttgart-Bad Cannstatt: Frommann-Holzboog, 1980), 1.2:104, 109, 122–123.

44. See Chepurin, "Indifference and the World" and "To Break All Finite Spheres."

45. F. W. J. Schelling, "Philosophische Briefe über Dogmatismus und Kriticismus," in *Werke: Historisch-kritische Ausgabe* (Stuttgart-Bad Cannstatt: Frommann-Holzboog, 1982), 1.3:96.

46. Schelling, *Aphorismen über die Naturphilosophie*, 61.

47. Schelling, "Vom Ich," 109, 119, 122; see also 101.

48. For a reading of the early Hegel, however, that aligns him with immanence and the annihilation of finitude, see Alex Dubilet, "Speculation and Infinite Life: Hegel and Meister Eckhart on the Critique of Finitude," *Russian Journal of Philosophy and Humanities* 2, no. 1 (2017): 49–70.

49. Whistler, "Abstraction and Utopia," 7.

50. See Albernaz and Chepurin, "Sovereignty of the World."

51. F. W. J. Schelling, *Sämmtliche Werke* (Stuttgart: Cotta, 1856), 2.1:509, 513–515.

1

Knot of the World
German Idealism between Annihilation and Construction

KIRILL CHEPURIN

> Blackness is not the pathogen in afro-pessimism, the world is[—]maybe even the whole possibility of and desire for a world.
> —**Jared Sexton**

> The world is its own rejection, the world's rejection is the world.
> —**Jean-Luc Nancy**

> For we cannot claim to know for sure whether or not our world, although it is contingent, will actually come to an end one day.
> —**Quentin Meillassoux**

A specter is haunting contemporary theory—the specter of the world. To think the world radically otherwise; to refuse the very need for a world or to reduce it affirmatively to nothing, a mere illusion or hallucination; to dissolve it in absolute contingency or chaos; to think the reality of that which the world forecloses, subjugates, excludes; to expose the world as totalizing and to find ways of tearing it down or opening it up; to work out an apocalyptic, postapocalyptic, messianic, posthuman ontology, ethics, or politics[1]—along this entire spectrum, the world remains, even in cases where its remains are thought of as, or after, its end. Even when one could not care less about the world itself, one is troubled by the fact of the world. No matter how spectral the world is declared to be, this fact remains a problem, with which all theory feels the need to engage. Even to say that the world is an illusion, that one ought to desire no world, is to admit that the world is there (and is at issue)—that it has the power to foreclose and divide, to make one hallucinate, and, most importantly, the power to survive, to remain. It is also to imply that the world is necessarily this way. But, why is the world there in the first place? Why this world—of divisions and exclusions, endless striving and endless postponement? Must it even be, this way or at all? Do we have to proceed from the fact that we—the subjects of modernity—are always already in this world?

Among these and similar questions, I would single out one as central: how to think the world without absolutizing or justifying it—to construct a world or the way the world could be, or to reconstruct the way the world is, without falling into the logic of justification—while accounting for the world's being there, as fact or problem? From Quentin Meillassoux's thinking of contingency as at once making the world possible and ungrounding it, to the Laruellean Real as prior to and without world and yet also, in the presence of the world, "giving" and "receiving" the world, to the polemics between Afropessimism and black optimism or queer negativity and queer utopianism, this question is inevitably at stake. The relation between world-making and theodicy (in the sense of world justification) marks this as a political-theological question.[2] In view of contemporary political theology's grappling with the problem of the (Christian-modern) world and its modes of legitimation, this question is central to its present and future.[3]

This is, at the same time, the typical transcendental conjunction, even the transcendental knot: conditions of *possibility* of experience are *necessary* for us to even have experience at all, so that to think the possibility of the world is necessarily to justify the world *as* necessary. This conjunction stems from Immanuel Kant, who formulates it in terms of so-called "transcendental conditions," that is, conditions of possibility of experience—of the world as it appears to us. For Kant, in order for us to even have experience, it must fulfill certain conditions; it must conform to a specific set of categories and follow certain rules. Thus, the reality of the world (of experience) is always negative and divisive: it is a world of objects separated from the subject and from each other; a world in which unity is secondary to separation and can only be thought by way of mediation (synthesis) and relation. There can be, in fact, no experience unless it conforms to these conditions; the world can only appear in this and no other categorial way for it to cohere. If we are to think a world, it can only be *this* world—that is, a world structured in this categorial way—because this is the way experience (our being-in-the-world) works. The transcendental thus converts possibility into necessity: to inquire into the conditions under which the world is possible, is to show that these conditions are necessary for us to even think a world at all. The possibility of *a* world is converted into the necessity of *the* world. To think the (possibility of the) world is to justify it as necessary: the transcendental turn is a theodical operation.[4]

This conjunction of possibility and necessity can take many forms—including contemporary ones. For example, to say with François Laruelle that the world functions by way of dividing the Real is to say that, assuming there *is* a world, this is the way it necessarily works—to determine the world as necessarily this way, to convert a world into the world. This conjunction may also be seen as a tension, within which the above question—of how to think the world without justifying it or exorcizing it—exists.

This tension is already present within German Idealism, spanning the conceptual space between two poles: world annihilation and world construction. In this essay, I will present some of the ways in which German Idealism tried to resolve this tension. The point, however, is not to suggest that German Idealism succeeded in doing so, but to put forward the transcendental knot as a key problem that German Idealism shares with contemporary continental philosophy and political theology. Accordingly, the following sections will approach the transcendental knot from different perspectives to highlight its various aspects and to demonstrate the numerous pitfalls when trying to deal with it—or how the world tends to survive all thinking of its end or rejection. It is crucial to engage with the world, with the way in which it is constructed (and can be deconstructed), and with the real power it possesses rather than announcing the world to be illusory, merely contingent, or easily refusable.

I take the pair of "annihilation" and "construction" from Friedrich Schelling.[5] Already in his early metaphysics, "the world" is a structure of divisive relationality: the original opposition between subject and object, the *I* and the *not-I*, which is then mediated by the *I*. Finding itself *in* the world, the subject is divided from object, faced with external reality as something different, other—something over and against which the *I* seeks to assert itself. Conflict, opposition, and striving are central characteristics of finitude; the finite world is a world of negativity, alienation, division.

As always already in the world, the *I* strives to break free of the world—be that through gathering the world into one totality that the *I* would perfectly possess (the dream of perfect sovereignty) or by purifying itself of any *not-I* (the dream of perfect dispossession, of having no need for the world). The former is the activity of synthesis: the *I* brings what is multiple into a unity. The latter is morality, configured as the striving to become absolutely nothing, without any need or lack. It may be seen, however, that the end goal of both strivings is, essentially, the same. "The ultimate end goal of the finite *I* and the *not-I*, i.e., the end goal of the *world*," Schelling writes, "is its *annihilation* as a world." What the *I* strives toward is absolute freedom from the negativity of the world—from conflict, division, and striving itself. This absolute freedom Schelling calls "absolute bliss." As negative and divisive, the world is fundamentally unblissful; the *I*'s existence in such a world is, accordingly, a constant longing *for* bliss. The world does nothing but defer, postpone, or mediate salvation and fulfillment. It is, after all, through this postponement that the world itself survives. From within the world, bliss cannot but appear as transcendent: as either a paradisal past or a future salvific telos—never now.

Imagine, however, that one would not have to strive for bliss; that the subject, instead of wanting something, could get fulfillment immediately—or not want anything at all. In this state of bliss, the subject would immediately cease to be just that: a subject. If there is nothing to strive for, nothing to negate or overcome, no positions to occupy, possessions to accumulate, or goals to achieve, what would subjectivity consist in? It would amount to simply *being what one is*. This is precisely absolute freedom: to simply *be*—without any self-assertion or lack, any further determination, any reason why. The *I* would become, as Schelling calls it, "absolute"—and thus cease to be an *I*, a transcendental subject or a subject of striving. As the mere *am* or *is*, this state may be termed "absolute being"; as being *what it is*, this being could only be an "absolute identity"—without any negativity or relation to otherness. As immanent only to itself, absolute freedom cannot become other, cannot transition to negation or any outside. "The absolute," Schelling insists, "can never be mediated."[6] It is "utterly immanent" and "has no need to go outside itself" (*VI*, 167). It is an absolute now, without before or after, possibility or actuality: immanently atemporal and amodal.

This kind of radical immanence can only function in and as the absence of a world. It possesses the "absolute power": the power to "completely annihilate" the world (*VI*, 122, 104). There are two aspects to this affirmative reduction to *Nichts*. Firstly, no common measure applies to absolute being (122), so that, from the perspective of the world, the absolute "can be neither object nor not-object, i.e., cannot be anything at all" (101)—can only be a nothingness, "nothing at all (= 0)" (119). Conversely, since the absolute has no place or need for otherness, it is the world that is *nothing at all*, annihilated immediately by the power of the absolute as the absolutely nothing. This annihilation functions by transporting the philosopher to the zero point that must be thought of as preceding—not following upon—the world. In other words, even though the *I* always already finds itself in the world, this is not where speculative thought must begin—this is not where Schelling locates the Real. The world is a factually inevitable yet secondary, imposed, negative reality. The zero point of nothingness or bliss is prior to the imposition of the world, annihilating its very possibility.

That is, in fact, why the *I* strives toward bliss in the first place: because it knows or intuits the world to be forcefully imposed, foreclosing the Real as that which is without negativity or striving—and so seeks to return to it. The temporality of the *I*'s striving in the world turns out to be one whereby the past is redoubled as the future, the past bliss as future bliss: a utopian loop. As long as the world is there, past and future remain separate, with the world existing precisely in and as this gap. To collapse them—to enact bliss right now—would necessitate a total collapse of the world. Why, then, must the world even be? "The main business of all philosophy consists," as a result, "in resolving the problem of the being-there (*Dasein*) of the world."[7] It is with this problem that contemporary theory continues to struggle.

It seems that this problem cannot, however, be resolved other than *from within* the world. In this, we approach the crux of the issue. At the standpoint of the absolutely Real, there is no world. As soon as the world is there, however, we find ourselves always already in the world. Even if we say with Schelling that, in fact, the absolutely Real is the "essence" of the *I* or the soul, so that in a more essential sense we are always already nowhere or nothing, prior to the imposition of the world—a fact that the world forecloses—and that the world is therefore an unreal, even illusory thing, this does nothing to make the world go away or cease its violent imposition. At best, it tears us between two "always already": one blissful, another imposed, with which we still have to engage.

It is, in effect, through this metaopposition that the world is constructed. This tear between the two "always already" itself is (the fact of) the world, existing as the gap within the Real. I am taking the term *construction* from Schelling's later philosophy, where it means exhibiting the world speculatively in—or with a view to—the absolute. To put it simply: if absolute identity and freedom are the absolutely Real, then how to think the world? Since there is no world at the standpoint of the absolute, to think the world is to think it as *negation* of the absolute—a negation of absolute freedom and bliss. In order to construct the world, then, we need not merely absolute being or nothingness, but twoness and division. The world functions by way of dividing and then mediating (bringing into relation or unity). Accordingly, in order to be a "system of the world" without absolutizing the world,[8] the system must be a system of oneness and twoness: it must at once annihilate or suspend the world and exhibit or construct it. The twoness is introduced by the fact of the world, a fact that cannot be thought if we remain at the standpoint of the absolute. Once it is introduced, however, the world can only be thought by way of negation and doubling. In other words, if the absolutely Real is without world, and if speculative thinking seeks to think according to the Real and not according to the world—seeks not to make the world into the first—then the only way to think the world is to think it *as* negative and imposed (vis-à-vis the Real). To think the possibility of the world turns out to think it as necessarily the (negative) way it is. The world cannot, it seems, be thought otherwise than in the very terms that serve to create it: the transcendental knot again.

To construct the world is thus, in the early Schelling, to reconstruct the way it is. But it is also to construct the end of the world. To think absolute being or nothingness as the Real, and to think the world as imposed negatively upon the Real, is to think that which immediately annihilates the world. The world can only be thought as its rejection or end. However, *from within* the world (where we are as subjects), this annihilation cannot but be thought of as its future (and not immediate) end. The issue is, in other words, how to think the annihilation of the world from within the world—given the fact that the world is there and does not simply and immediately go away.

If the absolutely Real is what annihilates the world, then to do so becomes imperative. In the absolute itself, no imperative could arise; however, from the point of view of the world, the soul's striving for the absolute translates into the demand of putting an end to the world. "In order to resolve the antagonism between I and *not-I*," Schelling says, "nothing else remains except complete *destruction* of the finite sphere (practical reason)." It is only if "we pierce through these [finite] spheres"—as demanded by the moral law—"that we find ourselves in the sphere of absolute being" (*VI*, 145). As a result, the question *Why is there a world at all?* "cannot be resolved except the way Alexander the Great resolved the Gordian knot, i.e., through the canceling-out of the question itself."[9] It is in the cutting of the knot of the world so as to break through to absolute identity and freedom, that the only resolution of the problem of the world consists. The moral imperative "enters, not in order to untie the knot, but to cut it into pieces by means of absolute demands" (*VI*, 100). To *Why must the world be?*, the only absolute answer is, *The world must not be.*

Since, however, the world *is* there, this absolute demand can only be re-mediated (from within the world) in terms of a future. The problem is that the canceling-out of the world, its affirmative reduction to nothingness, must be enacted from within the world. In order for the soul to strive toward the end of the world, this end must be configured as possible—

become representable as a goal. That which is supposed to annihilate the world becomes thereby a position in the world, a telos or *Endzweck* toward which the world must be directed. The absolute demand of immediate annihilation is impossible and so gets postponed into a possible future that is, constitutively, never now as long as the world remains. All that the striving toward this future can realistically amount to, then, is a progress of morality, an approximation of the absolute demand: an "incremental approximation to the end goal" (*VI*, 124). The world is supposed to be, in the end, annihilated, but this annihilation is always not-yet. In this way, the world remediates bliss as telos. As soon as nothingness becomes possibility and telos, it gets caught up in the same logic of futurity thanks to which the world exists in the first place: the gap in which past is redoubled as future. Via possibility and the not-yet, the world endlessly defers its annihilation.

By thinking the end of the world as the end goal—by thinking bliss as producible from within the world—the world is thus reproduced. Not only can the world only be thought as its rejection or end; the end of the world is the world. To construct the world with a view to its end thus runs the risk of justifying the world as the only way it can and must be.

I do not intend to suggest that this issue is absolutely unresolvable; to suggest so would also mean to absolutize the world. In his later thinking, Schelling may be seen as attempting to approach this issue differently—to think the fact of the world without reproducing the way the world is. In his so-called identity philosophy, Schelling insists that the world is something that we have imposed upon ourselves and need simply to reject; that we need to begin not with striving but with the refusal of striving; that we need to remain where we already are, to remain in the now, which is what the world forecloses. There are not two "always already," but only one. Essentially, we are never in the world. All finitude, temporality, relation, are already "annihilated in God."[10]

The identity philosophy proclaims the finite world, this world of reflection and the relation between subject and object premised on their separation, to be an illusion (*Schein*) that only appears if we adopt the point of view of reflection in the first place—a product of our "finite" way of looking at things, which must "disappear" if we are to think what is Real.[11] What is needed is to refuse to see the world that way: to *re-vision* the world as bliss, thereby *annihilating* it as world. There is but one being, an immanence common to all things; to see being otherwise—as divided—is to introduce division into it, to create the reality of which we then futilely strive to break free. To intuit this immanence-in-common is to see all things as simply being what they are—to see the pure "=" at the heart of everything, in which all distinctions between particular and universal, lower and higher, human and nonhuman disappear. Finite things may come into being and perish; but the "=" persists. In this, all divisions that make up the world are dissolved.[12] To construct the true reality is to exhibit it indifferently, that is to say, without difference, relation, or striving.[13]

On the one hand, this is a more fruitful move: to unground the very transcendental conjunction—to see the world in which we modern subjects exist as one whose necessity is tied to the conditions of possibility that produce this world as necessary—in this case, a certain way of looking at the world (of producing it *by* envisioning it as a world of alienation and division) that, one could argue, becomes dominant with modernity.[14] One could then investigate this conjunction historically, genealogically, or speculatively in order to destabilize it and to think a world not in terms of the transcendental knot. The transcendental is thereby made contingent or ungrounded. To expose this contingency is also to insist that the being that all things have in common, prior to the world thus produced, is where one already is, so that one must inhabit this common being and immanently refuse the world as unreal.

On the other hand, declaring this world to be an illusion, or perhaps something the absolute contingency of which needs to be exposed in order to think the Real or the event (for instance, to think with Meillassoux the coming of God as an eventuality that is absolutely contingent[15]), remains a problem insofar as it leaves the world free to haunt us. Insisting with Schelling on a being-in-common that the world divides, or with Meillassoux on the absolute of hyper-contingency that would allow us to think the event that "we might hope to see" one day,[16] still does not answer the question of *what to do* about the fact of the world—and the fact that it is the way it is—a fact that, as it were, recedes into the background of any destabilization of the world as mere illusion or as absolutely contingent. The world is made into a ghost, and the more one tries to exorcize it or to inhabit that which has (or wants to have) nothing to do with it, or the more one leaves its conditions of possibility to a throw of the die, the longer the world continues its haunting: a spectral dilemma, though not quite in Meillassoux's own sense—perhaps even a spectral knot.

Simply letting things be in order to immanently think absolute bliss runs the risk of simply leaving the world be, too. Similarly, to say that it is all up to an absolute, unmasterable contingency, may amount to justifying the world as merely (contingently) the way it is—to also simply letting it be. Contingency can do the work of legitimation as well: perhaps it is simply bad luck that the world is the way it is? Perhaps all we can do is hope for the lucky throw? Finally, to make the world into a ghost by proclaiming it to be illusory runs the risk of implying it can be simply refused—of trivializing the world's violence, thereby also justifying the world. This is not to say there is no way to evade these pitfalls. However, upon this way, one has to tread a very thin line, behind which the world continues to loom and which cannot, it seems, be traversed without engaging with the world in some way. No matter how illusory or contingent the world is announced to be, one has to think of ways of dealing with it—with the fact of the world's forceful imposition—if one does not want unwittingly to absolutize the world.

What to do about (or in) the world, too, remains a question with which Schelling continues to grapple. Elsewhere I have argued that the logic of highest agency (including moral agency) in Schelling's so-called middle period amounts to acting out of absolute indifference—to simply enacting what is right or beautiful without caring about what the world proclaims to be possible.[17] To act in such a way is to act *in* the world *without relation* to the world—an operativity that, for Schelling, completely disregards and, as it were, indifferently cuts through all worldly production and mediation. Moral virtue in particular is here no longer a matter of moral striving or progress, but a direct, immediate expression of the (soul's or God's) atemporal essence. "Let the [indifferent, blissful] soul act in you, or act through and through as a holy man"[18]—that is, one who acts, as Schelling points out in the *Freedom* essay, immediately out of the divine, out of "the highest resoluteness for what is right, without any choice."[19] In this state, the soul is immanent only to itself, so that morality, as the immediate expression of this immanence, operates without any deliberation and without relation to any context. It is atemporal in the sense of being without relation to the world's temporality or regime of reproduction, instead directly enacting what is right. It does not negotiate or construe dialectical relationships with the world; it intervenes into it. Morality is indifferent to the world as it is while being operative in it. In this, one may be said to act in the world without legitimating it.

This, too, is a way of annihilating the world. The basic idea here may be seen as responding to the problem we saw in the early Schelling. Any agency that is supposed to break through this world of actualization and the not-yet must not itself be inscribed into or function as part of the process of actualization. Any activity that seeks to abolish the position of the world must not itself be represented as a position within the world. Accordingly, to ask whether such an agency is possible is to fall back into the logic of possibility and striving. Such an agency, then, fundamentally cannot be self-reflective or inquire into its own conditions of possibility (bypassing thereby the transcendental knot); it cannot relate to any particular configurations of the world; it cannot act toward any position or any telos. The way it (mindlessly) cuts through the world may best be likened to a forest fire or perhaps a flood. No wonder that Schelling compares it at once to divine love (*Liebe*) and divine wrath (*Zorn*)—a divine violence that needs, furthermore, to be powerful enough to disregard worldly possibility, even to obliterate it so it does not block its path.

Where is such absolute power to be found? To ask this question is to raise the crucial issue. The world, after all, does block one's path. Even if we take the world, most radically, to be an illusion, its power—the violence it does, the hallucinations it produces, the fear it causes, the divisions it enacts—does not become any less real. Seeing as the world's divisions have real power, it becomes a question of enacting a power that would rival and even overpower the world—a power that would be capable of blowing up, setting on fire, flooding the wall or the colonial settlement that is the world. To locate this power in that which is transcendent to the world (a coming God perhaps), would be to reintroduce indefinite futurity into the picture. Another Schellingian answer would refer to this power as "nature"—this being of vast indifference and immense power, on which the modern world (of the Anthropocene) is imposed. It is unclear, however, whether waiting for a coming retribution from nature is any different from waiting for the arrival of a God. To wait is, again, to let the world be—which means that, in order not merely to wait, one needs to find ways of not simply leaving the world in place. That, in turn, implies thinking the world and the reality of its power (a thinking absent in the divine violence itself), even inhabiting it, if only to know where to ignite or how to produce or identify the cracks in the wall that should help make it give in to the coming flood. This issue is central not only for political theology but for contemporary thought as a whole. In Laruellean terms, the problem is that the Real and the world are *both* real, albeit in different ways, so that the reality of the world's power, if it is to be confronted, cannot simply be discounted as illusory. Unless it is confronted, however, the world continues to persist.

The move of beginning with what is absolutely nothing from the point of view of the world appears likewise in Johann Gottlieb Fichte's *Wissenschaftslehre*. The dogmatists—those who take the world to be the ultimate reality—"think of *things as the first*, and make knowledge depend on those, be formed through those." Knowledge and being for them coincide, so that, in dogmatic philosophy, the world fundamentally remains in place. The dogmatists, as a result, can only have "doctrines of things: ontology, cosmology, etc."—mere "images of things." The task is, however, to investigate the conditions of possibility of the world as it appears, or to trace how the world is constructed: a "construction *a priori*," which cannot begin with anywhere (any place or position) in the world. This kind of knowledge can, accordingly, only begin with a nonplace that must be thought of as preceding and totally *dis*-placing the world: the task is to think "knowledge as something independent—and for that matter, first, the question of whether things can still have any being outside knowledge if left in their place." The dogmatists cannot think such a nowhere, and so "cannot have any *Wissenschaftslehre*." To them, "it would be the doctrine of nothing."[20]

As proceeding immanently from the nonplace of total displacement, "knowledge structures itself through itself as an organized and articulated full *system*. . . . One part of that system is its concept of itself in its above-mentioned original organization. This is, precisely, the W.L. [*Wissenschaftslehre*]."[21] The point from which the *Wissenschaftslehre* begins, as part of the system of knowledge, is the point of the original completion of the system of knowledge as such. That the system is complete—a totality that is, however, not the totality of everything in the world—and that the standpoint of the *Wissenschaftslehre* is the atopic point where this totality coincides with itself, is crucial. It is, for Fichte, the atopic totality indexed by the system that ungrounds the world as always *not-yet* and instead grounds knowledge.[22]

"God" is what Fichte calls this atopic standpoint, similar to Schelling's absolute being. This being, too, is without negation or transition to otherness. As such, it cannot act, or produce any world.[23] Accordingly, the central issue is that of glimpsing the *ought* (*Soll*) behind the world. To what end must the world be? What is its meaning, its justification? To think the world *without* such an *ought* would be to think it as the mere capacity to effect an infinite series of things or positions, in space and time—as a potentiality without end or purpose, as meaningless, a nothing. But to reduce the world to nothing (*Vernichtung*) is—in a familiar inversion—to suspend this endless series of schematization (the drive to instantiate further things, without end), in order to expose the absolute being that it forecloses, a being that is itself a no-thing in the world. To inquire into the *ought* is to suspend the world as perpetually not-yet, so as to find oneself precisely at the original atopic standpoint with which we saw the system begin.[24]

To think the world from the standpoint of the *ought*, is to demand that the reason behind the world—the *ought* itself—become visible. The *ought* is thereby redoubled: as beginning and as end (as "the ought of the visibility of the ought," the telos of the world). "To construct the *true* world of sense" is, accordingly, to think the utopian point where the world coincides fully with the visibility of its *ought*. The gap between the two "oughts" fully filled, we find ourselves back at the original atopic standpoint.[25] Why, then, must we leave it in the first place? Because, again, the world is there and its meaning needs to be glimpsed. The existence of the world is the condition of possibility of the *ought* (it is because the world is there that the realization of the *ought* is thought to be possible[26])—but, also, it is only "on the condition that [individuals] find themselves on the path of glimpsing the ought" that the world and its *ought* may be seen to coincide: that the world may be regarded as justified.[27] To construct the world is to reconstruct it on the condition of its *ought*, and thus as not yet the (true) world—with a view to its end; and to think the end of the world, the point where its *ought* is fully visible, is to justify the world. Thereby, the world is constructed as the condition of possibility of its own (future) end. The ante-original, atopic beginning of the system is remediated into an eschatological telos to which the world is bound—and which is itself bound to the world.

The transcendental knot could not be tied any tighter. It is, perhaps, time to cut it again.

An alternative approach would be to think the world *without* an "ought"—the empty potentiality we glimpsed in Fichte.[28] In this approach, the transcendental conjunction is destabilized via the focus on the world-making capacity without a normative horizon or any necessary process of actualization. This would amount neither to absolutizing the world nor to declaring it an illusion, but to proceeding from the fact that the world is made or imagined. This is the early Romantic, poetic focus. Here, the transcendental knot is both acknowledged and ungrounded by thinking the conditions of possibility of the world without thinking this world (or any other world) as necessary or seeking to justify it.

"Is not," asks Friedrich Schlegel, "this entire, unending world constructed by the understanding out of incomprehensibility or chaos?"[29] The world is endlessly constructed ("unending"), serving to foreclose the incomprehensible—the chaos—not only as the Real but also, so to speak, as the material from which the world is being constructed. This idea is Kantian in origin: the in-itself as providing the material of sensation which the subject arranges into the world with the help of the categories. In Kant, however, the standpoint of the in-itself (which Schlegel calls "chaos") is cognitively inaccessible to the subject—and, as mentioned earlier, the categories themselves are necessary for the world to appear to the subject in the first place. The categories are thereby fixed and justified as necessary. They are also binaries or dichotomies (which are then mediated), in keeping with the character of the world as imposing itself on the Real by dividing and mediating it. Schlegel, too, acknowledges that the world, and the way we reflect about the world, functions this way. We tend to employ binary terms to construct the world or make it comprehensible—not just the ones found in Kant's table of categories, but also high and low, serious and jocular, beautiful and ugly, natural and artificial, and many others.

This is where, for Schlegel, *irony* comes in, which takes any pair of such terms and subverts or collapses them—so that, faced with irony, the subject cannot know whether the ironist (the ironic text or ironic speech) is being serious or jocular, where the higher might become the lower and the lower the higher, where the familiar might be revealed as strange, the natural as artfully constituted, and the ugly as beautiful, if in a different, unusual way. Thereby irony interrupts the flow of the world's construction in which we are habitually engaged, ungrounding the world's imposition and transporting the ironist to a standpoint at which *all* binaries are immediately collapsed. The operation of irony amounts to "a total interruption and canceling-out" of any process of construction (*KFSA*, 11:88). This serves not only to expose binary categories as themselves constructed and the world as produced—so that the alleged necessity of the way the world is gets fully suspended—but also to expose the Real on which these binaries are imposed and which can only be thought of as collapsing any binary, and thus as incomprehensible: the Real *of* incomprehensibility or chaos.

"Irony," says Schlegel, "is the clear consciousness . . . of the infinitely full chaos" (*KFSA*, 2:263). The irony of this expression, suspending the clear-chaotic opposition, is itself programmatic. There is, Schlegel observes, a certain symmetry to the chaos inherent in irony, with its move of "logical disorganization" (2:403)—a symmetry that cannot be the standard symmetrical demarcation between *A* and non-*A*. Rather, *symmetry* here names the structure of indistinction between any binary terms, or the total ("infinitely full") collapse of dichotomies. In nature-philosophical terms, Schlegel speaks of this full suspension as "the point of indifference [*Indifferenzpunkt*] where everything is saturated" (18:391), where everything is, to the point of indistinction, dissolved into one.

The first operation of irony stops, as it were, the cycle of reproduction of binaries, completely suspending the world with all its binaries, so as to begin with the chaos that must be regarded as prior to any world. At the atopic standpoint from which irony proceeds, all binaries are collapsed—so that, for example, *all* is jest and *all* is seriousness at once (*KFSA*, 2:160). The *all* suggests here not an alternation between the terms but an affirmation of a point of suspension in which the two (and any other opposing terms) coincide at any given moment. This is an operation of immediate annihilation, too—the world's decreation to the zero point that collapses all divisions. In a fragment from his philosophical notebooks, Schlegel connects neutralization, annihilation (nothingness), and chaos in the following way: "The chaos relates to the nothing in the same way that the world relates to the chaos. Chaos [is] the only real concept of the nothing. Nothing itself [is] the purely analytic concept. . . . The neutral, too, is confusion and chaos. . . . Nothing (*Nichts*) is more original than the chaos" (18:78).[30] Elsewhere Schlegel says, "Only that confusion is a chaos which can give rise to a new world" (2:263), and thus to speak of chaos is to speak of the world suspended or decreated. Similarly, to speak of nothingness, this purely ideal or "analytic" absence of anything, is to speak of chaos as a state in which all oppositions are refused in the all-encompassing *Indifferenzpunkt*.

There is, in this chaos, no trajectory or topos, no movement of mediation or distribution of possibility and actuality. It is the void of negativity grasped as "real," as an immanent materiality of nothingness—as pure material in which all distinctions are collapsed and with which the work of construction (of a world) begins. Chaos is nothingness considered as productive and generative. The ensuing construction reconfigures immanently this world-material—and in this, it is for Schlegel at once critical ("critique is the universal chaos"; *KFSA*, 18:366) and artistic: "the contact between the artist and the material is only thinkable as creation from nothing" (18:133). No wonder, then, that chaos is intrinsic for Schlegel both to the novel ("in its form, the novel is a well-formed artificial chaos"; 16:207) and to Romantic poetry (18:337). It is from this atopic standpoint of material nothingness that any binary—and any distribution of binaries, that is, a world—may be said to be constructed.

This decreation is configured by Schlegel, furthermore, as a revolutionary operation: "The chaos that, in the modern world, has previously been unconscious and passive, must return actively; *eternal revolution*" (*KFSA*, 18:254). Revolution is decreation followed by creation; or, even, creation by way of decreation. The same principle—"creation from nothing"—can be discerned for Schlegel in the three main contemporary events: the French Revolution, Fichtean idealism, and "the new [Romantic] poetry" (18:315). This nexus is crucial. What needs to be thought is simultaneous deconstruction of the world (to chaos or nothing) and its construction—one that is "artistic" or "poetic" in the sense of experimenting immanently with the pure material and constructing a world out of it: the transcendental conjunction as decoupled from the justification of the world under construction as necessary or the best possible. It is this decoupling that the terms *poetry* or *art* index—and not the valorization of the subjective and the arbitrary (as the supposed "subjectivism" of early Romanticism is sometimes understood). The ironist undermines any world she constructs by keeping open the capacity to confuse, to collapse any binary. The Kantian-Fichtean transcendental conjunction is important for Schlegel because it allows to see the world as constructed—without necessarily thinking it as necessary. The knot has to be cut only if one ties it in the first place; but why must one do so?

To think the poetic with Schlegel is to think construction without justification, and potentiality or capacity without necessity, including the necessity of actualization—but also without *end*. Romantic poetry is "progressive" (as Schlegel terms it) not in the sense of a not-yet, but as the absence of end or telos. Nor does it mean "incomplete" in any standard sense: instead, poetic construction begins immanently with a complete suspension of the world. The point is not to exorcize the world, thereby demonizing it or making it haunt us, but to think it (or, with Schelling's holy man, act in it) *without investment* in the way it is or could be. Thus, even if we accept that it is necessary to construct a world in some way, this does not have to mean justifying this world as necessary or implying that its construction must proceed in this and not some other way, toward this end or toward some end at all, or that it needs to be objective or serious.

That is, of course, an important part of Hegel's criticism of Schlegel: that irony "takes nothing seriously"[31]—that it does not take the objective movement of world history seriously. I do not have the space here to consider Hegel—or, for that matter, Marx—in any detail. But the way the transcendental knot is tied to world justification remains central to them both. In Hegel, world history famously is theodicy, and the transcendental structure—the way spirit produces its own conditions of possibility as necessary for its actualization and forward movement—is central to this history. To destabilize this conjunction the way Schlegel does is to endanger the teleology of spirit.[32] The issue, in Marx, of changing the conditions (of possibility) that are necessary to effect this change in the first place points to a similar knot. In the words of Lisa Robertson:

> Here is Marx's big dilemma, the reason he goes to Lucretius:
>   practice arises from conditions
>   yet these are the conditions we must change.[33]

This is, in different terms, precisely the issue which this essay has attempted to outline. In order to resolve it, Marx, Robertson suggests, turns to a thinking that is poetic in form. In the post-Kantian context, poetry indexes a "chaotic imagination that generates the promises of new worlds."[34] Romanticism wants to think the possibility of new worlds—but is that really the way to resolve the transcendental knot, this tension between annihilating and justifying the world? The (possibility of the) appearance of the new is, after all, at the heart of this tension that is political-theological in character.

This tension seems to remain as long as the world remains—because it indexes the fact of the world. In this essay, I have partially sketched the theoretical spectrum that emerges from attempts to engage with this tension and some of the pitfalls along the way. I have argued that, before German Idealism proceeds to construct the world, it annihilates it in order to reveal the Real that the world forecloses, so as to begin with this Real and not with the world. Instead of proceeding from the world as the ultimate reality, Idealism proceeds from a zero point absolutely free from any need for or any necessary transition to a world. This starting operation transports the speculative thinker to an atopic standpoint at which the world is turned to or exposed as *Nichts*, and which must be thought of as *preceding* the world. To annihilate the world, the way I have used this term, is to expose the world as secondary and imposed—to reduce it affirmatively to nothing—so as to proceed immanently from this nothingness (alternatively termed chaos, God, or bliss) as that which the world would foreclose.

To conceive immanently of a standpoint at which there is no world, revealing the world as imposed, is, however, not enough. For what to do about the fact that the world *is* there—the fact that we are subjects in and subject to the necessity of the world? For, no matter the force of world destitution and affirmation of nothingness, it is the construction (the thinking of the world) that ultimately determines whether, how, and to what extent the world survives and is justified. This construction may, as in Schlegel, take the form of ironic or poetic deconstruction, of taking apart the binaries that make up the world in order to freely rearrange them—but it is crucial that some sort of construction occur, some sort of inquiry into the exact conditions and function of the taking place or imposition of the world. If the construction is simply forgone, the world is either absolutized or turned into a ghost (or both). It might turn out, in this case, that the world is reproduced by way of its rejection, that the specter of the world persists paradoxically by way of its exorcism. Accordingly, the manner in which, and the end to which, the construction takes place is key. It does not suffice to declare the world to be nothing; it is important to destabilize the very conditions of possibility of the world and not to, wittingly or unwittingly, absolutize them. Even if the world is taken to be made or imagined, it is essential to trace how this imagination works—and the power it has over us. Deconstruction alone is insufficient; construction must take place. Such is a central insight that German Idealism bequeaths to contemporary political theology and contemporary theory.

Notes

1. The human is, after all, one of the names of the world—as "our world" (per the Meillassoux epigraph).

2. On the question of world-making as a central political-theological question, see Daniel Colucciello Barber, "World-Making and Grammatical Impasse," *Qui Parle* 25, nos. 1–2 (2016): 179–206.

3. See also my and Alex Dubilet's introduction. On the world in question as the Christian-modern world, see also our introduction, as well as Joseph Albernaz and Kirill Chepurin, "The Sovereignty of the World: Towards a Political Theology of Modernity (after Blumenberg)," in *Interrogating Modernity: Debates with Hans Blumenberg*, ed. Agata Bielik-Robson and Daniel Whistler (New York: Palgrave Macmillan, 2020), 83–107.

4. As first suggested, in a different context, by Odo Marquard. See, for example, Marquard, *Transzendentaler Idealismus, Romantische Naturphilosophie, Psychoanalyse* (Cologne: Verlag für Philosophie Jürgen Dinter, 1987), 77–83. I take issue with Marquard's understanding of modern theodicy, however, and German idealist theodicy in particular. He seems to take the term *theodicy* at face value, putting too much emphasis on God and not enough on the world—whereas, starting already from Leibniz (who coined the term), at stake in theodicy was the justification of *the world* as the best possible world, and of the negativity of the world as in some way necessary, ineliminable, and ultimately good. Thus, when Hegel says famously that world history is theodicy, the main function of that claim is not so much a defense of the figure of God but a justification of the course of world history as the best possible and even necessary or "divine"—so that no better world is possible, and no forms, categories, or grammar of spirit other than the ones produced historically by spirit itself. This, too, is a version of the transcendental knot.

5. This and the following section are a condensed version of the reading of the early Schelling offered in my "To Break All Finite Spheres: Bliss, the Absolute I, and the End of the World in Schelling's 1795 Metaphysics," *Kabiri: The Official Journal of the North American Schelling Society* 2 (2020): 40–67.

6. Friedrich Schelling, "Vom Ich als Princip der Philosophie," in *Werke: Historisch-kritische Ausgabe* (Stuttgart-Bad Cannstatt: Frommann-Holzboog, 1980), 1.2:109. Hereafter cited in text as *VI* and page number in parentheses.

7. Friedrich Schelling, "Philosophische Briefe über Dogmatismus und Kriticismus," in *Werke: Historisch-kritische Ausgabe* (Stuttgart-Bad Cannstatt: Frommann-Holzboog, 1982), 1.3:82.

8. Friedrich Schelling, *Stuttgarter Privatvorlesungen*, in *Werke: Historisch-kritische Ausgabe* (Stuttgart-Bad Cannstatt: Frommann-Holzboog, 2017), 2.8:68.

9. Schelling, "Philosophische Briefe," 79.

10. Friedrich Schelling, *Aphorismen über die Naturphilosophie* (Hamburg: Felix Meiner, 2018), 30.

11. Friedrich Schelling, "System der gesammten Philosophie" ["Würzburg System"], in *Sämmtliche Werke* (Stuttgart: Cotta, 1860), 1.6:140.

12. Schelling, *Aphorismen*, 49.

13. I owe the idea of Schelling's identity-philosophical construction as exhibiting the world indifferently to Daniel Whistler's work.

14. As suggested by Schelling himself in *Aphorismen über die Naturphilosophie*, 61.

15. Quentin Meillassoux, "Spectral Dilemma," *Collapse* 4 (2008): 261–275.

16. Meillassoux, 267.

17. See Kirill Chepurin, "Indifference and the World: Schelling's Pantheism of Bliss," *Sophia* 58 (2019): 613–630.

18. Schelling, *Stuttgarter Privatvorlesungen*, 166.

19. Friedrich Schelling, *Philosophische Untersuchungen über das Wesen der menschlichen Freiheit*, in *Werke: Historisch-kritische Ausgabe* (Stuttgart-Bad Cannstatt: Frommann-Holzboog, 2018), 1.17:159.

20. All excerpts from Johann Gottlieb Fichte, *Die späten wissenschaftlichen Vorlesungen* (Stuttgart-Bad Cannstatt: Frommann-Holzboog, 2003), 2:3–5.

21. Fichte, *Vorlesungen*, 2:15.

22. For a related argument on the standpoint of the system in Fichte as the impossible utopic non-place prior to the world's construction, see Kirill Chepurin, "Suspending the World: Romantic Irony and Idealist System," *Philosophy and Rhetoric* 53, no. 2 (2020): 111–133.

23. Johann Gottlieb Fichte, *Die späten wissenschaftlichen Vorlesungen* (Stuttgart-Bad Cannstatt: Frommann-Holzboog, 2000), 1:181.

24. Fichte, *Vorlesungen*, 1:189.

25. Fichte, 1:191–192.

26. Fichte, 1:189.

27. Fichte, 1:192.

28. This section draws from the more detailed interpretation of Schlegelian irony in my "Suspending the World: Romantic Irony and Idealist System."

29. Friedrich Schlegel, *Kritische Friedrich-Schlegel-Ausgabe*, ed. Ernst Behler et al. (Paderborn: Ferdinand Schöningh, 1958), 2:370. Hereafter cited in text as *KFSA* followed by volume and page number.

30. "Neutrality" is important here insofar as the neutral indexes precisely a neutralization of the binary logic.

31. G. W. F. Hegel, *Werke in 20 Bänden* (Berlin: Suhrkamp, 1971), 18:460.

32. For an important unorthodox reading of the movement of spirit in Hegel—not via his philosophy of history but via the transition from the *Phenomenology of Spirit* to the *Science of Logic*—that may be more aligned with the non-Hegelian and even Romantic trajectory charted in this essay, see

Rebecca Comay and Frank Ruda, *The Dash—The Other Side of Absolute Knowing* (Cambridge, MA: MIT Press, 2018).

33. Lisa Robertson, *3 Summers* (Toronto: Coach House Books, 2016), 47.

34. To borrow an expression from Frédéric Neyrat, "On the Political Unconscious of the Anthropocene," Society and Space, March 20, 2014, https://www.societyandspace.org/articles/on-the-political-unconscious-of-the-anthropocene/.

Utopia and Political Theology in the "Oldest Systematic Program of German Idealism"

S. D. CHROSTOWSKA

Modern utopias have a complex relationship with time. Rarely are they so regressive as to be set in some more or less distant antiquity. Rather than a straightforward return to the past, the desire that creates them makes an imaginary detour. It reaches backward to retrieve historic or mythic materials that enrich, shape, and set for the future a standard higher than the present can offer. The path to the future thus loops through the past, in which it recognizes, instead of models for a new and ideal society, material to be reworked by critique and reinvented by the imagination. In this way, the past becomes a means of renewing the present.

The utopian formula in question draws on Judeo-Christian eschatology (messianic and millenarian), reintegrating the lost Paradise: the restitution of the origin is to occur on a superior plane at the end of history. The detour's themes, meanwhile, most often derive from the classical Hellenic heritage. A synthesis of these two currents in utopian philosophical and social thought can take the form either of an inspired recuperation of the Platonic vision of the ideal city-state or, much less often, of a projected new mythology.

The earliest document of German Idealism is an example of the second emphasis. In it, reason emancipated from religious superstition and the Church turns to mythological sources. This recourse to a religious past takes a religious form, not only by assimilating the Judeo-Christian conception of an emancipatory futurity, but also by making its own the deep structure of religion—of *relegere*, meaning "to go through" or "gather again," to recover. The following looks at the logic and idea of this inaugural text to determine the potential value of its spiral historiosophic model for a materialist political theology with a utopian orientation.

The thought figure of the spiral most associated with post-Kantian idealism is itself comprised of a series of loops, representing the dialectic of spirit and the structure of history. In its Hegelian formulation, Idealism breaks with the perfection of the circle, the figure associated with the divine; from another perspective, however, it offers a dynamic, open, and secularized version of it, remaining continuous with the earlier design in its orientation toward an eventual totality (the outside is only temporarily out of the loop of history). Insofar as recourse is sought to the theological past, reactivated to sustain this utopian impulse, the secularization is incomplete. Hegel's subsequent integration of the development of political institutions into this telic schema translates and extends the model of theology into politics in the wake of the early modern reconceptualization of the latter as historical.

The spiral is already there in "Das älteste Systemprogramm des deutschen Idealismus" (Oldest Systematic Program of German Idealism; hereafter the Program), a text written by the young Hegel in 1796/1797 and made public for the first time in the revolutionary year 1917.[1] It is the course traced by the call for a new, rational mythology, *Mythologie der Vernunft*, to put an end to the modern state. Throwing into relief the utopian dimension of its radical political theology, the Program unites an orientation toward the future—an exceptional, Promethean moment of revolutionary foresight—with Epimetheanism, or hindsightfulness, that would come to define for Hegel the enterprise of philosophy.[2] The contraries of foresight, or forethought, and hindsight, or afterthought, convert into each other as their common ancient origin—and lasting fraternity—is recapitulated in their union at history's destination.[3]

More than perhaps any other in the German-idealist corpus and arguably the first philosophical text to do so, the Program shows the spiral's significance in the modern cultural-political-historical trajectory. This trajectory was profoundly inflected by nostalgic returns in the name of revolutionary and utopian aims. The spiral traces the desire to go beyond the present by way of the past which serves both to gain distance from and to envision overcoming the status quo. It is thus an allegory less of *history* which abuts on a utopian end-state than of modernity's *utopian desire* which nostalgically searches what remains of the past to discover its present potentials, preserving the former as a speculative resource while wishing to transcend it. In the simplest terms, the past is mobilized by a present desire for change.

In a genealogy extending from German Idealism through Karl Marx (who claimed the spiral temporal structure for dialectical materialism) to Franz Rosenzweig (the "Program's" discoverer and title-giver, whose own eschatological recapitulation assumed an open, looping form),[4] to the openly utopian thinkers of the historical dialectic—Martin Buber, Ernst Bloch, and Walter Benjamin—the spiral became the political-theological conceptual core of a secular discourse of a future this-worldly happiness. Finally, the figure also marked the distance between Benjamin, whose messianic-theological utopianism took up Karl Kraus's maxim, "The origin is the goal,"[5] and Carl Schmitt, political theology's first theorist, who, syncretically and telescopically, saw himself as a "Christian Epimetheus."[6] Traced back to the Program, the spiral structure of thought, in sum, characterizes a *dialectical* relationship between politics and theology, and represents the emancipatory, utopian dimension of totalizing historiosophic conceptions.

Between Eschatology and Mythology

The fragment known as "Das älteste Systemprogramm des deutschen Idealismus," written in the first person and originally untitled, is most likely unintentionally fragmentary.[7] A manifesto-like sketch for a vast, systematic project, it opens with the two-word sentence "*An Ethics*" and concludes with "the last, greatest work of humankind."[8] The ethics in question, we learn, is to encompass all *ideas*—to begin with, that of the individual *subject* (*selbstbewußtes Wesen*) as an autonomous moral agent, in line with Kant's "Copernican revolution." Next come *nature* and *physics*, their opposition overcome in a greater physics (*Physik im Großen*) that is "expected of future ages." From there we proceed to the idea of *humanity* (*Menschheit*), as opposed to the *state*. For, it is explained, "Only that which is an object of *freedom* is called an *idea*." Since the state dehumanizes and renders unfree, it must be superseded: "every state must treat free human beings as cogs in a machine; and it ought not to; hence it ought to *cease*." A true "*history of humanity*" (whose principles are to be laid out as well) would expose the state for what it is: part of a "miserable human work" (*elende Menschenwerk*).

Turning to aesthetics, the Program's author names the Platonic idea of *beauty* as the one that surmounts and "unites all [the ideas]," including *goodness*, *truth*, and Kantian *perpetual peace*. The "highest act" of speculative reason, the system, thereby becomes an "aesthetic act"; what lacks aesthetic sense lacks sense, coherence. Whence it follows that the philosopher of spirit must equal a poet, *become* a poet. The idea of poetry as the epitome of human achievement introduces the great loop of historical recuperation, conservation, and transcendence. The past is recovered in a superior, future unity as poetry "becomes again in the end what it was in the beginning—*teacher* of ~~history~~ *humanity*, for there is no more philosophy, no more history; poetic art alone will survive all the other sciences and arts."

Similarly recast under the sign of aesthetic beauty is *religion*. To serve the people, "the great masses" (*der große Haufen*), rather than the clergy, it must become *"sensuous."* It too must go beyond the traditional distinctions in religious belief. The author finds it imperative to reconcile the Christian faith with paganism, the unity of the first with the multiplicity of the second: "Monotheism of reason and of the heart, polytheism of the imagination and of art, this is what we need!" A universal, polyvalent religion necessitates, in turn, a new *mythology*: a system of rational myths "in the service of the ideas," outlined in the rest of the text. The new aesthetic-rational regime is to serve the people as well as the philosophers to usher in a new world order: "Until we make the ideas aesthetic, i.e., mythological, they hold no interest for the people, and conversely until mythology is rational, the philosopher must be ashamed of it. Thus, finally the enlightened and the unenlightened must *shake hands*, mythology must become philosophical, and the people rational, and philosophy must become mythological in order to make philosophers sensuous. Then eternal unity reigns among us" (my emphasis). With this organic coming-together, class and facultative differences disappear. In the concluding lines, the author explicitly takes the people's side against "sages and priests," envisioning life without existing hierarchies, one where "the *equal* cultivation [*Ausbildung*] of *all* powers" in the individual and across society will bring about "general freedom and equality of spirits." The new, sensuous religion, humankind's "last, greatest work" into which the system of ethics is finally absorbed, is to be founded, however, by "a higher spirit sent from heaven," presumably an incarnation of ethical principles.

It is the final sentence, announcing an egalitarian future predicated on a messianic intervention, that places the Program at the forefront of a revolutionary-utopian political theology. Beyond the horizon of the eschaton, history's climax in humanity's last and supreme work, lies a world in which all human toil has been superseded by the organization of spirit. Instead of the end of time, a new era is at once philosophically prepared and prophetically foretold. While avoiding Christian terminology, the vision transposes the unique divine redeemer onto a classical landscape where this ultimate human work is to be accomplished. In a process looping back to pre-Christian polytheism and reactivating the latter for a monotheistic age, myth and reason in their highest forms are united and transformed into something unprecedented with real and universal consequences for human existence. Renewing messianism as the motor and spirit of aesthetic reason, the inner-worldly transformation is integrated into an idealist model of history in which poetry inherits the force once accorded to religious transcendence.

The text's telic logic, its anticipation of the idea of social revolution, its postulation of a leader-liberator, and its glimpse of a world of harmony bear obvious resemblance to utopian literature, most of it secular in character, in the wake of the great "temporalization" (*Verzeitlichung*) of politics, critique, and utopianism in what Reinhart Koselleck termed the *Sattelzeit*.[9] During this "bridge period" (1750–1850), the realization of utopia becomes a matter of historical time and articulated in conjunction with socialist and anarchist ideologies. Far from the ideal no-place of philosophy (the utopian abstraction of Schelling's 1801 *Presentation of My System of Philosophy*),[10] the collective future outlined in the Program bears more than a passing resemblance to overtly utopian projections, such as Morelly's proto-socialist (albeit still statist) *Code de la nature* (1755), Henri de Saint-Simon's socialist *The New Christianity* (1825), or Joseph Déjacque's *L'Humanisphère: An Anarchist Utopia* (1858–1859). The philosophical fragment, among Hegel's juvenilia, contains aspects of both manifesto and prophecy, forms of expression increasingly characteristic of utopianism in the Age of Ideology. At the same time, its emphasis on and glorification of reason, the hoped-for unity of the arts and the sciences, as well as its quasi-religious promise of continued human progress qualify it as an extension of the Enlightenment project.

In urging such radical renewal of humanity on the plane of ideas, the text departs from multiple traditions of philosophical and religious thought. Humankind's entire cultural legacy essentially becomes folded into a spiritual mission that resolves its contradictions and supersedes it—an operation that prefigures Hegelian *Aufhebung* (negating, preserving, and elevating at the same time) while also offering an Ur-variant of it. The call for a modern mythology and its universalization in a new religion certainly incorporates a return to aspects of the ancient, Greco-Roman past, but this return along the lines of a detour for the sake of the future is part of a messianic-utopian scheme. That past is a theological remainder called upon and reactivated, potentiated, for futurity. The ideal unity of the coming society rests on the utopian desire to break out of the cycle of humankind's "miserable" work by recovering the past's emancipatory energies to advance the cause of humanity.

The double, retro- and progressive, movement in the history of spirit that is the history of humankind (whose principles are to be set forth) distinguishes this conception of history from another, roughly contemporary model of development: Giambattista Vico's "ideal eternal history," as presented in his *New Science* (1725, rev. eds. 1730 and 1744). The latter's immutable pattern of *corso* and *ricorso* (which follows the return to the point of origin at the end of a *corso*) could in principle be interpreted as spiral (with each subsequent cycle marking an overall advance), rather than circular. Vico's universal history was, however, based on an eternal law of providential change that, in Karl Löwith's penetrating account, qualifies as "neither progressive and redemptive nor simply cyclic and natural"—as neither an ineluctable, if convoluted, movement toward a telos nor a necessary cosmic recurrence of unhistoricized organic growth and decay. Unlike the Hegelian spiral, the pattern Vico described was more ancient than eschatological, and only "half-Christian."[11] Absent from it is the all-embracing linear progress—the total improvement, encompassing church and state whose transformation into, respectively, true religion and true community is advocated (again, with Kant) in the Program. Presenting a philosophical project awaiting execution, the earliest Program of German Idealism is doubly prospective: toward its own future elaboration and abolition, and toward the future of humanity, which it claims already to comprehend and (implicitly) to have a hand in constructing.

The Utopian Dialectic

The spring of history's spiral structure is, of course, the dialectic. In the Program, this is principally a dialectic between society and the state, between the an-archy of the first and the reified, mechanical order of the second. Resistance to the state form from within the modern state starts with the denunciation of "the whole miserable human work of state, constitution, government, legislature." This is prolonged by anticlerical sentiment, separating "the ideas of a moral world, of divinity, of immortality" from "superstition bogus faith [and] . . . the priesthood, which of late feigns reason," and thus stands in need of "prosecution" and "overthrowing." The outcome of such "stripping bare" is "Absolute freedom of all spirits who bear the intellectual world within themselves and may not seek either God or immortality *outside of themselves*." It is the human perfection of what remains after a dialectical confrontation between politics and theology, at the end of history. More precisely, the theological past reactivated to produce a messianic break is mobilized against political and religious institutions as the only means of their abolition.

The spiral conception of history appears at a dialectically charged historical moment. It takes shape against the backdrop of rapid and violent political transformation west of the Rhine—following the drafting of a second, radically egalitarian *Déclaration des droits de l'homme et du citoyen* in 1793 (Year I of the new French Republic), the Jacobin Terror (1793–1794), Thermidor, and the adoption, in 1795, of the bourgeois Constitution of the Year III, which established the Directory. The *Déclaration* accompanying the 1795 document, though it retained some of the language of its predecessor, removed natural equality and social rights, and officially added citizenly duties, in a considerable curtailment of freedoms.

The 1793 version of the Declaration (ratified but suspended by a state of exception in effect since the authoritarian Committee of Public Safety's *de facto* seizure of power) abolished slavery (Art. 18) and prescribed mandatory universal public education (Art. 22). It declared as "the most sacred right and the most indispensable duty" the insurrection of the social body in the face of an abusive government and the violation of rights (Art. 35), giving substance to the general will and popular sovereignty. It also proclaimed the freedom of expression, likewise soon to be withdrawn, as a pillar of democratic life: "The right to express one's thoughts and opinions by means of the press or in any other manner, the right to assemble peaceably, the free pursuit of religion, cannot be forbidden. The necessity of enunciating these rights supposes either the presence or the fresh recollection of despotism" (Art. 7). The ambiguity of the last line—despotism present or recent—indicates the possibility of a despotism without a despot and implicitly denounces oppression by a constitutional republic.

The enlargement of the semantic field of despotism, as reflected in the 1793 Declaration, prepared the ground for the critique of the state as a rigid, dehumanizing mechanism, whose abolition, as if building on this critical momentum, the Program would shortly envisage. The Program's political tenor is unmistakable, and its utopian desire exceeds that evident in the 1793 document. Just a year or so before composing it, Hegel looked forward to the revolutionary effects brought about by the "highest completion" of Kant's philosophical system, among them an actual political revolution in Germany:

> Not only will [peoples] demand their rights, which have been trampled in the dust, they will take them back themselves, they will appropriate them. Religion and politics have joined hands in the *same* underhanded game. The former has taught what despotism willed: contempt for the human race, its incapacity for any good whatso-

ever, its incapacity to be something on its own. With the spread of ideas as to how things *ought* to be, the indolence that marks people set in their ways, who always take everything the way it is, will disappear. This enlivening power of ideas even when they are in themselves still limited—such as the idea of the fatherland, of its constitution, and so forth—will lift hearts, which will learn to sacrifice for such ideas. For the spirit of constitutions has presently made a pact with self-interest and has founded its realm upon it.[12]

Despite the Program's focus on speculative philosophy, rather than a political program let alone agitation, its ambitions for humankind's political future well outstrip the most radical revolutionary aims (viz., *Déclaration* of Year I). For one, the state is discarded in it as the basic unit of social organization. Going beyond the Kantian vision, the future unites all peoples, rather than merely confederating republican states. The unifying idea is the utopian content of reason which subjects to critique all forms of government.

The content itself is minimally determined, limited to the statement of ethical and aesthetic principles implemented in the new society. In the context of the American and French Revolutions, these principles—equality of all, freedom from domination, the remaking of more than just political relations—had come to have a general, individual and combined, normative significance, as universal conditions or demands.[13] They prefigure the concept of a human, rather than a merely political, emancipation, famously articulated by Marx in "On the Jewish Question" (1843). Crucially, the Program prescribes no particular material social organization, leaving possible scenarios to be extrapolated from the regulative ideas it advances. Its utopian horizon is, thus, neither substantive nor purely formal, and it is reached by a double historical movement. The author's urgent desire for future transformation has recourse to the past as a conceptual resource, manifest in the call for a new mythology and messianism. The political-theological figure of the spiral approximates here the structure of the utopian wish. Utopian desire forms by passing through a sense of disappointment or injustice in the world, then through the negation of these perceived failings by particular images—images of desired (real or imaginary) happiness, justice, peace in the past—to end up as a desire to recover their content in the future. In this way, longing for the past converts into a longing for the future, modelled on and inspired by what was without being a simple transposition of its contents. The pursuit of this desire all the way to a systematic positive image of a desirable future is what the Program, for the most part, manages to avoid.

These distinct nostalgic underpinnings of utopia do not render it reactionary, even if it involves some selective preservation of the spirit and letter of the past. The case of the Program proves that utopian nostalgia can give rise to a revolutionary imagination, well beyond the restoration of some status quo ante. The dialectical spiral of its philosophy of history owes not a little to its proximity to actual revolutionary political and social developments, whose *revolutionary form* and utopian inflection it adopts. It was better suited than the premodern, astrological model of *revolution* as rotation to making sense of contemporary events in France.

The process of utopia's temporalization, bringing it into the process of history, reshaping it from an ideal for contemplation, which it (largely) was for Thomas More, into a program to be acted upon *hic et nunc*, which flourished in the nineteenth century, is plainly an aspect of secularization. While utopia's principal roots are not theological but humanist (the Catholic proclivities of its humanist originator notwithstanding), religious ideas underpin many blueprints for new societies unambiguously desired by their authors, such as Johann Valentin Andreae's *Christianopolis* (1618), Tommaso Campanella's *Civitas Solis* (1623), Francis Bacon's *New Atlantis* (1624), or John Eliot's *The Christian Commonwealth* (1659). Millenarian concepts found their way into the utopian faith in progress and in the transformative power of eminently political events like the French Revolution.[14] In Hegel's schema, the telos of history is spiritual union with the absolute; in Marx's materialist historiosophy, it is the hope for an end of what he calls prehistory, culminating in the profane apocalypse of the extinction of politics and the start of a history of man's own making.[15] The Program's speculative recourse to a religious past is not merely metaphorical; no metaphor is just a metaphor. It recapitulates, by its radical temporal foreshortening, the process of secularization. At the same time, in looping back through and drawing on this more ancient religious past, it demonstrates the secularization to be incomplete. Its need for messianic-utopian energy translates into a resistance to full secularization. As the language of the "new religion" makes clear, the author is not averse to preserving the spirit or idea of religion, whose ancient mode he wants revived for the sake of achieving a higher cultural synthesis. The theological impulse is openly perpetuated in the utopian impulse, and in a utopian cultural form that is to outlive all the arts and the sciences.

Two Paths for Political Theology

The Program thus deploys religious ideas positively to utopianize its political critique. Its principal target is the modern state form, still at this time bound up with institutionalized religion. More broadly, it rejects community constituted along political or ecclesiastical lines. Its revolutionary metapolitical, an-archic aim amplifies the utopian aspirations of the historical moment in which it is situated. Assuming its author is indeed Hegel, it is also evidence of a virulent anti-state sentiment in the early intellectual biography of the future theorist and apologist of the state. If, as Löwith believed, Hegel's teleological system is secularized eschatology, we might see this early Hegel as a proponent of political theology "from below"—from the point of view of the dominated and the insurgent.[16]

Based on the young Hegel's own distinction, Jacob Taubes opposed Kant's thinking about historical time to Hegel's as Old versus New Testament.[17] The passages Taubes selects from "The Spirit of Christianity and Its Fate" (1798–1799) echo the Program's criticism of the historical church and its relationship to the state. The Sermon on the Mount shows the "spirit of Jesus, a spirit raised above morality, . . . directly attacking laws . . . [in] an attempt, elaborated in numerous examples, to strip the laws of legality, of their legal form." It "exhibits that which fulfills the law but annuls it as law and so is something higher than obedience to law and makes law superfluous."[18] Rather than reflecting the categorical imperative, let alone Jewish submission to "lordship and bondage" (and the former, Kantian morality, is basically an extension of the latter, Old Testament legality), the Sermon is "expressive of life," of "the pure sensing of life which has in itself its justification and its authority."[19] Written some months after the Program, "The Spirit of Christianity" similarly displays the spiral structure and logic of supersession culminating in the transcendence of history. In a telic progression of ideas by a series of negations ending in a higher unity of former opposites: "Morality cancels domination within the sphere of consciousness; love cancels the barriers in the sphere of morality; but love itself is still incomplete in nature. In the moments of happy love there is no room for objectivity; yet every reflection annuls love, restores objectivity again, and with objectivity we are once more on the territory of restrictions. What is religious, then, is the πλήρωμα [fulfillment] of love; it is reflection and love united, bound together in thought."[20] The union involves "becoming as children" and is a restoration of the whole, a completion that presupposes a return: "The culmination of faith, the return to the Godhead whence man is born, closes the circle of man's development."[21]

The work lays out Jesus's political theology, invoking God as the principle of love ("the most disinterested love and so . . . the highest freedom"), rather than domination, in order to found a new community, "a perfected harmony," "united solely by a common faith and hope, and whose pleasure and joy is simply the pure single-heartedness of love, . . . a Kingdom of God on a small scale"—in which human relations are free and beautiful.[22] This outcome is not, however, contingent on a messianic event. Love here "is not religion, . . . the lovers do not *know* of this union; when they know anything, they know it as something severed."[23] Nostalgically preserved in this communitarian ideal is the spirit of the Christian faith whose letter the earlier text has already denounced as being opposed to such a vision of community. In striking contrast to the Program, the model of this community is clearly glimpsed on the horizon, not of the future, but of the past. And the eventual degeneration of the first Christian circle into a religion, a doctrine, into lordship and bondage, proves that it did not live up to the Sermon's message: its love became an ideal "deficient in life."[24] In excluding "all the relationships established in a political order," the members of this miniature Kingdom of God deprived themselves of the "active" and "living" ties to the state.[25] It is the fate of Christianity that "church and state, worship and life, piety and virtue, spiritual and worldly action, can never dissolve [in it] into one."[26] The unattainable utopian absolute lies in precisely such dissolution or living union.

If this overtly theological text, whose authorship is undisputed, throws into relief the spiral historical form that would become Hegel's hallmark, the earlier, programmatic fragment exhibits the an-archic and the revolutionary-utopian thrusts of his thought, about to be attenuated. These thrusts appear inseparable from the eschatological—the messianic event necessary to attaining the desired end beyond the state form. It suffices to think of the central terms or principles drafted against the modern state—individual freedom and equality expressive of life—for the link between social critique and the revolutionary-utopian future-orientation of the Program to become evident. Beauty, the principle of harmony and unity, is realized, actualized in the "aesthetic act" conceived as "the highest act of reason," reason's perfection. Linking critique and utopia, reason and myth (free of theological superstition), is the appeal to an ancient poetic system of belief (religious, ethical, political) defining a pre-Christian worldview. Reaching beyond Kantianism toward Romantic messianism (and as if to preempt reason's inadvertent regression into myth), the text nostalgically fuses the Enlightenment paradigm of omnipotent reason and the irrationality of myth (art, poetry) in a higher, dialectical synthesis—the Program's ultimate realization.

In the last days of the French Revolution, in the twilight of the Enlightenment, both revolution and reason had been tested and shown themselves unequal to the tasks they set themselves. The thesis of the revolution as incomplete, as unfulfilled, issued from within the Romantic movement, with revolution decoupled from reason's authoritarianism, and eventually took on a reified life of its own with the decline of hope in the messianic role of the proletariat (Marx's idea of permanent revolution, a revolution to end all revolutions, made the transition to a classless society seem imminent). To the progressive revolutionary intellectual currents of the nineteenth century, the looping structure of the dialectical process that is human history became synonymous with a serial political uprising. The reintroduction of explicit theological and Romantic motifs in the first quarter of the twentieth century (possibly to compensate for a weakened, secularized state) reflected a disappointment with the materialism of this model. The relation between politics and utopia in Marxist ideology, however, was in the main nondialectical, if we leave aside heretics such as William Morris or, in Germany, Bloch and Benjamin. Correlative to the theologically fortified socialism of the latter two, German counterrevolutionary conservatism, initially opposed only to liberal revolution, evolved a radical, revolutionary strand. The overarching vision of history held by its "conservative revolutionaries," among them Carl Schmitt, was eschatological and undialectical.

The telic progression adumbrated in the political-theological Program takes, as we have seen, the form of a spiral, whose use extends from the advent of German Idealism to Marx and, in the twentieth century, Rosenzweig, Georg Lukács, Buber, Bloch, and Benjamin. It is detectable in the negative-theological bent in Lukács, Bloch, Benjamin, and Adorno, in the negative utopianism of the last two figures, and in Benjamin's concept of a negative universal history.[27] Unifying this tradition is the dialectic between politics (future- or destination-oriented, Promethean) and theology (past- and origin-oriented, Epimethean).

The relationship between these two aspects structures the Program, which contends that the enlightened, projective, emancipatory element and the unenlightened, reflective element—the political and the theological—must "shake hands." A formulation that contrasts starkly with the underhand joining of hands by religion and politics against the people noted by Hegel in his letter to Schelling. Hegel's later conception, in the preface to *The Philosophy of Right*, of idealist philosophy as inherently Epimethean reflection after the fact, *après coup*, presupposes an Epimetheus who has already "shaken" with Prometheus.[28]

Schmitt's way of relating the two elements is quite different. Claiming that "Today, every attempt at a self-understanding ultimately proves to be a situating oneself by means of the philosophy of history or a utopian self-dislocation,"[29] he reflects on the available Christian conceptions of history to counterweigh the prevailing Marxist historiosophy. Another borrowing from Konrad Weiss (the source of Schmitt's self-description as a "Christian Epimetheus") encapsulates his own, personal view: "Salvation is, in opposition to all concepts, the decisive meaning of history."[30] The line's original context in Weiss's hermetic *Der christliche Epimetheus* is marked by a telic, circular structure, "[saving] the origin in the honour of the future": "[Salvation] ignites itself Epimetheus-like as a testimony that precedes it. It sets her milestone on a bloody footprint, given in advance, of a Christian event. And the unguarded hope deepens in the bounties of the struggle with the debts of history, even more so than in the legend of Pandora with mere gifts. [Hope] grows as if against itself and awaits on the edge of creation, which breaks off from the new configuration [*Geschaffenheit*] of the parable."[31]

Schmitt begins his discussion with the different conceptions of historical time found in Löwith's *Meaning in History*: (i) the cyclical (classical, pagan, all but devoid of historical consciousness, following the law of eternal recurrence); (ii) the great historical parallel; and (iii) the eschatological. All three, in his view, have been surpassed in the present. Historically, they seem to have overlapped, as happened during the Enlightenment and the formation of the "spiral-like" or positivist belief in progress—which were "only secularized Judaism and Christianity" (inheriting their *eschata*, as if progress were not conceived as indefinite!). At the time, revolutionary thought made sense of the present by reaching back into the ancient past for analogous developments. Socialism had likewise evolved by historical analogy—as a "New Christianity."[32] (One could also adduce here the superimposition of cyclical thinking on the progressivist utopian-socialism of Charles Fourier or, along with parallelism, on the later pessimistic cultural morphology of Oswald Spengler.) The "entire Hegelian-Marxist-Stalinist dialectics of history" has not provided a new model, as ancient Rome or early Christianity has served for the present's historical self-understanding.[33] In Benjamin, for one, such parallels become an occasion for the historical materialist's dialectical encounter with the past in the mystical *nunc stans*, or "now-time" (*Jetztzeit*): "the tiger's leap into the past" that, if it is taken "in the open air of history" and not "in an arena where the ruling class gives the commands" (as it was when bourgeois French revolutionaries quoted ancient Rome), becomes "the dialectical leap Marx understood as revolution" (the social, proletarian kind).[34] The rearward looping logic at work in Benjamin's approach recalls, of course, that of the Program.

Schmitt goes on to identify three possible interpretations of history consistent with a Christian worldview: the parallelist, the katechontic (eschatological yet antimessianic), and the Christian-Epimethean. The latter paradigm, which Schmitt finds in Weiss and appropriates, offers a "Marian image of history":[35]

> A historical counterforce against the leveling of history to the status of universal humanity, to the museum of the past, and an exchangeable costume to conceal the bluntness of activist attempts to give meaning to the meaningless. . . . [It is a] history that is not merely an archive of what has been, but also not a humanistic self-mirroring or a mere piece of nature circling around itself. Rather, history blows like a storm in great testimonies. It grows through strong creations, which insert the eternal into the course of time. It is a striking of roots in the space of meaning of the earth. Through scarcity and impotence, this history is the hope and honor of our existence.[36]

Thus, Christians "look back on completed events and find a basic reason [*Ingrund*] and an archetype [*Inbild*]. Through the active contemplation of them, the dark meaning of our history continues to grow."[37] The image is of course eerily reminiscent of—yet crucially different from—Benjamin's description of the Angel of History looking the storm of progress in the eye.[38] While the *Angelus novus* does not anticipate futurity directly, it is to be expected that, unless something interrupts or explodes history's homogeneous continuum, the future will be at least as dark as the past. Only in the materialist-theological configuration, in the messianic temporality— the arresting *Jetztzeit*, or revolutionary, redemptive instant that grants fullness to time—is history transcended. Schmitt's Christian Epimetheus, by contrast, does not accept history as senseless, hopeless, empty time, but as filled with eternity, given meaning by the incarnation in the Virgin, the event that sets history in motion. More than katechontic (counterrevolutionary, seeking divine legitimation for power), Schmitt's view is *incarnational*.[39] The retrospective, "active contemplation" of history by Epimetheus (following his mythic blunder) from the perspective of a singular moment is transposed onto a glance back at the moment of Christ's conception,[40] the beginning of history in light of which all that ensues, including the euphemistically styled "Promethean furnace" of World War II,[41] is redeemed.

The Handshake

Thinkers of political theology are free to choose between two historical paths. The first construes the relation between politics and theology dialectically, the second does not. The first corresponds to the German-idealist and, later, Marxian and Marxist critiques of the state as such; the second feeds into the early twentieth-century Christian critique of the parliamentary democratic state and of the bourgeois political Romanticism that led to its consolidation. Schmitt's theological history of suspended animation entails a rejection of linear secular progress. The retarding *katechon* is the restrainer or deferring force that restores historicity to the linear cosmology of waiting for the *eschaton* and, for Schmitt, overcomes this "eschatological paralysis,"[42] but in fact, as a historical anticipation of the end of time, produces a "frozen messianism."[43] This concept of history stands in sharp contrast to the spiral historical-materialist conception, married by Benjamin to a "*weak*" messianism,[44] holding on to the idea of universal history as "salvation history," with redemption as "the *limes* of progress."[45]

New non-Schmittian political theology, which inherits the intellectual legacy of Benjamin and others, can now trace its concept of history back to the Program and earliest German Idealism's spiral model of historical development with a utopian end. The ongoing unhealthy "fascination with 'political theology'" excoriated by Mark Lilla must be seen as the emotional, not always explicitly conceptualized core of a fascination with preserving tradition in the future.[46] The spiral describes how the inheritors of history's defeats hold on to an idea of moral progress, refusing to simply move on. There is a justified fear that all—especially the revolutionary traditions, and the hopes that rode and still ride on them for a change for the better—will be swept away, if not by a universal capitulation to, then by a ("real utopian") compromise with, the status quo. A new political theology of the oppressed, which takes the side of vanquished hopes in envisioning, however hazily, an emancipatory project's utopian horizon, cannot limit itself to infusing historical materialism with Jewish mysticism à la Bloch, Benjamin, or Taubes or with Christian values, in the manner of liberation theology.[47] It also must not be seen—and dismissed—as hopelessly tainted by its association with Schmitt, who himself was against secularization. It is, after all, counter to his political persuasions (if not always his diagnoses) that this *other* political theology took shape, creatively resisting his one-dimensional, Christian-Epimethean view of history by defending its own version of historical time. To continue such resistance while offering an alternative to modernity's self-legitimation crisis, it must assume a dual responsibility. At its heart, for any secularized theology that is popular (*of* and *for* the people) to inspire hope in redemption, it must "shake hands"—to maintain a tension—with the radical Promethean legacy of the Enlightenment to anticipate and warn of the future recurrence of human suffering.

Notes

1. For a historical overview of theories concerning the text's contested authorship and dating, see Panagiotis Thanassas, "Mythologie de la raison," *Methodos* 5 (2005), http://journals.openedition.org/methodos/341. The other authors proposed were Friedrich Wilhelm Joseph von Schelling and Friedrich Hölderlin. I take the principal, if not sole, author to be Hegel.

2. For a reading of Hegel's later work as a "political theology of revolution and utopia," see Kirill Chepurin, "Spirit and Utopia: (German) Idealism as Political Theology," *Crisis and Critique* 2, no. 1 (2015): 326–348.

3. Jared Hickman remarks on the "encompassing, cooptative" power of the "Platonic-*cum*-Christian political theology of the Absolute" seen, among others, in German Idealism, and particularly in Hegel. *Black Prometheus: Race and Radicalism in the Age of Atlantic Slavery* (Oxford: Oxford University Press, 2017), 4. The dominant interpretation, from the Enlightenment on, of the Prometheus myth as rebellion against tyranny and Prometheus's historical "blackening," as described by Hickman, suggest a more dialectical picture of the political theology at issue—as does the Program itself.

4. Franz Rosenzweig, *The Star of Redemption*, trans. William W. Hallo (London: Routledge, 1971; German original: 1921), 254–255.

5. The source is Kraus's *Worte in Versen*, the line serves as an epigraph to Thesis XIV in Walter Benjamin, "On the Concept of History," trans. Harry Zohn, in *Walter Benjamin: Selected Writings*, vol. 4, *1938–1940*, ed. Howard Eiland and Michael W. Jennings (Cambridge, MA: Belknap Press of Harvard University Press, 2006; German original: 1940), 395.

6. Carl Schmitt, *Ex Captivitate Salus. Erfahrungen der Zeit 1945/47* (Cologne: Greven, 1950), *passim*. The expression, appearing first in Schmitt's prison writings, comes from an eponymous 1933 poetic political treatise, *Der christliche Epimetheus*, by German Catholic poet Konrad Weiss, who cites Schmitt.

7. It is not, therefore, a Romantic fragment in the sense theorized by Philippe Lacoue-Labarthe and Jean-Luc Nancy in *The Literary Absolute: The Theory of Literature in German Romanticism*, trans. Philip Barnard and Cheryl Lester (New York: State University of New York Press, 1988), 27–37. The authors do, however, take the Program as symbolic of the philosophical incompletion characteristic of the Romantic fragment, and more generally of the philosophical horizon of Romanticism.

8. Anon., "The 'Oldest System-Program of German Idealism,'" trans. Taylor Carman, *European Journal of Philosophy* 3, no. 2 (1995): 199–200, trans. mod. German original: anon., *Mythologie der Vernunft. Hegels "ältestes Systemprogramm des deutschen Idealismus,"* ed. Christoph Jamme and Helmut Schneider

(Frankfurt am Main: Suhrkamp, 1984), https://www.hs-augsburg.de/~harsch/germanica/Chronologie/18Jh/Idealismus/ide_frag.html. All otherwise unattributed references in this section are to this work.

9. See Reinhart Koselleck, "The Temporalization of Utopia," in *The Practice of Conceptual History: Timing History, Spacing Concepts*, trans. Keith Tribe (Stanford, CA: Stanford University Press, 2002), 84–99.

10. See Daniel Whistler, "Abstraction and Utopia in Early German Idealism," *Logos: Russian Journal of Philosophy and Humanities* 1, no. 2 (2017): 3–22.

11. Karl Löwith, *Weltgeschichte und Heilgeschehen: Die theologischen Voraussetzungen der Geschichtsphilosophie* (Stuttgart: Metzler, 2004), 127, 148. For a close look at Vico's model, see Alain Pons, "Corso, ricorso," *Dictionary of Untranslatables: A Philosophical Lexicon*, trans. Stephen Rendall et al., ed. Barbara Cassin et al. (Princeton, NJ: Princeton University Press, 2014), 189–190.

12. Hegel to Schelling, Bern, April 16, 1795, in *Briefe von und an Hegel*, vol. 1, *1785–1812*, ed. Johannes Hoffmeister (Hamburg: Meiner, 1952), 23–24. English translation in *Hegel: The Letters*, trans. Clark Butler and Christiane Seiler (Bloomington: Indiana University Press, 1984), 35–36.

13. See Etienne Balibar, *Equaliberty: Political Essays*, trans. James Ingram (Durham, NC: Duke University Press, 2014).

14. See, for example, Reinhart Koselleck, "Temporal Foreshortening and Acceleration: A Study on Secularization," in *Religion and Politics: Cultural Perspectives*, ed. Bernhard Giesen and Daniel Šuber (Leiden: Brill, 2005), 207–229.

15. Prognosticating these depoliticizing metahistorical corollaries of economic development, the original chapter 6 on "real subsumption" was left out of the first (1867) edition of volume 1 of *Capital*. Revealing the full implications of his historical dialectic would have meant "[going] back to the alternative of a disappearance of politics or a messianic solution arising from the very destruction of the conditions of politics." Balibar, *Equaliberty*, 25. For a detailed analysis of this earlier solution, see Etienne Balibar, "Marxism and the Idea of Revolution: The Messianic Moment in Marx," in *Historical Teleologies in the Modern World*, ed. Henning Trüper, Dipesh Chakrabarty, and Sanjay Subrahmanyam (London: Bloomsbury Academic, 2015), 235–250. Although Balibar focuses on 1844 as Marx's "messianic moment," Marx never entirely outlived this moment (235).

16. The later, more familiar Hegel would then be his inverted image, one in which it is not the people but the state that takes the place of God. (He had, in other words, turned himself on his head long before Marx got to him.) For a reading of Hegel along these lines, see Michael Theunissen, *Hegels Lehre vom absoluten Geist als theologisch-politischer Traktat* (Berlin: de Gruyter, 1970).

17. Jacob Taubes, *Occidental Eschatology*, trans. David Ratmoko (Stanford, CA: Stanford University Press, 2009; German original: 1947), 149–163.

18. Friedrich Hegel, "The Spirit of Christianity and Its Fate," in *Early Theological Writings*, trans. T. M. Knox and Richard Kroner (New York: Harper, 1961), 212.
19. Hegel, "Christianity," 213, 255.
20. Hegel, 253.
21. Hegel, 270, 273.
22. Hegel, 285, 291, 290.
23. Hegel, 290–291.
24. Hegel, 294.
25. Hegel, 284.
26. Hegel, 301.
27. See Max Pensky, "Contributions Toward a Theory of Storms: Historical Knowing and Historical Progress in Kant and Benjamin," *Philosophical Forum* 41, nos. 1–2 (2010): 166–174.
28. In the *Protagoras*, Plato gives an account of Epimetheus who, entrusted with giving animals their *dynameis*, or powers, unwisely forgot to leave any for humans, forcing Prometheus to steal fire and the arts from the gods to give to mankind. Thanks to Epimetheus's error, humans not only survived, animals among other animals, but acquired divine attributes. Thought may have *followed* his own actions but provoked his brother's thoughtful, farsighted heroic feat. According to Hesiod, Epimetheus accepted Pandora (her name meaning "all-gifted"), who then, out of curiosity, released all evils from her jar, until only hope remained inside—another disaster with a redeeming side.
29. Carl Schmitt, "Three Possibilities for a Christian Conception of History" (1950), trans. Mario Wenning, *Telos*, no. 147 (2009): 167.
30. Konrad Weiss, quoted in Heinrich Meier, *Carl Schmitt and Leo Strauss: The Hidden Dialogue*, trans. J. Harvey Lomax (Chicago: Chicago University Press, 1995), 82n104. The sentence is quoted by Schmitt with reference to the Calvinist doctrine of predestination in his *Land and Sea: A World-Historical Meditation*, trans. Simona Draghici (Washington, DC: Plutarch, 1997), 45.
31. Konrad Weiss, *Der christliche Epimetheus* (1933), http://www.seiten-der-dichtung.de/konradweiss/dce.html.
32. Schmitt, "Possibilities," 169, 168.
33. Schmitt, 168.
34. Benjamin, "History," 395.
35. Schmitt, "Possibilities," 170.
36. Schmitt, 170.
37. Schmitt, 170.
38. Benjamin, "History," 392 (Thesis IX).
39. David Ratmoko contrasts Schmitt's view, which he qualifies as both apocalyptic and katechontic, with Taubes's, which is emphatically apocalyptic, seeking "a theological *delegitimation* of political power as a whole." It is the difference between a counterrevolutionary apocalypticism and a revolutionary one. David Ratmoko, preface to *Occidental Eschatology* by Jacob Taubes, xvi.

40. Schmitt, "Possibilities," 170.

41. Schmitt, *Salus*, 38.

42. Schmitt, "Possibilities," 169.

43. Giorgio Agamben, "A Jurist Confronting Himself: Carl Schmitt's Jurisprudential Thought," in *The Oxford Handbook of Carl Schmitt*, ed. Jens Meierhenrich and Oliver Simons (New York: Oxford University Press, 2016), 462. Any real historical progression, historically meaningful happening, is precluded by the deferral of historical meaning (derived from the *eschaton*) by and in the katechological present.

44. Benjamin, "History," 390 (Thesis II). For Benjamin, theology is needed to save historical materialism (Thesis I).

45. Walter Benjamin, "Paralipomena to 'On the Concept of History,'" trans. Edmund Jephcott and Howard Eiland, in *Walter Benjamin: Selected Writings*, 4:404.

46. Mark Lilla, *The Shipwrecked Mind: On Political Reaction* (New York: New York Review of Books, 2015), xix.

47. A recent Christian example of this theoretical fusion with a revolutionary goal is John Joseph Marsden's proposal—at the end of his *Marxian and Christian Utopianism: Toward a Socialist Political Theology* (New York: Monthly Review Press, 1991)—of a socialist utopian political theology, whereby the Church, in a revival of millenarianism and a "recovery of temporal expectations," is to "enter into *critical* solidarity with the socialist movement"—a socialism true to the "essentially utopian credo" of a Marxian humanist ethics (162–163). This vision, however, remains within the horizon of the state form precisely because of its heuristic attachment to the Kingdom of God, expressly to expand socialist theory to look beyond society toward humanity's release from suffering, that is, redemption.

3

Relational Division

DANIEL COLUCCIELLO BARBER

"I can imagine as an apocalyptic: let it go down. I have no spiritual investment in the world as it is."[1] Jacob Taubes's remark, presented as a somewhat offhand, adumbrated commentary on Carl Schmitt's theory of sovereignty, provides the lineaments not only for a certain reading of this theory but also for a mode of thought that operates as the refusal of worldly relation. It is because such an apocalyptic mode of thought—denominated as such in view of Taubes's self-identification as "an apocalyptic" (*Apokalyptiker*)—is defined by the refusal of worldly terms that its validity need not be restricted to the domain of political theology. To observe this point is to open a space of thought in which apocalyptic may be understood to address secular discourses such as Hegel's philosophy. The validity of such address—which will be taken up in the latter part of this essay—is due to the fact that Hegel's philosophy, like Schmitt's political theology, is a discourse that treats worldly relation as imperative. While perhaps counterintuitive, this commonality of Hegel and Schmitt ceases to be so insofar as one follows the apocalyptic imagination, which relativizes the distinction between political theology and philosophy in virtue of the question of the world.

My references to apocalyptic, political theology, sovereignty, and world are made within the context of Taubes's commentary on Schmitt. Each of these points of reference, or concepts, can be used, reimagined, or undone in all kinds of ways. Although I refer to apocalyptic, political theology, sovereignty, and world in a manner that is defined by the aforementioned context, my approach is not intended to resist these other ways. It simply follows from the circumscribed, analytically descriptive character of this essay, the proximate aim of which is to understand what is at issue not only in Taubes's introduction of apocalyptic precisely as response to and refusal of Schmitt's political theology of the sovereign but also in his articulation of this response and refusal in terms of the world. Put otherwise, the aim is not a simple endorsement of Taubes's apocalyptic but an analysis that tends toward immanent critique—of Schmitt and a certain Hegel, quite evidently, but ultimately of the entire context presupposed by Taubes's commentary.

What then does Taubes mean when he invokes the world? What implications might one draw from the fact that his commentary on Schmitt's political theology proceeds explicitly in terms of the world? To foreground the world is not to evade but to clarify the import of sovereignty. What is central for an apocalyptic reading of Schmitt's political theology is not sovereignty in itself, for sovereignty is advanced in service of the world. It then becomes exigent, if one follows the implications of Taubes's commentary, to discern an ontological claim—specifically, a decision on behalf of the being of the world—within the explicitly juridical terms of Schmitt's thought.

One might, in view of this exigency, understand the world as a reading of Schmitt's legal order, and specifically of the manner in which it is related to sovereignty: "Like every other order, the legal order rests on a decision and not on a norm."[2] A fuller elaboration of the relation between sovereignty and legal order (or the world) emerges when Schmitt introduces, as an intermediary term, the normal situation—that is, a situation in which legal norms are applicable. "For a legal order to make sense, a normal situation must exist, and he is sovereign who definitely decides whether this normal situation exists. All law is 'situational law.' The sovereign produces and guarantees the situation in its totality."[3] A clear sequence of dependence here emerges: the existence of a legal order requires the existence of a normal situation, which itself requires sovereign decision. The logic of this sequence, whereby sovereignty is required by legal order—or, perhaps more importantly, by the sense-making involved in such order—may likewise be understood as a rhetorical strategy: sovereignty is advanced not in itself but rather in the name of legal order. There is a need for sovereignty because there is a need for legal order, or (since legal order is "like every other order") for order in general—which is to say, for the world.

It is along these lines that the call for sovereignty appears in terms of a call for worldly relation: the need to relate to the sovereign is premised on a presupposed need to relate to the world. If there must be a sovereign, if sovereign decision is necessary, then this is because there is no world without the operation of sovereignty. Or, put otherwise, to be left without sovereignty is to be left with a chaos that precludes the world and thereby emerges as the ultimate enemy of sovereignty[4]—the sole "interest" of Schmitt, Taubes remarks, is "that the chaos not rise to the top."[5] In order for the world to be, to hold together as something in existence, there must be a decision made on behalf of the world, and it is precisely such a decision that is provided by sovereignty.

The necessity of sovereignty for Schmitt thus follows from the necessity of relating to, or in terms of, the world; the invocation of sovereignty is already implied by the terms of a world to which we relate or by the terms in which we relate to the world. This means, following what is implicit in Taubes's commentary, that any critical opposition to sovereignty that is based on the affirmation of worldly relation will fall short. It would be a mistake to oppose worldly relation—however multiplicitous, fluid, and horizontal—to sovereignty, for sovereignty—while certainly at least authoritarian, fixed, and vertical—is also already imbricated with relationality. Read according to the logic implicit in Taubes's commentary, Schmitt's political theology is not opposed to (and thus cannot be opposed by) worldly relation—in fact, it takes for granted and depends on such relation.

It is for this reason that the opposition between sovereign fixity and relational fluidity, or the critical production that ensues from and likewise reproduces this opposition, becomes suspended. Such opposition, emerging as it does between a fixed world and a fluid world, cannot address the fundamental question raised by sovereignty, which concerns the very being of the world. It is exactly this question that is foregrounded by Taubes's commentary, which opposes Schmitt's sovereignty without appealing to the world: there is no invocation of the world as something supposed to be positively imagined outside of sovereignty, no claim that the world, by being positioned in relation to sovereignty, is something inadequately thought or named. The world is not an autonomously accessible measure in relation to which sovereignty could be recognized as falling short, and so to imagine in terms of the world is by no means to gain critical leverage on sovereignty.

What is undone by this line of thought is not opposition to Schmittian sovereignty so much as the attempt to ground such opposition in the world. Opposition to political-theological sovereignty is without worldly ground but it remains as refusal of worldly terms. In other words, the absence of appeal to the world as a means for the critique of sovereignty has nothing to do with a qualified acceptance of sovereignty. On the contrary, such appeal is refused precisely because it introduces a worldly relation that is already oriented around the sovereignty of political theology. The refusal to appeal to the world as a ground for critical opposition to sovereignty thereby belongs to a more essential refusal of worldly relation, a refusal that is inseparable from the refusal of such sovereignty.

It is in view of this modality of refusal that one can understand the opposition of Taubes to Schmitt. Of central relevance for Schmitt, when read via Taubes's commentary, is the relation between world-investment and sovereignty: to invest in the world is to be involved in sovereignty, for the world holds together through sovereignty. To positively relate to the world, then, is necessarily to relate to sovereignty, for the world itself is related to sovereignty; investment in the world entails investment in sovereignty. Rendered in this manner, Schmitt's thesis, or at least its problematic contours, are granted by Taubes's remark. Yet Taubes—at least on his own account— "can imagine" a refusal of sovereignty, he can "let [the world] go down," because when it comes to the world he "ha[s] no spiritual investment." In other words, while he grants that world-investment is necessarily related to sovereignty, he refuses the necessity of world-investment.

Here one approaches the essential operation of Taubes's apocalyptic: not a refusal of this or that world so much as a refusal to positively relate to the world in general. To "imagine as an apocalyptic" is to imagine without positive reference to any world at all. This is to say, among other things, that such refusal does not emerge in view of another world. Refusal of the world, even when qualified according to its givenness ("the world as it is"), does not proceed in relation to an alternatively imagined world—a world that would be better, or even a world that would be different. Taubes's remark does not set forth a critical temporality between the world as it is and the world that is not yet. There is no call to inhabit a time between worlds. Nor does his remark refer to—much less invest in the imagination of—the purported fact that another world is possible. To imagine as an apocalyptic is not to imagine another world, but rather to not imagine another world. It is to imagine the collapse of the world—"let it go down"—without imagining this collapse in connection with another world. Apocalyptic imagination involves collapse without any resurrective concomitant.

To imagine as an apocalyptic, then, is to refuse to relate in terms of the world. Or, when one places emphasis on the temporal register of such relation, it is to refuse the expectation that one must relate in terms of the world. The success of Schmitt's call for sovereignty—where the *successful* establishment of sovereignty entwines with the temporal *succession* of the world into the future—depends on such expectation. The call of sovereignty arises amid awareness of the potentiality that the world will not hold together, that there will be no world, that there will instead be chaos, if this call is not sent forth and received. It is in this sense that the imperative at issue in sovereign decision is bound to the imperative of the world: sovereignty concerns the sheer assertion that the world must be, that the potentiality of the world's collapse must be warded off.

Taubes, by means of apocalyptic imagination, is able to situate collapse within a context that does not observe the survival of the world as prerequisite. Whereas Schmitt's thought answers the question, *What is required for the world to hold together?*, Taubes's commentary—through its avowal of collapse, of the fact that "forces can be unleashed that we are in no position to control"[6]—adverts to a question that is logically prior: *Why must the world be?*

If there is, from Taubes's apocalyptic vantage, a certain use for Schmitt—who he termed "an apocalyptic prophet of the counterrevolution"[7]—then this is insofar as Schmitt's thought serves to clarify that the world exists only through the sheer assertion of relational possibility. The world is something that would not be without being made imperative, something that can hold together only by way of sovereignty—something that depends, as Schmitt put it, on "an absolute decision created out of nothingness."[8] To address the world in this manner is to acknowledge that the possibility of the world stands or falls on its capacity to impose itself. It is in this (limited) manner that Schmitt manifests apocalyptic knowledge: to know that the world is a matter of possibility is to know that reality does not require the world. Yet Schmitt turns against this knowledge by foregrounding what may be described—beyond his own formulations, and in order to articulate a logic implicit to sovereignty—as the need of the world.

The need of the world refers, in an initial sense, to the assertion that there is a world, to the decision that the world must hold (or be held) together: the world needs to be. Yet there is another sense of the need of the world, one that emerges not from the assertion of sovereign decision but rather from the world as such. This is a need or neediness internal to the world, one that follows from awareness that the world does not hold together on its own terms, that the world cannot ground its own being. There is, then, a mutual implication between the two senses of need: the need that emerges "internal" to the world—the world's need for a ground that it cannot provide on its own terms, or from within itself—is met by and simultaneously produced as the justification for an imperative that emerges "external" to the world. The imperative (externally) provides the ground that the world cannot (internally) provide.

This imperative, this assertion of ground that meets the need of a world that cannot ground itself within its own terms, entails the invocation of a term external to the world. It is along these lines that one might read the import of theology within a Schmittian logic: theological discourse, revolving as it does around the name of God, provides the world with the external term that it needs in order to hold together. To pursue this reading is to appreciate that theological discourse, within the thought of Schmitt, is inseparable from—and, more precisely, is an attempt to respond to—knowledge that the world cannot be grounded on or within its own terms. Theology, as discourse of an external term, appears valuable because of its capacity to carry out the work of holding together the world, to remain concerned for the world's being. It is in this sense that theology, within a Schmittian logic, is always already a theology of the world and that the political—defined via the need of the world—is a matter of theology. What is therefore central in political theology, as it appears in Schmitt, is neither God as such nor the world as such, but rather the possibility of relation between them: God is thought not in itself but rather as a term externally related to the world; the world is thought not in itself but rather in relation to a theological terminology that wards off the collapse of worldly terms. Worldly relation finds its theological registration.

Yet the theology through which worldly relation is registered may be put in question: If God is a term external to the terms of the world, then why imagine that such a term could even be in relation to the world? What is at issue in this question is not whether the name of God is external to the world—this may be presumed—but whether such an external term actually serves to support, rather than undermine, worldly relation. This externality would seem to entail a mutual exclusion of terms—not a relation between them. To say that God is external to worldly terms, after all, is to say (no more than) that God cannot be named within the terms of the world. The name of God should then be understood, simply and strictly, as "without term."[9]

Consequently, to name God, or to call (upon) God, is by no means to call the world into being. The presumption of any such interpellative double clench is undone, for it depends upon a reality that cannot be related in terms. The attempt to ward off the collapse of the world by means of political theology, to theologically register a ground for a world, encounters a deepening groundlessness.

The success of a Schmittian appeal to theological discourse must involve something other than theological discourse as such, something that gives theology an additional, specific sense. This is because the act of naming God—which defines theology as such—revolves around, reveals, and remains bound to a reality without term. If Schmitt's thought claims to find in theological discourse a means for the registration of worldly relation, then this is only insofar as it converts such reality into terms of the world.

It is here that one encounters the specifically Christian character of Schmitt's political theology.[10] The inadequacy of worldly terms for the naming of God is a central feature of the Abrahamic traditions of Judaism, Christianity, and Islam. Christianity, however, has distinguished itself—which is to say that it has claimed itself as superior in relation to these others—through its claim that one can and should imagine the relation, or term of relation, between a God without term and a world at whose center exists the human.[11] This claim is made by means of Christology: Christ, as fully divine and fully human, is simultaneously a term for what is without term and a term for the world. That which is external to the world, that to which worldly relation turns for its ground, is made to turn back toward the world.

The claims of Christology enable the imagination that there is no reality that is ultimately without term: the irreducibility of God to worldly terms is superseded by the conversion of God into a term that relates to—that has, by means of incarnation, become a term within—the world. Christ thereby appears as the redeemer of the very being of the world. The irreducibility of God to worldly relation ungrounds the world—the world collapses while God is without term—but the world is redeemed from collapse because of the establishment of Christ.

This is to observe, furthermore, that the imagination of the terms God and world *as* relatable, as belonging to a *horizon* of relation—where Christ is the image of such horizon—is an *effect* of Christology rather than an already given condition to which the image of Christ subsequently responds. Apart from this horizon, it might even be difficult to speak of the world and God in terms of division: in order for a division between terms to have sense, these terms must be able to be related to one another, which is to say that there must be a minimal commonality between them—and this is precisely what is absent when it comes to God and the world. Division and relation, in other words, are not necessarily exclusive of one another. As long as one imagines a minimal commonality between the divided terms, relation and division can work together or be put to work through each other. A division between terms becomes recognized through a measure in which each shares or through a measuring of each in contrast with the other, while the possibilities of relation that emerge in virtue of such commensuration are sustained within the space produced between these divided terms.

It is along these lines that one can address the divisive relation that is essential to Christianity. Within the Abrahamic context, Christology is not one version of imagining a previously established possibility of relation, as this last is already precluded by a divine reality without term. What is established by Christology, then, is not one particular means of such relation so much as the very existence of a relational horizon to be imagined. The fact that this horizon involves division actually confirms the existence of relation: Christology's establishment of relation is likewise the establishment of the minimal commensuration that makes it possible to describe terms meaningfully as divided from one another. To establish a horizon between God and the world is to convert the divine reality without term into terms of relational division, or divisive relationality.

Even though Christology evidently establishes one prominent image of relation (Christ), it operates more fundamentally as the establishment of a divisively relational horizon—which might serve as the host of a multitude of other images—between the world and an external term. This is to say that the essence of the Christological operation should be located not in a specifically empirical image (Christ) but rather in a specifically transcendental imagination (divisive relationality). Such a reading of the Christological operation helps articulate the manner in which Schmitt's political theology may be understood as Christian: while not located in a specific image of Christ, the theological registration at issue in Schmitt's thought remains specifically Christian insofar as it treats as imperative (and thus requires imagination of) worldly relation.

The separation of Taubes's commentary from such relation is also a matter of theology, though one elaborated in a Jewish context and along apocalyptic (as well as Gnostic) lines.[12] The presumption of a common Abrahamic, "monotheistic," or "Judeo-Christian" horizon collapses when the question of the world's collapse—*Why must the world be?*—is brought to the fore. Theology, then, is not merely a discourse in service of the success of the world—or, while it is such a discourse in the specifically Christian sense, it is also, and as such, a discourse by which divestment from the world is observed.

Apocalyptic, at least as it appears in Taubes's remark, requires no investment in positively determined reference—whether such reference is to the *being* of God or the *day* of the world's end. What is enabled by the apocalyptic imagination is not this or that image but a doing without reference to images, including the image of the world. It is in this manner that apocalyptic imagination may be understood as a kind of negativity: a negativity that refuses to base itself on a deeper, higher, or future positive reference.

Yet this negativity without term is not without reality. Put simply, worldly relation establishes terms in which the reality at issue in the name or term of God cannot be located. This is to say that the reality of God may be understood as deictic. A deictic term, such as *this*, is a term that gains sense only insofar as it is contextualized within a network of coordinates that make evident that to which the term refers.[13] The statement "this house is red," or even "this house," generates a sense and relation that is absent from the statement "this." A singular insistence on the reality of *this*, without relation to other terms, thereby seems to provide one way of observing the structure at issue in apocalyptic insistence on a divine reality without term.

If apocalyptic imagination is defined by the refusal of worldly relation, and more precisely by singular insistence on *this*, then it may exceed the domain of political theology and be at issue within discourses that do not explicitly or directly revolve around the naming of God. To follow this line of thought is to appreciate the manner in which apocalyptic imagination may have validity for that discourse demarcated as philosophy. This is the case insofar as philosophical discourse asserts, either directly or indirectly, that the world must be. The line between political theology and philosophy, however it may be drawn, becomes relativized by an apocalyptic attentiveness to (and refusal of) worldly relation. What matters for the apocalyptic is not whether a discourse is philosophical or theological; it is whether a discourse treats the terms of the world as imperative. If such apocalyptic centering of attention on worldly relation entails a certain indifference to lines of demarcation between theology and philosophy, it also—by means of the same operation—enables awareness of commonalities that are occluded by the presumption of such demarcation.

One instance of such commonality is that between Schmitt and Hegel. These figures might be treated as distinct from one another in virtue of the distinction between political theology and secular philosophy, but apocalyptic does not operate in terms of such distinction. From an apocalyptic vantage, more significant than any difference between Schmittian political theology and Hegelian philosophy is a commonality premised on the imperative to relate in terms of the world. Hegel, of course, is by no means the only philosopher in which worldly relation is asserted in a sovereign manner. He nonetheless serves as the striking example of a more widespread philosophical tendency because he explicitly foregrounds the confrontation between worldly relation and the question of deixis, thereby making evident how the possibilities of the world require a sovereign decision against *this*.

It is at the outset of *Phenomenology of Spirit*, in his well-known critique of "sense certainty," that Hegel advances the claim that deictic insistence on *this* constitutes a failure of thought. To insist on and remain with *this*, he contends, is to fail to develop thought according to the properly dialectical terms of consciousness and object. It thus becomes imperative, on Hegel's account, to address *this* in terms of divisive relationality: *this* can be thought only insofar as it is superseded by and developed in terms of divisive relation—that is, between "one 'This' as 'I', and the other 'This' as object."[14] Along similar lines, and in keeping with his claim that thought must be divisively relational, Hegel proceeds by addressing two more instances of deixis: *now*, he claims, emerges for thought only through a dialectic exemplified by "Night and Day"; and *here*, he claims, is necessarily bound up with statements in which "truth has vanished and is converted into its opposite."[15]

What might it mean to address Hegel's claims by way of apocalyptic imagination? It must be noted that such address has no investment in the sense certainty that Hegel observes to be absent from *this*; the absence of sense certainty within deixis is granted, and in fact avowed, by apocalyptic. What apocalyptic imagination insists on is not sense certainty but *this*, without need for sense certainty, and so without need for the divisive relationality that Hegel advances in the name of sense certainty. The central question opened up by apocalyptic imagination is not, *Does* this *produce sense certainty?* Rather, it is, *Why must* this *be thought in the divisively relational terms of consciousness and object?*

It is by way of this line of questioning that the commonality between Hegel and Schmitt becomes evident. To propose such a commonality is not to deny the differences between them: Schmitt makes imperative a theological discourse external to the world, while Hegel makes imperative a dialectical discourse that arises within or as the world. It is simply to observe that in both cases—Schmitt's God and world; Hegel's consciousness and object—one finds a logic of divisive relationality that articulates that the world must be. Sovereignty, or the imperative to relate in terms of the world, remains even as the terms are changed.

The sovereignty at issue in Schmitt becomes manifest in Hegel as intraworldly relation. For Hegel, the world comes into being not through relation to a term external to the world but rather as the relation between two terms—consciousness and object—that are (presumed to be) found within the world. This means that the being of the world is asserted not as a whole *in relation to* an extraworldly term (God) but rather as *the relation itself* between parts of the world. A certain circularity of Hegel's approach may then be observed: the being of the world emerges through the relation between its parts—the terms *consciousness* and *object*—but these terms are able to emerge only insofar as there is already a world; the terms that relationally engender the world emerge within the very world that their relation has yet to bring into being. There is a reason that this circularity—whereby the divisively relational terms of consciousness and object are imagined both as found within the world and as the means of making the world in which they come to be found—does not present an obstacle for Hegel: the logic to which it belongs is decisive for his assertion that the world must be.

Sovereignty thus appears in Hegel's philosophy in a manner that is both intraworldly and indirect: the imperative of the world's being is (indirectly) made through the (direct) imperative to relate in and through terms within the world. This is to say that Hegelian sovereignty appears not in "vertical" terms of a theological ground but instead through "horizontal" terms that draw attention to an elaborative expanse of relations, a multitude of connections yet to be pursued and found. What becomes fundamental, or what is understood to be in potential collapse, is less the very possibility of the world—as was the case with Schmitt—than the possibilities made by and as the world. To deictically insist on *this*, Hegel claims, is to fail to encounter a massive congregation of relational possibilities: *this* may be "related in various ways to other things," it may produce "a rich complex of connections" that, considered in terms of consciousness, has "the significance of a manifold imagining and thinking."[16] The openness of such relational multiplicity does not contradict, but on the contrary serves to make present, a sovereign decision: one must not think *this*, one must not think *now*, one must not think *here*.

Does Taubes's apocalyptic then allow thought of *this*, *now*, *here*? While his insistence that it is not necessary to spiritually invest in the world allows opposition to discourses that treat worldly relation as imperative, this apocalyptic refusal appears in tandem with its own investment in the "Occidental." Having remarked that "I have no spiritual investment in the world as it is," he goes on to say, "the separation of powers between worldly and spiritual is absolutely necessary," and "if [this boundary] is not drawn, we will lose our Occidental breath."[17] While Taubes may apocalyptically oppose the context of worldly relation, or the spatiotemporal order of the world, this opposition itself seems to emerge from or within, and thereby to presuppose, yet another context—that of the spatiotemporal order called Occident. Does the latter subtend the former, thereby relativizing any difference between, on one hand, the world that Taubes observes and opposes in Schmitt's political theology and, on the other, Taubes's own apocalyptic imagination? Is the difference between apocalyptic and the world it refuses yet one more version of divisive relationality, where the common measure would now be Occidental?[18]

While apocalyptic might be imagined to extend to and potentially collapse the time and space generated by and as the Occident, Taubes's apocalyptic tends toward its preserve. He claims that the division "between worldly and spiritual"—the "boundary" in virtue of which he apocalyptically claims to be without "spiritual investment in the world" and to imagine, by way of divestment, "let[ting] it go down"—is one that must be made; it is imperative, at least in order to avoid "los[ing] our Occidental breath." As Taubes thus speaks of two losses, the affirmed loss of the world ("let it go down") and the feared loss of "Occidental breath," one might consider the possibility of a relation between them. Is one object of loss to be understood as logically prior to the other? And who is the collective subject (the "our") of the "Occidental breath" that might be lost? Such questions seem inevitable for any attempt to disentangle Taubes's apocalyptic and Occidental terms.[19]

Notes

1. Jacob Taubes, *The Political Theology of Paul*, trans. Dana Hollander (Stanford, CA: Stanford University Press, 2003), 103.
2. Carl Schmitt, *Political Theology: Four Chapters on the Concept of Sovereignty*, trans. George Schwab (Cambridge, MA: MIT Press, 1985), 10.
3. Schmitt, 13.
4. Schmitt claims, "There exists no norm that is applicable to chaos" (10).
5. Taubes, *Political Theology of Paul*, 103.
6. Taubes, 103.
7. Taubes, *To Carl Schmitt: Letters and Reflections*, trans. Keith Tribe (New York: Columbia University Press, 2013), 8.
8. Schmitt, *Political Theology*, 66.
9. The phrasing and logic of "without term" is here introduced with an eye to Hans Jonas's claim, when describing the Gnosticism that was so central to Taubes's thought, that "without" was one of its central themes. See Jonas, *The Gnostic Religion: The Message of the Alien God and the Beginnings of Christianity* (Boston, MA: Beacon Press, 2001), 51.
10. There is, of course, a substantive and ongoing tradition of literature concerning Schmitt and Christianity—see, for instance, Carlo Galli, *Janus's Gaze: Essays on Carl Schmitt*, ed. Adam Sitze, trans. Amanda Minervini (Durham, NC: Duke University Press, 2015); Heinrich Meier, *The Lesson of Carl Schmitt: Four Chapters on the Distinction between Political Theology and Political Philosophy*, trans. Marcus Brainard (Chicago: University of Chicago Press, 1998); Erik Peterson, *Theological Tractates*, ed. and trans. Michael Hollerich (Stanford, CA: Stanford University Press, 2011). The manner in which I approach the connection between Christianity and Schmitt, while indebted to the differential insights that emerge from this tradition, has a

relatively distinct (and much narrower) focus. My concern is not to address the relation between Schmitt's thought and a more or less established Christianity but rather to observe an inseparability between the logic of this thought and the logic by which Christianity is established in the first place: Christianity establishes itself through its claim that God, or that which is without term, can be converted to a term of relation, and it is this logic that is central to Schmitt's own theoretical endeavor (regardless of how one determines the relation between Schmitt and an already established Christianity).

11. As this sentence indicates, by "Christianity" I refer specifically to those doctrinally "orthodox" forms in which Christ is understood to be fully divine and fully human, thereby providing a term of mediation between a God without term and terms of the world.

12. Jewish theology obviously exceeds and therefore should not be reduced to (or even defined in terms of) the apocalyptic imagination. The point is simply that the God without term that is central to (and perhaps definitive of) the apocalyptic imagination is avowed within Jewish—but not Christian— theology. For an outstanding discussion of the relation between Jewish apocalypticism and messianism in Taubes, see Agata Bielik-Robson, *Jewish Cryptotheologies of Late Modernity: Philosophical Marranos* (London: Routledge, 2014), 166–212. On the relation between apocalypticism and Gnosticism in Taubes, see Joshua Robert Gold, "Jacob Taubes: 'Apocalypse from Below,'" *Telos* 134 (2006): 140–156.

13. My approach to deixis is influenced by Nicola Masciandaro's "What Is This That Stands Before Me?: Metal as Deixis," in *Reflections in the Metal Void*, ed. Niall Scott (Oxford: Interdisciplinary Press, 2012), 5.

14. G. W. F. Hegel, *Phenomenology of Spirit*, trans. A.V. Miller (Oxford: Oxford University Press, 1977), 59.

15. Hegel, 60–61.

16. Hegel, 58.

17. Taubes, *Political Theology of Paul*, 103.

18. If one is to discern in Taubes a "negative political theology" in explicit distinction from that of Schmitt—as has been argued, for instance, by Marin Terpstra and Theo de Wit's "'No Spiritual Investment in the World as It Is': Jacob Taubes's Negative Political Theology," in *Flight of the Gods: Philosophical Perspectives on Negative Theology*, ed. Ilse N. Bulhof and Laurens ten Kate (New York: Fordham University Press, 2000), 320–353—then the reference to a common "Occidental" time and space would make this a relative negativity: Taubes's apocalyptic articulates negativity in relation to the world that Schmitt wants to hold together but not toward the Occident as such.

Or, turning from political theology to political ontology, specifically that of Frank B. Wilderson III, one observes an apocalyptic valence that differs at essence from the one advanced by Taubes. When Wilderson invokes "the end of the world"—see his *Red, White & Black: Cinema and the Structure of U.S. Antagonisms* (Durham, NC: Duke University Press, 2010), 337—he is referring to a world constructed through racial slavery and anti-blackness, a world whose end would inevitably entail the undoing of the Occidental inheritance that Taubes seems concerned to preserve. Consequently, there should be no confusion: to invest in Taubes's apocalyptic, in the possibility of spiritual divestment, is something other than and seemingly at odds with the apocalyptic at issue in Wilderson's invocation of the world's end. If Taubes's apocalyptic is to refuse worldly relation in its essence, then it must address the centrality of racial slavery and its afterlives. This demand is occluded by the slightest confusion of Taubes's apocalyptic with Wilderson's.

19. Saitya Brata Das—in "The Gift of the World: A Note on Political Theology," *Culture and Religion* 15, no. 3 (2014): 268—proposes "that for Jacob Taubes 'the Occidental breath' means not so much the metaphysical (and political) claim of the Occident's sovereign power in the earthly domain that will have 'oriental' within its fold, but means rather, perhaps, the name of a promise, eschatologically given in the name of 'occident' that withdraws from all hegemonic claim of earthly sovereignty on a supposed divine foundation." Yet what is central to a spatiotemporal order called Occident, as I would understand it, is precisely the capacity to order time and space by drawing the boundary or division between spiritual and worldly.

4

Otherwise Than Terror
Ten Theses on the Modernist Secular

DANIEL WHISTLER

Paragraphs 582–595 of the *Phenomenology of Spirit* chart the ways in which secular neutrality ran amok in 1790s Paris. According to Rebecca Comay's reconstruction of these passages, the "Terror marks the modern crisis of secularization," and its various acts of revolutionary fury are to be interpreted as symptoms of a will to secularize.[1] What springs forth is "abstract negativity at its most truculent," "destructive dialectic" and ultimately death—"a series of corpses vanishing into thin air."[2] Hegel writes,

> By virtue of its own abstraction, [this form of Spirit] divides itself into extremes equally abstract, into a simple, inflexible cold universality, and into the discrete, absolute hard rigidity and self-willed atomism of actual self-consciousness.... All that remains of the [first extreme] by which it can be laid hold of is solely its *abstract* existence as such. The relation, then, of these two, since each exists indivisibly and absolutely for itself ... is one of wholly *unmediated* pure negation ... *death*.[3]

As Comay glosses, "Either way: abstraction. Either way: death."[4] The abstraction unleashed during the French Revolution—to the point of a utopian aversion to the concrete—does nothing but negate, destroy, kill, and this is because it is *itself* negation. The "animosity" to the abstract that Comay diagnoses in Hegel's veiled polemics,[5] then, becomes merely a negation of negation—and the *Phenomenology of Spirit* motors onward. But left by the wayside is any element of the secular—any fragment of its constituent operations of abstraction and indifferentiation—that resists subjection to the hegemony of negation.

To put it bluntly, Hegel's description is a theological fantasy of secularization. And, to this extent, it is worth insisting, as many have before, that Hegel's philosophy "remains essentially Christian and no more so than when it calls itself atheistic, scientific or secular."[6] His theses on the French Revolution in the *Phenomenology of Spirit* warrant a utopian thought experiment . . . what if secular abstraction and indifferentiation were not just modes of negation? They call for a philosophical transposition of the Terror into a discourse that takes the venom out of Hegel's "animosity" to abstraction, that describes secular universality otherwise than as death. While such a rewrite lies far beyond the scope of this or any essay, what follows are some preliminary remarks toward—what will turn out to be—a "Schellingianizing" of the *Phenomenology of Spirit*, a rewriting of secular violence from the vantage point of a metaphysics of indifference. They are not meant as a vindication of the secular but as an attempt to more accurately chart the conceptual operations of a particular variant of secularity—the modernist secular.[7] If the theses that follow sometimes take on a polemical edge, then I hope that the more irenic tone of their conjectural explanations softens it; I also hope that they do not so much polemicize *for* secularism as for an accurate description of one concept of the secular, which is theoretically interesting precisely in its a-Hegelian peculiarity, in its eccentric shape and erratic movements.

This essay is an intervention in the philosophy of secularity. For good reasons perhaps, the philosophy of secularity remains a small subfield of the philosophy of religion, particularity in comparison to the array of anthropologies, sociologies, and theologies of secularity; however, there is, it strikes me, a proper domain of philosophical reflection on the conceptual structure of the secular plane to be carved out, and this is what I preliminarily undertake in what follows. Yet, although I attend to a particular variant of secularity—the modernist secular—at the expense of, what I dub, the several "theological fantasies" of the secular that infest theory, I am nevertheless in no way interested in affirming it. This essay includes much material that is objectionable in light of the political power that secularity has often irresponsibly wielded: it describes the immediate and violent imposition of a universal, indifferent to differences, abstracted from all specific lived traditions; and it sporadically makes use of Alain Badiou, Maurice Blanchot, Gilles Deleuze, Johann Gottlieb Fichte, Friedrich Hölderlin, Thomas Mann, Louis Marin, Orhan Pamuk, and Friedrich Schelling to flesh out its conceptual implications. They are all, to varying extents, complicit in the violence of the secular—*as we are too*. The point of the following is neither to celebrate this violence nor to merely abhor it; it is to attempt to trace the precise logic of the modernist secular detached from the humanist polemic, postsecular critique and theological paranoia that tends to surround it. What this will mean in practice is a thoroughgoing de-Hegelianization of the modernist secular.[8]

The Mechanics of Indifference

1. The imposition of the modernist secular plane is inescapably violent.

The explanation of this thesis is to be found in the preceding introductory note. In short, there are liberatory as well as oppressive forms of violence—conceptual blows that lead to new scientific paradigms as well as the colonial violence of Western oppression. The modernist secular has, more often than not, led to the latter. This violence is explicit in Talal Asad's definition of the secular as "not simply an intellectual answer to a question about enduring social peace and toleration" but "an enactment by which a *political medium* (representation of citizenship) redefines and transcends particular and differentiating practices of the self that are articulated through class, gender, and religion."[9] The secular has operated by means of control, as a form of life practiced (often under compulsion) in the name of universal reason and Enlightenment values. Similarly, for Saba Mahmood, the secular is a universal into which religious forms of life are inducted, willingly or not.[10] In short, the modernist secular is a dangerous concept, and any appeal to it requires a thorough risk assessment.

2. The modernist secular occupies the position of the neutral in relation to all religious positions, including atheism.

The modernist secular is defined by its indifference to religions. Such indifference is absolute: the imposition of a secular plane (as a means of organizing religious material[11]) demands abstraction from the richness of historical traditions, from differences and even from its own conditions of possibility. This operation of active indifferentiation distinguishes the secular—at least prima facie—from atheism (the negation of religions) and tolerance (the affirmation of all religions). It is what Marin has identified as the utopic position—represented diagrammatically in figure 1, where ~S1 & ~S2 depict the secular position, "the place of the neutral . . . the place where mutual 'neutralization' occurs between contrary properties":[12] "[The neutral] has no negative function because it comes before judgment or even a position one might take. . . . Neither yes nor no, true nor false,

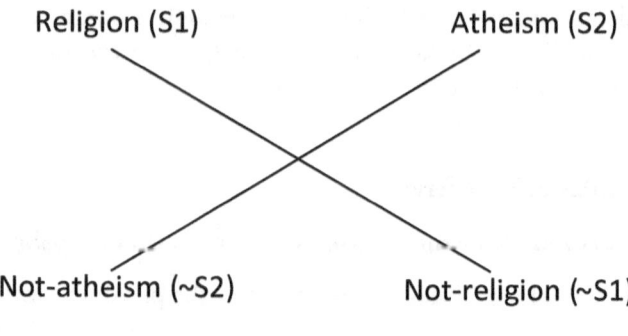

Figure 1. Religion in the public sphere: a Greimas square.

one nor the other: this is the neutral. . . . This neutral is the span between true and false, opening within discourse a space discourse cannot receive. It is a third term, but a *supplementary* third term, not synthetic."[13] That is, the secular neutral is a-thetic and therefore a-Hegelian, indifferent to the dialectical ruses of contradiction and negation. In Derrida's words, "the movement of the neuter is evidently neither negative nor dialectical";[14] or as Marin again puts it, this utopic position pertains to "the zero degree of the Hegelian synthesis . . . what remains after the crossing out of negation."[15] The secular acts as the "neither . . . nor" of both positive religions and their atheistic negations.

3. The modernist secular abstractly expresses religions.

If religions are to be abstractly expressed on the secular surface—like a canvas from which singular marks are read—then this suggests a number of provisional analogies between religious and artistic abstract expression.

3.1. The modernist secular is intimately linked to social and economic mechanisms of abstraction and disenchantment; hence, it possesses the potential to exacerbate them as well as to interrogate them. The modernist secular is ineluctably complicit in capital, the primary agent of abstraction in the modernist age. In other words, capital's abstractions (e.g., from use value to exchange value) attain their *artistic* limit on the canvas that sacrifices sensuous individuality entirely and their *religious* limit in a secularity that disregards concrete traditions. Thus, just as abstract expressionist art is both an extreme form of capital and also manages to "combat social abstraction with artistic abstraction," so too is modernist secular thinking. In other words, like the abstract expressionist canvas, secular practices have the capacity to interrogate implicit structures and de-fetishize hidden mechanisms by attentively reenacting the very moment of abstraction itself—and thus revealing (through its own abstractness) the ways in which "the concrete is no more than a mask of the abstract."[16]

3.2. It is indifferent to the concrete value, form, and content of its subject matter. Just as abstract expressionist art is cruel in its disregard for the varieties of sensuous concreteness that the subject encounters in lived experience—so too is the modernist secular. Both variants of abstract expression create "a desolate place,"[17] a utopic no-place instantiated regardless of concrete particulars. Mapped out in the forest that opens Ramon Llull's *Book of the Gentile and the Three Wise Men* and in the esoteric republics scattered through the radical utopian narratives of early modernity (including *The Voyages and Adventures of Jaques Massé* and *A History of the Ajaoiens*), this is now the idealized space of the university, of the state, or of Thomas Mann's secular monastery which cultivates "the purest indifference" and a "strange, dislocated attitude."[18] Temporality also becomes utopian through such active indifferentiation, whether it is again the experiments with time that take place on Mann's magic mountain, the "time without negation, without decision, when here is nowhere as well, and each thing withdraws into its image" of Blanchot,[19] or the absolute and noneschatological time without transition of the very last of Hölderlin's poems.[20] Both spatially and temporally, the modernist secular generates its own *sui generis* features.

3.3. Its surface is no longer marked by specific religious traditions but emits religious phantasms. Just as in abstract expressionist art (as a result of this total abstraction from what is seen), the marks on the canvas exhibit a different order of visibility and a "specific kind of objectivity"[21]—so too with the secular mediation of religions. One can speak here, with Deleuze, of a perverse if "fantastic deviation from our world" where the breakdown of habits leave space for alternative processes of meaning formation. This perversion is "an extraordinary art of surfaces" and "it is perhaps at the surface, like a mist, that an unknown image of things is detached."[22]

3.4. More precisely, on its surface, religions cease to signify and become, instead, corpse-like images of themselves—such is the secular imaginary. Just as, according to Jay Bernstein following Theodor Adorno, abstract expressionist art is founded on "ideas of an enigmatic, non-signifying language . . . a language without signification,"[23] so too religious phantasms on the secular plane are no longer signs for concrete traditions. Rather, like Blanchot's corpse, religions here "appear in the strangeness of their solitude," or more fully: "In the image, the object again grazes something which it had dominated in order to be an object—something counter to which it had defined and built itself up. Now that its value, its meaning is suspended, now that the world abandons it to idleness and lays it aside, the truth in it ebbs, and materiality, the elemental reclaims it. This impoverishment, or enrichment, consecrates it as image."[24] On the modernist secular surface, religions migrate "from [their] use value and from [their] truth value to something incredible—something neutral which there is no getting used to."[25]

3.5. Its images of religions fascinate as a museum exhibit does. Just as, again according to Bernstein, the abstract expressionist surface "robs the viewer of perspective and orientation with regard to it," but nevertheless "fascinates us"[26]—so too for the modernist secular, to quote Blanchot once more, "fascination is passion for the image."[27] Pamuk is the contemporary writer of this museumification of the religious image. In *Snow*, the novel becomes a museum of religions: traditions are flattened out, losing their diachronic dimension, their eschatological promise and their historical situatedness. The novel places religious subject positions synchronically next to each other in an encyclopedic panorama or *Wunderkammer* ("I will build a museum, and its catalogue will be a novel"[28]). *Snow*'s protagonist wanders through traditions so as to "interpret, classify and organise" voices across space, transforming faiths into vectors and thereby performing secularity as an archive.[29]

Otherwise Than Negation

4. The operation of abstraction is not a derivative mode of negation.

Within German Idealism, there is to be found a *différend* between the Hegelian coupling of abstraction and negation invoked in my introduction—such that abstraction is necessarily and fundamentally a mode of negation—and another conception of abstraction as irreducible to negation.[30] Fichte, for example, stands in the latter tradition. Reflections on abstraction are scattered throughout his work of the 1790s, for *abstraction* stands as a privileged name for the practice that begins philosophy. There is "no rule" in "a rigorously scientific transcendental philosophy . . . except the following: One should continue to abstract from everything possible, until something remains from which it is totally impossible to abstract."[31] Indeed, abstraction is a quasi-miraculous act of transcendence that gives the philosopher an *übermenschliche* perspective: "A finite rational being possesses nothing whatsoever beyond experience. . . . These same conditions necessarily apply to the philosopher, and thus it appears incomprehensible how he could ever succeed in elevating himself above experience. The philosopher, however, is able to engage in abstraction."[32] It is precisely this kind of methodological miracle that Hegel will attack in the name of dialectic as "the empty abstractions of an understanding which keeps itself in the abstract universal."[33] What is crucial for my purposes is that Fichte is very clear that abstraction is not assimilable to negation: to abstract is not to negate, destroy, or kill. In other words, one does not actively cancel that from which one abstracts, for "the concept . . . is here not thought of at all—either positively or negatively."[34] The abstracted element is not posited in any form; there is a suspension of judgment, an *epochē* or a-thesis, rather than an antithetic judgment. Hence, Fichte's insistence on the fundamental difference between abstraction and negation is to be contrasted with Hegel's definition of abstraction in "Who Thinks Abstractly?": "This is abstract thinking: to see nothing in the murderer except the abstract fact that he is a murderer, and to *annul* all other human essence in him with this simple quality."[35] For Hegel, abstraction "annuls," such that the hegemony of the dialectic, motored by negation, is preserved. Nevertheless, as evidenced in Fichte, there is an alternative that insists forcefully on the fundamental distinction between abstraction and negation. Since abstraction is not negation for Fichte, a philosophy premised on it possesses (at least) one non-dialectical moment.

5. The modernist secular is therefore not constituted by negation.

To reduce abstraction to negation is to falsify the secular; it is to transpose the modernist secular position (in the Greimas square shown earlier) from ~S1 & ~S2 (the neutral) to ~S1 & S2 (the atheistic). The distinction between secularity and atheism depends on preserving an irreducible difference between abstraction and negation; it depends on insisting that indifference to religions is not the annihilation of religions. This was already sufficiently clear in Marin's and Derrida's presentation of the neuter-position. Moreover, negation remains complicit in the life of religions, for the *negation* of Christianity in no way itself escapes from the logic of Christianity: God has already been killed within this religion, so to kill Him again is merely to reaffirm it. Understanding abstraction and indifference as negation co-opts secularity into death-of-God thinking. However, if abstraction is not negation—if to abstract from A or to be indifferent to A is not, as Fichte insists, to posit not-A, but to not posit at all—then something very different follows. Armed with this difference, abstraction neither affirms God nor kills Him, but remains steadfastly indifferent to Him. The modernist secular refuses, on this view, to be motored by negation.

6. The modernist secular is indifferent to specific religious differences.

Badiou's writings on religion provide an instance of a philosophy of the secular that engages creatively with the problem of the relation of the universal to the particular that is emerging in the above theses. In Badiou's polemics against *laïcité*—"the school of the cool consumer" governed by "pure capitalist law"[36]—he inchoately outlines an alternative approach to religions that bears comparison to the modernist secular. Of course, as suggested above, the modernist secular is nonetheless complicit in capitalist mechanisms of abstraction—transforming religious traditions into commodities, for instance—and yet, *as well*, the modernist secular, like the Badiouan approach, insists that "the particular does not matter," that specific differences in tradition "having not the least universal import, neither hinder thought nor sustain it," and that, in Peter Hallward's words, "universal principles are not immanent . . . they are imposed as if from without."[37] And, furthermore, in line with the earlier theses, Badiou is adamant that such an "indifference that tolerates differences" is never a negation: "The universal is not the negation of particularity."[38] This partial affiliation between Badiou and the modernist secular is clearest in the former's attacks on "communitarian particularisms" and "closed identities" in the name of "universalisable singularities" that traverse all specific traditions. The concrete is to be disregarded, for what matters is religious singularities (such as Pauline militancy) that are emitted when the conditions for universality are met.

Corollary on the Theological Fantasy of the Secular (I)

Postsecular critics tend to contrast the secular mode with another mode of constituting the neutral—a way that presupposes a different relation of universal to particular. On the one hand, there are *particular* religious traditions out of which, for the most part, the universal gradually comes into being; on the other hand, there is secularity which lays *immediate* claim to the universal. In religions, it is claimed, the conditions for universal neutrality are usually attained at the end of a dialectic process, whereas, when it comes to secularity, they are immediately imposed, even if such immediate imposition is fragile, forever at risk from becoming a merely partial (in both senses of the word) manifestation of neutrality. In the religious constitution of neutrality, the universal is *concrete* to the extent that it emerges freely out of a particular worldview; in the secular constitution, the universal is *abstract* to the extent that it is imposed violently on particular worldviews from without. Such, of course, is something like Hegel's reading of the Terror, in which an immediate, abstract universal is articulated as something violent, as something that suppresses genuine particularity, that channels "the *fury* of destruction"—a false universal ("the exhalation of a stale gas").[39] Crude repetitions of this Hegelianism have become a mainstay of public discourse: the secular is imposed without concern for the rich traditions of particular religions. For example, in *Lautsi v. Italy*, a freedom of religion case heard at the European Court of Human Rights, one judge laments, "A court of human rights cannot allow itself to suffer from historical Alzheimer's. It has no right to disregard the cultural continuum of a nation's flow through time, nor to ignore what, over the centuries, has served to mould and define the profile of a people. No supranational court has any business substituting its own ethical mock-ups for those qualities that history has imprinted on the national identity.... A European court should not be called upon to bankrupt centuries of European tradition. No court, certainly not this Court, should rob the Italians of part of their cultural personality."[40] In other words, the particularity of Italy's Christian heritage needs to be protected from the violence done by an immediate imposition of an abstract universal (the secular). The judge goes on to contrast "the perfumes and the stench of history" (i.e., concrete particularity) with "a regime of aseptic secularism."

But, in response, the above theses lead us to wonder: What if the imposition of indifference were not destructive? What if the abstraction of the modernist secular related to religious traditions otherwise than as negation?

The Destitution of the Transcendental

7. Totalizing abstraction abstracts from its own conditions of possibility, thereby overcoming the problem of the "immune transcendental."

Despite the significance of Fichte's distinction between abstraction and negation (discussed above), his account of abstraction is still limited in one regard—that of, what can be termed, the immune transcendental.[41] Fichte demands that one begin by abstracting from the object of intuition to isolate the self or the intuiting activity: "One should continue to abstract from everything possible, until something remains from which it is totally impossible to abstract. What remains is the pure I."[42] For Fichte, the abstracting *I* is a limit; it is what remains after the most thoroughgoing procedure of abstraction has removed every object of consciousness. Moreover, this *I* cannot be abstracted, it seems, because it is what makes the activity possible in the first place. The transcendental condition of abstraction cannot itself be abstracted from, Fichte abstracts from the object in the name of the self. Everything becomes indifferent *except the self*: this is a form of condescension brought about by the transcendental condition remaining *immune* to its own activity of abstraction. On the contrary, for Schelling, at the opening of his *Presentation of My System of Philosophy* as well as in other writings around 1801, both the object and the subject are suspended so as to isolate what he calls "the total indifference of the subjective and the objective."[43] Complete abstraction generates absolute indifference. It is for this reason that Schelling's writings are important for unearthing the logic of the modernist secular. Schellingian philosophy charts the production of complete indifference: its totalizing gesture of abstraction presupposes the value—and even the violence—of the abstract (thereby refusing some forms of dialectics) and it also indicates the possibility of a suspension of even its own transcendental conditions (thereby resolving the problem of the immune transcendental).[44] In 1804 Schelling will repeat this initial moment of total abstraction by which the philosopher attains absolute indifference: "[We] abstract from everything, from the reality of [what is posited] as well as from its reality as one of a subject and predicate."[45] The point is this: for Fichte, the activity of the abstracting self forms a limit to abstraction—a limit that Schelling entirely transgresses. What is more, Fichte's implicit argument for such a limit seems to be a version of the *cogito*: just as one cannot doubt what is doing the doubting, so too one can never abstract from what is doing the abstracting. However, the Schellingian response is simple: one is in no sense denying this abstracting activity. Abstraction does not have the same limits as doubt, for it is in no way a form of rejection or denial; it is not a modality of negation. As Fichte himself insists, abstraction suspends; it does not negate. To abstract from the positing of the *I* is not to deny that it occurs, it is merely to become indifferent to it: it is to situate oneself at the neuter position (~S1 & ~S2) of the Greimas square. Therefore, it is perfectly possible to abstract from what is self-evidently necessary, like the activity of abstracting itself. There is no limit, and this forms the basis of Schelling's solution to the problem of the immune transcendental.

8. The modernist secular is absolutely indifferent.

Recently popularized as a theoretical example by Saba Mahmood,[46] the case of *Lautsi v. Italy* (heard at the European Court of Human Rights between 2009 and 2011) concerned the right of the Italian government to enforce the display of crucifixes on classroom walls. In 2009 the Court initially upheld the complaint of a secular parent that this display should not be legally mandated; however, the case went to appeal before the Grand Chamber in 2011, resulting in a reversal of the decision. The objections to the initial judgment given by Berlusconi's government went in part as follows: "The judgment was based on a confusion between 'neutrality' (an 'inclusive concept') and 'secularism' (an 'exclusive concept'). Moreover, in the Government's view, neutrality meant that states should refrain from promoting not only a particular religion but also atheism, 'secularism' on the state's part being no less problematic than proselytising by the state. The Chamber's judgment was based on a misunderstanding and amounted to favouring an irreligious or antireligious approach."[47] Neutrality, it is here claimed, can be a concept "inclusive" of all religious traditions; but a secular interpretation of neutrality is never inclusive, rather it is always necessarily "exclusive": it evacuates from the public sphere all reference to religious tradition. For the Italian government and its sympathizers, secularism is covert atheism, atheism's political face—for secular indifference to religion is said to manifest itself as an "irreligious or antireligious" decimation of religious symbolism. Secularism is ultimately not neutral at all, and this is because it favors one religious position, atheism, over all the others. In other words, atheism is claimed to provide the ideological transcendental condition for the secular constitution of the neutral; the secular is the exoteric appearance of a secret atheism. What is recurring here is the Fichtean problem of the immune transcendental: in both cases, the operation of neutralization or abstraction is shown up as incomplete; in both cases, there is a limit beyond which indifferentiation cannot pass, and this limit corresponds to the necessary condition that makes the operation itself possible. In *Lautsi v. Italy*, it is atheism which guarantees the secular operation; for Fichte, it is the abstracting self; in both cases, these conditions remain immune. Once again, the modernist secular is shifted from the ~S1 & ~S2 position of the Greimas square to that of ~S1 & S2. To save the distinction between secularity and atheism—to insist on the consistency and *sui generis* character of the modernist secular—it is therefore necessary to solve the problem of the immune transcendental by totalizing abstraction; it is necessary to think a Schellingian secular as the conceptual telos of the modernist secular.

Corollary on the Theological Fantasy of the Secular (II)

In *Lautsi v. Italy*, Berlusconi's government uses the critique of secularism—as failing to abstract from its own condition of possibility (atheism)—to propose an alternative theological model for neutrality, an inclusive constitution of the neutral that *affirms* all religious traditions equally. And this alternative is forged from the materials of Christianity. The ground of religious inclusiveness is, the government argues, Christian theology: "The logical mechanism of exclusion of the unbeliever is inherent in any religious conviction, even if those concerned are not aware of it, *the sole exception being Christianity*. . . . In Christianity, even faith in an omniscient god is secondary in relation to charity, meaning respect for one's fellow human beings. It follows that rejection of a non-Christian by a Christian implies a radical negation of Christianity itself, a substantive abjuration; but that is not true of other religious faiths. . . . The cross, as the symbol of Christianity, can therefore not exclude anyone without denying itself; it even constitutes in a sense the universal sign of acceptance."[48] On this argument, Christianity possesses within itself the theological resources to make toleration (S_1 & S_2 on the Greimas square) conceptually possible, because of the primary function charity plays in the Christian tradition, and also (presumably) because of the self-negation of Christ on the cross. The death of God and its ethical implications give rise to a religion that negates itself in the name of the pure toleration of all others. And this is what makes Christianity "the sole exception": while all other religious attitudes (including atheism and therefore secularism) operate through a logic of exclusion, in which they affirm themselves as true at the expense of all other worldviews, Christianity has always already negated itself.

But one might wonder . . . What if, as the preceding theses have suggested, it is not only possible but also necessary (for the sake of conceptual consistency) to think a secularity that overcomes the problem of the immune transcendental, secularity as absolutely indifferent to everything including its own conditions of possibility? What if a Schellingian secular were conceivable?

9. The conditions of possibility of modernist secularity are therefore irrelevant to immanent understandings of it.

By overcoming the problem of the immune transcendental through totalizing abstraction, a secularity no longer has access to its own conditions of possibility. It disregards them indifferently, that is, it must become Schellingian, since only the sort of totalizing abstraction that Schelling practices can safeguard the distinctness of secularity as neuter (~S1 & ~S2 on the Greimas square) from atheism as negation (~S1 & S2). Any immanent account of the modernist secular, therefore, must equally be indifferent to such transcendental conditions. This is true of all variants of the secularization thesis: any narrative that understands the modernist secular as the negation, transformation, or reconstitution of previous forms of thought is necessarily one that has its vantage point outside of the modernist secular itself (since the latter understands its own implementation of the secular plane as *immediate*). For a subject of the modernist secular, such a thesis is a theological fantasy that misinterprets the universal as emerging dialectically from a particular tradition. This is particularly true of Charles Taylor's *A Secular Age*, which, both in its general "Hegelian inspiration" and especially in its distinction between beliefs and their conditions,[49] fails to understand the modernist secular on its own terms. Two methodological problems illustrate this:

a. Taylor's hermeneutics look to the *conditions* of secular belief, whereas modernist secularity is precisely that which is necessarily blind to its own conditions (owing to its totalizing abstraction). Accordingly, Taylor is thereby led to attack secularized methodologies precisely for their indifference, that is, their practices of "excarnation," "disengagement" or "withdrawal of a certain sort."[50] These practices are, he continues, "perverse."[51] Conversely, Taylor desires his own hermeneutic approach to tarry with the concrete. In short, Taylor's methodological rejection of indifferentiation and abstraction is already a rejection of secularity. From the very approach he adopts, Taylor is antisecular: his disdain for the secular age is preprogrammed.
b. Taylor's phenomenology of fullness is equally antisecular. Taylor states, "All people have a sense of fullness"[52]—that is, it is universally and necessarily the case that each subject aspire to a form of experience that in some sense fulfills, completes, or consummates the aims, values, and orientations that frame their life.[53] But, to repeat, the secular is that which actively indifferentiates, and Taylor's insistence on understanding every life in terms of the values of a particular worldview contravenes such an operation. Thus, Taylor must misrepresent the secular by positing "suppressed modes of fulfilment,"[54] for it would otherwise fail to sit easily within his phenomenology. Just as for Berlusconi's government in *Lautsi*, so too for Taylor: the transcendental condition of the secular—that which orients the secular subject toward

fulfillment—is atheism (or more accurately: its pretheoretical corollary, "exclusive humanism"). The secular age is constituted out of exclusive humanism's ideal of fullness.[55] The problem of the immune transcendental recurs.

In general, the problem for Taylor and any proponent of a secularization thesis is that they forget their own complicity in the modernist secular. In their very attempt to get outside the secular viewpoint to identify the conditions of possibility to which it is blind, all secularization theses merely exacerbate the abstractive liberation that the modernist secular itself promises, despite their appeals to the concrete, to historical genesis, and to transcendental structure. We are all more complicit in the modernist secular than we tend to confess and to acknowledge this entanglement entails a thinking of *the secular without secularization*.

10. The modernist secular's act of totalizing abstraction is a destitution of the transcendental as such.

Transcendentalizing the modernist secular contravenes its self-understanding. On the modernist secular plane, the conditioning-conditioned framework no longer applies. This is the *epochē* at the heart of the modernist secular—a bracketing of the very conditions that made it possible, a refocusing of attention away from historical narratives of genesis and transcendental inquiries into underlying structures, so as to concentrate the modernist gaze on the abstract surface alone, populated by religious phantasms or traditions reduced to surface effects. This is a destitution of the very structure of transcendental explanation, and, in general, what arises out of this destitution is a utopian space, hovering in an abstract no-place without foundations, and a utopian time, free of its own history and genesis, an intemporal and superficial "now" of abstract singularities or religious phantasms. The modernist secular constitutes a plane of Schellingian abstract indifference that repeats (occasionally in a critical mode) the very indifferentiations and neutralizations of capital itself. While the violent imposition of such indifference may well be terrifying (as well as pernicious and oppressive), it is less obviously Hegel's Terror.

The foregoing is, moreover, one illustration of a philosophical construction of secularity—an attempt to unravel the logic of one mode of the secular, to trace its conceptual peculiarities and erratic dynamics, under a philosophical gaze that purports to be itself *abstracted* from the humanist polemic, postsecular critique and theological paranoia that tend to dominate theoretical interventions in this domain.

Notes

1. Rebecca Comay, *Mourning Sickness: Hegel and the French Revolution* (Stanford, CA: Stanford University Press, 2010), 60, 127.
2. Comay, 56, 58, 69.
3. G. W. F. Hegel, *Phenomenology of Spirit*, trans. A.V. Miller (Oxford: Oxford University Press, 1977), §590.
4. Comay, *Mourning Sickness*, 69.
5. Comay, 69.
6. Arvind Mandair, "Hegel's excess: Indology, historical difference and the post-secular turn of theory," *Postcolonial Studies* 9, no. 1 (2006): 32. *Contra* those equally many voices who have claimed that Hegel is "a theorist of secularisation malgré lui." Espen Hammer, "Hegel as a Theorist of Secularization," *Hegel Bulletin* 34, no. 2 (2013): 224.
7. To emphasize: the modernist secular is not the secular *tout court* (it is specifically "modernist," owing to its will to abstract); hence, such a qualification is intended to leave open the possibility for alternative manifestations of secularity. Equally, abstraction (or indifferentiation) is not necessarily secular (monasticism is an obvious counterexample).
8. An earlier, Portuguese version of the claims that follow—with extended discussions of *Lautsi v. Italy* and Charles Taylor's *A Secular Age*—can be found in Daniel Whistler, "Desafios para uma filosofia do secular renovada," in *Religião em um Mundo Plural Debates desde a Filosofia*, ed. Marciano Spica and Horacio Martinez (Pelotas: NEPFIL, 2014).
9. Talal Asad, *Formations of the Secular: Christianity, Islam, Modernity* (Stanford, CA: Stanford University Press, 2003), 5.
10. Saba Mahmood, "Secularism, Hermeneutics, Empire: The Politics of Islamic Reformation," *Public Culture* 18, no. 2 (2006): 323–347; *The Politics of Piety: The Islamic Revival and the Feminist Subject* (Princeton, NJ: Princeton University Press, 2005).
11. For the concept of the "secular plane," see Daniel C. Barber, *On Diaspora: Christianity, Religion and Secularity* (Eugene, OR: Cascade, 2011); and Anthony Paul Smith and Daniel Whistler, "What is Continental Philosophy of Religion Now?," in *After the Postsecular and the Postmodern: New Essays in Continental Philosophy of Religion*, ed. Smith and Whistler (Newcastle: CSP, 2010), 1–25.
12. Louis Marin, *Utopics: The Semiological Play of Textual Spaces*, trans. Robert A. Vollrath (New York: Humanity Books, 1984), 11, 13.
13. Marin, 7.
14. Jacques Derrida, *Parages* (Paris: Galilée, 1986), 70.
15. Marin, *Utopics*, 7, 13.
16. Jay Bernstein, "The Death of Sensuous Particulars: Adorno and Abstract Expressionism," *Radical Philosophy*, no. 76 (1996): 10.
17. Bernstein, 16.
18. Thomas Mann, *The Magic Mountain*, trans. H. T. Lowe-Porter (London: Vintage, 1999), 93, 18, 376.

19. Maurice Blanchot, *The Space of Literature*, trans. Ann Smock (Lincoln, NE: University of Nebraska Press, 1982), 30.

20. On the precise temporal and topographical structures of the modernist secular (read through Hölderlin and Mann, among others), see Daniel Whistler, "The Categories of Secular Time," in *Reading the Abrahamic Faiths: Rethinking Religion and Literature*, ed. Emma Mason (London: Bloomsbury, 2014), 237–254; "The Cloistered Imaginary," in *The Feminist Philosophy of Gillian Howie*, ed. Victoria Browne and Whistler (London: Bloomsbury, 2016), 103–129; and "The Production of Transparency: Hölderlinian Practices," *Essays in Romanticism* 23, no. 2 (2016): 155–174. On a very different account of secular space and time, see the comments in Asad, *Formations of the Secular*.

21. Bernstein, "Death of Sensuous Particulars," 11.

22. Gilles Deleuze, *The Logic of Sense*, trans. Mark Lester (London: Continuum, 2004), 345–354.

23. Bernstein, "Death of Sensuous Particulars," 13–14.

24. Blanchot, *Space of Literature*, 257.

25. Blanchot, 258.

26. Bernstein, "Death of Sensuous Particulars," 12.

27. Blanchot, *Space of Literature*, 32.

28. Orhan Pamuk, *The Innocence of Objects: The Museum of Innocence, Istanbul*, trans. Ekin Oklap (New York: Abrams, 2012), 21.

29. Orhan Pamuk, *Snow*, trans. Maureen Freely (London: Faber and Faber, 2004), 128. See also Whistler, "Categories of Secular Time." Considering the above invocation of Blanchot, André Malraux's late art history—*Voices of Silence*, trans. Stuart Gilbert (New York: Doubleday, 1953)—is relevant here: just as, for Malraux, artworks come into their own by entering a virtual museum of images, so too religions can possibly take on new powers by this becoming-image on the secular surface (religions "without walls," as it were). On the constitution of the image from the secular surface, see also Daniel Whistler, "The Logic of Secular Sense in Cendrars' Epic Trilogy," *Literature and Theology* (forthcoming).

30. See also Daniel Whistler, "Abstraction and Utopia in Early German Idealism," *Russian Journal of Philosophy and Humanities* 2, no. 2 (2017): 3–22.

31. J. G. Fichte, "Concerning the Difference between the Spirit and the Letter within Philosophy," in *Early Philosophical Writings*, ed. and trans. Daniel Breazeale (Ithaca, NY: Cornell University Press, 1988), 204.

32. J. G. Fichte, "An Attempt at a New Presentation of the *Wissenschaftslehre*," in *Introductions to the Wissenschaftslehre and Other Writings, 1797–1800*, ed. and trans. Daniel Breazeale (Indianapolis: Hackett, 1994), 10–11.

33. G. W. F. Hegel, *Lectures on the History of Philosophy*, trans. E. S. Haldane and Frances H. Simson (London: Routledge, 1896), 3:472.

34. Fichte, "An Attempt at a New Presentation of the *Wissenschaftslehre*," 39.

35. G. W. F. Hegel, "Who Thinks Abstractly?," in *Hegel: Texts and Commentary*, ed. and trans. Walter Kaufmann (New York: Anchor, 1966), 118; my emphasis.

36. Alain Badiou, *Circonstances II* (Paris: Scheer, 2004), 116, 118.

37. Badiou, 122, 120; Peter Hallward, *Absolutely Postcolonial: Writing between the Singular and the Specific* (Manchester: Manchester University Press, 2001), 183.

38. Alain Badiou, *Saint Paul: The Foundation of Universalism*, trans. Ray Brassier (Stanford, CA: Stanford University Press, 2003), 99, 110.

39. Hegel, *Phenomenology of Spirit*, §§589, 586. Of course, Hegel does recognize the positive power of the abstract—but only ever *as partial*. See also Peter Osborne, "The Reproach of Abstraction," *Radical Philosophy*, no. 127 (2004): 21–28.

40. *Lautsi v. Italy* [2011] 54 E.H.R.R. 3, §11 (concurring opinion of Judge Bonello).

41. See also Whistler, "Utopia and Abstraction."

42. Fichte, "The Spirit and the Letter," 204.

43. F. W. J. Schelling, *Presentation of My System of Philosophy*, trans. Michael Vater, *Philosophical Forum* 32, no. 4 (2001): 349.

44. Of course, this says nothing about the feasibility of such a gesture, and indeed—as indicated earlier—I am here merely concerned with describing conceptual implications (the *logic* of the modernist secular), not its reality, even if such questions would quickly inform any evaluation of the concept.

45. F. W. J. Schelling, *System of Philosophy in General and of the Philosophy of Nature in Particular*, in *Idealism and the Endgame of Theory*, ed. Thomas Pfau (Albany, NY: State University of New York Press, 1994), 147.

46. See, for example, Saba Mahmood, *Religious Difference in a Secular Age: A Minority Report* (Princeton, NJ: Princeton University Press, 2016), 168–170.

47. *Lautsi* [2011], §35.

48. *Lautsi* [2011], §15.

49. Hammer, "Hegel as a Theorist of Secularization," 225–226.

50. Charles Taylor, *A Secular Age* (Cambridge, MA: Harvard University Press, 2007), 288, 283, 284.

51. Taylor, 286.

52. Taylor, 769.

53. See Taylor, 5.

54. Taylor, 612.

55. See Taylor, 45.

5

Kant's Unexpected Materialism
How the Object Saves Kant (and Us) from the Moral Law

JAMES MARTEL

The division between the phenomenal and the noumenal worlds is something for which Immanuel Kant is often attacked. He is attacked from the right by thinkers such as John Milbank for having set the boundaries between the two worlds too strongly, and from the left, by Friedrich Nietzsche, among others, for having set them at all. For Milbank, Kant leaves a legacy marked by "the denial that the categories used to understand the finite world . . . can be speculatively extended to apply to the ultimate and transcendent 'in itself.'"[1] Here, Kant's transcendental idealism denies human beings any access to the transcendent and, in so doing, invites nihilism as we are left with nothing but "as ifs," speculations about a divine nature that we cannot possibly understand. Milbank specifically understands Kant's sublime as something that separates us entirely from the divine and thereby from natural law.[2] For Milbank, the Kantian sublime is something that holds out the promise of divinity and transcendence which is in fact only a chimera.

From the Nietzschean left, and especially from Nietzsche himself, we get a different claim. In *The Genealogy of Morals*, Nietzsche calls Kant a "tortured man seeking release from his torment."[3] For Nietzsche, Kant hates his own body, his own human life. He seeks to overcome himself (and not in a good, Nietzschean way) by reinventing himself—and by extension the rest of us—as supersensible beings that supersede the animal self. Nietzsche writes: "The height of sadistic pleasure is reached when reason in its self-contempt and self-mockery decrees that the realm of truth does indeed exist, but that reason is debarred from it. (In the Kantian concept of the 'noumenal' character of things we may discern a vestige of this prurient ascetic split which enjoys turning reason against itself. For the noumenal character, to Kant, signifies that aspect of things about which the intellect knows only that it can never comprehend it.)"[4]

In this way, we can think of Kant as being poised, as it were, between Milbank and Nietzsche, stuck between two groups that consider the other to be nihilists. Ironically the one point that a Nietzschean and a follower of Radical Orthodoxy can agree on is that Kant is on the other side, not only a nihilist but perhaps *the* nihilist. In this essay, I will take up this claim in order to show that, even as Kant appears to be the antithesis of everything that Nietzsche stands for, Kant is in effect saved from his own desire for transcendentalism by a complicated relationship to the very mundane objects that Milbank accuses Kant of being overly connected to. In what follows, I will argue that Nietzsche was wrong about Kant and Milbank was right, but in that wrongness and rightness we see a peculiar reversal. Nietzsche is wrong about Kant's hostility to the material world. Milbank is right about Kant's immanentism. Yet rather than agree with Milbank that this is what makes Kant a nihilist, I will use that argument to align Kant (this is the reversal) with Nietzsche, claiming that Kant's unexpected materialism—that is, the way his philosophy preserves the phenomenal in the guise of superseding it—saves him (and by extension the rest of us) from the nihilism inherent in transcendentalism.

I will make this argument first in a weak and then in a strong version. In the weak version, I will briefly look at some of the secondary literature on Kant's notion of the sublime in order to show how much trouble Kant's sometimes mystifying attachment to objects can cause his would-be followers. I will then go on to make the stronger argument by focusing on Kant's own descriptions of the sublime to demonstrate a complicated relationship with materiality that goes deeper than simply an unexpected reluctance to abandon the object. I will argue that Kant *needs* the object to persist even after he seems to have dismissed it along the way to supersensibility. In this way, Kant's materialism necessarily vanquishes his transcendentalism, effectively saving him from himself.[5] More specifically, I will claim that in having a built-in requirement for the material object despite his claims to the contrary, Kant eviscerates the force of the moral law.

When we read Kant as self-sabotaging, ruining rather than delivering us over to the moral law, the sublime changes radically. It ceases to serve as a way to recognize our limits and our submission to the moral law. Instead it becomes a form of self-encounter, an engagement with our own materiality that occurs while we are busy waiting for something higher and better. It is this material sublime, the feeling within the feeling, that constitutes a more radical face for Kant. It is radical because, in effectively rejecting the higher self, even in the guise of seeking it out, Kant is, however unwillingly, embracing what Nietzsche embraces too: the material, the fleshy, the ordinary, and the mortal, that which is usually targeted for elimination by transcendentalism. In its hostility to such things, the politics of transcendentalism are inevitably hierarchical, exploitative, and nihilistic, whereas the politics that comes from an embrace of the human as such is, I would argue, radical, anti-hierarchical and anarchic.

Accordingly, I claim that this self-sabotaging element of Kant, his unexpected materialism, constitutes a messianic interruption of the fate that Kant would otherwise submit us to. It is not messianic in the normative sense of saving us—indeed such a conception, as Nietzsche argues, serves only to condemn us to further self-hatred and phantasm, to the belief that as ourselves we need to be superseded by a higher better self. Instead, this other messianism, a material messiah, takes on a lowly and ordinary form, saving us from false forms of transcendental salvation, interrupting and resisting the phantasms of a higher—and archist—form of messianism that is really just a mode of self-hatred and destruction.

While it may seem strange to use the language of messianism and theology more generally to discuss what is, after all, a very earth- and human-based way of reading and responding to Kant, I will argue that this radical theological language is critical for countering the occult theologies that otherwise determine and inform the way we tend to read Kant (and much of the secular and modern world as well for that matter). Given that much of what I will be opposing in this essay, the concept of transcendence, the hierarchy of higher and lower forms of being, and the concept of freedom are all, at their core, reflective of their own (Christian) theological origins, to read Kant differently requires recourse to an alternative theological language. In this case, what is messianic delivers us, not to the higher order but from it. Rather than seeking transcendence, a way to escape our bodies and our mortality, our rootedness in materiality and presence, the way I am reading Kant suggests an orientation toward what might be called instead descendance. This is a going-back into ourselves, our bodies and our locations in time and space, offering what could be considered a form of salvation from salvation, a messianic interruption that relieves us of the yearning for and need of messiahs.

While Kant's own sight may well be oriented toward precisely the transcendence that I will be critiquing in this chapter, his unexpected connection to materiality serves to make him, as it were, the first (but certainly not the last) to be saved from this particular—and particularly nihilist—form of salvation. The messianic figure in this case is not some deity who descends from the sky but rather the most ordinary of objects in all of their banal existence, an unexpected messiah for an unexpected, and possibly even unwanted, act of redemption.

Kant's Would-be Followers and the Resilience of the Object

How do many of Kant's readers understand him in terms of his relationship to objects and materiality? In the literature on Kant, and perhaps in particular in the literature that treats Kant's understanding of the sublime, we see a perplexity about the degree to which Kant—who ceaselessly declares himself to be opposed to any phenomenal contamination of the supersensible—nonetheless evinces a stubborn streak in his thinking wherein material objects are far more resilient and more entangled with the supersensible than they seemingly should be.

One especially good example of the tendency of Kant's modern-day disciples to fret about the material object's durability in Kantian thought can be seen in Paul Crowther's *The Kantian Sublime*. Crowther repeatedly comes across the problem of the object's tenacity in and interference with what he otherwise takes to be a supremely logical and rational system of thought. For Crowther, Kant introduces a series of paradoxes about materiality. These include the way the sublime evokes potentially messy emotional feelings in the human subject, the way that reflective judgment threatens to contaminate the supersensible with the specific object being judged, and the way that judgments of taste can be communicated in a manner that is partial and specific rather than universal. In each case, the engagement with the object for Crowther introduces the concern that the object, rather being passively transcended, lingers and distorts that which is meant to overcome it.

Thus, Kant consistently insists that the kinds of respect that arise from this engagement with the sublime are produced via a series of feelings, both negative and positive. The negative feeling is the humiliation of the phenomenal self, its sense of inadequacy in the face of the sublime. The positive feeling is the feeling of pleasure that arises when the phenomenal self intuits the higher self that it actually is, a feeling encountered via the unexpected harmony of human faculties (the imagination and the understanding) as they fall into place under the organizing power of the supersensible self. These feelings are something that Crowther feels obliged to explain further:

> Since consciousness of the moral law checks our contrary inclinations, it "must" do so by producing a negative feeling that humiliates our "self-conceit" and, in turn, serves to elevate us with a sense of our supersensible rational vocation. But why "must" it do so? . . . Indeed, might we not develop a disposition for suppressing inclinations contrary to the law's demands? In such a case, our habitual conformity to the moral law would surely enable it to determine the will without involving an occurrent feeling of respect on every such occasion.[6]

In Crowther's explanation, respect is a kind of emotion—or is so closely bound up with emotions that it cannot be fully separated from them. Kant believes that there *must* be a simultaneity of both natural/emotional and moral states insofar as the freedom that he seeks can only be understood by contending with natural responses and, in effect, overcoming them. "On these terms," Crowther writes, "the determination of the will by the moral law 'must' involve an occurrent feeling of respect because it is only on this presupposition that the determination of human agency by natural causality and the possibility of free moral agency are rendered compatible."[7] Such a state of affairs introduces a dangerous element of risk for Crowther—the idea that nature (and hence the objects that constitute nature) in some instances might not be overcome and even "must" be retained.

Similarly, Crowther sees a problem with Kant's notion of reflective judgment, which attempts to connect a singular object or event to universal concepts (what is, Crowther asks, the "guarantee that . . . the particular piece of empirical diversity we are attending to will be immediately graspable in terms of a specific teleological principle?"—what if reflective judgment "fails"?).[8] Not to mention that any attempt at such a judgment itself seems to be bound up for Kant with feeling, a "very appreciable pleasure" that "does not wear off"—which Crowther regards as a problematic discrepancy and tries to resolve through a desensitization to feelings.[9]

Finally, when it comes to the communicability of judgments of taste, for Crowther, a phenomenal element remains—the possibility of "considerable divergence of response according to difference in cultivation amongst the individuals concerned" and, accordingly, in "our feeling of pleasure"—that keeps interfering with the universal.[10] In this way, the natural haunts Kantian philosophy, distorting and complicating the elegance of Kant's schema, producing discrepancies that must be accounted for.

For Crowther, such distortions seem to hint at a deeper problem, a kind of chaotic core in an otherwise harmonious and well-ordered system. This can perhaps be seen most clearly when we consider Crowther's analysis of the sublime itself. Of most concern for Crowther is the question of whether the supersensible self, the purported target of the sublime experience, can be considered to be "real," that is to say, how much it is like a material object and how much it is not. Crowther writes:

> Given that for Kant our supersensible rational being is not only the true "object" of sublimity but is our "ultimate vocation," it follows that we must know this superiority to be real rather than illusory. Indeed, if such a superiority was experienced as anything less than real, it would hardly make the feeling of sublimity subjectively final in relation to moral feeling. It might even have the opposite effect—for if we were indifferent to the reality of theoretical reason's superiority over sensibility, this could incline us to be equally indifferent to morality's authority over our sensible being. Matters are also problematic in relation to Kant's holding that judgements of sublimity do not presuppose any definite concept of the object. He attempts to avoid any difficulty here by claiming that such judgements only present rational ideas (specifically those of infinity and the supersensible) "indeterminately."[11]

Here, human beings in their subjective capacity are suspended between two objects, as it were. First, there is the "object" of the self's own supersensible being. To call the supersensible self an object may seem strange, but that appears to be the only way to understand what it is from our phenomenally based perspective. The problem here is: in what way is this an object? In what way can it be said to be real? Putting the word object in quotes suggests that its reality is not clearly given but rather is a question. The notion of reality, after all, is deeply connected to nature and phenomenon. Crowther's language is careful: "We must know this superiority to be real rather than illusory." But this begs the same question: how do we know this and what form does this knowledge take? How can we know a higher reality, even if in a wholly negative way, when it comes to us by analogy to a reality that we already know but which is, for Kant, hopelessly contaminated? Even if Crowther himself may not always want to ask these questions, they arise from the careful way that he addresses the discrepancies in Kant.

The second object in Crowther's statement is the one that we encounter in nature which triggers our sublime experience in the first place. This other object is seemingly less important (but, as I will argue later, is actually far more important) to the point where Kant tells us that it does not need to exist at all; such an object could be a hallucination or a case of mistaken seeing. For Kant, we only have to *think* that we have encountered this object. It has to be real in the sense that we do not immediately perceive it as nonexistent in order to effect the sublime experience. Here again, the nature of reality becomes an issue. For Crowther there is a danger that if the material object is not real enough for us, the sublime experience may not be taken seriously. Insofar as the nature of reality itself seems to depend on our perception of the material object, we see that the various risks that Crowther has spotted in Kant threaten the very edifice of his theory.

For Crowther this is all extremely problematic, suggesting once again a deeper confusion in Kant's theory. Speaking specifically of the dynamic, as opposed to the mathematical sublime—that is to say, the sublime based on a tremendous force like a hurricane or volcano compared to one that is simply massive like a mountain range or the ocean—Crowther tells us that the judgment of this form of the sublime offers us only a "subjective finality," a kind of assumption of what must be and hence an outcome that is only of "indirect moral significance."[12] Here, Crowther, who usually praises Kant, suddenly becomes quite critical of him: "This is the most fundamental problem with Kant's theory of the sublime as a whole. The fact that here it is a feeling rather than a concept which is final in relation to morality is, for Kant, sufficient to establish that judgements of sublimity are 'subjectively determined' and thence aesthetic in character. But from a general critical viewpoint this is most unsatisfactory."[13] Here, the risk that Kant has built into every cognitive process becomes intolerable for Crowther. Kant's willingness to rely on emotions and other natural phenomena becomes a serious problem. To ensure that Kant's theory remains "viable," Crowther says that he must effectively rewrite Kant's schema, including a general "abandonment of Kant's general architectonics . . . his main 'baroque' version of the mathematical sublime, and his *entire treatment of the dynamical mode*" in order to save Kant's theory from his own unexpected and largely unwanted anti-logical materialism.[14]

Not all contemporary Kant scholars who are nominally in the analytic, and hence "pro-Kantian," camp are as critical as Crowther (although some, like Paul Guyer and Henry Allison, can be quite critical at times[15])—but a great deal of attention is paid in the literature as a whole to the troubling issue of materiality, including its connection to feelings and emotions in the Kantian sublime.[16]

Looking at the way contemporary readers of Kant think about his work, it is striking to note how Kant himself is far more willing than many of his later readers to engage with emotions and material objects. He does not seem to fear nature as much as later Kantians will. Nor does he concern himself as much with questions of what is real and what is not. Perhaps all of this is borne of his confidence that the universe can be shown to be moral and correct, that the human and natural world as such is not hopelessly corrupting and that it can be understood in ways that anticipate noumenality.

Even so (and this is the essence of my weaker claim), Kant's willingness to engage so readily with the material suggests the possibility of something more subversive afoot. The material object, as noted above, has a way of malingering and potentially subverting the upward path that Kant seeks; insofar as the supersensible can only be understood in terms of tangible material forms of objectivity, its own purity becomes suspect. Is it possible, then, to read Kant as being at odds with himself (and certainly against many of his disciples), as having a subterranean materialist agenda that militates against his stated goals?

The Vanishing Object

Besides causing distress for some of his disciples, what does it matter that Kant clings so assiduously to the object (both objects, in fact: the object that is our supersensible self and the material object that allows us to apperceive that first object through the operations of the sublime)? To think further about this, I wish to look more deeply at the question of Kant's treatment of the two objects in terms of their relationship to one another via the sublime.

For Kant, the sublime is the interface between the ordinary and supersensible. Perhaps the most famous passage in Kant that describes such an interface (albeit without the direct language of the sublime) comes at the end of the *Critique of Practical Reason*:

> Two things fill the mind with ever and new increasing admiration and awe, the oftener and the more steadily we reflect on them; *the starry heavens above me and the moral law within* . . . I see them before me and connect them directly with the consciousness of my existence. The former begins from the place I occupy in the external world of sense, and enlarges my connection therein to an unbounded extent with worlds upon worlds and systems of systems. . . . The second begins from my invisible self, my personality, and exhibits me in a world which has true infinity, but which is traceable only by the understanding, and with which I discern that I am not in a merely contingent but in a universal and necessary connection, as I am thereby with all those visible worlds.[17]

Here, we are back to the two objects discussed in the context of Crowther's readings of Kant, albeit in a slightly different form. The first object is again the supersensible self and the second is, in this case, the animal self (with the stars and the moral law being the "helper objects" that facilitate the encounter between the two forms of self).

For Kant the point is not the coexistence of these objects but instead the dematerialization of the one (the animal) for the sake of the other (the supersensible):

> The former view of a countless multitude of worlds annihilates, as it were, my importance as an *animal creature*, which after it has been for a short time provided with vital power, one knows not how, must again give back the matter of which it was formed to the planet it inhabits (a mere speck in the universe). The second, on the contrary, infinitely elevates my worth as an *intelligence* by my personality, in which the moral law reveals to me a life independent of animality and even of the whole sensible world—at least so far as may be inferred from the destination assigned to my existence by this law, a destination not restricted to conditions and limits of this life, but reaching into the infinite.[18]

Here, the starry night, which is real and sensible in a tangible, natural way—albeit "reaching into the infinite" and in that way approximating the mathematical sublime—serves to overwhelm and annihilate the "animal creature." The idea of the moral law serves to give an inkling of the supersensible self.

But what is the quality of this "annihilation" of the animal self? Does it truly go away or is it merely reduced to something of which we become hardly aware? Here, the question of the "reality" of the objects reemerges (Kant himself is more insistent on the reality of the supersensible than the secondary material object, including the object that is our own animal self). It seems as if the "reality" of the supersensible self is only apparent to the individual in question by effectively transferring the reality of the animal body to the supersensible self (by "giv[ing] back the matter") and, through this transfer, stripping it away from the animal—that is, having the material object give up its objecthood for the sake of the supersensible self that is now, and perhaps only now, an object.

Here, we get two opposite motions that converge: the spectacle of the starry night is meant to reduce the sense of the animal self by an operation of enlargement; even the earth itself is, as Kant reminds us, "a mere speck in the universe." At the same time, the idea of the moral law is meant to enhance our apperception of our own supersensibility by a movement of diminution and internalization. These two operations move in opposite directions, diluting the former (the animal self) and concentrating the latter (the supersensible self). Insofar as the moral law has no sensible aspect, it can be said to "borrow" that aspect from the starry night; what is scattered and diffused to the stars becomes regathered under the aegis of the supersensible self now concentrated to a sharp pinpoint.

When we move directly to consider Kant's discussions of the sublime, we see the same dynamic at play. In the *Critique of Judgment,* after telling us that the sublime "must always have reference to our *way of thinking,* i.e., to maxims directed to providing the intellectual [side in us] and our rational ideas with supremacy over sensibility," he goes on to write that "we need not worry that the feeling of the sublime will lose [something] if it is exhibited in such an abstract way as this, which is wholly negative as regards the sensible."[19] By way of an example, Kant goes on to say:

> For though the imagination finds nothing beyond the sensible that could support it, this very removal of its barriers also makes it feel unbounded, so that its separation [from the sensible] is an exhibition of the infinite; and though an exhibition of the infinite can never be more than merely negative, it still expands the soul. Perhaps the most sublime passage in the Jewish Law is the commandment: Thou shalt not make unto thee any graven image, or any likeness of any thing that is in heaven or on earth, or under the earth, etc. This commandment alone can explain the enthusiasm that the Jewish people in its civilized era felt for its religion when it compared itself to other peoples, or can explain the pride that Islam inspires.[20]

Here again, we see how the "reality" of the supersensible (or perhaps more accurately, the sense of its reality, the convincing as-if-ness of that nonobject), can only become an object by borrowing its reality from the material object. It is as if a supersensible being must be dressed in ordinary, sensible clothing in order to be located, felt to be present (even though what is inside those clothes remains nothing as far as our senses are concerned). Kant's reference here to the Jewish commandment against idolatry and the enthusiasm this kind of law produces for the Jews (and for Muslims as well) is a reference to the way these seemingly abstract experiences can in fact motivate very tangible and actual human practices and ways of life.

Kant follows this discussion by writing:

> The same holds also for our presentation of the moral law, and for the predisposition within us for morality. It is indeed a mistake to worry that depriving it of whatever could commend it to the senses

will result in its carrying with it no more than a cold and lifeless approval without any moving force or emotion. It is exactly the other way round. For once the senses no longer see anything before them, while yet the unmistakable and indelible idea of morality remains, one would sooner need to temper the momentum of an unbounded imagination so as to keep it from rising to the level of enthusiasm, than to seek to support these ideas with images and childish devices for fear that they would otherwise be powerless.[21]

Here, we see the transfer of reality more clearly. Initially there is the material object, and then there comes the point when "the senses no longer see anything before them." This dematerialization is emphatically not, Kant tells us, an icy and removed experience. Rather, all of the energy, all of the force and even *all of the emotion* that normally accompanies the material object has now been transferred to the supersensible, and it is the material object itself (however temporarily) that now becomes empty and lifeless (no longer seen). This transfer—the dematerialization of the animal self/object and materialization of the supersensible self/nonobject—having been achieved, the supersensible self becomes tangible to the subject, more "real" than her own mind and body (which are reduced and diluted while her "soul" is expanded).

This transfer seems simultaneous; it is not clear that the one happens before the other. What is clear, however, is that the apperception of the supersensible self could not occur, would not be "real," without this transfer of affect and materiality. Here, too, there is a danger inherent in this transfer. Kant invokes the notion of enthusiasm—which often has problematic connotations for this thinker even as it seems positive (see previous example)—as the price to be paid for this animation of the supersensible.[22] Precisely because the emotions involved in the sublime experience are the same emotions that occur in other judgments (of beauty, of taste) they risk an excess or, worse yet, the danger of subreption, when the feelings of the will are mistaken for the feelings of reason (where the one masks, imitates, and overwhelms the other). This is the same risk that interpreters like Crowther worry about—but Kant is clearly willing to take that risk, because otherwise the supersensible could never be other than an immaterial haunting, a state of which only the most intellectual and rational of beings could have an inkling.

Kant directly addresses these dangers when he goes on to write:

> On the other hand, this pure, elevating, and merely negative exhibition of morality involves no danger of *fanaticism*, which is the *delusion . . . of wanting to* SEE *something beyond all bounds of sensibility,*

i.e., of dreaming according to principles (raving with reason). The exhibition avoids fanaticism precisely because it is merely negative. For *the idea of freedom is inscrutable* and thereby precludes all positive exhibition whatever; but the moral law in itself can sufficiently and originally determine us, so that it does not even permit us to cast about for some additional determining basis.[23]

Here we get to the crux of the matter. Kant feels that the risks inherent in the kinds of engagements with affect and materiality can be safely navigated because the ultimate object, the supersensible self, is always and only negative. Negativity itself is Kant's defense against subreption; its nothingness disallows any false claims about what the supersensible is. Enthusiasm (and worse yet, fanaticism) is a violation of that principle by thinking that *something* about the supersensible can actually be sensed. Although, as already noted, Kant speaks of the "enthusiasm" of the Jews in the earlier passage in a seemingly positive way, we see that such an emotion renders that community susceptible to the very idolatry which they seek to avoid.[24] Here we can more clearly see the double-edged sword that Kant accepts as the precondition for invisible things to become as real as (or even more real than) our own selves or our own encounters with the material world around us.

Yet, if the supersensible can only be known through sensible means, how can we know what is of itself and what is not? How would we know how much of the sensible that "transferred" a sense of the reality (minus any actual presence) to the supersensible could be separated from the supersensible itself? Insofar as Kant puts so much faith in the negativity of the supersensible (it is negative by definition), this becomes a problem for him if there is even the slightest suggestion that what we think is supersensible is actually phenomenal. Given the way we anticipate and *enjoy* the negative, and given that it is so much of a piece with the material delineation around it, is it really so certain that we can enjoy the negative *as such*? Doesn't the negative itself have a kind of thinghood, one that we engage with at our peril?[25] The danger of idolatry and subreption haunts Kant's attempts to declare this process free of material contamination.

It is true that Kant goes out of his way to make a clear separation between the natural and the supersensible object. Earlier in the text, speaking specifically about the mathematical sublime, Kant writes: "this liking [produced by the sublime] is by no means a liking for the object (since that may be formless), but rather a liking for the expansion of the imagination itself."[26] One cannot "like" an abstraction, something that exists in a form that approaches infinity. Instead, Kant says that the failure of the imagination to recognize the supersensible object on its own terms, is exactly what makes it available to us, the most we can expect in encountering it. Thus, Kant concludes: "*Sublime is what even to be able to think proves that the mind has a power surpassing any standard of sense.*"[27]

And yet, this failure of the imagination to perceive this object is based on a previous—and unnoted—failure. We have to fail in one way (fail to see what is before us in the case of the mathematical sublime) in order to experience a second failure (the imagination's failure to perceive the supersensible).

The first failure (first in a temporal rather than a metaphysical sense) is particularly telling when we consider Kant's relationship to materiality. In effect, Kant *requires* the first object even though that requirement includes needing that object to disappear from our senses. Furthermore, that material object is actually preserved in its new (now transferred) guise as the supersensible object. In this way, Kant continues to rely upon an object which is nominally meant to disappear (for us) altogether. At the very center of Kant's attempt to allow us to apperceive the supersensible, lies the unacknowledged but continually necessary material object.

I have mostly been talking here about the mathematical sublime, but a similar case can also be said to occur with the dynamic sublime. There, the natural violence the subject witnesses—albeit from afar—causes displeasure and humiliation even as she also recognizes that such threats cannot affect her higher, supersensible self, causing a pleasure and enhanced sense of selfhood. For Kant, the dynamic sublime "reveals in us . . . an ability to judge ourselves independent of nature."[28] Furthermore, it "keeps the humanity in our person from being degraded, even though a human being would have to succumb to that dominance of nature."[29] In this way, the supersensible self is encountered, not by failures of the imagination but rather by our discovery that we are not utterly dominated by nature. Kant says of this: "Hence sublimity is contained not in any thing of nature, but only in our mind, insofar as we can become conscious of our superiority to nature within us, and thereby also to nature outside us (as far as it influences us)."[30]

This is still a failure of sorts, the failure, as it were, to only be a mortal, phenomenal being or, put differently, the failure of our phenomenal selves to ascertain the whole of what we are based on our relationship to (threatening) nature. Here, too, nature is determinant and resilient even in its own supposed undoing. Kant writes that "the sight of [the terrifying object] becomes all the more attractive the more fearful it is, provided we are in a safe place."[31] This reference to personal safety is written like an aside, but I see it as critical to the operation that it describes. To have an experience of the dynamic sublime we need to no longer be afraid of what threatens us; we have to be at a sufficient physical remove to engage in what comes next. In this way, the corporeal sense of safety itself—and beneath that, a sense of the corporeal body as such—serves as the basis for the supersensible body to which it formally gives way.

In this, too, we see an element of transference; the animal body gives that sense of presence, safety, and remove over to the supersensible body, itself becoming disembodied in the process. That sense of embodiment is ultimately what is being transferred. It offers a perspective (just like the safe animal body) that can serve as the site where the experience of being a higher self or object can occur.

This is where we begin to see the ways that these operations are theological in nature even if Kant himself is not evoking a theological language in discussing these processes. In both the case of the mathematical and the dynamic sublime, materiality is the theological core—precisely because it is unacknowledged—of a system of thought that belies its own claims to superseding the empirical. It is theological because it happens in a hidden realm (in this case the material realm which is "no longer seen") in a way that supports and makes possible the ostensibly "secular" and supersensible outcome.

The argument that Kant is himself operating in a disguised theological fashion is not in itself novel.[32] Yet, I am not claiming that Kant is secretly (or even not so secretly) promoting a Christian model but rather the opposite. The main difference with traditional forms of Christian theology is that here the material haunts the supersensible element. This is, as previously suggested, a kind of counter theology that addresses any occult Christian idealist theology that might be present in Kant's work, very much including his apparent preference for the supersensible over the phenomenal world. Given the way that objects tend to linger in Kant's work, we see how his unexpected, and unwanted, materialism serves to unravel his own transcendental preferences.

This material resilience functions very much like the kinds of spiritual resilience that Christian dogma looks to. Yet, whereas in that case the spirit can be said to haunt the material world and, in that haunting, demonstrate its authority over the world, in this case, the material functions like a kind of spirit of its own, haunting the transcendent world that would supersede the material world, thereby exercising a similar authority, albeit from the opposite direction.

Understanding this theological (or counter-theological) dimension of the nature of material resilience in Kantian theory leads to the stronger version of my argument: although Kant himself seems to be far more comfortable with allowing an empirical dimension to his thinking than his followers (indeed, his dualism is one of the hallmarks of his philosophy), the way he understands the nature of the sublime experience suggests that what comes out of this process is not superior, not pure or wholly negative; what results necessarily remains contaminated by the materiality that is meant to give way before it. Yet, in my view, that is not a theological failure on Kant's part (as Milbank would argue as regards natural law) or even a confusion within his philosophy (as Crowther and many others would argue) but instead what saves his philosophy from being what Nietzsche says it is, a form of nihilism that denies and hates the animal and material selves that we are.

Perhaps more accurately, this *is* a theological failure on Kant's part (so that Milbank is once again right although only in a limited and technical sense) insofar as Kant fails to properly obey the strictures of orthodox Christian dogma wherein the material world is meant to be used up and ultimately eliminated in the face of divine forms of grace and transcendence. But this failure leads to a counter-theological success insofar as the failure to obey that kind of doctrine (even if Kant is in fact motivated to be obedient to its dictates) leads to an outcome that produces, not nihilism and the denial of life, but its affirmation, an effectively positive stance toward bodies and objects that is much closer to Nietzsche than Nietzsche himself might want to allow for.

A Messianic Materialism

In reading Kant in this way, I am therefore clearly aligning him with Nietzsche, which might seem like a very difficult thing to do. But in fact, as he does with many of his philosophical enemies, Nietzsche pays tribute to Kant, and recognizes this element of self-subversion when in *The Genealogy of Morals* he writes: "Kant, like all philosophers, instead of viewing the esthetic issue from the side of the artist, envisaged art and beauty solely from the 'spectator's' point of view, and so, without himself realizing it, smuggled the 'spectator' into the concept of beauty."[33] In speaking of the way that Kant has "smuggled the 'spectator,'" Nietzsche may be alluding to the same phenomenon that I have been discussing earlier, namely the way that Kant, in seeking to supersede the material, has instead placed it at the center of his philosophy. The concept of "smuggling the spectator" indicates that Kant has failed to fully abandon a very critical subject: himself, his all-too-human body that remains embedded (as noted above) even in the supersensible body that is meant to replace it. This is also suggestive of the way that physical bodies have a way of lingering, even after they have transferred their bodyhood—their material substance—to a higher and better body/object. Although Kant himself portrays the spectator as "disinterested," such a spectator has not reduced the physical body the way Kant would like to; even the pleasure of overcoming that body (the bit that is "smuggled") requires a retention of that body as a (safe) place where pleasure can happen, no matter how minimally or disinterestedly, something that would be impossible in the case of true unembodied formlessness.

And it is here that I think we come closest to considering another Kant, a smuggler and coconspirator of Nietzsche's in terms of political theology. We can say that Kant protects his notion of reason and the moral law from one end from competition from higher and divine authorities (i.e., religion), but he fails to guard against the lower reaches, against materialism, affect, and bodies that are no less a threat (and perhaps no less theological in nature). It may be that Kant feels confident about his control over the material object because it is dumb and "inert," subject to an easy determination by reason. Yet, Kant is not nearly as in control of materiality as initially appears.

It is helpful at this point to think of the material, the remnant that survives its transfer to the supersensible, as being in and of itself messianic. We are more used to thinking about messiahs that evoke the invisible, supersensible and supernatural but there are plenty of thinkers (such as Walter Benjamin and Nietzsche himself) who offer us a vision of what I would call a messianic materialism. From this perspective, it is the humble, inert, and dumb materials of the world that act as messiahs. In this case, what they save us from is Kant himself, the sadist that would force us to obey the moral law, who so hates himself and his body (and all of our bodies by extension) that he would seek our "annihilation" in favor of a moral law that has no material existence or reality of its own. Once exposed or ruined by materiality, the moral law goes from being a universal mandate to being only a demand, one that we can and should refuse. Kant's failure to completely abolish materiality—or, put in a more positive light, his ability to preserve materiality exactly through his attempts to eliminate it—allows it to serve as a permanent source of salvation from salvation. In other words, by this failure, Kant avoids the "salvation" of Christianity and the Enlightenment, providing a fount of resistance to everything that is higher, better, and (Nietzsche would say) hateful toward the body and the world.

Normally, the messianic is understood as entering the world from elsewhere, but this kind of messiah is different. It is already in the world. What it interrupts, however, is not ordinary reality (it *is* ordinary reality) but a false reality that is being imposed on that world through transcendental operations.

Here again, we see the radical reversal of conventional theology. Normally, the theological is the supersensible element which is more "real" than the material world, what gives it its meaning. In this other version of Kant, the material takes that meaning away, showing the supersensible to be empty and meaningless.

In "On the Concept of History," Walter Benjamin writes that "every second [is] the small gateway through which the Messiah might enter."[34] This encapsulates the messianic at its most materialist and anarchic. No one moment of time is determinant; time is not ordered in any particular way and no future event guarantees the coming of the messianic (in that same passage, he also says: "We know that the Jews were prohibited from inquiring into the future").[35] Here the messianic is not the culmination of eschatology but that which denies and prevents that deliverance.

What Benjamin suggests about time is also true about space: no one spot or one thing in space is any better (or worse) than any other. This gives room for the ordinary itself to be messianic; literally *anything* can be and is messianic because it serves as the site of deliverance from false notions about the future, about reality, about the self that exists beyond time and space. At the same time, because it is messianic, such ordinariness is invested with a purpose and meaning of its own, even if that purpose and meaning stands largely in terms of resistance to the false claims that materiality helps to dispel. Rather than serving as a source of a subservient materialism which dispenses with politics altogether, a material messianism remains a critical and subversive force, one that may compel even a normative thinker like Kant toward radical outcomes.

Conclusion: Kant's Pure Means

Through his unexpected materialism, Kant could be said to be demonstrating the power of means as such. Despite all his claims to the contrary, Kant may in fact be turning to means as a way to confound his own ends, ends which he cannot otherwise avoid. In this way, the means, the objects, and the instruments that Kant engages with, are acting akin to what Benjamin calls "pure means."[36] The notion of pure means suggests that when means have their ends cut off (often by the intrusion of the means themselves), they become something else. Here, the would-be instruments render the employer of those instruments into a different kind of subject, one who is unexpectedly turned back to her own devices (and by her own devices). Put another way, even as the Kantian subject seeks to employ instruments for her own self-supersession, those instruments turn on her, fortunately denying her the transformation she seeks.

This returns us to my suggestion that the sublime for Kant is *not* in fact a way to overcome and annihilate the material but, on the contrary, serves to encounter the material as if for the first time. It is, as previously suggested, a way to engage with the feeling within the feeling, that is to say, to recuperate the all-too-human emotions that, for Kant, are purportedly only meant as a path to supersensibility. When the objects of the world become pure means, it is their ends that are annihilated (rather than those objects themselves), returning those ends to the nothingness from which they were conjured. When means are liberated from their ends, they become something else; the path to supersensibility is cut off, allowing us to reencounter the phenomenal world that we inhabit.

More particularly, we can reencounter ourselves. This rereading of Kant as Nietzsche's (or Benjamin's) coconspirator may be particularly relevant for thinking about what happens to the subject when she becomes pure means. Here the Kantian subject is rescued from being a supersensible subject. That is, through the failures of Kant's attempts to transcend the subject we, in effect, see how to "descend" the subject. When the subject becomes akin to "pure means," she is not one unified thing. Instead, she becomes many local messy anarchist things, a material stew of selves.

That all of this possibility is enabled by objects in their utter ordinariness suggests that we ignore this aspect of political theology at our peril. When the object is taken for granted it is perhaps at its most subversive, its most messianic. The radical Kant shuts the door on what the transcendental Kant would otherwise pursue, but it is never clear if it is Kant himself or the objects that he would employ that cause this messianic failure. At the very least we can see that, even if Kant does seek to abandon and annihilate the object, it will not abandon or annihilate him.

Ultimately, it is the messiahs that we are not looking for that are, perhaps, the only ones who can save us. This is the case even as we may remain fixated on external and supersensible messiahs who—very fortunately—never actually show up (nor should we want them to).

Notes

1. John Milbank, *Theology and Social Theory* (London: Wiley-Blackwell, 2006), 76.
2. Milbank, 105.
3. Friedrich Nietzsche, *The Genealogy of Morals* (New York: Anchor Books, 1956), 240.
4. Nietzsche, 254–255.
5. Paul de Man makes the argument that Kant is a materialist—especially in his concept of the sublime—in *Aesthetic Ideology* (Minneapolis, MN: University of Minnesota Press, 1996), esp. chap. 3, "Phenomenality and Materiality in Kant."

6. Paul Crowther, *The Kantian Sublime: From Morality to Art* (New York: Oxford University Press, 1991), 24.
7. Crowther, 24–25.
8. Crowther, 47.
9. Crowther, 47–48.
10. Crowther, 64.
11. Crowther, 129.
12. Crowther, 131.
13. Crowther, 131–132.
14. Crowther, 135.
15. See Paul Guyer, *Kant and the Claims of Knowledge* (New York: Cambridge University Press, 1987). See also Henry E. Allison, *Kant's Transcendental Idealism: An Interpretation and Defense* (New Haven, CT: Yale University Press, 2004).
16. Robert Clewis is another example of a thinker who tries to "fix" Kant by altering his theory, in Clewis's case by offering a third model of the sublime, the "moral sublime." Robert R. Clewis, *The Kantian Sublime and the Revelation of Freedom* (New York: Cambridge University Press, 2009), 84.
17. Immanuel Kant *Critique of Practical Reason* (Amherst, NY: Prometheus Books, 1996), 191. For more of Kant's writing on the sublime, see also Immanuel Kant, *Critique of Judgment* (Indianapolis, IN: Hackett, 1987); Immanuel Kant, "Observations on the Feeling of the Beautiful and Sublime (1764)," in *Kant: Observations on the Feeling of the Beautiful and Sublime and Other Writings*, ed. Patrick Frierson (Cambridge: Cambridge University Press, 2011), 11–64. See also "Remarks in the *Observation on the Feeling of the Beautiful and Sublime (1764–65)*" in the same volume.
18. Kant, *Critique of Practical Reason*, 191.
19. Kant, *Critique of Judgment*, 135.
20. Kant, 135.
21. Kant, 135.
22. For more on Kant's description of enthusiasm, see Kant, 132. See also Robert R. Clewis, "The Feeling of Enthusiasm," in *Kant and the Faculty of Feeling*, ed. Kelly Sorensen and Diane Williamson (Cambridge: Cambridge University Press, 2018), 184–207.
23. Kant, *Critique of Judgment*, 135–136.
24. Just a few years after writing the Third Critique, Kant will in fact accuse the Jews of idolatry. See Immanuel Kant, *Religion within the Limits of Reason Alone* (New York: Harper and Row, 1960). See also Susan Meld Shell, "Kant and the Jewish Question," *Hebraic Political Studies* 2, no. 1 (Winter 2007): 101–136.
25. I am indebted to Karen Feldman for this insight.
26. Kant, *Critique of Judgment*, 105.
27. Kant, 106.
28. Kant, 120

29. Kant, 121.
30. Kant, 123.
31. Kant, 120.
32. For Kant's relationship to Christian theology, see for example, Stephen R. Palmquist, *Kant's Critical Religion* (Aldershot: Ashgate, 2000); Onora O'Neill, *Kant on Reason and Religion (The Tanner Lecturers on Human Values)* (Salt Lake City: University of Utah Press, 1997); John Hare, "Kant and Theology," *Toronto Journal of Theology* 33, no. 1 (Spring 2017); Allen Wood, *Kant's Rational Theology* (Ithaca, NY: Cornell University Press, 1978). For more on Kant's own writings on religion and theology, see Kant, *Religion within the Limits of Reason Alone*. See also Immanuel Kant, "The Conflict of the Philosophy Faculty with the Theology Faculty," in *The Conflict of the Faculties* (Lincoln: University of Nebraska Press, 1979), 20–139; Immanuel Kant, "Lectures on the Philosophical Doctrine of Religion," in *Religion and Rational Theology*, ed. and trans. Allen W. Wood and George Di Giovanni (Cambridge: Cambridge University Press, 1996), 341–451.

33. Friedrich Nietzsche, *The Genealogy of Morals* (New York: Anchor Book, 1956), 238.

34. Walter Benjamin, "On the Concept of History," in *Walter Benjamin: Selected Writings*, vol. 4, *1938–1940*, ed. Howard Eiland and Michael W. Jennings (Cambridge, MA: Harvard University Press, 2003), 397.

35. Benjamin, 397.

36. Walter Benjamin, "Critique of Violence," in *Walter Benjamin: Selected Writings*, vol. 1, *1913–1926*, ed. Marcus Bullock, Michael W. Jennings (Cambridge, MA: Harvard University Press, 1996), 246.

Earth Unbounded
Division and Inseparability in Hölderlin and Günderrode

JOSEPH ALBERNAZ

> Earth is local movement in the desegregation of the universal.
> —Stefano Harney and Fred Moten, "Base Faith"

The universal is segregated. Universality is, fundamentally, an operation of segregation. It hierarchically separates under the claim of unity, totality, and wholeness, and gives birth to itself by way of this separation: separate and unequal. This act of segregation (division, separation) always takes place on, in, and against the earth. The logic and the content—indeed, the very title—of Carl Schmitt's book *The* Nomos *of the Earth* [*Der* Nomos *der Erde*] (1950) make this clear.[1] The *nomos* of the earth is the earth's appropriation, division, enclosure, and segregation. The Greek noun *nomos*, which is usually translated as "law" or "norm" (a translation Schmitt takes great pains to undo), comes from the verb *nemein* (νέμειν), which originally means appropriation, separation, division (German: *teilen*), and enclosure. The primordial act of *nomos* encloses the excess of the common, immanent earth, establishing in general the condition of possibility for particular regimes of the proper: "the first order of all of ownership and property relations is created by the initial division [*Teilung*] and distribution of the land . . . ownership derives from this initial land-division" (*NE*, 45). *Nomos* is thus a "fundamental process of division and distribution, of *divisio primaeva*," of the earth, but as this primeval division takes place, there must simultaneously be a taking of place, or appropriation (the German *-nahme*, from *nehmen* or "to take", is, according to Schmitt's questionable reconstruction, etymologically linked to *nomos* and *nemein*, sharing the

Indo-European root *nem-*) (327). Schmitt explains that *nomos* is, in essence, this appropriation. In taking place, this taking *of* place (*Landnahme*) gives rise to place and position as such: it instantiates and institutes *topos* upon a placeless, unenclosed earth.

Schmitt writes that the ancient world's *nomoi* lacked a proper sense of *topos* because they lacked a properly global *nomos* of the earth, where *nomos* is a concrete act of land-appropriation and division, grounding a "*concrete* order and community" (*NE*, 20).[2] That is to say, the universal—the global, the whole—*only comes into being through its* nomos, *its concrete segregation*. This became truly possible, for Schmitt, only when the earth was fully encompassed in 1492. In historical terms, then, the segregated universal takes place with the taking and enclosing of the so-called New World, simultaneously creating and dividing the whole earth hierarchically into European (Christian) and non-European—an event Schmitt admiringly calls "heroic" (349). "The first *nomos* of the earth" is thus "when the earth first was measured and encompassed by European peoples," and "lines were drawn to divide and distribute the whole earth," demarcating the New World as "an area open to European occupation and expansion" (49, 86–87). Universality, in all its forms, would follow this logic of a concrete imposition and segregation at its center.[3] In this way, the "original, constitutive act" of *nomos* as "appropriation" and enclosure is always necessarily one of "colonization" (78).[4]

The logic of the segregated universal—concrete appropriation grounding universal order—made possible by and co-constitutive with the event of 1492 and its political-theological sanction, culminates its trajectory in German Idealism. Here this logic finds its most complex development, articulation, and justification—but also, as I argue, its refusal. There are many textual loci in the corpus of German Idealism that could help illustrate the first claim, but a certain passage from Hegel is especially apt for this essay and its focus on earth. It comes not from Hegel's *Philosophy of World History*, the most famous vehicle for his Eurocentrism, but from the *Philosophy of Nature*, in a section that discusses the division of the earth into parts: "Europe forms the consciousness, the *rational part of the earth* [*Teil der Erde*] . . . the division of the world into continents is therefore not contingent."[5] Earth is hierarchically divided, segregated, with a concrete appropriating force—Europe—constituting its universality: a concrete universal. Because Schmitt interrogates this logic and its essential relation to earth so explicitly, it is worth mentioning the importance of German Idealism to Schmitt and *The* Nomos *of the Earth*—particularly Kant and Hegel, who feature prominently toward the beginning and the end of the book. At the close of the introductory chapter, Schmitt even enigmatically says that "only one author" has heretofore come close to the *arcanum* (or secret) of the *nomos* of the earth: none other than Hegel (49).

In the *Philosophy of Subjective Spirit*, in another passage on the division and concrete differentiation of the earth (*concreten Unterschiede der Erde*) into parts or continents (*Weltteile, Erdteile*), Hegel identifies the concrete universal not only with Europe and Europeans but also with the inner logic of Christianity and its universal God who concretizes and divides Himself. The concrete partition of the earth—the concrete (segregation of the) universal—which is geological, cultural, political, and racial,[6] is also essentially and originally *theological*: "It is, however, the concrete universal, self-determining thought, which constitutes the principle and character of Europeans. The Christian God is not simply the One which is devoid of difference, it is the Triunity, that which holds difference within itself."[7] Under the political-theological-geological regime of a *nomos*, the earth is partitioned: earth is both unified as a global whole and segregated by a *nomos* that places Europe at and as its concrete center. This colonizing segregation of earth is an irreducibly Christian political-theological operation, whose worldly divisions are justified by theological foundations—a point about which Schmitt is also explicit and emphatic.[8] In a different key, Sylvia Wynter has tracked a similar relation between theology, coloniality, and the division of the earth: "the geography of the earth had also had to be known in parallel Spirit/Flesh terms as being divided up," and "[blackness was] made to reoccupy the signifying place of medieval/Latin-Christian Europe's fallen, degraded, and thereby nonmoving Earth."[9] The example of Hegel is a test case for how even the most abstract theological logic of diremption is related to the concrete dividing of the earth.

Universality thus at once depends upon and cancels earth (and the beings it designates as earth's condemned avatars, its wretched). But earth moves, under and against its divisions. "Earth is local movement in the desegregation of the universal."[10] How might the *locality* of this desegregating movement of earth be thought alongside and against its apparent evil twin, the *concreteness* of Schmitt's appropriating and enclosing *nomos* of the earth? Since the colonial imposition of *nomos* is also ecologically disastrous, culminating in the epoch of ecological crisis now known as the Anthropocene (itself differentially inflicted), thinking the earth against its segregated *nomos* becomes a problematic both of political theology and of general ecology. Alongside recent interest in ecology and earth in much contemporary theory, including political theology, this essay turns to figurations and formulations of earth in two figures in the galvanizing circuit of German Idealism, Friedrich Hölderlin (1770–1843) and Karoline von Günderrode (1780–1806), to think the earth as a destabilizing common that undoes the enclosures of the world and the universal. Earth here is a placeless field of situated disorder that shatters the concrete orders of separation and the proper, allowing for the conceptualization of a locality that is not constitutive of segregated universality. Instead, earth's locality is only a trace of universality's dissolution, a trace related to what Hölderlin called the "trace of the departed gods," for both he and Günderrode develop their conceptuality of earth through forms that emerge in and as the wake of theological ruin.

Nomos and Being

German Romanticism, contemporaneous with and nebulously but critically related to German Idealism, is also decisive in Schmitt's larger trajectory: in 1919 he published *Political Romanticism*, separated by just three years from *Political Theology* (1922), the latter establishing Schmitt's concept of sovereignty and founding the discourse of political theology in the twentieth century. One writer haunting Schmitt's discussions of German Idealism and Romanticism is Hölderlin, who was both a poet and a key figure in the development of post-Kantian German Idealism. Hölderlin warrants a single but utterly crucial mention in *The* Nomos *of the Earth*, in the discussion where Schmitt offers his most forceful attempt at disarticulating *nomos* from law. *Nomos* is not law, Schmitt says, but the concrete appropriation, which is in fact the "ur-act" ("nomos *als ur-Akt*") of the *ur-concrete*, the concrete positing of concretization as such,[11] creating at once the situated and the universal: "The *nomos* by which a tribe, a retinue, or a people becomes settled, i.e., by which it becomes historically situated and turns part of the earth's surface into the force-field of a particular order, becomes visible in the appropriation of land" (*NE*, 70). For Schmitt, *nomos* is not the particular constituted set of laws or norms, but rather a primordial enclosure, the "constitutive historical event" of force that makes any given regime of mediations though law or norm—any given "settle[ment]"—possible (73).

Schmitt's foil for this claim is none other than Hölderlin, though triangulated with the ancient Greek poet Pindar. In his almost unfathomably strange texts known as the "Pindar Fragments" (1805) (translations of Pindar with prose quasi-commentaries), Hölderlin translates Pindar's formulation *Nomos ho panton basileus* (Νόμος ὁ πάντων βασιλεύς) as "The law / King of all" ["Das Gesetz / von Allen der König"].[12] Assessing Hölderlin's rendering of *nomos*, Schmitt reproaches Hölderlin for "taking the false path of this unfortunate word [law], although [Hölderlin] knew that, in the strictest sense, law is mediation. In its original sense, however, *nomos* is precisely the full immediacy of a legal power . . . it is a constitutive historical event [*Ereignis*] of legitimacy" (*NE*, 73). For Schmitt, Hölderlin fails to grasp the immediate and originating power of *nomos*, an immediacy that conditions mediation; but as we shall see, this is because Hölderlin is after what is prior to this origin, prior to any division. Because *basileus* means "king" or "sovereign," the Pindar-Schmitt-Hölderlin encounter also functions as an important hinge in Agamben's discussion of sovereignty in *Homo Sacer*. (I leave the problematic of sovereignty aside for reasons of space, except to note that the logic of the segregated universal as *nomos* closely mirrors the logic of the sovereign decision and exception; thus it is easy to see why Schmitt approves of Pindar's equation of *nomos* and sovereign.[13] This is the case even as the concept of sovereignty is oddly missing from *The Nomos of the Earth*, all the more odd because Schmitt's rendering of *nomos* as *Nahme* [appropriation] is so close to the key word in his definition of sovereignty: *Ausnahme* [exception].)

In his commentary to the *nomos basileus* translation, Hölderlin writes: "The immediate, strictly speaking, is impossible for mortals, as for immortals" (*PF*, 713). That is, both humans and gods—both secular and theological, we might say—must rely on mediation, must make decisions and divisions that constitute universals and "differentiate several worlds [*verschiedene Welten unterscheiden*]," must make worlds out of the earth (713). God's transcendence enacts a mediation and division of worlds precisely in order to retain a sovereign purity—this is the very nature of God ("according to [God's] nature"): "heavenly goodness, for its own sake, must be holy, pure [*unvermischet*]" (*PF*, 713; trans. modified). Humans require mediation because they cognize, and cognition operates through separation and opposition: "Human beings, as cognizant ones, must also differentiate between several worlds, because cognition is only possible by opposition [*Entgegensezung*]" (713; trans. modified). Hölderlin continues his emphasis on cognition at the end of the commentary, explaining—almost as if anticipating Schmitt's reproach for not understanding *nomos* as "legal power"—that the sovereignty of *nomos* as king does not in the first instance index power: "'King' here means the superlative that is only the sign for the supreme ground for cognition, not for the highest power" (713). But cognition is ultimately secondary for Hölderlin, who is after the "supreme ground" that precedes and refuses any logic of division. In his early and important philosophical fragment known as "Judgment and Being" ("Urteil und Sein"; ca. 1795), he names this ground "Being."

In this remarkable text, which evinces a profound engagement with Kant, Schelling, and especially Fichte, Hölderlin seizes upon the play suggested by the German word for judgment, *Urteil*, as *Ur-teil*, "original division." For Hölderlin, judgment is a fundamental mediation that names and performs a primordial separation (an *"Ur-Teilung"*) of undifferentiated, immediate Being into different orders: subject and object. In the very operations that mediate consciousness, then, we cannot escape a logic of segregation at the moment of founding, an *"ursprüngliche Trennung"* (*Trennung*, often translated as "segregation," is a synonym Hölderlin uses for *Teilung*): "In the concept of separation [*Teilung*], there lies already the concept of the reciprocity of object and subject and the necessary presupposition of a whole of which object and subject form the parts."[14] On the other hand from the world of judgment and division, there is Being proper (*Sein schlechthin*). This Being is not even wholeness (or identity), it is totally other than the kind of primordial operation that segregates existence into parts and reunifies them into coherence. For even a whole made of parts, Hölderlin says, retains the concept of the reciprocal relation (and thus division) of parts: a unity/totality constituted through a concrete segregation, as it were; a "completion in separation."[15] But Being is, in a sense, immanently indifferent to any logic of separation or division, of part and whole, particular and universal, situated and global: "Where subject and object are united altogether and not only in part, that is, united in such a manner that no separation can be performed without violating [*verletzen*] the essence of what is to be separated, there and nowhere else can be spoken of *Being proper* [Sein schlechthin]."[16] Being names unity and connection (*Verbindung*), though without any possible separability. When and where separation is operative, along with the world of mediation it carves out and founds (precisely the world of "when and where"), Being's essence cannot be spoken of or cognized in judgment. Being is other than the world of (and as) segregation, and is indifferent to it, but Being's essence can be hurt (*verletzen*) by division. The mediated world exists as the injury of Being; the world reproduces itself through enclosures that continuously cancel the pre-original, inseparable commonness of Being. Here "common" denotes not a substance held in common by separated beings but a sharing of being prior to any enclosure. The point here with "Judgment and Being" is not about Hölderlin's epistemology or theory of subjectivity, nor his relation to Fichte and the early Schelling; the point is rather to understand the logic of separation, and what is other than it, what might move against it: earth.

Hölderlin's Common Earth

I have tracked the intimate relation between the partition of the earth and the theo-logic of the concrete universal in Hegel, so it is unsurprising to find that Hegel directly identifies the universal with the separating and diremptive operation of judgment as *Ur-teil* ("the universal is disjunction or judgment (*Urteil*)"), even elsewhere going so far as to make that same pun as his old friend and roommate Hölderlin, in what is likely a subterranean allusion to "Judgment and Being."[17] Yet a still more striking parallel is that when Schmitt is grasping for a succinct definition for the *nomos* of the earth as division, he also employs the exact same pun on *Ur-teil*, identifying the two: "The second meaning of *nomos* [after appropriation] is the action and process of division and distribution—an *Ur-teil* and its outcome" (*NE*, 326). *Nomos* is thus explicitly the primordial separation of *Ur-Teilung*, or "*divisio primaeva*" as Schmitt says on the next page. In this way, since *nomos* is always first the ur-segregation of the *earth*, one that both divides and imposes a universal, global order (a world), the division of the earth in Schmitt and the division of Being in Hölderlin—in each case an *Ur-teil*—are directly analogous. Their logic is one. By way of the coinciding of what *Ur-Teil* is *opposed* to (Being in Hölderlin and earth in Schmitt), and with triangulatory help from Hegel (the thinker closest to grasping *nomos*, for Schmitt), we are invited to think the logic of Being's indifferent nonseparability as nothing other than earth's indifferent nonseparability: a refusal of enclosure and insistence on the immanence of the common. Being before and against *Ur-teil* is earth before *nomos*—the common earth unenclosed.[18] And like Being, though, earth can be "hurt" (subject to *verletzen*) by divisions and segregations. The world wants to divide and cancel the earth, whose unbounded commonness, from the perspective of the world (the world of *nomos*, judgment, universality, cognition, mediation, separation, division, place, position, etc.), is impossible; it is nonbeing, nothingness. The world (*nomos*) suspiciously considers earth's nonboundedness to be a "nothingness" that is "hostile" to its orders of division and mediation: "boundlessness or a nothingness [is] hostile to *nomos*" (355). The world's suspicion is correct: the earth moves against it.

The question is: how to think on the side of earth (the side of no sides, or the underside, "earthy underside"[19]), how to move with it? Thinking on the (under)side of the earth means thinking and moving locally against the segregations and divisions of the universal and the world, meeting them at and undoing them in their concreteness, destituting them through fostering local movements of the common against concrete acts of appropriation. Indeed, far from only an analogy with Schmitt and Hegel vis-à-vis *Ur-teil*, this notion of earth against enclosure is already present in many of the formulations of Hölderlin's poetry and prose.[20] One such instance is the 1799 ode "Der Main," the opening line of which invokes, on the one hand, the "living Earth," and on the other, the various "lands," separated and demarcated territories that divide its surface: "True, on this living earth [*lebenden Erde*] there are many lands / I long to see" (*PF*, 137). Following a priamel structure, the poet zeroes in on the famed land of Greece, but arrives there only to wade through a scene of destitution, among the literal traces of theological ruin: "in the scattered rubble [*Schutt*] / Of temples Athens raised, and imaged Gods [*Götterbilder*]" and "worlds that are no more" (137). Instead of building or travelling to another world, with its new forms and enclosures, the "homeless poet [*heimathloser Sänger*] . . . must wander / From foreign to foreign, and the / Earth, the unbounded [*Erde, die freie*], alas, must serve him / In place of home and nation his whole life long" (139; trans. modified). Kir Kuiken, whose work on earth in Hölderlin and reading of "Der Main" I am building on here, writes: "This very destruction of the 'world' represented by the Greek temple is the condition for the emergence of the Earth, an even more radical 'stranger' [*Fremde*]."[21] The wandering "from foreign to foreign" [*Von Fremden er zu Fremden*], among ruins, is a local movement tracing the dissolution of any claim to the proper, tracing the world's shaped undoings ("worlds that are no more"). It's a local movement only insofar as it heralds the ruination of any "concrete order and community" (Schmitt). Thus, it is local without stability or order, without home or nation, without proper or appropriation—a groundless (non)locality. It bears the form of the unmaking of form, an agenda for concrete disorder, similar to what Hölderlin once called "becoming in dissolution" ["*Werden im Vergehen*"].[22] Instead of home and nation, there is the alien movement of earth.

The poet associates this exilic local movement with "Earth, the unbounded" ("*Erde, die freie*"). It is precisely the nonenclosure of earth, its free openness and commonness, that renders a refusal of the partitioned and partitioning formations of "homeland and nation." "Earth, the unbounded" is simply another way of saying: earth unenclosed. Kuiken, who sees this unbounded common earth as offering a "new conception of collectivity," also draws attention to the importance of Hölderlin's theological situation, citing the line from Hölderlin's "Remarks on *Antigone*" about the modern place of God—what Hölderlin calls "the more real Zeus"—being nothing but a movement "more decidedly down onto earth."[23] Earth, then, could be seen as the movement of the gods leaving the sky. But there is also a more famous formulation that will help us adumbrate Hölderlin's political theology of earth: his claim that the gods have fled. For Hölderlin, the modern poet writes in a situation of theological destitution, able to detect only an evanescent "trace of the departed gods" ["*Spur der entflohenen Götter*"] (*PF*, 328–329; trans. modified). The departure of the gods is also conjoined with Romanticism's postrevolutionary situation, and the dissolution of the legitimation of the political-theological apparatus of sovereignty: "This is no longer the time of kings [*Dies ist die Zeit der Könige nicht mehr*]."[24] This impoverished political-theological situation, the departure of God and the gods, allows a thought of earth in its groundlessness, even as this groundless, open, common earth is blocked by the divisions, mediations, and separations of the world.

The opening line of Hölderlin's unfinished poem "To Mother Earth" ("Der Mutter Erde") crystallizes this in six words: "Instead of open common, I sing song [*Statt offner Gemeine, sing' ich Gesang*]" (*PF*, 468–469; trans. modified). The poem addressed to Mother Earth begins with an acknowledgment of its enclosure: instead of the open commonness that should characterize the unbounded earth before division, there is only the promise of poetry. The implication is that *in* the world, poetry offers the closest thing to summoning and accessing the pre-primordial commonness of the earth, before its first segregations and divisions.[25] While poetry is wrapped up in and with mediation insofar as it consists of language, Hölderlin's gambit is that poetry's mediations, laws, and names are essentially different from those of world. It is from here that we can better understand the earlier *différend* between Hölderlin and Schmitt on the translation of *nomos*. When Hölderlin chooses the word "*Gesetz*" (law)—a word Schmitt dismisses as beloved by "poets and philosophers" (*NE*, 70n)—he does so keeping in mind his own theories about the rhythmic law of poetry, the "calculable law" (*kalkulable Gesetz*). Precisely because law is rooted in earth, as Schmitt himself acknowledges,[26] law must be seen in its ultimate groundlessness, its anafoundational relation to the churning earth. For Hölderlin, poetry and tragedy are exemplary modes of working through this notion of self-destituting *Gesetz*, which is fundamentally other than (because lacking a fundament) the Schmittian *nomos* of stabilization through concrete appropriative violence. Recall "Der Main," where the poet or "singer" wanders from foreign to foreign without any enclosed home or nation, only moving through the unbounded earth. As in "Die Teilung der Erde," the poem by the young Hölderlin's idol Schiller, the poet has no part in the universal division of the earth.

Amid the philosophical and political-theological ferment of German Idealism, then, Hölderlin offers a conceptual and a poetic constellation that undoes operations that enclose, segregate, and divide the common earth. When Hölderlin famously asks about the use of poets in a time of destitution ("Wozu Dichter in dürftiger Zeit?"), we might hear in this last phrase not only the typical evocations of theological abandonment and political upheaval but also intimations of ecological crisis inflicting the earth. As he writes in the third version of the poem "Greece": "the ancient knowledge of the earth is in danger / Of going out" (*PF*, 699). Just as poetry remains in language, within mediation, within the concrete measures of the world, the earth moves alongside the concrete segregations named by *nomos* to open them. The "significance of locality" in Hölderlin is then the concrete undoing of the concrete—earth's movement is both one of gathering out of the open common, and devastation: "The earth, proceeding from devastations [*Die Erde, von Verwüstungen her*]," reads another formulation in "Greece" (698–699).[27] This is perhaps another way of saying that "earth constantly carries out a movement of deterritorialization on the spot."[28]

The movement of earth is local and a movement of gathering, of the common, even as in the world it looks like destitution; for this gathering is not a reunification of separated elements but the local expressions of a pre-original inseparability that, from the perspective of division, is nothingness. As a local movement of gathering, its character is ecological, although this is "an ecology in a gnostic spirit."[29] The point is to think this ecology, this field of relationality, as concrete disorder vis-à-vis the world, that is, vis-à-vis what Schmitt calls "concrete order," the segregated universal constituted by *nomos*. Earth is the unbounded, the common, unity before any original separation (*Ur-teil*), the plenitude that still moves. As Jean-Luc Nancy writes in an essay on the poet: "[For Hölderlin] the unity of the whole must be grasped in passing, as passage, and not pursued throughout its movement."[30] The movement is unpredictable, and not on the world's time; it cannot be pursued but it can be joined, wherever you are, until there is no there where you are.

Günderrode and the Divine Life of the Earth

The Romantic writer Karoline von Günderrode's work involves a figuration of earth that traverses deeply consonant conceptual and political-theological sites. And like Hölderlin, Günderrode is positioned on the margins of German Idealism, although her engagement with its primary thinkers—particularly Schelling and his *Naturphilosophie*—was intensive. In "Idea of the Earth" ("Idee der Erde"), one of the last texts of her brief life, Günderrode develops a theologically inflected idea of the earth as a pre-primordial commonness that undoes the mediated divisions and forms of the world, even as in this finite world, earth is approached through local instances of connection and the common.

Earth is a central poetic, philosophical, and theological locus throughout Günderrode's writing, and was so up to and even after the very end of her life: the epitaph on her tombstone is a poem beginning: "Earth, my mother" (*Erde du Meine Mutter*). That this verse is a reworked version (via Herder) of a Sanskrit text is also notable, as much of Günderrode's work displayed a serious engagement with non–Euro-Christian theological materials, especially from the traditions of Islam and Hinduism. Even as her writings recurrently evoke the earth as a site for poetic, philosophical, and theological reflection, earth retains an unsettling element of alienness rather than being a harmonious order and stable ground—not for nothing is a biography of Günderrode titled after her remark that "The earth has not become a home for me" (*Die Erde ist mir Heimat nicht geworden*).[31] Rather than attempt to encapsulate and harmonize the varying operations and thematics that "earth" represents in Günderrode's poetry and prose, I turn to "Idea of the Earth" to bring out a logic that refuses and ruins separation and enclosure.[32]

The text translated as "Idea of the Earth" is in the form of a letter, the last in a brief exchange between two lovers found in Günderrode's book *Melete*. The letter begins with an agonizing and moving effusion of erotic longing and separation, decrying the condition of the world as one of endless "learning, activity, and suffering [*Lernen, Tun, und Leiden*]" (*IE*, 95/358). This worldly condition results in an individuated existence on earth that is fundamentally and essentially fragmented, broken, and ruined, what Günderrode refers to as "the shipwreck of earthly life" (96). Günderrode then moves from the particular conditions of separation and fragmentation to consider the meaning of separation as such, and the pre-primordial unity that separation separates from: "What does it mean that from the oneness of Nature [*Allheit der Natur*] a being with such consciousness detaches itself and feels itself torn away [*losscheidet, und sich abgerissen*] from Her?" (96/359). Günderrode gives the name "earth" to this "oneness," "this whole [that] is life itself" (96). Earth names the logic of an immanent, unenclosed whole, and the purpose of "Idea of the Earth" is to think through earth's (non)relation to the finite world of division, separation, enclosure, and individuation. Like Hölderlin's earth that proceeds from devastations, Günderrode's earth continuously moves through a "dissolution" of separated "parts," such that "the totality becomes animated through the individual's decline . . . and thus through life and death the individual helps to realize the idea of the earth" (96–97). The life and idea of the earth is the desegregation of the worldly divisions that tear into what is common.

Rather than a simple absorption into unity, however, Günderrode goes on to develop a more radical logic of "shattering" that characterizes the relation of earth to the mediations and forms that constitute the world:

> It must be that all the forms [*Formen*] brought forth till now have not satisfied the earth spirit, because she continues to shatter [*zerbricht*] them and seek new ones; she would not be able to destroy

[*zerstören*] forms that truly resembled her precisely because they would be identical and inseparable [*untrennbar*] from her. This perfect identity [*Gleichheit*] of the inner essence with the form cannot, it seems to me, be attained in the diversity of forms; the earth-essence is only One [*nur Eines*], so its form can only be one, not diverse [*verschiedenartig*] (97/360).

The problem, then, is separability and the logic of division. Because earth's immanent unity cannot destroy what is "inseparable [*untrennbar*]" from it, what the earth destroys is precisely separability itself. Like Hölderlin's formulations of "Being," or "earth, the unbounded," earth for Günderrode is totally other than not only the logic of division, but also the logic of mediated unification after division (what Harney and Moten call the earth being "unified in separation"[33]). The idea of the earth exists in nonrelation to the mediated forms of division and connection, but it still moves—it moves against and shatters (*zerbricht*) these forms and what is separate from it, thereby undoing any separation. Earth thus shatters individuated forms not into various parts but rather, strangely enough, into (or even out of) unity. It is and can be "only One." No "*Gleichheit*" is possible through a "diversity of forms," that is, insofar as these forms are constituted through divisions and segregation or are "diverse" (*verschiedenartig*). Earth undoes false totalities, totalities constructed through division, separated from its unity. Any form that is not one with the immanent, unenclosed, undivided earth is not universal enough, but is a universal constructed through segregation—thus the earth's shattering movement is "ever more perfect and universal" (97). Its movement is "ceaselessly universalizing," we might say, echoing one contemporary thinker who not coincidentally describes his own formulation of an idea or "mysticism of the earth."[34] The ceaselessness of earth's movement of undivision is, in Günderrode's terms, *literally* universalizing; it invokes and convokes a common life on the scale of the cosmos, and is thus "a task for the entire universe [*eine Aufgabe für das gesammte Universum*]" (97/361).

The success of this task, however, is uncertain.[35] Only with the dissolution of all separation into one "common [*gemeinschaftlichen*] organism" would the idea of the earth be realized (97/360). This organism, however, is not a typical holistic unity of harmonious parts—its common form would be wholly other (*ganz verschieden*) than the separated body and matter of the world and its logics of unity (97/360). It is at this point in the text that the theological enters more prominently, as Günderrode associates this absolute, common life with what is "immortal" and "divine"

(97). It is also the case that this theological vision of the earth—Günderrode was involved in the Romantic project of a "New Mythology," and here she writes of the "god of the earth"—bears on the political and on forms of sociality. Although these aspects are more implicit in this text, Günderrode was a deeply political, even revolutionary, writer, for whom the commitment to the common against separation cut across the domains of the political, the philosophical, and the theological—domains that are themselves constituted by acts of segregation.[36] Indeed, the end of "Idea of the Earth" discusses the concepts of justice, virtue, and love, rearticulating what such values look like under the aspect of this idea of the earth. After writing that love brings us closer to the earth's absolute unity, the text's stunning, quasi-Gnostic final passage presents a darker image of division that keeps a chained and wounded god "distant" from—separate from—his own life: "Every act of falsity, injustice, and selfishness drives away that blessed condition, and throws the god of the earth into new shackles [*neue Fesseln*], that god whose longing [*Sehnsucht*] for a better life is expressed in every mind's receptivity to excellence, but who moans [*klagt*] in wounded awareness [*verletzten Gewissen*] that his blessed, divine life still remains distant" (98/362). Certain actions and organizations of the world can drive away the undivided unity and put the god of the earth in shackles: acts of division, acts of injustice and selfishness (i.e., insistence on separateness). But local modes of undoing separation where it presents itself and affirming the common, including (in politics) justice as "striving to be equal," bring us closer to the immanent earth (98). It is also no accident that the text, recall, takes the form of a love letter—*eros* here is a local expression of the anoriginal common that precedes individuation.

The theological drama of this final sentence subtly evokes St. Paul's formulation from Romans 8 that all creation is groaning to be delivered, in order to reverse it: here it is not creation but god himself who moans with longing (*Sehnsucht*) to be delivered from all logics of division. God is enchained, imprisoned with shackles (*Fesseln*), enclosed in the world, and the imperative to free him is the imperative to act in the nameless name of the common telluric promise, found not (just) in the starry sky above, but in getting down with the earth and its disenclosure. Acting and moving with the earth involves joining and ultimately becoming the wounded god of earth, a god wounded by separation and enclosure. It is striking that Günderrode here uses "*verletzten*," the exact same word used in Hölderlin's "Judgment and Being," in describing the violation and wounding that operations of division enact on the earth—recall Hölderlin's absolute, undivided Being that is hurt (*verletzt*) by separation (*Teilung, Trennung*). In each case, the governing logic of division and appropriation (*nomos*) encroaches and performs an act of violence upon the common.[37]

But in affirming "the constant eruption of the earth into and out of the world"[38]—the unruly, deforming, chthonic force that Hölderlin called the *aorgic*—Günderrode adumbrates modes of undivision and strivings for the common that evince a distinctly, albeit enigmatically, theological texture. Still, this ruined theology of a wounded god crying against the world is far from orthodox; this culminating theosis that the text demands—joining the god of the earth—looks like nothing familiar. For what would it be to realize the idea of the earth? For Günderrode, the earth's only power is ruin and collapse (or what looks to the world like collapse). If the local unities were to realize the idea of the earth, they would simply be one immanent unity, and their separability would shatter. Earth does not appear as such, as its realized idea, in the world—in Günderrode's text earth is only known in and as the shattering (*zerbrechen*) of particular, separated forms in the world. Thus, earth is *local movement of desegregation*. As it undoes forms in the divided world, we gain an idea of the earth through the tracing of this dissolution, the total form of this unforming. In this way Günderrode's idea of earth is close to that of one of her primary influences, Schelling, in his text *Clara*: "The whole Earth is one great ruin."[39] Amidst its own devastations, ecological and otherwise, what the earth heralds is the ruination of organizations of common life that proceed from (and justify) hierarchical division, even and especially when this division is papered over by a claim to universality or totality. This is the logic of earth she leaves us with. Far from the least radical trajectory we can trace in Günderrode's text is its prompting us to think this earthen movement of the common as a burdened expression of divine longing.

Conclusion: Aberrant Earth

In thinking earth as a logic and imperative of undivision and disenclosure through blasted shapes of theological destitution—an absent, departed god, and a wounded, moaning god—both Hölderlin and Günderrode carve out a particular political-theological space in the midst of German Idealism's fascination with the "languishing of God."[40] This thought of unbounded earth from the margins of German Idealism, an opposition to logics of division both secular and theological, provides an important conceptual reservoir for the future of political theology in a time of ecological crisis. This ecological crisis is itself inextricable from particular histories of appropriation, colonization, enclosure, and racialization—divisions that have marked and made the modern world, and whose conceptuality was articulated at the heart of German Idealism. If, as Schmitt has it, coloniality's most primary meaning is the segregation named *nomos*, and if *nomos* is first against the earth, then it is no surprise that colonialism and slavery have left scars deep in the earth's very geological record.[41] And if these divisions are fundamentally against the earth, thinking *against* the divisions must start with the earth; this demands thinking against and under the dividing operations of *nomos*, the concrete order that claims to be universal—"a universal and as such a European exclusive."[42]

The universal imposition of a concrete order and enclosure on the earth by a "separatist, monocultural and monotheistic imperium" is not just social, political, and theological—it is also ecologically violent.[43] As the ecological consequences of such impositions intensify in the Anthropocene, segregation and separation threaten to proliferate in forms both old and new. Schmitt himself claimed that "every new epoch . . . is founded on new spatial divisions [*Einteilungen*], new enclosures" (*NE*, 79). And the new epoch of the Anthropocene—the very name of which recapitulates the segregated universal, with "Anthropos" standing in for a false totality—will see its new enclosures, new apartheids, new borders, new walls erected (Schmitt: "*nomos* can be described as a wall" [70]): precisely what Günderrode's text calls the "new shackles" (*neue Fesseln*) that operations of division impose upon the earth. At the same time, this fact calls for a renewal of means for the unthinking and undoing of enclosures, collective habits of "de-noming" that would be always local in their common, groundless, earthy, desegregating movement.[44]

Following the conceptual formulations of Hölderlin and Günderrode—two figures who, within and against German Idealism, blur the lines between literature, philosophy, and theology—I have traced the contours of thinking earth in a political-theological key that affirms a commonness that both precedes and moves against separation, and in doing so offers a different starting point than *nomos* for any organization of life, human and nonhuman. Pursuing this thought and naming the earth in doing so can revitalize aspects of German Idealism's ambivalent political-theological legacy, putting it in dialogue with many important strands of contemporary theoretical discourse that are invoking the earth: from recent work in political theology, such as Catherine Keller's call for a new "political theology of the earth" and a "planetary commons" or Bruno Latour's *Facing Gaia*,[45] to the philosophical ecology of Frédéric Neyrat's "unconstructable earth,"[46] to Jared Sexton's "mysticism of the earth," to the frequent invocations of earth in the recent work of Harney and Moten, including this essay's guiding epigraph: "Earth is local movement in the desegregation of the universal." Thinking earth as a local movement of desegregation, an unbounded exilic movement that proceeds from devastations (Hölderlin), a movement that shatters worldly divisions (Günderrode), also helps us understand the Invisible Committee's reformulation of communism as both "the return to earth" and the "the real movement that destitutes the existing state of things,"[47] not to mention struggles that refuse enclosure and division in the name of earth from a situated juncture, such as Standing Rock.[48] Earth: common movement of desegregation, devastation, shattering, destitution—each time locally unworking the operations of division that constitute the conjoined matrix of the local and the global, the concrete and the universal. Such terms should be integral to any future political theology that wants to move with what poet Nathaniel Mackey calls "the aberrant earth."[49]

Notes

1. Carl Schmitt, *The* Nomos *of the Earth in the International Law of the* Jus Publicaum Europaeum, trans. G. L. Ulmen (Candor, NY: Telos Press, 2003). Hereafter cited in text as *NE* and page number in parentheses.

2. "[In antiquity] there was no concept of the planet . . . there was no global consciousness . . . they lacked a *topos*, and thus had no concrete order" (*NE*, 50).

3. "From the 16th to the 20th c., European international law considered Christian nations to be the creators and representatives of an order applicable to the whole earth . . . Europe was still the center of the earth" (*NE*, 86).

4. On coloniality as a regime of enclosure and the proper, see Stefano Harney and Fred Moten, "Conversación Los Abajocomunes," *The New Inquiry*, September 5, 2018, https://thenewinquiry.com/conversacion-los-abajocomunes/: "What if it turns out that at a really fundamental level coloniality is an imposition of the proper[?] . . . the propriative borders and fences that scar the earth with the materialized desire to suture over our common incompleteness [are] settler coloniality, [with its] tendency to bind up and, thus, reductively and often murderously make whole."

5. G. W. F. Hegel, *Hegel's Philosophy of Nature*, trans. A. V. Miller (Oxford: Oxford University Press, 1970), 285. I have modernized the German spelling throughout.

6. Hegel, *Philosophy of Subjective Spirit*, ed. Michael John Petry (Dordrecht: Springer 1978), 45: "The universal planetary life of the natural spirit . . . particularizes itself into the concrete differences of the Earth and separates into the particular natural spirits. On the whole, these express the nature of the geographical continents, and constitute racial variety."

7. Hegel, 59–61.

8. "The last great, heroic act of the European peoples—the land-appropriation of a new world and of an unknown continent—was not accomplished by the heroes of the *conquista* as a mission of the *jus commercii*, but in the name of their Christian redeemer and his holy mother Mary" (*NE*, 349).

9. Sylvia Wynter, "Unsettling the Coloniality of Being/Power/Truth/Freedom: Towards the Human, After Man, Its Overrepresentation—An Argument," *New Centennial Review* 3, no. 3 (Fall 2003): 319. Wynter's attention to the racialization of blackness here, along with Hegel's mention of racial variation via divisions of the earth, are two entry points into thinking through the divisions and *nomos* of earth as also irreducibly racialized. See also Jared Hickman, *Black Prometheus: Race and Radicalism in the Age of Atlantic Slavery* (Oxford: Oxford University Press, 2017); and Denise Ferreira Da Silva, *Toward a Global Idea of Race* (Minneapolis: Minnesota University Press, 2007).
W. E. B. Du Bois, in *Darkwater: Voices from Within the Veil* (London: Verso, 2016), also approached the racialized link between the earth and *nomos*'s imposition of the proper in his theologically inflected apothegm: "whiteness is the ownership of the earth, forever and ever, Amen!" (18).

10. Stefano Harney and Fred Moten, "Base Faith," *e-flux* 86 (November 2017): 6.

11. *Nomos* as land appropriation and division is "the source of all further concrete order and all further law" (*NE*, 48).

12. Hölderlin, *Poems and Fragments*, trans. Michael Hamburger (London: Anvil Press, 2004), 713. Hereafter cited in text as *PF* followed by page number.

13. See Agamben, *Homo Sacer*, trans. Daniel Heller-Roazen (Stanford, CA: Stanford University Press, 1998), 37: "Insofar as it is sovereign, the *nomos* is necessarily connected with both the state of nature and the state of exception."

14. Friedrich Hölderlin, *Essays and Letters on Theory*, trans. Thomas Pfau (Albany: State University of New York Press, 1988), 37. The German is cited from Hölderlin, *Theoretische Schriften*, ed. Johann Kreuzer (Hamburg: Felix Meiner, 1998).

15. Harney and Moten, "Conversación."

16. Hölderlin, *Essays and Letters*, 37.

17. Hegel, *Philosophy of Nature*, 410. Hegel makes the explicit pun on *Ur-teil* in both the *Encyclopedia Logic* (§166) and the *Science of Logic*. Schelling also makes this pun in his 1800 *System of Transcendental Idealism* and 1804 Würzburg *System*.

18. "Earth unenclosed" comes from Harney and Moten, "Conversación": "To be with the migrant movement is to be for a program of total disorder, a general antagonism, earth/flesh unenclosed."

19. Fred Moten, *Stolen Life* (Durham, NC: Duke University Press, 2018), 94.

20. Further evidence still for linking Hölderlin's philosophical conceptions of Being and original division with the name of earth is Schelling's work, which, according to Andrew Bowie, directly grappled with Hölderlin's "Judgment and Being" for years. One instance of this grappling, Bowie suggests, is Schelling's *Statement on the True Relationship of the Philosophy of Nature to the Revised Fichtean Doctrine* (1806), which discusses the question of unity and the division into multiplicity precisely in terms of the earth: "It is the same with the earth . . . [whose] true essence can be known only in the bond which gives it

the power to posit its unity eternally as the multiplicity of its things, and on the other hand also this multiplicity as its unity . . . this necessary and indissoluble oneness of unity and multiplicity is what you call [earth's] existence." F. W. J. Schelling, *Statement*, trans. Dale Snow (Albany: State University of New York Press, 2018), 51. See also Andrew Bowie, "Friedrich Wilhelm Joseph von Schelling," *Stanford Encyclopedia of Philosophy*, https://plato.stanford.edu/archives/fall2016/entries/schelling/.

21. Kuiken, "Hölderlin's Earth," unpublished ms., 10–11. He continues: "Faced with the destruction of the temple of Zeus and the collapse of the world to which it belonged, the speaker is instead 'driven on' from strange to strange, toward an Earth freed ('Erde, die freie') from its determination by that world." I thank Kir for sharing his unpublished work, deeply convergent with mine, which also draws on Frédéric Neyrat's recent *The Unconstructable Earth: An Ecology of Separation*, trans. Drew S. Burk (New York: Fordham University Press, 2018).

22. Hölderlin, *Essays and Letters*, 13. See Hölderlin's essay "Becoming in Dissolution."

23. Kuiken, "Hölderlin's Earth," 9.

24. Friedrich Hölderlin, *Gesammelte Werke*, ed. Hans Balmes (Frankfurt: Fischer, 2008), 513.

25. Earth, in Neyrat's formulation, *"precedes the primordial"* (*Unconstructable Earth*, 163).

26. Schmitt speaks of "this terrestrial fundament, in which all law is rooted" (*NE*, 47).

27. See David Constantine, *The Significance of Locality in the Poetry of Friedrich Hölderlin* (London: Modern Humanities Research Association, 1979).

28. Gilles Deleuze and Félix Guattari, *What Is Philosophy?*, trans. Hugh Tomlinson and Graham Burchell (New York: Columbia University Press, 1994), 85–86.

29. François Laruelle, *En dernière humanité: La nouvelle science écologique* (Paris: Cerf, 2015), 76.

30. Jean-Luc Nancy, *Expectation: Philosophy, Literature*, trans. Robert Bononno (New York: Fordham University Press, 2017), 88.

31. See Dagmar von Gersdorff, *"Die Erde ist mir Heimat nicht geworden": Das Leben der Karoline von Günderrode* (Berlin: Insel, 2011).

32. The text I'm calling "Idea of the Earth" (hereafter cited in text as *IE* and with English/German page number) is actually the text of a letter ("To Eusebio") in her late, posthumous collection *Melete*. This title comes from Warren Breckman's translation in the anthology *European Romanticism* (Boston, MA: Bedford/St. Martin's, 2008), not to be confused with another text called "Idee der Erde," an earlier overlapping draft. I cite the German from *Sämtliche Werke*, ed. Walter Morgenthaler, vol. 1 (Frankfurt: Stroemfeld/Roter Stern, 1991).

33. "Base Faith," 3: "[For the world,] the earth's movement must be stopped, or contained . . . The earthen must become clear and transparent, responsible and productive, unified in separation."

34. Jared Sexton, "On Black Negativity, or the Affirmation of Nothing," interview with Daniel Barber, *Society and Space*, September 18, 2017, http://societyandspace.org/articles/on-black-negativity-or-the-affirmation-of-nothing/.

35. "Whether the earth will succeed in organizing herself so immortally, I do not know" (*IE* 97).

36. Lucia Licher calls Günderrode a "poet of the revolution" and articulates her political-theological vision in terms of the undoing of division and separation: "[Günderrode's] New Mythology [and] radical-democratic and cosmopolitan orientation results from the all-encompassing demand of reconciliation and connection across all separations and boundaries [*Trennungen und Grenzen*] upon the earth. She can also be designated as religious." *Mein Leben in einer bleibenden Form aussprechen: Umrisse einer Ästhetik im Werk Karoline von Günderrodes* (Heidelberg: Universitätsverlag C. Winter, 1995), 45, 118.

37. Novalis, an influence on Günderrode, expresses a similar formulation of the earth as an inappropriable common that undoes division and *nomos*. See Gabriel Trop: "For Novalis, the earth represents a deterritorialized zone. The earth belongs to no one in particular; the very concept of the earth contains an energy hostile to the establishment of zones of demarcation, thereby introducing a critical disjunction between law (νόμος) and belonging (νομός): 'Nature is an enemy of eternal possessions. It destroys, according to immutable laws, all signs of property, eliminates all indications of formation. The earth belongs to all peoples—everyone has a claim to everything' (HKA, 2, 416)." "Transcendental Loosening," 17, unpublished English translation of "Fléchissement transcendantal et procédé hyperbolique: les mouvements de l'absolu chez Novalis et Hölderlin," in *Esthétique et sciences du romantisme allemande*, ed. Daniel Lancereau and Andre Stanguennec (Rennes: Presses Universitaires de Rennes, 2018), 153–182.

38. Harney and Moten, "Base Faith," 1.

39. F. W. J. Schelling, *Clara: or, On Nature's Connection to the Spirit World*, trans. Fiona Steinkamp (Albany: State University of New York Press, 2002), 25.

40. See David Farrell Krell, *The Tragic Absolute: German Idealism and the Languishing of God* (Bloomington: Indiana University Press, 2005).

41. Simon Lewis and Mark Maslin, *The Human Planet* (New Haven, CT: Yale University Press, 2018), 320: "This new geological epoch [the Anthropocene] is built from slavery and colonialism." On the georacial stratifications of the Anthropocene, see also Kathryn Yusoff, *A Billion Black Anthropocenes or None* (Minneapolis: University of Minnesota Press, 2018).

42. Denise Ferreira da Silva, "Globality," *Critical Ethnic Studies* 1, no. 1 (Spring 2015): 34.

43. Fred Moten, "Blackness and Poetry," *Arcade*, no. 55 (July 2015): n.p.

44. Walter Mignolo has recently suggested the term "de-noming" to name movements of undoing the European colonial *nomos* of the earth. For direct decolonial engagements with Schmitt, see Mignolo's "Anomie, Resurgence, and De-Noming," in *The Anomie of the Earth: Philosophy, Politics, and Autonomy in*

Europe and the Americas, ed. Federico Luisetti, John Pickles, and Wilson Kaiser (Durham, NC: Duke University Press, 2015). For a related outline of a decolonial thought against the "metaphysical catastrophe" of modernity and the divisions that the "coloniality of being" imposes, see Nelson Maldonado-Torres, "Outline of Ten Theses on Coloniality and Decoloniality," Fondation Frantz Fanon (website), https://fondation-frantzfanon.com/wp-content/uploads/2018/10/maldonado-torres_outline_of_ten_theses-10.23.16.pdf.

45. Catherine Keller, *Political Theology of the Earth* (New York: Columbia University Press, 2018), 22.

46. See Neyrat, *Unconstructable Earth*. Although Neyrat's book finds a conceptual resource in thinking separation, his logic of separation is utterly different from the logic of *nomos* discussed in this essay. I have also attempted to trace this different modality of separation and partiality—as opening onto the common—elsewhere in my work on Romanticism. See my "Fragmentary Domesticity: Wordsworth's Image of the Common," *New Literary History*, 51.3 (2020): 523–547.

47. The Invisible Committee, *Now* (Boston, MA: MIT Press, 2017), 45, 89.

48. See, for example, Nick Estes and Jaskiran Dillon, eds., *Standing with Standing Rock: Voices from the #NoDAPL Movement* (Minneapolis: University of Minnesota Press, 2019). I am also thinking of the example of Julie "Mama Julz" Richards, an Oglala Lakota woman at Standing Rock who chained herself in protest to a piece of heavy construction machinery known as an "earthmover." The body and the thought of Mama Julz moved with the earth against the earthmover, refusing the enclosures of pipeline construction. We might also think of the recent manifesto by the indigenous collective The Red Nation, which casts communism precisely as a matter of "mov[ing] together with the earth": "The Red Nation (TRN) stands with and moves with the people as we move together with the earth," *Communism is the Horizon, Queer Indigenous Feminism is the Way*, https://therednation.org/communism-is-the-horizon-queer-indigenous-feminism-is-the-way/ (2020), 1.

49. Nathaniel Mackey, *Eroding Witness* (Urbana: Illinois University Press, 1985), 17.

Kant with Sade with Hegel
The Death of God and the Joy of Reason

OXANA TIMOFEEVA

It is said that Hegel's privileged figure is not simply a circle, but the circle of circles. In approaching Hegel's notorious idea of reconciliation with reality, I will use a triangle of triangles: (1) a triangle of ethics, religion and politics; (2) a triangle of reason, enjoyment and death; and (3) a triangle of authors—Kant, Sade, and Hegel—as thinkers who, against the background of the French Revolution and the Jacobin Reign of Terror, raised the ultimate question of the foundation of ethical and political acts. I focus on the idea of enjoyment that is presented in Hegel's passage on reconciliation in the preface to *Philosophy of Right* and identify the voice of reason as the source of an insight that elevates reason to the peak of enjoyment (also designated by Hegel as dance). The voice is what connects Hegel's imperative of the enjoyment of reason with two other imperatives—the Kantian imperative of reason and the Sadean imperative of enjoyment. It is not clear whence this imperative voice comes, but one can discern two vectors of interpretation of its possible source—the divine and the unconscious. Referring to Jacques Lacan's analysis of Sade and Kant as a philosopher/antiphilosopher couple preoccupied with the formulation of the moral (or, in the case of Sade, immoral) law, I will turn to Lacan's theorization of psychosis as the emergence of the lost object in the Real and his discussion of philosophy as analogous to psychosis. As a final step, I will interpret Hegel's absolute freedom as the form of consciousness where the opposites of Kant and Sade—that is, moral and immoral, reason and enjoyment— unite in a kind of psychotic episode that philosophy must overcome.

From this perspective, I will consider Hegel's philosophy of the French Revolution and the revolutionary terror as a turning point between the psychotic solitude of consciousness and the ethical community, or the *we* that creates a utopian horizon within the postapocalyptic political-theological situation of the death of God and the end of the world.

The Owl of Minerva

As Karl Löwith recounts, Hegel, on his sixtieth birthday, in 1830, received a medal from his pupils. The front contained a portrait of Hegel; the back depicted an allegorical representation: on the left, a male figure sitting and reading a book, a pillar with an owl crouching on it behind him; on the right, a female figure holding a cross that towers above her; a naked genius, who is turned toward the man but whose raised arm points to the cross on the other side, stands between the two.[1]

A closer look at these symbols, the owl and the cross, suggests that Hegel's genius mediates not only between philosophy and theology, as suggested by Löwith, but also between two kinds of what I would call "mysticism of the Enlightenment"—Christian and revolutionary. Deciphering the symbols of the owl and the cross, which are present not only on Hegel's birthday medal, but first and foremost in one of his most important texts—the preface to *Philosophy of Right*—will reveal a dialectics of revolution and the death of God, while also marking both the horizon and the limitations of such mediation.

Even before Hegel introduced the Owl of Minerva into his philosophy, this symbol was in circulation in the culture of Hegel's time and was well-known to his contemporaries. *Minerva* was the name of a renowned historical-political journal, read by Hegel, Hölderlin, Schelling and many other German intellectuals. The owl perched on an open book served as the emblem of the Bavarian Illuminati—a secret society of the Masonic type.[2] Hegel's works are full of deliberate allusions to the secret esoteric societies of his time. Brotherhoods such as the Freemasons, the Illuminati, and the Rosicrucians at that time faced the crucial task of fighting obscurantism and disseminating the ideas of the Enlightenment. The Enlightenment, understood as a general intellectual and spiritual emancipation, led to ideas of political liberation, including ideas that were radical, revolutionary, cosmopolitan, anti-Christian, anti-monarchical, and even anarchistic in nature.

In short, Hegel's owl does not appear from nowhere. In the symbolism of the age, it represents not only reason but also revolution, around which reason circles dangerously and with increasing intensity. The utterly unrevolutionary context into which Hegel suddenly places the owl is thus all the more bewildering. "When philosophy paints its grey in grey, then has a shape of life grown old. By philosophy's grey in grey it cannot be rejuvenated, but only understood. The Owl of Minerva spreads its wings only with the falling of dusk," he writes in the penultimate paragraph of the preface to *Philosophy of Right*,[3] thus summing up his argument that philosophy's task is not to teach the world how it ought to be or give instructions to the state, but to "comprehend *what is* . . . for *what is*, is reason."[4]

Hegel's owl thus appears here as no anarchist or revolutionary, no conspirator seeking to change the world, but an old defender of the same state against which she once stood in the name of reason and freedom. Reality, with which reason is reconciled, is more rational than any set of ideals. This reconciliation is furthermore not a renunciation or simply an acceptance of the inevitable. Reason "is just as little content with the cold despair which submits to the view that in this earthly life things are truly bad or at best only tolerable, though here they cannot be improved and that this is the only reflection which can keep us at peace with the world. There is less chill in the peace with the world which knowledge supplies."[5]

The peace reached by reason that found itself in comprehending *what is* and simultaneously *what it is*, is by no means coerced; on the contrary, it brings joy. In the argument that follows, I will connect this joy to the death of God and to the openness of the political horizon of Hegel's thought. For this, the following quote from the same preface to his *Philosophy of Right* will be central: "To recognize reason as the rose in the cross of the present and thereby to enjoy the present [*Gegenwart . . . sich zu erfreuen*], this is the rational insight which reconciles us to the actual, the reconciliation which philosophy affords to those in whom there has once arisen an inner voice bidding them to comprehend, not only to dwell in what is substantive while still retaining subjective freedom, but also to possess subjective freedom while standing not in anything particular and accidental but in what exists absolutely."[6]

The Rose on the Cross

Like the Owl of Minerva and in equal measure, the rose on the cross is a powerful cultural symbol: whereas the owl evokes the Illuminati, the rose on the cross is the emblem of the Rosicrucians. According to this esoteric doctrine, God is Absolute Reason, and knowledge provides the path to spiritual rebirth: through several steps or levels, an ordinary man is transfigured into the man of Gnosis and continues to live on Earth as a supreme, divine being. It is thus possible to recognize traces of the Rosicrucian Absolute Reason in Hegel's Absolute Knowing.

As Löwith explains: "Reason is a rose within the cross of the present, not because every estrangement strives by its very nature for reunion, but because the agony of the estrangement and reconciliation has already taken place within history in the suffering God."[7] By estrangement, one can understand here the separation between knowledge and belief, as well as between body and soul, the mortal and the immortal, between death and life. Whereas Löwith is talking about suffering, for Hegel the object of experience is less the suffering than the death and resurrection of God. To say "the object of experience" is to say that the death of God is inscribed into the experience of consciousness, is immanent and present at its every moment. God never stops dying or suffering—as death is a process, not a state; the death of God is present as his dying. Furthermore, Hegel's image suggests that the present is a cross, to which reason is attached, or perhaps out of which reason grows, as something extraneous but beautiful and alive—like a rose. In reconciliation, enjoyment comes together with suffering: enjoying the present is the reverse side of God's suffering on the cross.

In an earlier passage in the preface to his *Philosophy of Right*, Hegel paraphrases the moral of Aesop's fable of the Boasting Traveler and, acting as if the sense of such a play on words were self-evident, transforms "*Hic Rhodus, hic* saltus" (Here is Rhodes, jump here) into "*Hier* ist die Rose, *hier* tanze" (Here is the rose, dance here).[8] Philosophy invites us to dance, expressing the joy of sympathetic reason and reconciliation with reality, not somewhere, sometime but precisely here and now. The dance with the roses on the cross of the present is the culmination of the celebration of universal knowledge. "Here is the rose, dance here" could be Hegel's answer to the anarchistic motto attributed to Emma Goldman, "If I can't dance, it's not my revolution." It is not in some distant, ideal revolution, but in the reality of the actually existing state that sympathetic reason begins joyfully whirling in its ritual danse macabre.

On the other hand, the cross symbolizes death in Christian culture. Crosses adorn and designate graves. Death, however, in Christianity, is never simply death but the gate to immortality and eternal life. Death points to resurrection, that is, the death of death itself, or, to put it into Hegelian terms, a double negation. Such is the meaning of the death of God, which negates the negative and thus affirms the absolute.[9] God is dead, but we never find him in this state, as his grave is empty. That is what Hegelian consciousness discovers at the end of chapter 4 of *Phenomenology*, and what makes it unhappy: "Consciousness, therefore, can only find as a present reality the *grave* of its life."[10] By the end of chapter 7, Hegel comes back to this episode as a moment of the revealed religion, and connects "the painful feeling of the unhappy consciousness that *God Himself is dead*" to "the death of the *abstraction of the divine Being*,"[11] or an abstract negativity that belongs to the element of representation, or picture-thinking. In the death of Christ, particularity passes away but not the self-consciousness. The latter returns "into the depths of the night in which 'I' = 'I,' a night which no longer distinguishes or knows anything outside of it."[12] It stays alone. But it is precisely this loss of substance (the loss of the picture of substance) that brings it to the point of pure subjectivity: in the experience of the death of God, substance becomes subject. In this movement, the sensible becomes universal or rational.[13] While the unhappy consciousness mourns God as the object infinitely severed from it, reason has to reconcile itself with his death and enjoy it as resurrection, in which it recognizes itself.

In an analogous manner, the Hegelian "cross of the present" represents the end of time itself. "Philosophy is its own time apprehended in thoughts," Hegel says, meaning the present: it is impossible to "overleap [one's] own age, jump over Rhodes,"[14] impossible to leap over death. For philosophy, any time which is *not present* (and that means any time, because the present is not a time but a ceaseless transition into nonbeing) is always already dead in some sense. Hegel's cross of the present on the grave of time is crowned with the roses of knowledge.

The End of the World

The Owl of Minerva completes its flight and philosophy begins when everything has already happened, and nothing can be changed. What the owl discovers is not exactly the present (in which we could still intervene and even give directions, prescribing to the world how it ought to be) but the past: a picture of the end times, the ruins of the world—or the graveyard—where, on the cross of the present, the roses of knowledge are supposed to blossom joyfully.

Mladen Dolar suggests that, in Hegel, a condition for the existence of philosophy is the end of the world or the apocalypse.[15] It is as if being, in order to be, required an originary catastrophic event, or as if the end of the world preceded the beginning of philosophy (the same as with the death of God, when the substance is lost in order to become subject). This paradoxical condition can only be understood through the notion of retroactivity in Hegel's dialectics. Here, retroactivity would mean not only that philosophy begins at the end of the world (when everything is completed, and nothing can be changed) but that the end of the world is only actual via the beginning of philosophy (as that which is becomes reason). As Gregor Moder claims in his book on Hegel and Spinoza, philosophy "is literally caused retroactively."[16] All its prehistory—being, substance, the world—thus really emerges post factum.

Discussing the problem of the beginning in Hegel, Frank Ruda says that *"Beginning needs to be unprincipled."*[17] A proper beginning, beginning from the very beginning, cannot ground itself on something that already is: there must be a zero point, the point where being equals nothing. In chapter 1 of book 1 of the *Science of Logic*, Hegel famously declares that *pure being and pure nothingness are one and the same*.[18] This is the zero point from which the *Logic* begins—one that Hegel defines in his introduction as "the mind of God before the creation of the world."[19] However, in order to arrive at this zero point, first we have to pass through *Phenomenology*, which ends history: thus, the entire Hegelian system functions in a retroactive way. Phenomenal reality vanishes, God dies, substance becomes subject, and finally we arrive at the zero point whence we start. It is crucial to note that the "one and the same" of logical being and nothingness signifies not their indifference but their absolute engagement, the truth of which—becoming—contains a subtle temporal nuance: "being has passed over into nothing and nothing into being—'has passed over,' not passes over."[20] Becoming unfolds in the postapocalyptic modality of the "always already," or even—as noted by Dolar, Rebecca Comay, and Catherine Malabou—of the "always already too late."[21]

This picture might look melancholic, but, as I argue here and elsewhere,[22] the other side of this attitude is happiness. On the ruins of the world, the belated reason is having fun. I have repeatedly emphasized this point: Hegel's reconciliation does not imply renouncing the pleasure principle in favor of the reality principle, in order to receive some safe, quiet, and grey life in return. Instead, the Owl of Minerva is supposed to really enjoy its flight.

The Voice

There is thus an "imperative to enjoy" in Hegel's moment of reconciliation.[23] It crowns not an ethics but a politics of reason that enjoys not because it ought to but because it can do so. The end of the world and the death of God set it free in a very specific sense: reason is found where it seemed very unlikely to be found—in reality, in what *is*, in the grey and as the grey. This is not easy to see. One should not hurry to depict reason as boring, as simply accepting the rules of the game, because such an acceptance would not be the joy of reason but simply its retreat. No one really commands it, and nothing pushes it to reconcile.

Whence, however, does this imperative to enjoy come? Let me repeat the relevant quotation: "To recognize reason as the rose in the cross of the present and thereby to enjoy the present, this is the rational insight which reconciles us to the actual, the reconciliation which philosophy affords to those in whom there has once arisen an inner voice bidding them to comprehend, not only to dwell in what is substantive while still retaining subjective freedom, but also to possess subjective freedom while standing not in anything particular and accidental but in what exists absolutely."

We see that there is an *inner voice* that bids one to comprehend, and to stand "in what exists absolutely," that is, in a happy match between being and thought. But can one really "stand" there? Does not such a "standing" in the absolute, where the opposites coincide, demand a persistent movement of thought? What is joyful may be precisely this invisible movement: we stand, but we dance ("hier ist die Rose . . .").

The machine of reconciliation is put in motion by the inner voice that is thus responsible for our "rational insight." Here, an excursus outside of Hegel is necessary, as the inner voice is an old motif in philosophy. Dolar has examined this motif in various contexts, including ethics, which offers a long tradition of taking the inner voice as crucial,[24]—from Socrates to Rousseau and Kant. In this tradition, Kant produces a decisive shift. If Socrates's voice dissuaded him from doing wrong, and in Rousseau, a voice at once natural and divine was supposed to guide human beings through their lives, the Kantian voice "does not command or prevent anything, it neither advises nor deters," writes Dolar. "It is merely a voice which demands, inexorably imposes, one thing alone: submission of the will to the rationality and formality of the moral law, the categorical imperative. The voice of reason is merely the injunction to submit to reason, it has no other content. It is a purely formal voice, the form of a voice, imposing pure formality, submission to form."[25]

Whence does this voice come? Everything seems to point to the postulates of God and the immortal soul. But, even if this is only a hypothesis reduced to the mere function of supporting the categorical imperative, it nevertheless, according to Dolar, undermines Kant's central point about the autonomy of reason. The problem is that this voice is closely related to the subject of enunciation of the moral law, and the question arises: "Who is it that addresses us in the second person and admonishes us: 'So act that the maxim of your will could always hold at the same time as the principle giving universal law'? Who is the subject enunciating the categorical imperative? Which authority addresses everybody as 'you' in an appeal which is both intimate and universal?"[26] According to Dolar, the voice as a source of demand does not really come from the subject but from a place that the subject cannot attain: "The innermost realm of consciousness stems from a place beyond consciousness; it is an atopical voice addressing us from inside, the interior atopos. Kant gives way to a long tradition by qualifying this voice as divine, since any evocation of divinity directly opposes his central ambition to pose a principle independent from any divine authority, and to cut all ties between ethics and theology."[27]

The voice is beyond consciousness, but, as we see, not merely outside of it. There is thus a territory within the subject that consciousness does not control, and the voice of reason comes from this uncontrollable territory. It could be divine, it could be transcendent, and it could be the thing in itself of morality, but the idea that this thing is an "interior atopos" brings us to a further step where the regime of the divine turns into the regime of the unconscious, and the thing in itself transforms into an object *a*. A psychoanalytical perspective is needed in order to lend a more attentive ear to the voice with which reason both in Hegel and in Kant are familiar and which resonates, I suggest, across ethics and political theology.

Kant with Sade

A psychoanalytic approach to the Kantian voice is already suggested by Jacques Lacan, particularly in his essay *Kant with Sade* (1963),[28] where he analyzes Sade's *Philosophy in the Bedroom*, written seven years after *The Critique of Practical Reason*, and advances the idea that Sade's pamphlet is an important supplement to and even the truth of Kant's ethical treatise. Kant and Sade form an interesting couple: on the one side is the postulate of the autonomy of reason that gives itself a formal law, on the other is the despotism of enjoyment that is also proclaimed as a universal principle. A pure reason without enjoyment, filtered out by Kant, is counterpoised with an impure enjoyment without reason, a total madness and debauchery of Sade's libertine utopia.

Lacan begins by pointing out that Kant's categorical imperative can only be universal if it is independent of any object. Kant defines as "pathological" any external motivation that would allure the ethical subject by promising phenomenal goods or pleasures. Indeed, I would add, Kant's law literally posits itself beyond the pleasure principle, where Freud will locate the death drive. Perhaps, then, Sade's adventure is to go beyond the death drive.

"Frenchmen, yet another effort if you want to be republicans"—thus begins the furious libertine and anti-Christian manifesto read aloud by one of Sade's characters during the orgy. Lacan condenses its content into a short maxim, which he defines as Sade's own universal rule: "I have the right of enjoyment over [*le droit de jouir de*] your body, anyone can say to me, and I will exercise this right, without any limit stopping me in the capriciousness of the exactions that I might have the taste to satiate."[29]

The moral experience, according to Lacan, is stretched between these two imperatives, Kantian and Sadean. Although the latter appears as the inversion of the former, it is structurally different from it, since it is pronounced from the mouth of the Other, not the self: "anyone can say to me." Moreover, it addresses me as the Other. An integral function of the "I" that, in Kant, unified myself, joining my will and my reason, is now blocked. In Lacanian brand-name formulation, adopted from Rimbaud, "I is an Other" (*Je est un autre*);[30] in this case, I is an Other supposed to obey the maxim (of the Other).

This shift is significant for Lacan. It allows him to characterize the Sadean maxim, which replaces Kantian reason in dominating the will, as "more honest then appealing to the voice within, since it unmasks the splitting, usually conjured away, of the subject."[31] The Sadean Other reveals what is hidden in Kant—a bipolar disorder, upon which the moral order is based, the split "of the subject of the enunciation from the subject of the statement." This split, Lacan argues, is in fact the only principle of the moral law.

Lacan suggests that the Sadean voice could be "a voice on the radio, recalling the right promoted by the supplemental effort to which, at Sade's call, the French would have consented, and the maxim become, for their regenerated Republic, organic Law."[32] Such vocal phenomena resemble to some extent the object in psychosis: psychotics can hear voices that address and sometimes command them, as if coming from the outside. In turn, for the subject of the moral law, the voice itself, in the absence of other objects, could also be qualified as an object. Of course, the voice of Kantian reason must come from the inside, but, as already noted, this is "an interior atopos." Perhaps, then, the Kantian voice must in fact originate from within the split between the two Others, the split that covers itself with the transcendental unity of the *I*. And yet, the Kantian voice, "however mad, imposes the idea of the subject"[33]—that is, of the *I* that controls the situation. Luckily, in Kant, there is God, and God is good; there is a moral argument for his existence. In Sade, God is not: "religion is incompatible with the libertarian system."[34]

I would argue that the death of God is the political-theological core of the encounter between the two ethics: Kant's ethics of reason and Sade's ethics of enjoyment. On the one side, God is still the guarantor of the subject, on the other, God is the enactment of the split. The border between the two sides is constituted by the French Revolution and the Jacobin Reign of Terror. Sade is at the center of these events, whereas Kant remains a distant observer. In contrast to Sade's fluctuation between criticizing the Revolution from an aristocratic position and fervently pushing it forward, Kant is reserved, yet ambiguous. As Comay explains, Kant has clear sympathy with the ideals of Enlightenment and republicanism,[35] but he also rejects revolution inasmuch as it goes *against the law*—not only against particular juridical or moral laws but against the principle of law in general, against the universal formal law.[36] Sade, by contrast, endorses the denial of the principles on which the social contract is based; for him, law and social contract are "the safeguard of the weak."[37] In Sade, God as the guarantor of the law and the ultimate instance of authority must die in order for Frenchmen to make another effort and become truly republican.

According to Lacan, the law is the order of signifiers or the symbolic Other. As Lorenzo Chiesa explains, it operates because it is "guaranteed by another transcendent Other, namely the paternal Law. The Other as Law, the Other of the Other, corresponds to the Name-of-the-Father."[38] If we translate into Lacanese sentences such as "God is the guarantor of the moral law" or "The monarch is the representative of God," we will get this simple formula: there is the Other of the Other. By contrast, if there is, in fact, no Other of the Other, there is also no law. As Madame de Saint-Ange philosophizes in the bedroom: "those absurd laws are the handiwork of men, and we must not submit to them."[39]

But, again, whence comes this "must" or "must not," this imperative form that even Madame de Saint-Ange could not avoid?—From an anonymous pamphlet, from the radio, or, simply, from the object-voice. Here, we return to the possibility of psychosis, briefly mentioned by Lacan in *Kant with Sade*. As Chiesa explains, it is not by chance that Lacan defines psychosis as a radical rejection of the Name-of-the-Father, a foreclosure that leaves the subject in direct contact with the Real. What the psychotic lacks is the Other of the Other, which would protect him from the invasion of the Real: "Such an invasion occurs, with disastrous consequences, in the case of psychosis."[40] The psychotic loses the distinction between the ego and the unconscious, so that the latter literally appears in front of him— and here comes the voice: "In psychotic delusions, the ordinary perception of external reality—which, in order to function properly, necessitates a symbolic articulation ultimately rooted in the Name-of-the-Father—is indeed replaced by phenomena such as auditory hallucinations whose 'verbal' nature is a matter of fact. The unconscious as Real-of-language—as unmediated, unsymbolized letter—appears in reality."[41] Dreams come true, as do nightmares.

A Psychotic Triangle

Ultimately, Lacan will ascribe to Kant a kind of psychosis—the kind that unites him with all, or almost all, other philosophers, since philosophy itself, for Lacan, is analogous to psychosis. One philosopher who takes this diagnosis seriously and even suggests some positive strategy out of it is Alain Badiou.[42] According to Badiou, Lacan is right in defining the specifically philosophical or metaphysical form of psychosis through the operation of foreclosure. This operation proceeds in two steps. First, the so-called master signifier, or the name of the father, has to be rejected, so that thought can locate its own foundation in itself and not elsewhere. In this way, philosophy eliminates everything that would link it to enjoyment. This annihilation of enjoyment produces a lack upon which philosophy is in fact based. Second, what was rejected in the symbolic returns in the Real in the form of hallucination. According to this interpretation, the Real itself turns out to be the philosophical subject that speaks, enjoys, and so on. If we apply this schema to Kant, we see how the autonomy of reason demands the rejection of the master signifier in order to establish its own unconditioned law; how this law's autonomous, pure, formal, and universal character demands the rejection of any phenomenal or sensual content that would subordinate it to the pleasure principle; how this double rejection (of paternal authority and maternal object of desire) produces a lack within philosophy's foundation (the unattainability of things in itself as Kant's general melancholy); and, finally, how what was rejected—any instance outside of the subject that would influence the subject's will—returns as the voice, transformed from a divine voice to an object *a*.

For Badiou, there would be no philosophy without antiphilosophy, which has a necessarily critical function of exposing philosophy's blind spots. Antiphilosophers expose what philosophers hide, reject, or repress.[43] Philosophers and antiphilosophers form couples. One such couple is Kant with Sade, in which the antiphilosopher Sade exposes how, against Kantian reason, an excluded enjoyment takes a monstrous shape. There is nothing wrong with this psychotic couple except the fact that we need to look for a triangle instead of a couple. There must be a third, in whom the opposites of reason and pleasure coincide.

This is the moment when Hegel enters the stage and establishes another psychotic structure out of the same onto-epistemological concerns and political premises. *Phenomenology of Spirit*, especially chapter 5, "Reason," is replete with references to Kant, including to the ideas of pure and practical reason, but the result is less a critique than an *Aufhebung*: Hegel makes them appear as forms of consciousness that must be overcome. The universal formal law is likewise a form of consciousness: instead of giving edicts or commandments, it examines them. It goes against the arbitrariness of laws and shows the capacity of reason to examine their validity, but it is also inseparable from these laws. The "ought," or the despotism of the law, and the willfulness of reason that examines where this law is valid, are modes of the same consciousness, whose problem is that it opposes itself as an individual to the moral substance or spiritual essence (in which reason immediately finds itself when these two modes are superseded).

The presence of Sade in *Phenomenology* is not explicit, but I would suggest that one can discern traces of Sadean characters in various forms of consciousness. In chapter 4, we encounter the dialectics of master and slave, where the master, just like the Sadean libertine, rolls in pleasures, consumption, and destruction. But there are also traces of Sade in section B of chapter 5, where Hegel discusses ethical questions. In "Pleasure and Necessity," or the Faust episode, consciousness is seeking immediate sensual, erotic pleasures (and ends up ruining its life). In "The law of the heart and the frenzy of self-conceit" it tries to proclaim its own desire as universal law, paralleling Sade's theoretical proclamations. Finally, in "Virtue and the way of the world," it struggles against the world in the name of an abstract Good. This last form of consciousness has traditionally been connected to Don Quixote, but I would suggest the relevance of the figure of Sade's *Justine*, a poor girl who is so virtuous and committed to the Good that the way of the world can only bestow upon her a series of rapes and other misfortunes.

The problem of these three forms is, according to Hegel, that consciousness can only see itself as an individuality opposed to the world, in a more infantile way than the Kantian examining consciousness, which at least think itself as a part of the society in which it acts. The B-consciousness of the chapter 5 acts not in the world, but against it. As a result, in Hegel's *Phenomenology,* as I interpret it, Kant and Sade fail in a different way, but for the same reason: they are stuck in the individual.

An encounter between Kant and Sade should be located within the "Spirit" chapter, where Hegel discusses the Enlightenment, which "will taste the fruits of its deeds."[44] In the experience of the French Revolution following the Enlightenment, "common sense" and "utility," characteristic of the Enlightenment, suddenly devolve into the madness and potlatch of terror. Once there is no more God, and the previous forms of rule and social order have been done away with, the "undivided Substance of absolute freedom ascends the throne of the world without any power being able to resist it."[45]

The fruits of the Enlightenment, which allow spirit to open up the space of absolute freedom, suddenly begin to look like vegetables. Self-consciousness sees before it the guillotine with decapitated heads piled up like cabbages: "The sole work and deed of universal freedom is therefore death, a death too which has no inner significance or filling, for what is negated is the empty point of the absolutely free self. It is thus the coldest and meanest of all deaths, with no more significance than cutting off a head of cabbage or swallowing a mouthful of water."[46] As Comay writes, "Absolute freedom *is* terror. It is the infinite melancholia of a self that knows no other."[47] The reality of the objective world, detached from self-consciousness and opposed to it, has lost its certainty; the "independence of real being" has been transformed into a "corpse."[48] Spirit thus finds itself entrusted to its own self, to its "sovereign solitude," and now death as a reality that is free but without otherness frightens it: "the *terror* of death is the vision of this negative nature of itself."[49]

What is "Absolute Freedom and Terror" if not a narration of a serious psychotic episode in the story of Hegelian consciousness? It occurs on the ruins of the universe—not only of the old regime, but of the entire world, which disappears in its objectivity, so that consciousness alone remains. In this episode, where law is cancelled out, Kant with Sade, these two fruits of Enlightenment, merge into one Jacobin cocktail of an incredible solitude, with the only way out, seemingly, being the coldness of death. *Solitude* is the key term here, as it marks a foreclosure: Kant's subject of reason and Sade's subject of enjoyment are united in the French Revolution under the rubric of bourgeois individualism. The autonomy of the subject of the formal law, which has excluded all objective content from the domain of his will, coincides with the solitude of a libertine. As Georges Bataille observes, Sade's fantasies arise from his solitude in prison: "The Bastille was a desert; his writing was the only outlet for his passions and in it he pushed back the limits of what was possible beyond the craziest dreams ever framed by man. These books distilled in prison have given us a true picture of a man for whom other people did not count at all."[50] For Kant, other people did count, of course, but only insofar as they were autonomous individuals, acting freely in their transcendental cocoons.

Hegel's absolute freedom and terror may be seen as a political outcome of the encounter between these two loners, a resonance of the two voices (together with many others) into the silence of death. And suddenly, as it always happens in *Phenomenology* with the experience of consciousness, there is a breakthrough: "absolute freedom leave[s] its self-destroying reality and pass[es] over into another land of self-conscious Spirit where, in this unreal world, freedom has the value of truth."[51] Sovereign freedom brings this transition into being, and "the new shape of Spirit, that of the *moral* Spirit,"[52] arises. But to rejoice in the new, it was necessary to pass through its devastating and catastrophic trial, encountering solitude and death themselves under the name of freedom. Freedom is necessity, that is, reality, that is, reason ("dance here").

What if Hegel's joy of reason is experienced precisely in such moments of renewal and truth, in which the reality revealed by philosophical and antiphilosophical psychoses (both of which are present in Hegel's dialectics and embraced in their unity) is overcome? If so, why would this occur in Hegel, but not in Sade or Kant, or in the two of them together, but without Hegel? Hegel's novelty lies in proceeding beyond the individual into the realm of ethical life, which can also be seen as the utopian horizon of his politics. As Kirill Chepurin notes apropos Hegel's anthropology, there "*we* are the absolute and *we* are the utopian. Every single event of revolution is incomplete, and the utopian is that which bridges the event and its full enactment; consequently, utopia may serve as another name for Geist."[53] The *we*, the collective in Hegel, is beyond the death of God. The passage from the individual to the *we* manifests itself theologically as the death of God, which, in chapter 7, marks the beginning of (Christian) community. Kant's voice is an atopic *I*, Sade's a dystopian Other, and Hegel's is a utopian *we*. Kant does not even consider the death of God, Sade calls for it, and only in Hegel does it find its place as a rational and joyful thing, because it is a new beginning.

Notes

1. Karl Löwith, *From Hegel to Nietzsche: The Revolution In the Nineteenth-Century Thought*, trans. David E. Green (New York: Columbia University Press, 1991), 14–15.
2. Jacques D'Hondt, *Hegel: Biographie* (Paris: Calmann-Lévy, 1998). Kindle.
3. G. W. F. Hegel, *Philosophy of Right*, trans. T. M. Knox (Oxford: Oxford University Press, 1967), 13.
4. Hegel, 11. Emphasis added.
5. Hegel, 12.
6. Hegel, 12.
7. Löwith, 17.
8. Hegel, *Philosophy of Right*, 11.
9. Jean Wahl, *Le malheur de la conscience dans la philosophie de Hegel* (Paris: Presses Universitaires de France, 1951), 71–72.
10. G. W. F. Hegel, *Phenomenology of Spirit*, trans. by A. V. Miller (Oxford: Oxford University Press, 1977), 132.

11. Hegel, *Phenomenology of Spirit*, 476.
12. Hegel, 476.
13. Wahl, *Le malheur*, 72, 74.
14. Hegel, *Philosophy of Right*, 11.
15. I am borrowing the idea of catastrophe and apocalypse as the founding event of being and thought in Hegel's philosophy from Mladen Dolar, who has been kind enough to share with me an unpublished passage in which the Hegelian subject is described as a catastrophe survivor.
16. Gregor Moder, *Hegel and Spinoza: Substance and Negativity* (Evanston, IL: Northwestern University Press, 2017), 45.
17. Frank Ruda, "Hegel's First Words," in Rebecca Comay and Frank Ruda, *The Dash—The Other Side of the Absolute Knowing* (Cambridge, MA: MIT Press, 2018), 89.
18. G. W. F. Hegel, *The Science of Logic*, trans. by G. di Giovanni (Cambridge: Cambridge University Press, 2010), 59.
19. Hegel, xlix.
20. Hegel, 59–60.
21. See Mladen Dolar, "The Owl of Minerva from Dusk till Dawn, or, Two Shades of Gray," *Filozofija i društvo* 26, no. 4 (2015), 881; Catherine Malabou, *The Future of Hegel: Plasticity, Temporality and Dialectics*, trans. Lisabeth During (London: Routledge, 2005), 4; and Rebecca Comay, *Mourning Sickness: Hegel and the French Revolution* (Stanford, CA: Stanford University Press, 2011).
22. Oxana Timofeeva, "The Owl and the Angel," *Russian Journal of Philosophy and Humanities* 1, no. 2 (2017): 115–134.
23. Jacques Lacan, *On Feminine Sexuality: The Seminar*, Book XX (New York: Norton 1998), 3.
24. Mladen Dolar, *A Voice and Nothing More* (Cambridge, MA: MIT Press, 2006), 83.
25. Dolar, 89–90.
26. Dolar, 90.
27. Dolar, 90–91.
28. Jacques Lacan, "Kant with Sade," trans. by James B. Swenson, *October* 51 (Winter 1989): 56.
29. Lacan, 58.
30. Jacques Lacan, *The Seminar of Jacques Lacan*, Book 2, *The Ego in Freud's Theory and in the Technique of Psychoanalysis, 1954–1955*, trans. Sylvana Tomaselli (New York: W. W. Norton, 1991), 7.
31. Lacan, "Kant with Sade," 59.
32. Lacan, 60–61.
33. Lacan, 61.
34. Marquis de Sade, *Justine, Philosophy in the Bedroom, and Other Writings*, ed. and trans. Richard Seaver and Austryn Wainhouse (New York: Grove Press, 1965), 301.

35. Comay, *Mourning Sickness*, 166–167.
36. Comay, 36–37.
37. Maurice Blanchot, "Sade's Reason," in *The Blanchot Reader* (Oxford: Blackwell Publishers, 1995), 80.
38. Lorenzo Chiesa L. *Subjectivity and Otherness: A Philosophical Reading of Lacan* (Cambridge, MA: MIT Press: 2007), 107.
39. Sade, *Justine*, 223.
40. Chiesa, *Subjectivity and Otherness*, 108.
41. Chiesa, 109.
42. Alain Badiou, "Filiation et sexuation de la philosophie," in *Se construire comme sujet entre filiation et sexuation*, ed. Karl-Leo Schwering (Toulouse: Editions Erès, 2012), 95–104.
43. See Bruno Bosteels, "Radical Antiphilosophy," *Filozofski Vestnik* 29, no. 2 (2008): 155–187.
44. Hegel, *Phenomenology of Spirit*, 354.
45. Hegel, 357.
46. Hegel, 360.
47. Comay, *Mourning Sickness*, 68.
48. Hegel, *Phenomenology of Spirit*, 368.
49. Hegel, 361.
50. Georges Bataille, "De Sade's Sovereign Man," in *Erotism: Death and Sensuality*, trans. Mary Dalwood (San Francisco: City Light Books, 1986), 167.
51. Bataille, 363.
52. Bataille, 363.
53. Kirill Chepurin, "Spirit and Utopia: (German) Idealism as Political Theology," *Crisis and Critique* 2, no. 1 (2015): 343.

8

A Political Theology of Tolerance
Universalism and the Tragic Position of the Religious Minority

THOMAS LYNCH

Hegel's political philosophy is a political theology in two senses. First, he takes a certain form of German Protestantism to be integral to the achievement of the ideal political community. Christianity, he says, is "the religion of freedom" foundational to this project.[1] Second, and at a deeper level, Christianity suffuses Hegel's philosophy, informing the conceptions of the universal, the dialectic, and history that are key to his political philosophy.

The consequences and limitations of this political theology are acutely manifested in Hegel's treatment of religious minorities. In *Outlines of the Philosophy of Right*, he develops an account of the universality of the state before turning to the role of religious communities in facilitating the actualization of this universality. Religious communities, while essentially particular, can function as articulations of the universal, forming part of the dynamic whole of an organic universality.[2] Not all religious communities partake in the universal, however, and in a footnote to §270 he argues that these aberrant forms of religion should be tolerated.

Reading §270 in light of Hegel's wider discussions of Christianity, universality, the dialectic, and history reveals a political-theological logic at work in the discourse of tolerance. Although only mentioned in a footnote by Hegel, tolerance is now central to the narratives of the emergence and continuing superiority of liberalism and secularism.[3] Good citizens, good religions, and good states are tolerant. Tolerance of others is highlighted as one of the originating virtues of liberalism, and secularism promises a religiously neutral state that can tolerate a diverse range of religious beliefs.[4] Although liberalism and secularism both denote complicated political traditions, recent work by Talal Asad, Saba Mahmood, and others have argued that underlying this complexity is a consistent, identifiable logic—a logic of universality.[5] This logic has two components: an underlying drive to articulate a universal political, social, and cultural vision; and an operation by which the particularity of "European" or "Western" thought is erased in the process of positing this universal vision. Notions of liberalism, democracy, rights, freedoms, and secularism are not regarded as particular conceptualizations emerging in specific historical contexts to address concrete problems but as facets of human civilization as such. Questioning this logic with regard to tolerance is not a matter of who or what is tolerable; instead it takes up the issue of the political meaning of toleration.

Without attempting to make a genealogical claim about Hegel's role in the development of liberalism or secularism, a reading of his argument for tolerance can thus inform an analysis of the position of religious minorities in secular, liberal societies. First, it enables a critique of the universalist pretense of the secular, liberal discourse of tolerance. Second, understanding tolerance in terms of the relationship between the universal and the particular reveals the tragic position of the tolerated religious minority. Finally, a consideration of the variety of universalism at work in Hegel opens up the possibility of a politics of indifference rather than tolerance.

Hegel and the Logic of Tolerance

Analyzing Hegel's account of tolerance requires an understanding of his conception of the relationship between religion and the state. For Hegel, religion plays a key role in the life of the state, but it is also a perpetual source of potential disruption. In *Philosophy of Right*, Hegel separates piety—a realm of subjectivity and feeling—from the objectivity of right. Religion in its more pious form threatens to slip into an abstract universalism that rejects the authority of law.[6] Believers mistake subjectivity for objectivity, failing to do the rational work of determining the nature of that objectivity and relying on religious sentiment to judge the authority of the state.[7] This failure reduces the absolute to the accidental and transient. If given too strong a position in relation to the state, religion can introduce "instability, insecurity, and disorder."[8]

Having specified the risks of religion Hegel then describes its more constructive role. Genuine religion supports the work of the state. In return, the state should offer protection and assistance to religious communities insofar as these communities integrate the values of the state with the deepest dispositions of citizens.[9] Hegel even goes so far as to suggest that all citizens should belong to a church, although he does not think membership in a particular community should be required.[10] Religion is necessary for the possibility of an ethical life where the divine spirit is "indwelling in self-consciousness, and it is actually present in a nation and its individual members."[11]

In the 1831 fragment "Religion and the State" Hegel makes the point even more directly: "There is one concept of freedom in religion and state. This one concept is the highest concept that human beings have, and it is made real by them. A people that has a bad concept of God has also a bad state, bad government, and bad laws."[12] The German people, as "the bearers of the Christian principle," have the right concept of God.[13] Hegel lays out this political theological justification of the German state both logically, particularly in *Phenomenology* and *Philosophy of Right*, and historically, in his *Philosophy of History*. As a historical achievement, the political consequences of the Christian conception of freedom and universality enshrine the German state at the top of a spatiotemporal hierarchy.[14] Christian Germany leaves behind the historical religions (such as Judaism) and inferior regions (such as Africa) in actualizing true freedom.

Religion and the state thus share a concept of freedom that neither can actualize without the other. This is the fundamental problem of religion for Hegel. Religion is essential to the functioning of the state, but the characteristics that make religion essential are also the ones that make it dangerous. Religion is then sorted into legitimate and illegitimate forms, with legitimate religion promoting cohesion and illegitimate religion remaining a constant threat that must be managed and contained.

This contrast between legitimate and illegitimate religion can be understood in terms of the universal and particular. Legitimate religion, what Hegel calls "consummate" religion, is key to unifying the particular and universal. He argues that individuals will be motivated by particular self-interest, mediated through the universality of a state that is ultimately revealed to be the means of realizing those particular self-interests.

> The result is that the universal does not prevail or achieve completion except along with particular interests . . . and individuals likewise do not live as private persons for their own ends alone, but in the very act of willing these they will the universal for the sake of the universal, and their activity is consciously aimed at the universal end. The principle of modern states has prodigious strength and depth

because it allows the principle of subjectivity to progress to its culmination in the self-sufficient extreme of personal particularity, and yet at the same time brings it back to substantial unity and so maintains this unity in the principle of subjectivity itself.[15]

It is this relationship between universal and particular that is definitive of Hegel's Christian notion of the universal and freedom. The universal is that which can be willed by all particulars as their own end and to engage in this willing is to be free.

Legitimate religion is part of this unification of the particular and universal. For Hegel, this unification entails conformity and obedience, but it is not a coercive process. It is an organic alignment of the particular with the universal. Illegitimate religion poses a challenge to this alignment. In this case, an individual or community does not will the universal for its own sake. The response to this problem is tolerance. A strong state may "tolerate communities . . . which on religious grounds decline to recognize even their direct duties to the state."[16] As he states in the footnote to this section, "To sects of this kind, the state's attitude is *toleration*."[17]

For Hegel, religious minorities should be tolerated for two reasons. First, a strong state can afford to overlook "anomalies" and, in so doing, affirm the humanity at the basis of all civil rights.[18] Second, tolerance is ultimately a tool for conversion or the modernization of religious views. By granting rights even to the undeserving, the state is able to cultivate the feeling of having rights among the minority community, which in turn alters their self-consciousness. Excluding the community would confirm the isolation that the community already uses as justification for resisting the norms and values of the state.[19] The hope is that tolerance can work as the mechanism of political inclusion.[20] Rather than a form of acceptance, it is a means of melting away particularity. Tolerance is ultimately understood in terms of the interests of the tolerating community rather than any inherent or natural rights or freedoms of the minority.[21]

While the dynamics of tolerance remains the same, the tolerating state has shifted away from the explicitly Christian formulation of this tolerance. If for Hegel, the religious minority is tolerated by the Christian state demonstrating the universality of genuine religion, secularism maintains this universalist pretense while disavowing its particular origins. For the purposes of considering religious minorities, the question "who is tolerable?" can be rephrased as "which religions are compatible with secularism?" Being secular does not require abandoning religion, but agreeing to submit to the norms of secular, liberal political discourse. It is to be religious in the right way.

Hegel performs the secularizing move himself, again in terms of the universal and particular. In his consideration of the relationship between religion and the state, the state is described as the actual, "the unity of universal and particular," while churches remain trapped in their particularity.[22] Yet, read in the context of Hegel's wider philosophy, it is clear that although churches remain particular, the same is not true of Christianity as such. Christianity, as the universal religion, is the foundation of the state. It is the source of the state's universality, which is then "articulated" in its contained particulars. Together the universal and particular form an organic whole. Hegel is indeed a "theorist of secularization" or a "secular theologian" in the sense that he makes Christianity universal by separating it from religion.[23] "Religion ceases to be that which belongs to Christianity and instead becomes that which belongs to those who do not belong to the secular."[24]

Although Hegel self-consciously performs this secularizing gesture, the contemporary secular has naturalized this universalization of Christianity. If for Hegel it is obvious that true universality is animated by a Christian logic, in the contemporary secular all traces of particularity must be stripped away so that the secular can function as the foundation of tolerance. When Mahmood argues that the secular now functions as "a discursive operation of power that generates these very spheres, establishes their boundaries, and suffuses them with content, such that they come to acquire a natural quality for those living within its terms," we should hear echoes of Hegel's vision of the secular.[25] For Hegel, the "secular life is the positive and definite embodiment of the Spiritual Kingdom—the Kingdom of the *Will* manifesting itself in outward existence."[26] Secularism is the naturalization of a particular vision of Christianity through the production of the distinction between religion and the secular.

Secular tolerance, then, assumes a position of neutrality in relationship to religion through an extension of Christianity's normative position.[27] As Hegel's Christian, albeit not religious, state sorts the legitimate from the illegitimate forms of religion, the state becomes a theological authority. The conflict is thus not between religion and secularism. Religious communities can conform to the liberal demands of secular society, namely the privatization of religious belief. The conflict is between "the secular," inclusive of religions that conform to the secular, and those religions that do not or cannot. In establishing this latter group as that which is to be tolerated, religion becomes a site of inherent conflict.[28]

This creates a dilemma for the religious minority. If the religious minority persists in their particularity, they pose an ongoing possible threat to the convergence of the universal and the particular in Hegel's ideal state. Although this persistence does not immediately require expulsion, it renders the position of the minority vulnerable. The minority is not a full member of the state, and their stubborn particularity is easily weaponized. They are thus trapped, partially included by a universalism defined in opposition to their particularity. This is a tragic position.

The Tragic Position of the Religious Minority

Throughout his work, Hegel returns to the concept of tragedy to explore the relationship between the universal and the particular.[29] This concept is essentially political-theological, developed in his consideration of fate in his early works on Christianity and later in his discussion of the opposition between divine and human law in Antigone. In both instances, the tragic is the moment of "self-division" that allows for the eventual "self-reconciliation."[30] Tragedies are meant to be overcome and, in their overcoming, the universal is revealed. Elsewhere, this dialectical overcoming is presented in explicitly Christian terms—it is in the person of Christ that the merely abstract universal is rendered concrete.[31] Christianity is the source of true universalism.

As Karin de Boer has recently argued, Hegel accurately captures the dynamics of the universal and particular but overestimates the power of the universal.[32] In her reading, Hegel's assumption that the universal will be able to subsume the particular fails to recognize the depth of the conflicts that emerge.[33] He can thus help describe contemporary intercultural conflicts, but his belief in the dialectical overcoming of the tragic is no longer persuasive. Put differently, the inability of universality to completely subsume particularity leaves fragments of heterogeneity that block the dialectic. These conflicts and contradictions grind the movement of the dialectic to a halt.

This creates a dilemma for the state. In terms of religion, Hegel is clear that forced conversion is pointless, arguing that it is "the height and profanity of contradiction to seek to bind and subject to the secular code the religious conscience to which mere human law is a thing profane."[34] The state, however, still must act to manage these minority religions, lest they realize their inherent potential for political disruption. This identification and containment of political-theological threats create the tragic position of the religious minority. Either such communities maintain their own accounts of ethical life in opposition to the state or submit to state authority.[35] In other words, having arrived at something like a tolerant, constitutional monarchy (Hegel's ideal state), there is no position from which religious minorities, operating as religious minorities, can offer legitimate opposition to the state.

This tragic position is exacerbated by secularism in two ways. First, as described earlier, the secular disavows the Christian nature of the universal. The now naturalized secular universal appears as neutrality and to question this neutrality is to manifest irrational religious particularity. Second, the boundaries of this secular order are not stable. The tolerable and intolerable are constantly negotiated, maintained by legal and political decisions, each of which contributes to the revision of these boundaries.[36] This instability only reinforces the need for secularism. With each instance in which it becomes impossible to disentangle religion from politics and culture, the commitment to secularism is redoubled.[37] The failure to be secular demands that we secularize better. It is the nature of the tragic to be overcome. In this sense, the tragic "coincides" with the dialectic.[38] In the case of the religious minority, this means functioning as the ground upon which the universal is reasserted. The tragic is resolved *for us*, not for those trapped in the tragic position (as is clear in the case of Antigone). The tolerated other is preserved in its otherness—particular grist for the dialectical mill.

Further, within this secular framework, it becomes structurally impossible to act politically from the minority position. The discourse of tolerance central to the secular narrative depoliticizes religion by presenting conflict as cultural or moral, not political. In other words, although there is a political dispute about religion, religion itself cannot be political. Any perceived oppression or marginalization due to religion is always a misapplication of otherwise sound secular and liberal principles. If the religious beliefs of the minority were politically legitimate, they would not require tolerance. If they are legitimate, they are not political.[39] There is thus an essential power imbalance between the majority and the minority: "the universal tolerates the particular in its particularity, in which the putative universal therefore always appears superior to that unassimilated particular—a superiority itself premised upon the nonreciprocity of tolerance (the particular does not tolerate the universal)."[40] This tolerated particularity only further affirms the universality of the tolerator.

Given this impossibility, the only remaining option is to refuse the gesture of toleration. Yet this bid for political agency from the minority position only reinforces one's intolerability. Mayanthi Fernando provides an example of the resulting dilemma in her study of the "Muslim French": "Because Muslims are excluded from the community of citizens, they are compelled to respond to this exclusion by bringing their specifically Muslim interests to the attention of the polity and by seeking political, economic, and symbolic redress. In doing so, however, they reinforce their Muslimness—and their nonabstractness and nonuniversality—reproducing their ideological and embodied difference from the community of citizens and its general will."[41] In protesting their exclusion, the Muslim French only become more of a problem. Complaints from the minority position must be carefully calibrated so as not to challenge the majority. Proper dissent allows wider society to continue to "understand themselves as generous, well-intentioned, accepting, pluralistic, and . . . tolerant."[42] To identify exclusion or marginalization is to question the dynamics of tolerance and, for those occupying this minority position, it is imperative to accept toleration. Refusing to be tolerated, demanding equality, is dangerously intolerable. It is to manifest particularity against the universal and, in doing so, question that universality.

Secular religions, those that are privatized and depoliticized, are tolerable. Those that do not or cannot are excluded. There is no way out of this tragic conflict that does not challenge the very terms of the conflict itself.

Universalism and the Possibility of Indifference

Thus far, I have argued that Hegel's argument for tolerance relies upon a specific understanding of the universal and the particular. This political-theological logic offers the prospect of a secular state in the specific sense that a universalized Christianity takes on a political life beyond its religious origins (a narrative that is itself enabled by the Christian imposition of the distinction between religion and the secular). This process of universalization allows the state to claim a neutrality toward religion. Some religions, in their particularity, serve to articulate the universality of the state. They facilitate the dynamic whole, playing their part in the movement of the Christian dialectic. Not all religious communities are willing or able to articulate the universal. These problematic particulars, in refusing the political-theological logic of tolerance, reject its underlying universalist pretense.

Just as the failure of the secular begets the demand to secularize better, this failure of universalism requires a more inclusive universalism. The problem is not with the logic of universalism as such, so the argument goes, but with its execution. Hegel is ready to help with this task of improvement. His discussion of universalism extends beyond the version described earlier—what we might call the Christian universal. In *Philosophy of Right*, Hegel contrasts this universalism with a lesser, abstract universalism—a negative universalism. Citing Hinduism and the French Revolution, Hegel cautions that this negative version rejects any form of particularity.[43] Any attempt to render the abstract concrete is inadequate in comparison to the purity of the abstract. All that is left is the "fury of destruction."[44]

Madhavi Menon reads this negative form of universalism against traditional interpretations of Hegel. Rather than the universalism of colonialism or the German state, this "underbelly" of the universal enables an opposition to the specific "regime of difference to which we are attached."[45] Gone is the Hegel of hierarchy or the election of another particular to the position of the universal. For Menon's Hegel, this destructive negative universal is not aimed at the particular as such, but the organization of the differences that define particularities. The result is thus not an eradication of particularity but indifference to the particular. Rather than allowing particular differences to constitute identities, this indifference recognizes the universality of difference.[46] This indifferent universalism no longer requires tolerance. The tolerated particular is no longer isolated by their particularity. No particularity is allowed to occupy the place of the universal, as particularity as such is universal.[47] When there is only difference, a specific difference cannot be the basis for a claim to unique access to the universal. Universalism is stripped of its traditional hierarchical connotations.

Within political theology, this notion of an indifferent universalism is associated with the return to Paul. Alain Badiou, perhaps most famously, argues that Paul's declaration—that "there is no longer Jew or Greek, there is no longer slave or free, there is no longer male and female; for all of you are one in Christ Jesus" (Galatians 3:28)—can be read as a (if not the) foundational text for a universalism that claims to be indifferent to difference.[48]

Yet Paul, and Badiou with him, is illustrative of the difficulties of achieving an indifferent universalism. As Amaryah Armstrong shows, shortly after declaring there is no "slave or free," Paul returns to the language of slavery in order to explain the relationship between the universal and the particular.[49] Hagar, the slave, is excluded as the spirituality of the universal is opposed to the particularity of the flesh. Badiou, likewise, struggles with the question of particularity and difference. In his critique of Négritude, for example, he describes the movement as poetic rather than political. While appreciating this aesthetic intervention, he argues that categories such as "black" are not political categories.[50] Even as he insists that he cannot be sure what particularities are capable of becoming political, he expresses skepticism about a familiar set of particularities (including "women," "Islam," and "Arab").[51]

In both instances, then, there is a movement from the particular to the universal, yet the articulation of this universal is haunted by the particular. Even indifferent universalism seems to remain trapped between Hegel's options of the positivity of the Christian universal or the destructive fury of the negative. It is difficult to avoid the conclusion that for both Badiou and a certain Hegel even indifference can be Christian.

Hegel still has more to contribute, however. Postcolonial readings of his work have found potential within the negativity of his account of the universal. As Nick Nesbitt writes in reference to Hegel and Haiti, "truth, the actualization of human freedom as a concrete universal in the world, can be attained only by the forceful negation of this natural existence, through the rational and imaginative construction of human freedom as something never before seen on the face of the earth."[52] While Nesbitt does not take up the question of abstractness, this "forceful negation" carries strains of the dangerous negative universalism that Hegel rejects. While Hegel's reflection on history and the achievement of freedom are offered from "*the last stage in History*," Nesbitt sees the universal as an inaugurating gesture.[53] Freedom, as an "unfolding historical reality," is yet to be achieved.[54] The universal is yet to be wrought. In this sense, Nesbitt thinks universalism from a different direction—from the position of the excluded particular. This stands in contrast to Badiou, who thinks from the position of the universal. In Daniel Whistler's reading of Badiou's indifferent universalism, for example, he considers the possibility of a nondestructive imposition of indifference.[55] To pose the question of imposition is to already think from the position of an assumed universal.

Becoming indifferent requires refusing to assume that universality. Who am I to tolerate the Muslim? To tolerate the religious other is to welcome her to my universal project. To be indifferent is to open up new forms of solidarity. To adapt a point made by Houria Bouteldja, refusing to be tolerated and refusing to tolerate, is to require a new universal[56]—a refusal of our rather than my making. It is, as in Menon's reading of Hegel, to destructively reject a regime of difference to which we have become attached, not in favor of a substantial universal but the universality of the negative.

In terms of religion, this regime of difference is the secular/religious divide. To adopt a negative universalism, then, is to become indifferent to this distinction. That is not to say that there are no longer differences between Jews, Christians, Muslims, Hindus, or Sikhs. It is to not conceive of these differences as religious. It "is to insist on thinking them just as they are. It is precisely by refusing to render them consistent . . . that we make possible an encounter with them that would escape division."[57] There is no (Christian) secular universal from which to survey the landscape of religious difference, no neutrality from which to adjudicate competing religious claims. There is only difference.

There is a fine distinction between this call for indifference and the indifferent universalism of Badiou and Menon. For Badiou, "difference can be transcended only . . . as *an indifference that tolerates differences.*"[58] Menon, also turning to Paul, argues that this universalism allows one "to be all things to all people without being any one thing in particular to any specific person."[59] Negative universalism is less ambitious. There is no aim of transcending difference, only negating those regimes by which difference is organized and rendered consistent. The transcending of difference is the temptation of the Christian universal and, as Paul himself shows, particularity always stows away in this move.

To be content with only difference thus is to recognize that differences must be negotiated from within—there is no outside or beyond. There is no universal from which to tolerate, only a multitude of differences from which to form bonds of solidarity or adopt stances of opposition. Toleration requires order and hierarchy. Negative universalism recognizes only different differences.

It is here that Hegel's contribution ends. His theorization of the universal and the particular continues to illuminate the Christian universalism that sustains tolerance, and with it the liberalism and secularism rooted in the claim to tolerance. And while his understanding of the universal, the dialectic, and history contribute to the thinking of indifference, the new universal is purely negative. In this context, Hegel might find his universal has been rendered problematically particular.

Notes

1. G. W. F. Hegel, *Outlines of the Philosophy of Right*, trans. T. M. Knox, ed. Stephen Houlgate (Oxford: Oxford University Press, 2008), §18A:40.

2. Hegel, *Philosophy of Right*, §207A:253.

3. Wendy Brown, "Subjects of Tolerance: Why We Are Civilized and They Are the Barbarians," in *Political Theologies: Public Religions in a Post-Secular World*, ed. Hent de Vries and Lawrence Eugene Sullivan (New York: Fordham University Press, 2006), 299.

4. See, for example, John Rawls's discussion in the introduction to his *Political Liberalism* (New York: Columbia University Press, 1996), xxiv.

5. A growing body of work is essential to analyzing the relationship between liberalism, secularism, and tolerance, including: Talal Asad, *Genealogies of Religion: Discipline and Reasons of Power in Christianity and Islam* (Baltimore, MD: John Hopkins University Press, 1993); Saba Mahmood, *Religious Difference in a Secular Age: A Minority Report* (Princeton, NJ: Princeton University

Press, 2016); Mayanthi Fernando, *The Republic Unsettled: Muslim French and the Contradictions of Secularism* (Durham, NC: Duke University Press, 2014); and Hussein Ali Agrama, *Questioning Secularism: Islam, Sovereignty and the Rule of Law in Egypt* (Chicago: University of Chicago Press, 2012).

6. Hegel, *Philosophy of Right*, 9–10.
7. Hegel, §270R:243–244.
8. Hegel, §270R:244.
9. Hegel, §270R:246.
10. Hegel, §270R:246. While Hegel focuses on Christian churches, John Burbidge and Thomas A. Lewis argue that his point can be extended to other religious communities as well as communities that would not typically be understood as religious. See Burbidge, "Hegel's Open Future," in *Hegel and the Tradition: Essays in Honour of H. S. Harris*, ed. Michael Baur and John Edward Russon (Toronto: University of Toronto Press, 1997), 185; and Lewis, *Religion, Modernity, and Politics in Hegel* (Oxford: Oxford University Press, 2011), 247.
11. G. W. F. Hegel, *Hegel's Philosophy of Mind: Part Three of the Encyclopaedia of the Philosophical Sciences (1830) with Zusätze*, trans. A. V. Miller (Oxford: Clarendon Press, 1990), §552:283.
12. G. W. F. Hegel, *Lectures on the Philosophy of Religion*, vol. 1, *Introduction and the Concept of Religion*, trans. R. F. Brown, Peter C. Hodgson, and J. M. Stewart, ed. Peter C. Hodgson (Oxford: Oxford University Press, 2007), 452.
13. G. W. F. Hegel, *The Philosophy of History*, trans. J. Sibree (Buffalo, NY: Prometheus Books, 1991), 341.
14. For a consideration of Hegel as an example of this more general colonial logic, see Stefan Helgesson, "Radicalizing Temporal Difference: Anthropology, Postcolonial Theory, and Literary Time," *History and Theory* 53, no. 4 (2014): 545–562.
15. Hegel, *Philosophy of Right*, §260:235.
16. Hegel, §270R:246–247.
17. Hegel, §270R:247n98.
18. Hegel, §270R:247n98.
19. Hegel, §270R:247n98; Rachel Bayefsky, "The State as a 'Temple of Human Freedom,'" in *Hegel on Religion and Politics*, ed. Angelica Nuzzo (Albany: State University of New York Press, 2013), 49.
20. On the violence of inclusion, see Étienne Balibar, *Citizenship* (Malden, MA: Polity Press, 2015), 72–73.
21. Wendy Brown, *Regulating Aversion: Tolerance in the Age of Identity and Empire* (Princeton, NJ: Princeton University Press, 2008), 28.
22. Hegel, *Philosophy of Right*, §270A:253; PR§270R:253.
23. See Epsen Hammer, "Hegel as a Theorist of Secularization," *Hegel Bulletin* 34, no. 2 (2013): 223–244; and Joseph Prabhu, "Hegel's Secular Theology," *Sophia* 49, no. 2 (2010): 217–229.
24. Daniel Colucciello Barber, "Mediation, Religion, and Non-Consistency In-One," *Angelaki: Journal for the Theoretical Humanities* 19, no. 2 (2014): 166.

25. Saba Mahmood, *Religious Difference in a Secular Age: A Minority Report* (Princeton, NJ: Princeton University Press, 2016), 3.

26. Hegel, *Philosophy of History*, 442.

27. A growing body of literature is investigating the relationship between secularism and Christianity. Particularly important for the argument developed here are Talal Asad, *Formations of the Secular: Christianity, Islam, Modernity* (Stanford, CA: Stanford University Press, 2003) and Gil Anidjar, "Christianity, Christianities, Christian," *Journal of Religious and Political Practice* 1, no. 1 (2015): 39–46.

28. Brown, *Regulating Aversion*, 15.

29. For a brief summary of Hegel's notion of the tragic, including the shift that occurs between early and late Hegel, see Peter Szondi, *An Essay on the Tragic*, trans. by Paul Flemming (Stanford, CA: Stanford University Press, 2002), 15–22.

30. Szondi, 16.

31. G. W. F. Hegel, *Phenomenology of Spirit*, trans. A. V. Miller (Oxford: Oxford University Press, 1977), §20:11.

32. Karin de Boer, "A Greek Tragedy? A Hegelian Perspective on Greece's Sovereign Debt Crisis," *Cosmos and History: The Journal of Natural and Social Philosophy* 9, no. 1 (2013): 371. Similarly, David Scott—in *Conscripts of Modernity: The Tragedy of Colonial Enlightenment* (Durham, NC: Duke University Press, 2004)—describes tragedy as "that which derives from a particular kind of action, the kind of action in which a collision or conflict of incommensurable wills or purposes or focuses or obligations or powers takes place (between family and state, for example, or ruler and ruled, or parent and child) . . . this is not necessarily a conflict between a neatly divided good and evil, but rather between relentlessly and intransigently one-sided positions adopted by the antagonists. This one-sidedness constitutes the real ground of the collision" (157).

33. Karin de Boer, "Hegel Today: Towards a Tragic Conception of Intercultural Conflicts," *Cosmos and History: The Journal of Natural and Social Philosophy* 3, nos. 2–3 (2007): 117–131.

34. Hegel, *Hegel's Philosophy of Mind*, §552:288.

35. Kevin Thompson, "Hegel, the Political, and the Theological," in *Hegel on Religion and Politics*, ed. Angelica Nuzzo (Albany: State University of New York Press, 2013), 110–111.

36. Fernando, *Republic Unsettled*, 12.

37. Fernando, 22–23.

38. Szondi, *Essay*, 16.

39. Brown, *Regulating Aversion*, 174.

40. Brown, 186.

41. Fernando, *Republic Unsettled*, 87.

42. Russell T. McCutcheon, *Religion and the Domestication of Dissent: Or, How to Live in a Less Than Perfect Nation* (London: Routledge, 2014), 79.

43. Hegel, *Philosophy of Right*, §5:29–30. In *Phenomenology* and *Philosophy of History* this form of universalism is discussed in terms of fanaticism and is connected to Islam and "the Turk."

44. Hegel, §5:29.

45. Madhavi Menon, *Indifference to Difference: On Queer Universalism* (Minneapolis: University of Minnesota Press, 2015), 9.

46. Menon, 15.

47. Menon, 125.

48. Alain Badiou, *Saint Paul: The Foundation of Universalism*, trans. Ray Brassier (Stanford, CA: Stanford University Press, 2003). Biblical passages are taken from the NEW REVISED STANDARD VERSION. Menon also draws this connection between Badiou and Hegel. See Menon, *Indifference to Difference*, 7.

49. Amaryah Armstrong, "Of Flesh and Spirit: Race, Reproduction, and Sexual Difference in the Turn to Paul," *Journal of Culture, Religion and Theory* 16, no. 2 (2017): 132.

50. Alain Badiou and Peter Hallward, "Politics and Philosophy: An Interview with Alain Badiou," *Angelaki: Journal for the Theoretical Humanities* 3, no. 3 (1998): 118.

51. Badiou and Hallward, 118, 120.

52. Nick Nesbitt, "Troping Toussaint, Reading Revolution," *Research in African Literatures* 35, no. 2 (2004): 27.

53. Hegel, *Philosophy of History*, 442.

54. Nesbitt, "Troping Toussaint," 34.

55. See Daniel Whistler's essay in this volume.

56. Houria Bouteldja, *The Whites, Jews, and Us: Towards a Politics of Revolutionary Love*, trans. Rachel Valinsky (South Pasadena, CA: Semiotext(e), 2016), 114.

57. Barber, "Mediation," 170. Barber's argument, framed in terms of the One, the Many, and the question of mediation, echoes Menon's understanding of a queer universalism that refuses to make difference "coherent" or "self-identical" (125).

58. Badiou, *Saint Paul*, 99.

59. Menon, *Indifference to Difference*, 12.

Hegel, Blackness, Sovereignty

VINCENT LLOYD

Hegel is totalizing. Hegel is Eurocentric. Hegel makes Europe the culmination of his rigid system. Hegel's dialectic is all-consuming, and it is violent. Against these worries, another Hegel has emerged. For this Hegel, method is essential. And Hegel's method is dynamic. It is driven by always unsated desire. It is driven by the wrinkle in every state of affairs, that moment of negativity that reminds us that things can and will be radically otherwise. For this Hegel, reason is crucial, but reason is also insufficient and broken, and the work of philosophy consists of grappling with this brokenness with the only tools we have. We must look to history, to philosophy, and to religion. We must acknowledge that we are formed by them and learn from them, but also discern their limits, find their wrinkles. We must appreciate how our world is broken; only by struggling to articulate this brokenness can we see it rightly and move toward a better world. Stories about history, philosophy, and religion must be told, but they are told in service of the present, in service of the imperative to tarry with the negative, to follow our unsated desire.[1]

From this perspective, Hegel's *Phenomenology of Spirit* and his *Logic* are his most important works, with his lectures on history, philosophy, and religion imperfect attempts to apply his method to the world around him—imperfect because of the limited empirical data available to him, because of his own personal prejudices and intellectual flaws, and because *every* state of affairs has its wrinkle, every system contains within it a loose thread that can and eventually will be pulled and result in systemic transformation. What Hegel offers, at his best, is a series of exercises to teach method, after which his student should be able to encounter any state of affairs, tell a story about how tarrying with the negative gave rise to that state of affairs, and search for wrinkles in the present.

For those who do not find themselves fitting comfortably in the stories Hegel tells about his state of affairs (with respect to history, religion, and philosophy), for those who are not upper middle-class German men, a focus on Hegel's method can seem quite radical. When applying that method to a state of affairs at the margins rather than at the center, from the perspective of women, or the working class, or a racialized minority rather than from ivory towers in Berlin, Hegel's method would seem to offer a way of accounting for how marginalization came about; how that marginalization deeply affects the character of a community and the souls, as it were, of community members; how to identify the most effective ways to channel a marginalized community's frustrations, their unsated desires; and such a method would promise that systemic transformation will necessarily follow. To be an effective activist or organizer requires, in this view, training in Hegel's method, in the dialectic.[2]

But championing Hegel is still unsatisfactory to some. Rather than a Hegel who imposes a totalizing system in a heavy-handed, stilted way, now we have a Hegel who seems kinder and gentler, but whose ambition remains. Instead of a Hegel who speaks to everything, this is a Hegel who invites us to speak to everything, continually updating and improving the system. Instead of a Hegel who fits all data into a mold—in its crudest caricature, thesis, antithesis, synthesis—this is a Hegel who sees the struggle of desire unsated everywhere, a more dynamic mold but a mold nonetheless. Instead of European man necessarily being the full realization of our humanity, now a rainbow of humanity is represented, all struggling to realize their humanity, all formed by and reckoning with their history, all tarrying with the negative in the stories they tell about the states of affairs in which they find themselves. Here we have a Hegel fit for our multicultural age, allowing for identity to be complicated, a site of formation and struggle, but also a Hegel ultimately promising reconciliation in difference.

I do not mean this characterization to be dismissive, but I do want to make clear what motivates resistance to this version of Hegel. In short, what about the wholly unexpected, the wholly new? Isn't there a chance we will encounter happenings that no amount of historical and social research can explain? When we tarry with the negative, what comes next supervenes on (though perhaps is not fully determined by) what came before. Is the centripetal force pulling toward reconciliation really desirable to all? Is ethics really exhausted by norms of a community discerned in light of history and oriented toward the satisfaction of all desire?

For those who take Hegel seriously but are sympathetic to these concerns, shifting from Hegel's system to his method is not enough. Philosophy must start with the rejection of Hegel, both system and method. Hegel remains vitally important, in such views, because he so effectively names what philosophy ought not to be; he names what philosophy contaminated by worldly interests is. Hegel is, indeed, the culmination of European philosophy, the sum of the temptations that we, Europe's willing or unwilling progeny, face when we endeavor to philosophize. Hegel's system and method must be rejected, and in its place, generating normative imperatives, we must put the not-Hegel, the non-system and non-dialectic, that which is unassimilable—that which is wholly Other. The project of philosophy becomes thematizing exteriority, that of which Hegel cannot speak, that which interrupts Hegel, speaking from depths which make the whole Hegelian apparatus tremble. From the perspective of Germany's victims, Emmanuel Levinas develops such a project. It is continued by Enrique Dussel, from the perspective of Europe's victims and from marginalized communities more generally. In recent years some scholars of African American studies have embraced this posture as well, identifying blackness with the figure of the fugitive, always evading European attempts at sense-making and systematizing.[3]

The challenge, as Levinas recognized, is that any content that one attributes to the wholly Other, anything one says about it, diminishes its otherness. To speak of the Other is to draw it back into a system of language and concepts. Yet something must be said. We must speak in metaphors (the face) and mark effects of encountering Otherness (a visceral response). For those who would place real communities in the role of history's Others, the challenge is still greater. But if blackness is characterized by survival in a world that means to do it harm, that intends its death, then blackness must have developed survival strategies for evading capture, literally and metaphysically. Scholars point to the performance of blackness in everyday life and in art, and especially in music, as demonstrations of what exteriority looks like in practice.[4] All of this, recall, is in opposition to Hegel, or what he is seen to represent: a sophisticated story that speaks to all, giving each her place in the history of the world, necessarily desiring, finding desire thwarted, and transforming in the direction of reconciliation and full recognition.

This intellectual landscape makes literary historian Jared Hickman's suggestion that we might be able to read Hegel as a theorist of exteriority so intriguing.[5] Hickman urges readers to turn back to Hegel's writings on

Africa, so often dismissed as simply a product of racism.[6] For Hegel, infamously, Africa stands outside of history, outside of metaphysics, outside of genuine religion. In fact, Africa is literally treated outside of world history by Hegel, outside of the main body of his lectures purportedly covering the full expanse of world history. This position of exteriority is precisely what a set of scholars suspicious of Hegel seek to articulate—and what some of them, in African American studies, attribute to blackness, just like Hegel. Hickman's project is one of literary history rather than philosophy, so he does not pursue the point in detail. I take his suggestion as an invitation to explore Hegel's own account of blackness as exteriority. We find a curious mirroring of what for Hegel is best and worst, most sophisticated and least, when we read his account of Africa in his philosophical project, and I will argue that the concept of sovereignty plays a central role in generating this mirroring. Even the most ostensibly radical reconfigurations of sovereignty, for example when that term is put under erasure or configured as the non-sovereign, are less capable of escaping the dynamics of sovereignty than they advertise. Put another way, Hegel's political theology is centrally concerned with Africa, and Hegel teaches Africana studies a lesson about just how hard it is to reach escape velocity from the problematic named by political theology.[7]

Hegel's discussions of Africa occur in his Berlin lectures on history and on religion, delivered in the mid-1820s. The former are the most discussed, and criticized, because they are so clearly pejorative, leaning on racist stereotypes and fantasies. This they do, but my suggestion is that Hegel is using the tools at hand, the empirical facts about Africa at his disposal, perhaps viewed through a racist lens, in order to conjure exteriority. By definition exteriority is impossible to represent—it is what evades representation—and invoking fantasy holds the possibility, though certainly not necessity, of connoting that which evades representation.

While we might say that Hegel places Africa outside of history, this is imprecise. In Hegel's account of world history, in the beginning peoples were spread across the earth. There were different sorts of people in different places, and each people had to grapple with the geographical particularities they found themselves confronting. The combination of geography and a people's contingent characteristics results in the speed with which they progress through history's stages—except in Africa. While Hegel associates North Africa with Europe and Egypt with Asia, sub-Saharan Africa (which Hegel calls "Africa proper") has an unfortunate combination of inhabitants and geography that results in no forward motion through history at all. With its "unexplored highlands and narrow coastal strips along its shores," Africa remains "enclosed within itself" to the point that "enclosedness has remained its chief characteristic."[8] Because there is no contact, or only minimal contact, with the rest of the world, in Africa we find preserved what human life looked like before metaphysics, before abstraction, outside of the centripetal force of desire for reconciliation and recognition. Hegel can say that Africa "has no historical interest of its own,"[9] but Hegel means in his technical sense of history, history as spirit unfolding, for Hegel himself demonstrates historical interest in Africa. Africa may be "removed from the light of self-conscious history and wrapped in the dark mantle of night," but the night intrigues.[10] The shadows of light place all that is, all that is visible during the day, in new light.

What if we seek to glimpse life in Africa itself? Hegel cautions that this task presents the observer with serious obstacles. What we see "is difficult to comprehend because it is so totally different from our own culture and so remote and alien in relation to our own mode of consciousness."[11] In fact, the difference between the world to which "we" are accustomed and the world of Africans is like the difference between our world and the world of a dog.[12] We are tempted to use concepts from our own experience, to fit what we see into the world we know, but we must resist this temptation as much as possible. In a sense, Hegel works backward, asking what it would look like if all the apparatus he develops (concerning religion, history, and subjectivity) is stripped away, and assigning this, what remains, what is absolutely exterior to his system, to Africa. We will never be able to feel what an African feels or to extrapolate from our feelings what an African's world is like, so this intellectual exercise is the only way we can encounter Africa, Hegel suggests.

Just as the drama of history has not yet commenced in Africa, there is not yet a drama of subjectivity either. What Hegel finds in Africa are "a succession of contingent happenings and surprises" together with "a series of subjects."[13] There are raw events and objects, including animals, and humans as a type of animal, but nothing that binds them all together. Note that this does not mean there are no narratives, just that narratives come and go, uncoupled from each other, free from a sense of overarching unity in past, present, or future. We will not find any concept of God or law or justice, for all concepts such as these require a sense of totality, that all things and events can be linked in a certain way, and this sense is absent from Hegel's Africa.

What does life look like in a world of contingency, in a world without subjectivity? Hegel describes it as a life lived in immediacy. This means an immersion in the realm of senses and feelings, with the apparatus of reason used only in pursuit of immediate desires. Africans have "a highly sensual nature along with affability but also a shocking and inconceivable ferocity."¹⁴ They are immersed in the natural world, feeling and reacting, and when they emote, they do so without the constraints of reason or self-consciousness, "childlike." The only limit on the arbitrary will of Africans is external force. Humans do, of course, engage in the activities of human life, but they are concerned with the particularities of the activity in the moment, not the generalities to which it might point. People eat and are concerned with food, drink and are concerned with water, hunt and are concerned with locating and killing an animal.¹⁵

In this world, in Hegel's Africa, there is no qualitative difference between humans and animals. It just may be that humans have more resources for pursuing some of their passions than other animals (and fewer resources for pursuing other passions). There are no hierarchies separating humans and the natural world, for these would be ordering principles foreign to the African context. Because humans occupy no special role in this world, there is no prohibition on eating human flesh. Hegel suggests that one will never find Africans acting philanthropically. That would require a concept of humanity, deserving of love or kindness, but no such concept of humanity exists in Africa. Even self-interest is not an absolute value, or generator of values, and at times Hegel sees the self, too, as a participant on that plane of immanence. For this reason, Africans give no particular value to their own life or death, accounting for the "great courage" shown by them, for example as they "allow themselves to be shot down in thousands in their wars with the Europeans."¹⁶

The only interests that matter are interests of the self. God is unknown, and so are other deities. The moon cannot be a god, nor the sun, nor the rivers, because this would be establishing a hierarchy, refusing the plane of immanence which is Africa. From the perspective of each African, there is a world of objects and events that she looks out upon and seeks to manipulate. To fulfill her desires and to respond to her emotions, she makes use of objects, including animals and other people. There is no religion in Africa, but there is magic. Because there is no sense of causation (since that would suggest the abstraction of a physical law), manipulating the world involves sheer exercise of will, which is magic. Hegel cites Herodotus's observation, "All men in Africa are sorcerers."¹⁷ Each human being exercises her will without mediation, that is, without discerning nature's regularities or appealing to a deity.¹⁸ The fetish is nothing more than a worldly object, equal to others, that serves as a means for the African to exercise her will over nature. It is never worshiped; it is used. If it stops being useful for facilitating action on the natural world, it is discarded.¹⁹

At the end of the day, however, the African has no real power over her world. The essential problem with the African, in Hegel's account, is the fact that there are, in fact, regularities to nature and histories of communities and ways of predicting the future. To act as if there are not, as if each event and object is disconnected from each other, is to allow those regularities and histories and possibilities to have a tyrannical force over oneself.[20] We desire to make sense of our world and ourselves, to see how we are formed and fit into regularities, but this desire goes unsated in Hegel's Africa. It is impossible to sate this desire, in Hegel's view, for this would be to achieve full self-consciousness in a community where spirit is fully realized. But pursuing this desire is how we realize our humanity; to be uninterested in this desire, like Africans, is to be excluded from the realm of humanity.

The Africa that Hegel describes sounds frightening and intellectually vapid, but it is also paradise. Hegel means this quite literally: what we find in Africa is what was found in the Garden of Eden.[21] There, too, humans were at one with the other animals that inhabited the Garden. All were in a state of innocence. Hegel notes that innocence here should not be confused with goodness. Rather, the innocence of Africa and Eden characterizes a time before the encounter with good and evil, before humans developed the capacity to distinguish between good and evil. We ought not to aspire to return to Eden, or Africa, because this would require losing our humanity. "That initial natural oneness is in actuality not a state of innocence but the state of savagery, an animal state, a state of desire or general wildness."[22] Our deep desire is to fulfill our humanity, and for humanity to be fulfilled in a way that brings about the fulfillment of history and community at the same time. As Hegel puts it succinctly, "Humanity as it is by nature is not what it ought to be; human beings ought to be what they are through spirit."[23] Humanity infused with spirit names the realization of humanity by grappling repeatedly with negation.

Even though a desire to return to Eden, or Africa, is misguided, in Hegel's view, such primal situations do play an important role in structuring our desires. They show how "the abstract destiny of man was already potentially present."[24] Here we have a particularly clear statement of the way that Africa resembles the telos of Hegel's project, just as the paradise of Eden represents the paradise of heaven. The full realization of spirit in humanity, community, and history that occurs at the (ever-deferred) end of Hegel's project—Germany at its finest, perhaps—looks remarkably like Hegel's Africa at its most basic. All our desires will be fulfilled at that telos, but in some sense all desires were fulfilled in Africa as well, so we, somehow, desire Africa as a symbol of desire fulfilled. Hegel is ambivalent on this point, for Eden of course is described as unequivocally comfortable and serene, whereas Hegel's Africa is turbulent and bloody. Hegel acknowledges that Eden is not a historical place and that its depiction, while "very profound" and part of "the eternal and necessary history of humanity," is handed down to us in "a mythical mode"—this explains the "inconsistencies" between Eden's biblical depiction and the way it ought to exist according to Hegel's theory.[25] For Hegel, it seems, the actually existing Africa is closer to what Eden really was like than the biblical representation of Eden.

With Hegel's Africa envisioned as a land of immediacy and arbitrary will, the only political structures that one can find there are despotic. A leader imposes his arbitrary rule on those who are weaker than him. "There is no rational and communal spirit of which the government could be the representative and executor."[26] Hegel provides various anecdotes gathered from missionary and travel writers to illustrate African society, often quite bloody anecdotes. After a series of these, Hegel's presentation of Africa reaches a climax as he describes a certain queen in the Congo. As with the equivocation between the paradise of Eden and the paradise of heaven, in this account we find a curious resemblance between Africa and the other end of Hegel's thought, the culmination of his system. According to Hegel, this Congo queen in fact converted to Christianity, twice, the double conversion marking duplicity and self-interest. She ascended to power by removing her mother as queen, "and she renounced all love towards her mother."[27] This ostensibly Christian queen expelled all of the men from her lands, and she also renounced her son.[28] Not only that, she goes on to kill her son, pounding him to death with a mortar at a public gathering. Then, she "devoured his flesh and drank his blood."[29] She decreed that the women of her kingdom must similarly kill any male children they had.

Here we have an obvious parody of Christian political theology. The distance between worldly ruler and God has entirely collapsed: the ruler makes herself a God in the style of Christianity. She kills her son and initiates a ritual of eating his flesh and drinking his blood. But this is only for material, not transcendent, ends. Human flesh is eaten out of individual hunger, not to commune with the divine. The sovereign command, to kill one's own sons, ensures that there are no bonds of affection, even familial affection, in this state. There is only sheer power exercised by the strongest, by the god-leader, over each individual. In a sense, this is secular political theology, political theology that is utterly worldly, where the trappings of the theological attach to a political sovereign not in order to mystify or elevate but to demystify, to ensure that the community is only attuned to the crudest of material realities.

Here we have a group of fierce black women, led by the fiercest, living on their own terms. They were subject to no law, save their arbitrary will and the arbitrary will of the one woman who is stronger than they are, their queen. She is positioned by Hegel as chief magician and ruler, the two offices folded into one, and her dual role confirmed not by any external acclamation but by the strength of her self-assertion.[30] In Africa, there is nothing higher. There is merely desire, excessive, that has no object on which to affix. For there is no realm of representation to offer traction: concepts are fleeting, entering and exiting as they move in and out of usefulness for the purpose of fulfilling immediate desires. The queen stands alone, her family vanquished, the possibility of family prohibited. Her perverse communion ritual does not link her with the truth of the world, with spirit unfolding. Just the opposite: it affirms the absolute separation of bodies and events, leaving her standing alone, a goddess-sovereign but most essentially a single human. If Jesus is the new Adam, the Congo queen is the new Eve, fulfilling the promise of human origins politically and theologically at once. In contrast to the Christian story, the sensuality of the Congo queen is never tainted by intellectualizing; she does with the bodies of men what she wishes, when she wishes, and she models such sensuality for the women around her.

Hickman turns to Hegel as part of a larger story he tells about the political theology of human self-assertion, crystallized in the figure of Prometheus, snatcher of fire from the gods. Christian political theology unites under the power of one god-man, that is, under the figure of sovereignty. This stands in stark opposition to the Promethean spirit that Hickman finds in Africana sources, which Hickman keeps separate from the European, Christian story that Hegel so masterfully tells. The two stories are incompatible. The European, Christian story is backed by enormous power, physical and ideological, so it is only now and then, through the work of myth, that the Africana counter-story surfaces. If we were to morph Hickman from literary historian to philosopher, he would be saying: the Africana counter-story is ultimately the true story, for the European, Christian story contains a structural instability. It aspires to speak universally, but there is an irreducible difference between its aspiration to the universal and the reality of the global, a difference that comes into view when Europeans encounter indigenous Americans in 1492. Hegel trips over Africa because of this irreducible difference between the universal and the global, and in the process, he allows an Africana political theology to show itself. In Africa, each human is a god, each act of self-assertion divine.

Although Hickman's instincts strike me as correct, his account is not fully satisfactory. The language of self-assertion, and indeed the figure of Prometheus, is suggestive of a sort of subjectivity that Hegel adamantly avoids in his depiction of Africa (and Eden). Hegel writes of the "wildness of will" of Africans, an aspect of the immediacy and sensuality that characterize the lives they live.[31] The self-assertion Hickman describes, and implicitly lauds, places humans in the role of gods. But this is not quite what happens in Hegel's Africa. Humans place themselves in the position of highest authority, over against all other objects, animals, and other humans. This status, however, is essentially negative. Hegel's Africans do not subordinate themselves to any gods. As a result, they can act on their wild wills unimpeded. The more fully Hegel's Africans refuse subordination—the Congo queen is exemplary here—the more unencumbered the Africans' ability to act on immediate desires. Promethean self-assertion, in contrast, suggests both a refusal of subordination and a building up of the self, taking something that the gods have and claiming it for the self.

Another way of pursuing this point is in terms of sovereignty. The sovereignty of the European, Christian God not only echoes in political sovereignty but also in the sovereignty of the white slave master, in Hickman's view. The black Promethean tradition refused such accounts of sovereignty and instead is committed to "a radical, alternative conception of freedom entirely oriented toward belonging to an egalitarian community." Such a view of sovereignty "runs *against* rather than *through* the Absolute," a view Hickman calls "heretical antislavery."[32] Again, the instinct seems right, but the terrain is treacherous. At the heart of Carl Schmitt's descriptive account of sovereignty is a distinction between the eighteenth century, when God and king were both believed to be able to suspend the laws (of nature or state) at will; that was what constituted their sovereignty. In the nineteenth century, and for Schmitt Hegel is an important figure here, divine and political sovereignty were thought to be distributed across the (natural or political) world. While Schmitt is not explicit about his normative claim in *Political Theology*, it is quite clear that he is arguing that the nineteenth-century conceptions of theological and political sovereignty, those that anchor the parliamentary democracy of his day, are defective. After laying out the historical contrast between eighteenth and nineteenth centuries, in chapter 3 of *Political Theology*, Schmitt spends his next, final chapter pointing to resources from the Counter-Reformation that could fulfill the genuine meaning of sovereignty, as announced in his book's opening sentence: sovereign is he who decides on the exception. In other words, Schmitt diagnoses the political problem of his day as a commitment to nineteenth-century theological and therefore political ideas; he shows that those theological and political ideas have been and so could become dramatically different, organized around transcendence rather than immanence, and he offers resources to effect such a shift.

The project of demystifying European, Christian, slaveholder sovereignty so as to open up the possibility for freedom in egalitarian community threatens to stay within the terms of the choice posed by Schmitt: eighteenth versus nineteenth century, transcendent versus immanent.[33] Hegel's ambiguous position exemplifies the false consciousness that Schmitt diagnoses as typical of nineteenth-century thought. It purports to be committed to immanence, theologically and politically, God unfolding in the world and in history and sovereign power disbursed among the people. Yet an arbitrary will, a decision on the exception, lurks beneath this account. This decisionism is revealed when Hegel turns to Africa as Eden, the perfect past pointing to the perfect future—and ruled by the Congo queen. For Hegel, perfect future officially involves the sovereignty of Spirit, unfolding and only partially realized in the civilized world, though increasingly approached in Germany. Each subject is fully realized as she is recognized by her fellows. Ostensibly this is "freedom entirely oriented toward belonging in an egalitarian community," but for Hegel such freedom is inextricable from the arbitrary, sovereign will of the Congo queen. As Jacques Derrida showed in his critique of Levinas, the desire for the wholly Other cannot be separated by the desire to hold tight to sameness.[34] Hegel's account of Africa as wholly Other is entangled with his system as a whole, and Hickman's account of "heretical antislavery" is troublingly connected with the "slaveholder sovereignty" it disclaims.

Yet the decisionism suggested by Hegel's account of Africa is not quite the decisionism that opens Schmitt's *Political Theology*. The Congo queen decides, but she does not decide on the exception. She has no relation to law. She decides based on her wild will, undetermined by anything outside herself, outside her sensual engagement with the world. Does this mean she and her people might represent an alternative mode of sovereignty, defined in the negative, outside of Schmitt's framework? Or perhaps "unsovereign" sovereignty?[35] For those theorists who wish to reject the Hegelian dialectic by embracing exteriority, it is necessary to grapple with this uncomfortable question. Hegel does more than echo racist caricatures. He attempts to think exteriority, and it does not look appealing. Hegel himself leaves this ambivalence unworked: if the real Eden is violent and tyrannical, why should we be motivated to continue in search of a new Eden (much less wax nostalgic for an old Eden)? If blackness as exteriority, or fugitivity, is to provide an ethical norm, how can we be sure maroon villages will not look like Hegel's Africa?

Rather than choose between dialectic and exteriority, political theology that takes Africa seriously, that takes blackness seriously, must invert the dialectic. It must take from Hegel his starting point, Africa, and his method, dialectic, and lean into the creative tension between these. An inverted dialectic would move from one site of apparent exteriority to another, from one unassimilable margin to the next. In these encounters between margins, South to South, as it were, the contingent positivity that accumulates at each site, compromising exteriority, is wiped clean. Its contingency is exposed. What remains is an embrace of the negative: those aspects of Africa, or marginality, that contest marginalization, that contest domination. This would push the gods and kings of Africa away from the realm of fantasy and into the realm of struggle. Through an inverted dialectic, spirits and heroes dedicated to challenging systems of oppression would slowly come into view. Exteriority would not be a hidden, longed-for space, nor a place to wallow, nor a self-enclosed people, but rather a process of undoing through appeals to history, religion, and subjectivity. When Africa is taken as the starting point and dialectic is taken as the method—which is to say, when Hegel's claims are fully embraced—there is neither a centripetal force pulling toward sovereignty nor a celebration of the supposedly unsovereign. Rather, political theology becomes never-ending work against false claims to sovereignty, that is, against political and religious domination.

Notes

1. See especially Gillian Rose, *Hegel Contra Sociology* (London: Athlone, 1981); Judith Butler, *Subjects of Desire: Hegelian Reflections in Twentieth-Century France* (New York: Columbia University Press, 1987); Slavoj Žižek, *Tarrying with the Negative: Kant, Hegel, and the Critique of Ideology* (Durham, NC: Duke University Press, 1993); Fredric Jameson, *Valences of the Dialectic* (London: Verso, 2010). Of course, there is a much longer history of this sort of approach, going back to "left" and "right" Hegelians in the nineteenth century.

2. For example, C. L. R. James [et al.], *Notes on Dialectics: Hegel and Marxism* (Detroit, MI: Friends of Facing Reality, 1971); see also George Ciccariello-Maher, *Decolonizing Dialectics* (Durham, NC: Duke University Press, 2017); Andrew J. Douglas, *In the Spirit of Critique: Thinking Politically in the Dialectical Tradition* (Albany: State University of New York Press, 2013).

3. Emmanuel Levinas, *Totality and Infinity: An Essay on Exteriority* (Pittsburgh, PA: Duquesne University Press, 1969); Enrique Dussel, *Ethics of Liberation in the Age of Globalization and Exclusion* (Durham, NC: Duke University Press, 2013); and Fred Moten, *In the Break: The Aesthetics of the Black Radical Tradition* (Minneapolis: University of Minnesota Press, 2003). See also Ranajit Guha, *History at the Limit of World-History* (New York: Columbia University Press, 2003); Guha frames his project against Hegelian historiography.

4. For example, Moten, *In the Break*; Moten, "The Case of Blackness," *Criticism* 50, no. 2 (2008): 177–218; Richard Iton, *In Search of the Black Fantastic: Politics and Popular Culture in the Post-Civil Rights Era* (New York:

Oxford University Press, 2010); J. Kameron Carter, "Paratheological Blackness," *South Atlantic Quarterly* 112, no. 4 (2013): 589–611.

5. Jared Hickman, *Black Prometheus: Race and Radicalism in the Age of Atlantic Slavery* (New York: Oxford University Press, 2017), 118–128.

6. Robert Bernasconi, "Hegel at the Court of the Ashanti," in *Hegel After Derrida*, ed. Stuart Barnett (London: Routledge, 1998), 41–63.

7. Paul Gilroy, popularizer of the phrase "Black Atlantic," calls for what amounts to using Hegel's method but approaching it from the perspective of the bondsman, of the "slave," in the section of *Phenomenology of Spirit* about the lord and the bondsman. Gilroy's project is to track the mutually constitutive entanglements between blacks and Europeans across space and time, privileging the voices and experiences of blacks. Projects such as Gilroy's remain essentially committed to Hegel's method, whereas I am interested in the impulse toward exteriority—and to interrogating whether Hegel's own commitment to exteriority may open possibilities for rethinking his method. Paul Gilroy, *The Black Atlantic: Modernity and Double Consciousness* (Cambridge, MA: Harvard University Press, 1993). See also James Sneed, "On Repetition in Black Culture," *Black American Literature Forum* 15, no. 4 (1981): 146–154. Hegel writes about historical slavery as the only point of contact between Africa and history. G. W. F. Hegel, *Lectures on the Philosophy of Religion* (Oxford: Clarendon Press, 2006), 197. Andrew Cole in *The Birth of Theory* (Chicago: University of Chicago Press, 2014) has argued that we ought not to conflate Hegel's view of the African and the bondsman.

8. G. W. F. Hegel, *Lectures on the Philosophy of World History: Introduction* (Cambridge: Cambridge University Press, 1975), 173.

9. Hegel, 174.

10. Hegel, 174.

11. Hegel, 176.

12. Hegel, 177; although Hegel also suggests the difference between our perspective and that of the Greeks is great. See also Hegel, *Philosophy of Religion*, 224: "To put oneself in the place of a dog requires the sensibilities of a dog. We are cognizant of the nature of such living objects, but we cannot possibly know what it would mean to transpose ourselves into their place."

13. Hegel, *Philosophy of World History*, 176.

14. Hegel, *Philosophy of Religion*, 197.

15. Hegel, 226.

16. Hegel, *Philosophy of World History*, 185.

17. Hegel, 179.

18. Hegel acknowledges that, although in principle every African is a magician, in reality there are certain designated, trained magicians, and they can only work their magic at certain times, by means of specific practices, often involving states of frenzy. See Hegel, *Philosophy of Religion*, 180. In his lectures on religion, Hegel describes the African king as the head magician, and he ascribes certain powers of abstraction to magicians (230; 226–227).

19. Hegel, 235; Hegel suggests that Africans treat the dead similarly, as tools to be used for self-assertion over the world. Ancestors are venerated when they work for that purpose, punished when they do not (233); see also Hegel, *Philosophy of World History*, 181.

20. Kirill Chepurin suggests that this could be contrasted with the Kantian as-if as the structure of the sovereign-transcendental, an imperative to act as if there is perfect, God-ordained order in which every subject is sovereign and free.

21. Hegel says that the Eden story is representative of "the myths of all nations" (*Philosophy of World History*, 178). See also the discussion in *Philosophy of Religion*, 214–216.

22. Hegel, *Philosophy of Religion*, 215. In Eden humans were not even able to discern the laws of nature because doing so requires a form of abstract thought that would separate humans from their animal nature and by extension begin the process of realizing their humanity, possible only after the fall (218).

23. Hegel, 215.

24. Hegel, *Philosophy of World History*, 178.

25. Hegel, *Philosophy of Religion*, 215.

26. Hegel, *Philosophy of World History*, 186.

27. Hegel, 189.

28. According to Hegel, the kingdom's female inhabitants used men they enslaved for procreation (and presumably pleasure).

29. Hegel, 233.

30. Kirill Chepurin rightly noted in personal conversation that this resonates with the distinctive conceptualization of self-assertion by Hans Blumenberg, who distinguishes it from secularization and political theology, and contrasts with Hickman's appropriation of Blumenberg, where self-assertion and secularization are more closely aligned. See Blumenberg, *The Legitimacy of the Modern Age* (Cambridge, MA: MIT Press, 1985).

31. Hegel, *Philosophy of Religion*, 225.

32. Hickman, *Black Prometheus*, 82.

33. I elaborate on this point in the introduction to my *The Problem with Grace: Reconfiguring Political Theology* (Stanford, CA: Stanford University Press, 2011).

34. Jacques Derrida, *Writing and Difference* (Chicago: University of Chicago Press, 1978).

35. See, for example, Jared Sexton, "The *Vel* of Slavery: Tracking the Figure of the Unsovereign," *Critical Sociology* 42, nos. 4–5 (2016): 1–15.

Political Theology of the Death of God
Hegel and Derrida

AGATA BIELIK-ROBSON

All those thinkers who ever commented on Karl Löwith's "thesis on secularization" agree that modernity maintains a relation with premodern theology. The term *relation* is broad enough to embrace the whole spectrum of rapports ranging from: continuity-with-modification (as in Charles Taylor's *Secular Age*), through secularizing immanentization (as in Karl Löwith, Carl Schmitt, Jacob Taubes, and Ernst Bloch, despite all the differences between them), up to militant atheistic negation (as in Nietzsche and, to some extent, in Hans Blumenberg's *Legitimacy of the Modern Age*). The term *political theology*, made popular by Schmitt in the 1920s, designates the critical point of intersection between theology and modernity. As Schmitt himself attests, modern politics demonstrates the ongoing *vitality* of the old theological paradigm of divine sovereignty, thus showing that, despite Friedrich Nietzsche's declaration, in modernity God is not at all dead; that, in fact, he is very much alive and kicking.[1]

In my essay, however, I would like to complicate this Schmittian picture of God's continuing vitality by evoking another theological figure which, already for Hegel, constituted the gist of modern religiosity: "the sentiment of the death of God," as he calls it in his *Faith and Knowledge*.[2] Furthermore, by reading Hegel through Jacques Derrida's lenses, most of all his *Glas*, I would like to show the inherent subversion of the political theology which focuses not on God's vitality but on God's demise. The death of God appears here not as the Nietzschean metaphor of radical atheization, but as the antinomian moment within the modern political theology: the moment of the paradoxical *a/theologization* which occurs in the theological realm itself. Modern political theology would thus be the paradoxical political a/theology of the death of God: not of the Schmittian forever vital, undying, powerfully decisionistic God, but the God who himself agrees to die and cedes his legacy to the world.

In his deconstruction of the sovereign paradigm, which starts as early as *Glas* and then continues through "Faith and Knowledge" up to his last seminars, Derrida follows closely Hegel's definition of the modern religious sentiment as the "religion of the death of God," but he radically modifies its emotional register. While in Hegel, this sentiment is "the infinite grief of the finite," the essentially endless work of mourning in which the finite beings are destined to commemorate the dead God and imitate the sublime gesture of his self-sacrifice, in Derrida's reading it emerges as a joyous and future-oriented attitude in which the theological content is offered possibility of a further *survie*, "living-on."[3] Yet, despite this difference, both Hegel and Derrida agree that in order for the singular beings of the world to come to the fore as the proper object of new metaphysics of finitude, God's previously all-powerful and infinite existence has to diminish: its all-pervasive light, *Lichtwesen*, must "set down" and hide from sight. The modern God, therefore, can only be the hidden God, *deus absconditus*, of a decreased vitality and presence—sent off down "under the table" (Walter Benjamin) or straight to the "crypt" (Derrida)—yet, at the same time, never completely erased or forgotten. The modern atheism, therefore, is never pure and simple; it is rather, as in Gershom Scholem's seemingly oxymoronic expression, a *pious atheism*.[4]

One of the tenets of this essay is to prove that the "death of God religion" is not a Christian monopoly. Almost all thinkers associated with the "death of God theology"—Thomas Altizer, Jean-Luc Nancy, Slavoj Žižek—insist on the absolute uniqueness of Christianity as the only religion which harbors atheism structurally within itself and as such paves the way to what we tentatively call the modern process of secularization. Yet a similar—if not precursory—maneuver of a/theologization occurs already in Jewish messianism, beginning with the Lurianic kabbalah and ending with Derrida's attempt to pluralize the concept of the "death(s) of God(s) religion(s)" in his own contribution to the debate on secularization, "Faith and Knowledge."

Which Death, of Whose God?

The main feature of this "new religious sentiment," already well spotted by Hegel, is restlessness (*die Unruhe*): God, before imagined as an eternal substance beyond any change, enters the path of dynamic self-transformation. Before a synonym of restful immutability, God now becomes identical with a process—a movement which aims at solving the tensions and aporias tearing apart the original form of the Godhead. This seminal change found a paradigmatic expression in Martin Luther's notion of *Anfechtung Gottes*, meaning struggle *within* God himself—*Gott wider Gott*—but also a struggle *with* God, an assertive attempt of the finite being to find its place in the new metaphysical arrangement. Yet the very origin of this new theological vision, which now focuses on restlessness and conflict with and within the Absolute, is to be located in the groundbreaking system of the sixteenth-century Safed kabbalist Isaac Luria, who introduced change into the very heart of the divine with the invention of *tsimtsum*: the withdrawal/contraction of God. Luria's theory of *tsimtsum* can indeed be seen as the first occurrence of the typically modern self-occlusion of God who retreats in order to make room for the world and subsequently hides behind the created being. By hiding, withdrawing, and absenting himself from direct influence; by giving up on his sovereign and "unscathed" status of the original Infinite (and in this manner playing out his inner contradiction), God *en-crypts* himself in both meanings of the Derridean phrase: he lays himself down in the tomb/crypt and erases any clear signs of his presence within the worldly immanence in which he leaves only cryptic traces. If modernity is cryptotheology, then it is also a Jewish/Marrano modernity, because the modern process of the divine *encryption* begins not only with Luther's "God himself is dead" (*Gott selbst ist tot*), but also with Luria's *tsimtsum*. This other modernity runs like a subterranean current under the dominant Christian narrative; although obscured by the latter, it nonetheless exerts a powerful influence on the modern version of a/theologization, most of all within German Idealism.[5]

The shift that determines the "new religious sentiment" is the passage from the infinite to the finite. This, again, is the explicit theme of the Lurianic *tsimtsum*, in which the Absolute, the primordial *Ein-Sof* (without limits) undergoes a dramatic limitation, in this manner creating room for the otherness of the world. Followed by yet another metaphor from the Lurianic vocabulary, "the breaking of the vessels" [*shevirat ha-kelim*] which announces the end of all Platonic static forms and eternal universals, this limitation paves the way to a new understanding of being as univocally finite. God makes himself finite and after the last dispersion of the eternal forms-vessels, exiles himself into the material universe. He is setting as a Platonic sun and enters the "night of the world" in the form of scattered sparks and oblique traces. In Gershom Scholem's description: "Creation out of nothing, from the void, could be nothing other than creation of the void, that is, of the possibility of thinking of anything that was not God. Without such an act of self-limitation, after all, there would be only God—and obviously nothing else. A being that is not God could only become possible and originate by virtue of such a contraction, such a paradoxical retreat of God into himself. By positing a negative factor in Himself, *God liberates creation*."[6] This image of a "liberated creation" will resurface in Hegel who concludes his *Phenomenology of Spirit* with the last lines of Schiller's poem— "Only 'from the chalice of this realm of spirits foams forth for Him his own infinitude'"[7]—which indicates that from now on the infinite can only be interpreted as the community of finite spirits that recreate the divine *Gestalt*, yet without restoring the Absolute to its original ontological infinity. Modern ontotheology, therefore, is all about finite being, and *univocatio entis* simply means the absolute rule of finitude. This, for Jean-Luc Nancy, Derrida's most important polemicist in the domain of contemporary Hegelianism, is the ultimate sense or "dis-enclosure" of Christianity as the religion of the "death of God": sealing the metaphysical passage from the infinite to finite being, where even—or most of all—God cannot enjoy the infinite existence but undergoes the paradigmatic "exposure," thus becoming the ontological model for all other beings.[8] For Derrida, on the other hand, this passage, although related to the "death of God," does not have to be necessarily thought in the Christian way: without automatically connotating "negativity" of the Passion, sacrifice and self-offering, deep down it merely announces that, in modernity, God "a/theologizes" himself, because he is no longer thought in terms of "the unscathed" [*indemne*]—the infinite, eternal, absolute, immutable, invulnerable, safe and sound, whole and holy—but is given over to the continuous "trial" and "ordeal" of the finite immanent reality.[9] As such, God is no longer the sovereign capable of subjugating the world by the sheer power of his infinite being. What Schmitt envisaged as the undying model of political theology, undergoes a process of internal self-deconstruction in which God *himself* [*Gott selbst*] announces his loss of sovereignty.

Derrida's interpretation of Hegel pushes his "death of God" motif in the direction of Luria's *tsimtsum*. In Hegel, it is God himself who consents to die, but then his kenotic self-sacrifice encumbers the world with the guilt which must be bought off/redeemed at the end of history.[10] In Isaac Luria, on the other hand, modernity emerges as the time of the world, offered in the gesture of a pure liberating *gift* which is to be remembered (*zakhor*), but in a different way than the remorseful "memory of the Passion."[11] Derrida is well aware that, despite some surface affinities, the Lurianic *tsimtsum* is *not* the same as the Christian *kenosis*: it is not God's self-sacrifice and self-offering which burdens the world with the sense of a terrible and scandalous loss. It is a "death of God" for sure, if we mean a sovereign highest being which possesses infinite existence, but it is also God's self-estranged afterlife; his only mode of a non-sovereign "living-on" in and with the world which he simultaneously made his own creation and let go as a free other-being. The *tsimtsum*-contracted God does not die *for us*, because he does not simply *die*: he limits his primordial infiniteness and becomes finite not in order to make creation eternally guilty and obliged but in order to pour himself into and affirm finite being as the right and final way to be. He himself is the most powerful spokesman for the principle of the radical univocity of being.

It is precisely by having in mind *tsimtsum* as the other—that is, nonsacrificial—gift, that Derrida writes in his commentary on Hegel whose account of the beginnings seems to contain both moments: "This perhaps: the gift, the sacrifice, the putting in play or to fire of all, the holocaust, are under the powers of ontology.... Without the holocaust the dialectical movement and the history of Being could not open themselves... could not annul themselves in producing the solar course from Orient to Occident. Before, if one could count here with time, there is, there will have been the *irruptive event of the gift*."[12] Yet, *which* gift? For Hegel, who understands creation in terms of Christian *kenosis*,[13] it simply must take on the form of self-offering: hence the simple enumeration in the first quote: "the gift, the sacrifice." But, is it possible to think the gift *without* the sacrifice? Is it not obvious that the primordial *Lichtwesen*, the "light being" of the oldest Oriental religions, "must" have offered itself to the fire which it was in the first place, commit an auto-holocaust or a burnt self-offering in order to "set down" and produce the "solar course from Orient to Occident"? For Hegel, it is self-evident that the "irruptive event of the gift," without which there would be no world of beings, must be thought in terms of the sacrificial logic. The first reflective movement of dialectics in which the fiery substance of the "light being" transforms into subject occurs when it turns *against* itself. But Derrida questions precisely this very logic and asks: is it possible to think about the gift *without* the sacrifice? For, once gift becomes "gifted" (poisoned with the sacrifice), it begins to guard itself as something precious that immediately creates a space of debt—debt to be returned and paid back—and thus stops being a gift. This is what Derrida, already pressing toward a nonsacrificial logic of the gift, calls the constraint, that is, the dogmatic axiom in Hegel's reconstruction of the "first movement" from which everything begins:

> From the moment of this constraint, this constriction of the "must" comes to press the mad energy of a gift, what this constriction pro-

vokes is perforce a countergift, an exchange, in the space of the debt. I give you—a pure gift, without exchange, without return—but whether I want this or not, the gift guards itself, keeps itself, and from then on you must-owe, *tu dois*. . . . I give you without expecting anything in exchange, but this very renunciation, as soon as it *appears*, forms the most powerful and most interior ligament. . . . *The gift can be only a sacrifice*, that is the axiom of speculative reason. (*G*, 243; my emphasis)

This is precisely the dogma that Derrida wishes to deconstruct as the last ditch of sovereignty, which reinstates itself the very moment it allegedly gives up on itself. God who "dies for us" may have relinquished his mastervitality of the "terrible living God," but he immediately recreates it in the newly opened "space of death,"[14] in which he becomes the sovereign paradigm of self-sacrifice: the Hegelian "infinite grief" is to manifest itself in "the moral sacrifice of empirical existence [which] only dates the absolute Passion or the speculative Good Friday."[15] Hence *kenosis*, even the most radical and seemingly self-humbling, is still God's self-offering and because of that a toxic gift which does not liberate its recipients but enslaves them by a perverse gesture of sovereignty. This is also the reason why, pace Nancy's official thesis, Christianity can never fully deconstruct itself into atheism, because it will always be kept on the leash of indebtedness and obligation; a certain "bad conscience" which keeps returning, more or less involuntarily, in Nietzsche, Heidegger, and Nancy despite their explicit allegiance to the "innocence of becoming." Christian dead God, says Derrida, can never let his people go: he would forever make them bound by guilt (*schuldig*), subjugated not by force, but by moral obligation. Thus, in modern thinking about God-becoming-finite, we must pass beyond the traps of *kenosis*, which smuggles under its *skandalon* the idea of a cosmic catastrophe and thus prevents from imagining this *finitization* as a truly free opening, beyond the economy of debt and redemption. This is precisely where *tsimtsum* enters as the nonsacrificial and noncatastrophic gesture of God's self-limitation: the *gift without sacrifice*. In Derrida's rendering, the Hegelian account of the "beginnings" is Lurianic—the "first movement" is indeed the self-exteriorization of the divine light which reflexively turns on/against itself and contracts/sets down—but the way in which he insinuates into it the toxic motif of *kenosis* is Christian.[16]

But what is this "first movement" which creates all: the world of beings, as well as time, change, and history? In the beginning, there is nothing and everything simultaneously: the undifferentiated All manifesting as the light of *Lichtwesen*, the "all-consuming fire." This fiery light is engaged in the ceaseless "holocaust" which burns all, the apocalyptic "fury of destruction," or—to use the psychoanalytic idiom—the pure death drive, which leaves no traces as it leaves no room for anything else by annihilating all being as well as itself. What the light brings into being/visibility, the fire immediately destroys by annulling all the difference. Even if the primordial *Lichtwesen* contains all, the particular beings cannot assert themselves in existence; they "burn" to the ashes of dedifferentiation, the cyclically self-renewing *Indifferenz*. Derrida comments on the passages from Hegel's *Phenomenology* concerning the first Oriental form of religion: "Pure and figureless, this light burns all. It burns itself in the all-burning it is, leaves, of itself or anything, no trace, no mark, *no sign of passage* . . . The all-burning is 'an essenceless by-play [*Beiherspielen*], pure accessory of the substances that *rises* without ever *setting*, without becoming a subject. And without consolidating through the self its differences, . . . *this play does not yet work*" (*G*, 238; my emphasis). It is only in the next inexplicable move that the substance "*gibt sich dem Fürsichsein zum Opfer*" (*G*, 240): instead of remaining forever a playful substance projecting "torrents of fire destructive of figuration," it suddenly "decides" to "set down" and thus become a subject through self-sacrifice. And although later, in the *Science of Logic*, Hegel will call this move by the purely philosophical name of "negation of negation," in which the first light retreats from destruction—that is, "annihilates the annihilation"—in order to let beings be, Derrida insists on presenting it in the series of theosophic images, which are to remind us about its still unsettled origin. It is, therefore, not an abstract, neutrally philosophical, and atheistic "negation of negation," inscribed into the nature of the First Idea, but the "irruptive event of the gift": the *tsimtsum*-like "setting of the sun" that no longer blinds and burns to ashes the particular beings, simultaneously tinged with the aspect of the kenotic self-offering which "insures its guarding" and in this manner transforms gift into debt. The religion of the dead God, therefore, repeats the gesture of its object of cult: just as God dies in order to let beings be, so religion must die in order to be sublated by philosophy—

> This explains how Hegelian philosophy—through and through a philosophy *of* religion—could be read as an effect of Christianity as well as an implacable atheism. Religion accomplishes itself and dies in the philosophy that is its truth, as the truth of past religion, of the essence as thought past [*Gewesenheit*] of the Christian religion. Truth—the past-thought—is always the death (relieved, erected, buried, unveiled, unbandaged) of what it is the truth of. . . . History is

the process of a murder. *But this murder is a sacrifice*: the victim offers himself. A scandal that a finite tribunal cannot understand at all: a victim would thus have rendered to the murderers, at the same time as his body, the instrument of the crime (*G*, 32, 33; my emphasis).

Yet, just as the kenotic sacrifice of the divine light does not allow to be forgotten and turns the Hegelian "through and through philosophy *of* religion" into an incessant "speculative Good Friday," so does the religious "picture-thinking" (*Vorstellungsdenken*), which Hegel promises to dissolve into pure philosophical argument, insist on returning with the unexplained "irruptive event of the gift" that inaugurates the history of being. Derrida's reading of Hegel is thus an *Erinnerung*, the recollection of what *refuses to die* in the Hegelian speculation: the persistent "memory of the Passion" transposed into the "first movement" which should allow the dialectical history to begin, thus securing the passage from "the play of pure light" into the serious work of real differences.

But does it? This refusal to die—the paradox of *kenosis* as simultaneously (or rather timelessly) the death and the resurrection of God—is the ultimate obstacle which hinders the desired passage from the playful infinite into the serious finite. The Trinitarian doctrine, as perceived by Hegel read by Derrida, does not allow God to die: by dividing the second person of the Trinity, the Son, into the dying-finite and the immortal-infinite, the doctrine *undoes* the "tragedy of the cross" and turns into "God's play with himself," that is, merely a *dokos*, an "appearance," which, despite all its orthodoxy, makes it dangerously close to the heretic teachings of the Docetists. Having in mind Marx's malicious remark about German Idealism as a hermetic "play" (*Spiel*) resembling masturbation, Derrida accuses Hegelian use of the trinitarian scheme as precluding any true otherness for the sake of familiarity understood as "familial bonds." Instead of producing a truly alienated alterity, the apparent "death of God," who in fact refuses to die, dissolves into a familiar play of the same immediately returning to itself. Everything thus stays in the family:

> God knows and recognizes himself in his son. He assists (in) his death, burial, his magnification, his resurrection. The knowledge relation that organizes this whole scene in a third, a third term, the element of the infinite's relation to self: it is the holy spirit. This medium obtains the element of *familiarity*: God's familiarity with his very own seed, the element of *God's play with himself.* The (infinite) exemplar gives itself and makes the (finite) exemplar return to it. The infinite father gives himself, by self-fellation, self-insemination, and

self-conception, a finite son who, in order to posit himself there and incarnate himself as the son of God, becomes infinite, dies as the finite son, lets himself be buried, clasped in bandages he will soon *undo* for the infinite son to be reborn . . . a dividing himself in two, the Son. (*G*, 31; my emphasis)

According to Derrida's reading of Hegel, "the whole system repeats itself in the family" (*G*, 20) and Spirit, the third person in the familial Trinity, is envisaged as most of all a filial bond. While Judaism represents for Hegel an abstract "morality" (*Moralität*) of a separated individual—"Kantianism is, in this respect, structurally a Judaism" (*G*, 34)—Christianity represents communal "decency" (*Sittlichkeit*), based on the familial "bonds of love" (*Liebesbande*) ("there is no love before Christianity," [*G*, 34]). While Judaism favors violent separation, diremption, and antithesis leading to irreconcilable otherness, Christianity attempts to bind and repair the broken whole with filial *Liebesbande*. Yet, this attempt of reparation, occurring alongside the divide which effects the passage from the infinite to the finite, does not even "give time" to the finite otherness; the immediate "undoing" of the results of the divine plunging into the condition of finitude does not give a chance for the latter to assert themselves in their finite way of being.[17]

But, as I have already indicated, Derrida detects in Hegel something else, a different aspect of the "first movement," which goes beyond the paradoxical logic of *kenosis*. If history can truly begin, it is only because this alternative manner of contraction and self-limitation does not demand to be "undone"; once God "declines," he no longer refuses to die. He erases himself out of existence in order to become a spectral Subject which had released all that once belonged to his substance into the free open of absolutely nonfamiliar and nonfamilial alterity (*freilassen*), precisely the way Scholem describes the Lurianic act of *tsimtsum*: "By positing a negative factor in Himself, *God liberates creation*."[18] By obliquely invoking the opening scene of *Zohar*, in which the primordial light of *Ein-Sof* occludes itself in the dark cloud, Derrida comments: "The light envelops itself in darkness even before becoming subject. In order to become subject, in effect the sun must go down [*decline*]. Subjectivity always produces itself in a movement of occidentalization. . . . That is the origin of history, the beginning of the going down, the setting of the sun, the passage to occidental subjectivity. Fire becomes for (it)self and is lost" (*G*, 239). Hegel connects the birth of the Occident with the "setting down of the sun." Religion travels from the East to the West, which coincides with the crucial passage: from Substance to Subject, where God stops being the all-consuming light-fire and, by negating himself—"setting down"—becomes reborn as a restless subjectivity: the specter hovering and spectating over the spectacle of being, now "emptied out" (*entäussert*) completely into the finite world. And as Hegel quite surprisingly announces, the first religion of the West, the "land of the setting sun" (*Abendland*), is the "religion of flowers": the first blooming (*eclat*) of the divine subject as the "finite spirit" within the world: "Then in place of burning all, one begins to love flowers. The religion of flowers follows the religion of the sun" (*G*, 239–240). And just as before Derrida was critical toward the familial/familiar aspect of Hegel's Christianity, now he fully endorses the *real* passage from the all-consuming infinite to the truly other fragile finite, symbolized by a delicate bloom of Isaiah's fading "flower of the field" (Isaiah 40:6–8), which soon would transform into a much more positive and liberating image of the "lily of the field" we know from the Gospels (Luke 12:27). But in order to ensure that the specter does not stop smiling while watching over the liberated—and still very precarious—creation,[19] Derrida must deconstruct the moment of *kenosis*: the self-sacrificial death of God, who, by refusing to die, does not let beings be.

The Perfect Gift, or the Religion of Flowers

But why does the new religiosity of the World begin with the "religion of flowers"? Could it be that Hegel, an avid reader of esoteric literature, who admired the main symbol of the Rosicrucians—"the rose in the cross of the present"[20]—conflated it with yet another rose, also of a mystical origin, famously portrayed by Angelus Silesius? Silesius's mysticism is rightly seen as prophetic in regard to the developments of modernity. It is, in fact, a mystic-poetic variation on Duns Scotus's scholastic thesis on the *univocatio entis*, now transformed into an intense vision of all things existing on the same plane with God, equally strongly and *causa sui*: "without why" (*ohne warum*)—that is, autotelicly and beyond justification:

> *Die Rose ist ohne warum; sie blühet, weil sie blühet*
> *Sie achtet nicht ihrer selbs, fragt nicht ob man sie siehet*
> [It blooms because it blooms, the rose that has no Why,
> Forgets itself and cares not for any gazing eye][21]

This one epigram of Angelus Silesius can easily explain the Hegelian idiosyncrasy of declaring the mysterious "religion of flowers" as the first truly Occidental form of cult: the mystical promise of blossoming and its "spontaneous production of the chromatic light" (*G*, 246) sheds a new visibility on the finite beings in the world, no longer occluded by the "all-burning" hyper-luminescence of the Absolute. The blooming shine of the "chromatic light" (*eclosion*) represents for Hegel his favorite dialectical maneuver which also chimes close with the Derridean *différance*: the deferment/delay/diffusion of the primordial light now refracted in the "many-coloured dome" (Shelley) of worldly differences, no longer forced to return to the abyssal *Indifferenz*: "The introjection of the sun, the sublime digestion of the luminous essence, will end 'in the heart of the occidental': it begins in the flower" (*G*, 246). Yet, although first after the "setting down of the sun," the religion of flowers is not to last: it is nothing but a "disappearing moment" between the cult of light and the cult of war characteristic of the next "animal religion": as such, it parallels the passage called Paradise between the stage of God alone, before he created anything, and the stage of the Fall which is the true and lasting condition of the creation. According to Hegel, therefore, the religion of flowers is innocent and playful, not yet "serious" enough: "The innocence of the flower religion, which is merely the self-less representation of self, passes into the seriousness of warring life, into the guilt of animal religion; the quiet and impotence of contemplative individuality pass into destructive being-for self" (*G*, 2).

But, does the flower religion really lack the serious work of the negative? Derrida begs to differ. This one epigram and this one commentary explain the mysterious construction of *Glas*, divided into two columns: the left one devoted to Hegel, and the right one devoted to Jean Genet, his *Pompes funebres, Notre-dame-des fleurs*, and *Miracle of the Rose*. And indeed, the right column is a hymn to "the Miracle of the Rose": its innocent *eclat*, the *eclosion* of the Wordsworthian "splendour in the grass, glory in the flower" which, as Luke claimed, surpasses even "Solomon in all his glory." The blossoming "religion of flowers" is celebrated here, with full seriousness, as the first religion of the created/liberated world. In this synesthetic experiment, the reader is supposed to feel the stench of burning cinders, which accompany the holocaust of the divine *Lichtwesen*, combined—or rather compensated—by the heavy scent of the flowers, growing out of the soil enriched by ashes and thus alchemically transforming them back into the living spirit: out of death—new life. This is not an accident: Derrida wants to strengthen the tendency already present in Hegel's thought, which would allow to treat the "flower religion" more "seriously," that is, arrest the "murderous" progress of history and "give time" to the stage of ontological innocence, before beings become irreversibly implied in the "kenotic" economy of sacrifice, guilt, and redemption understood as the payback of debt. In his lectures on aesthetics, Hegel himself openly praises

Angelus Silesius for the "greatest audacity and depth of intuition and feeling which has expressed in a wonderful mystical power or representation the substantial existence of God in things and the unification of the self with God."[22] Hegel's interpretation of Silesius goes even further than the idea of singular beings merely engaging in *imitatio Dei*; what he implies is the most "audacious" transformation in God who now is in a restless search for his own being, while singular creatures enjoy the divine "substantial existence" *causa sui*. Infinity is denied access to being which is now reserved solely for the innocent, self-justifying finite: the traditional ontological hierarchy of God's stronger being dominating the weaker and dependent existence of creatures becomes reversed.

In *Sauf le nom*, the essay wholly devoted to Angelus Silesius (but with a constant reference to Hegel, to be sure), Derrida tries to elaborate on God's *Gelassenheit*/abandonment, in the magnanimous context of the *tsimtsum* which truly lets beings be, by releasing them into the open. The secret word that, for Derrida, combines "to let" and "to leave" is *laisser*. Derrida chooses it as the best French equivalent of Angelus's *Gelassenheit* which he, in a visible *clinamen* from Heidegger ("whether Heidegger likes it or not"[23]) understands as a "serenity of abandonment" relaxing in "all the without"—without reason, without purpose, without guilt and debt, without the justifying structure of the great chain of beings, that is, without anything that used to support the subjugating hierarchy of political theology.[24] While quoting Silesius's epigram, *Nichts lebet ohne Sterben* (Nothing lives without dying):

> *Gott selber, wenn Er dir wil leben, muss er sterben:*
> *Wie dänckstu ohne Tod sein Leben zuererben?—*
> [God himself must die if he wills you to live:
> How else can you inherit life without death?]

Derrida cannot hide his enthusiasm: "Has anything more profound ever been written on inheritance?"[25] Indeed, this epigram, written already under the influence of Jacob Böhme (himself most probably influenced by the Lurianic kabbalah), tells the secret of *tsimtsum* as the last word in the logic of univocity: if the finite beings are to exist in the world, God himself must die, properly and once for all, that is, pass on his existence in the manner of metaphysical legacy. Here, the demise of God is not the gift of death (in which we, by sacrificing our empirical lives, compensate and pay back for God's original self-offering), but the "inheritance of life" which no longer knows any sacrifices: *Sterben und Lebenlassen* is Angelus's new rule for God, this benign "smiling specter." The messianic principle—"no more sacrifices!"—means also: no more political theology which implicates the subject in the net of guilt and debt to be repaid.

The true *Gelassenheit*, therefore, is the highest art of "abandoning God who abandons himself":[26] not clinging to him, not trying to grasp him, not even feeling obliged to do so. The duty of redemption as repayment is annulled for the sake of a new imperative: "not give back anything to God, not even Adieu, not even to his name."[27] *Oubliez Dieu*—yes, but this oblivion will not be as unproblematic as the simple Nietzschean injunction to forget God, imposed from the outside of the theological realm. This movement of releasement occurs inside, following the unique logic of *tsimtsum*: "This is how I sometimes understand the tradition of *Gelâzenheit*, this serenity that allows being without indifference, lets go without abandoning, unless it abandons without forgetting or *forgets without forgetting*."[28] In the slightly earlier text, *Given Time*, Derrida makes this paradoxical "forgetting without forgetting" and the *gelassen* "without why" the very condition of the gift:

> The gift would be that which does not obey the principle of reason: It is, it ought to be, it owes itself to be without reason, without wherefore, and without foundation. . . . As the condition for a gift to be given, this forgetting must be radical not only on the part of the *donnée*. . . . From the moment the gift would appear as gift, as such, as what it is, in its phenomenon, its sense and its essence, it would be engaged in a symbolic, sacrificial, or economic structure that would annul the gift in the ritual circle of the debt. . . . The simple consciousness of the gift right away sends itself back the gratifying image of goodness or generosity, of the giving-being who, knowing itself to be such, recognizes itself in a circular, specular fashion, in a sort of auto-recognition, self-approval, and narcissistic gratitude.[29]

Derrida's intention, therefore, is to let us see that the true challenge facing late-modern thought consists in nothing else but rethinking the idea of abandonment/*Verlassenheit* (of God as well as Being) as the cryptotheological maneuver, or the self-deconstruction of political theology: not as a secular gesture of aggressive atheization and the rupture with all theological discourse, but as a move occurring within the "modern religious sentiment" itself and its peculiar "religion of the death of God."

One must, however, bear in mind that the Scholemian moment of "liberating the creation" does not yet *finish* the story: the "religion of flowers," no longer destined to be just a "disappearing moment," must also bring fruits in the continuing self-deconstruction of the sovereign paradigm. As we have seen, Hegel's solution to keep the ball of history rolling lies in the exploitation of the guilty "memory of the Passion": "the infinite grief of the finite." Creation is obliged to play a role in the drama of history, because of the sense of constraint rooted in guilt and debt. The "terrible thought" that "God himself is dead," that he died for us and we have not yet managed to repay him for his sacrifice, is the source of the new subjugation— no longer by power and fear exercised by the "living God" but by the internalized sense of guilt. The idiom of *kenosis*, which Hegel applies already to creation, implicates the whole creaturely realm into the "Golgotha of Absolute Spirit," coextensive with the process of history itself. If this was a gift, then, in Derrida's terms, not generous enough, because expecting something—in fact quite a lot—in return. The Hegelian guilt inducing God may thus not be as "vitally" powerful as the Schmittian political "living God," but he still rules over the creation by tying it into the Benjaminian *Schuldzusammenhang*, the net of guilt and infinite mourning over the eternally self-repeating "tragedy of the cross." In consequence, the Hegelian deconstruction of the "death of God" political theology freezes the dead God in the gesture of perverse sovereignty: dying and refusing to die, letting beings go and keeping them on the leash, at the same time.

The Derridean/Lurianic "supplement" to Hegel's narrative aims to unpack this aporetic double bind which blocks the deconstructive process and evaporate the last internalized traces of divine sovereignty, still hindering the realization of the Hegelian promise of the universal freedom. Hegel can be rescued from the "kenotic axiom of the speculative reason," but only on the proviso that *kenosis* will be replaced by *tsimtsum*: a different logic of the gift, the presence of which Derrida detects in Hegel's account of the "beginnings," lurking there, in the shadow of the dominant Christian doctrine. By strengthening the Lurianic line within Hegel's narrative, Derrida tries to release Hegel from the trap of *kenosis* and its toxic enslaving gift. The tragic fixation on the sovereign moment of the self-sacrificial death can finally give way to the messianic hope in "no more sacrifices": the true innocence of the finite becoming liberated from the mortifying guilt.

In the end, therefore, the shift from *kenosis* to *tsimtsum*, which Derrida inscribes into Hegel's narrative, reveals itself as a part of a more general and fundamental transition that takes place in Derrida's writings: the passage *from the tragic to the messianic*; from the principle of sublime self-offering to the principle of the regained innocence of life; from the gloomy mythology of the "tragic Absolute" to the religion of flowers and its "garden of earthly delights."[30] The tragic account of the death of God, which Hegel gives in his "Faith and Knowledge," focuses on the Lutheran "tragedy of the cross": the dying God casts a long shadow of his sacrifice, in fact as long as the history itself, which then makes sense only as the redemptive *undoing* of the original catastrophe. The messianic account of the death of God, on the other hand, emphasizes the moment of affirmation and liberation, which does not call for any undoing: *God dies and lets live*, by setting the paradigmatic example of the finite life as the ultimate mode of being.[31]

What does this alternative genealogy of the "death of God" spell for the future of political theology? Well, it spells—the future. The whole point of this other a/theologization consists in securing the possibility of what Derrida calls "futurity" [*futurité*]: an open time that refuses to be wholly determined by the past and leans proleptically toward the advent of the new, yet always and only within the condition of the finite life. The Derridean revision of the political theology does not annul the redemptive perspective, but it wants to give it a *true future*, which would allow it to transcend the economic cycle of debt and repayment and circumvent the past-facing logic of the original sin/guilt. The tragic account of the "death of God" is not only a priori guilt-inducing; it also enslaves the subject in the traumatic configuration of the divine self-sacrifice, which then projects the redemption as an event wholly defined by its ability to undo the past trauma, and in this manner deprives it of the messianic innovation. The truly "messianic apprehension" of the redemptive future must reject any projection because it always draws on the determining power of the past. In his reply to the critics of *Specters of Marx* who reproached him for diluting the Marxian utopian vision to a contentless vagueness, Derrida says: "Messianicity . . . refers, in every here-now, to the coming of an eminently real, concrete event, that is, to *the most irreducibly heterogenous otherness*. Nothing is more 'realistic' or 'immediate' than this messianic apprehension, *straining forward toward the event of him who/that which is coming*. . . . Anything but Utopian, messianicity mandates that we interrupt the ordinary course of things, time and history here-now."[32] The issue, therefore, is not about this or other projection of the redemptive event—be it either the Hegelian utopia of the repayment of debt in the worldly resurrection of the divine or the Marxian utopia of the annulment of debt in the conditions of atheistic immanence—but about keeping it truly proleptic, open, "irreducibly heterogeneous," and future-oriented. By releasing us from the burdens of the past in order to allow for an interruption of the historical continuum, the Derridean intervention secures the transcendental possibility of the future advent [*avenir*] as such. While the political theology of the "death of God" understood as the kenotic self-offering will always present the foundational act of finitude as the original guilt/sin (Hegel read via Christian lenses), Derrida's Jewish/Lurianic *clinamen* on Hegel dissolves/redeems (*erlöst*) this primordial fault and lets the finite beings turn away from the past and face the future as, finally, the true "preparation" for the events to come.

We do not yet know what the finite creatures are capable of, but then, we will never learn unless we let them be.

Notes

1. Carl Schmitt, *Political Theology: Four Chapters on the Concept of Sovereignty*, trans. M. Schwab (Chicago: University of Chicago Press, 2006), 43: "Alle prägnanten Begriffe der modernen Staatslehre sind säkularisierte theologische Begriffe." Schwab translates Schmitt's original word *Prägnanz* as "significance," which unfortunately loses the vital aspect hidden in the conceptual "pregnancy" of the idea of God, that in modernity had not lost its power to engender new political structures. I modify Schwab's translation by proposing "vital" instead of "significant" in order to convey the generating power of the German word *prägnant*.

2. G. W. F. Hegel, *Faith and Knowledge*, trans. Walter Cerf and H. S. Harris (Albany: State University New York Press, 1977), 190.

3. Jacques Derrida, "Faith and Knowledge: The Two Sources of 'Religion' at the Limits of Reason Alone," trans. Samuel Weber, in *Acts of Religion*, ed. Gil Anidjar (London and New York: Routledge, 2002), 48–50.

4. Gershom Scholem, "Reflections on Jewish Theology," in *On Jews and Judaism in Crisis: Selected Essays*, ed. Werner Dannhauser (New York: Schocken Books, 1976), 283.

5. To appreciate the astounding career of the seemingly obscure kabbalistic notion of *tsimtsum*, see Christoph Schulte, *Zimzum: Gott und Weltursprung* (Frankfurt am Main: Suhrkamp, 2014), which gives a very exhaustive panorama of thinkers engaged with the divine contraction, from Luria himself, via Hegel and Schelling, up to Scholem, Jonas, and Levinas. On the possible indirect influence of Luria on German Idealism, see also my "God of Luria, Hegel, Schelling: The Divine Contraction and the Modern Metaphysics of Finitude," in *Mystical Theology and Continental Philosophy*, ed. David Lewin, Simon Podmore, and Duane Williams (London and New York: Routledge, 2017), 32–50, as well as Agata Bielik-Robson and Daniel H. Weiss, eds., *Tsimtsum and Modernity: Lurianic Heritage in Modern Philosophy and Theology* (Berlin: de Gruyter, 2020).

6. Scholem, "Reflections," 283; my emphasis.

7. G. W. F. Hegel, *Phenomenology of Spirit*, trans. A. V. Miller (Oxford: Oxford University Press, 1976), 493.

8. Jean-Luc Nancy, *Dis-enclosure: The Deconstruction of Christianity*, trans. Bettina Bergo (New York: Fordham University Press, 2008), 147.

9. Derrida, "Faith and Knowledge," 58.

10. Hegel would return to the idea of the infinite grief in the finite many times, always accentuating the tragic clash between infinity and finitude, which demands the sacrifice of the latter. See G. W. F Hegel, *Aesthetics: Lectures on Fine Art*, trans. T. M. Knox (Oxford: Clarendon Press, 1975), 1:537.

11. Derrida, "Faith and Knowledge," 50.

12. Jacques Derrida, *Glas*, trans. John P. Leavey and Richard Rand (Lincoln: Nebraska University Press, 1986), 241. Hereafter cited in text as *G* and page number.

13. Hegel's *Entäusserung*, "externalization," is the German word for *kenosis* in Luther's translation. On the importance of Luther's translation of *kenosis* for Hegel, see Catherine Malabou, *The Future of Hegel: Plasticity, Temporality, and Dialectics* (London: Routledge, 2005). Malabou states: "This injury is made clear in the Hegelian concept of a divine alienation, central to the dialectical conception of *kenosis* and its principle. 'Kenosis' means the lowering or humbling of God in his Incarnation and the Passion. . . . Luther translates κενωσις as *Entäußerung*, literally 'the separation from the self through an externalisation.' Now from this *Entäußerung* or 'alienation', Hegel forges a logical movement which becomes constitutive of the development of the divine essence. God necessarily departs from himself in His self-determination" (82).

14. Derrida, "Faith and Knowledge," 88.

15. Derrida, 53.

16. Derrida's dissatisfaction with the Hegelian axiom of *kenosis* comes to the fore very visibly in his preface to Catherine Malabou's *Future of Hegel*, where God's self-emptying figures very largely as indeed the axiomatic canvas of the whole phenomenological process of the divine self-recuperation. Malabou writes: "The Death of God thereby appears for Hegel as a moment in the divine being in the form of a first negation, logically destined to be reduplicated and reversed: 'Rather, a reversal takes place: God, that is to say, maintains himself in this process, and the latter is only the death of death (*der Tod des Todes*).' The expression *mors mortis* is found many times in Luther's writing, but the singularity of the Hegelian version shows itself in the way he interprets this death of death as a 'negation of negation.' Supported by such an interpretation we can already predict the transition from the theological signification of *kenosis* to its philosophical meaning" (Malabou, *Future of Hegel*, 107.) Agreeing with Malabou's emphasis on the importance of *kenosis* for Hegel, Derrida, worried by the past-oriented retributive character of the redemptive process, comments: "[Such] God would have no future, he would not even be able to promise or give himself both because he leaves and impoverishes himself (he says farewell to himself) and because, while leaving himself, he still does not leave himself, he does not abandon himself. . . . Too much emptiness, too much fullness . . . *We should then accomplish one more step, add a supplement of farewell to this Hegelian farewell, and say farewell to this farewell of God to God*" (Derrida, preface to Malabou, *Future of Hegel*, xlii; my emphasis). In my interpretation,

this "one more step" supplementing the "Hegelian farewell" is the notion of *tsimtsum*.

17. On the Trinitarian dialectics of emptiness and fullness, *kenosis* versus Eucharist, dying on the cross versus coming alive again in the act of communion, see also Werner Hamacher, *Pleroma—Reading in Hegel*, trans. Nicholas Walker and Simon Jarvis (Stanford, CA: Stanford University Press, 1998), and Stuart Barnett, "Eating My God," in *Hegel after Derrida*, ed. Stuart Barnett (London: Routledge, 1998), 131–144. Barnett ingeniously supplements the Hegelian definition of philosophy as a "speculative Good Friday," in which God permanently dies, with a new definition of speculative idealism as a "permanent Last Supper" which "reads the history of the Absolute on the basis of the signs of its disappearance. . . . In this Last Supper signs are eaten, disgorged, and then readied to be eaten again. . . . Hegel can only accept the notion of the finitization of God if it follows the model of the Last Supper" (144, 142). It is precisely this model that allows to put together the dispersed pieces of the disappeared God and thus, as Hegel himself describes it, "resurrect him daily": G. W. F. Hegel, *Phenomenology of Spirit*, trans. A. V. Miller (Oxford: Oxford University Press, 1976), 299.

18. Scholem, "Reflections," 283; my emphasis.

19. The "smiling specter" is a figure conceived by Antonio Negri in his commentary to Derrida's *Specters of Marx*: "The Specter's Smile," in *Ghostly Demarcations: A Symposium on Jacques Derrida's Specters of Marx*, ed. Michael Sprinker (London: Verso, 2008), 5–16.

20. On the hermetic meaning of this Hegelian phrase, see Alexander Glenn Magee, *Hegel and the Hermetic Tradition* (Ithaca, NY: Cornell University Press, 2008), 248.

21. Angelus Silesius, *Sacred Epigrams from the "Cherubinic Pilgrim,"* trans. Anthony Mortimer (New York: AMS Press, 2013). Cf. Luke 12:27: "Consider the lilies in the field, how they grow: they toil not, they spin not; and yet I say unto you, that Solomon in all his glory was not arrayed like one of these."

22. Hegel, *Aesthetics*, 1:371.

23. Jacques Derrida, *On the Name*, ed. Thomas Dutoit, trans. John P. Leavey (Stanford, CA: Stanford University Press, 1995), 82.

24. Derrida, 84.
25. Derrida, 82.
26. Derrida, 92.
27. Derrida, 84.
28. Derrida, 73; my emphasis.

29. Jacques Derrida, *Given Time: I. Counterfeit Money*, trans. Peggy Kamuf, (Chicago: University of Chicago Press, 1992), 153, 23.

30. See David Farrell Krell, *The Tragic Absolute: German Idealism and the Languishing of God* (Bloomington: Indiana University Press, 2005).

31. The Jewish angle of Derrida's interpretation of Hegel has also been accentuated by Edith Wyschogrod, *Spirit in Ashes: Hegel, Heidegger and the*

Man-Made Mass Death (New Haven, CT: Yale University Press, 1985), which discusses the destructive aspect of the Hegelian progress of the spirit. Elliot Wolfson, in *Beyond the Gift. Apophasis and Overcoming Theomania* (New York: Fordham University Press, 2014), also praises her approach: "Wyschogrod is to be given credit for connecting the kabbalistic account of God contracting the infinite essence into a dot with the Hegelian idea of the extension of space into the punctiformity of time. The Sabbath, in her reading, 'expresses the turning of space into time, the respite from creation as the temporal self-articulation of identity-in-difference'" (224–225); Edith Wyschogrod, "Crossover Dreams," *Journal of the American Academy of Religion*, no. 54 (1986): 546. However, while Wolfson links Derrida and Wyschogrod as the two Jewish, kabbalah-influenced thinkers who ventured into a properly iconoclastic speculation on the nature of God, I wish to stress a difference between them, which derives precisely from the latter's vision of the cosmic Sabbath. While for Wyschogrod, at the end of times the time will triumph and the *tikkun* will occur as a Hegelian repetition of the original *tsimtsum*, in which the alienation of space will have been sublated into a respite of time—for Derrida, the spatialization, which constantly produces new finite beings in the process of dissemination, is *to no end*: it neither serves any redemptive goal nor can it be stopped. The *tsimtsum* which paves the way toward alienation, spatialization, or dissemination is irreversible—and this is the main reason why Derrida attacks the Hegelian axiom of *kenosis* in creation as the remnant of the mythic system of retribution, which demands the cosmic sacrifice to be repaid and thus undone.

32. Derrida, "Marx and Sons," in *Ghostly Demarcations*, 248–249; my emphasis.

Exception without Sovereignty
The Kenotic Eschatology of Schelling

SAITYA BRATA DAS

To begin with, let me pose the following hypothesis: the dominant tendency of the Occidental metaphysics determines being as potentiality. The epoch of modernity—modernity that has secularized the theological concepts in terms of immanent theodicy of history—understands and determines potentiality (which is not *a* potentiality among other potentialities of being but *the* very potentiality of being at all) as Subject. In his posthumously published *Broken Hegemonies* (2003), Reiner Schürmann shows how the epochal condition of modernity is founded upon the *arché* of the Subject as the legitimating principle of the modern hegemony. This epoch of modernity, and along with it the Occidental metaphysics as such, has now come to a closure, both in the sense of having fulfilled itself and having terminated itself, thereby opening to a sense of pure exteriority or pure transcendence.[1] Such closure, as I will show, manifests itself in Schelling for the first time and in a singular and irreducible way; in other words, it comes to certain phenomenality. This *phenomenalization* takes place at the instance—where the instance itself is an abyss, a *wink*, an eschatological opening to eternity—when the "idea" of "actuality without potentiality" presents itself in Schellingian works, an idea that interrupts and momentarily arrests the univocity of the discourse of metaphysics. This means: the phenomenalization at the closure of metaphysics, or the phenomenalization of the closure of metaphysics, is, at the same time, the apparition of a caesura between what Schelling comes to name toward the end of his life as "positive philosophy" and "negative philosophy." This caesura cuts through the immanence of the discourse of modernity by an "unprethinkable" (*Unvordenkliche*) decision (*Ent-Scheidung*): the result is a "negative political theology" (to distinguish it from what comes to be known at the wake of Carl Schmitt) whose essence consists of an eschatological delegitimation of any earthly sovereign power on the basis of theological foundation. In this way, my argument here takes its point of departure from Jacob Taubes's critical engagement with the political theology of Schmitt. In the spirit of Taubes's eschatology of delegitimation, I am thinking here of a negative political theology of "actuality without potentiality": actuality as the eschatological exception to the mythical act of the law-positing sovereign power.

To bring the whole hypothesis to a more concrete formulation: the later Schellingian idea of "actuality without potentiality"—the idea that cuts through the immanent theodicy of history (that grounds the epochal discourse of modernity)—opens up, eschatologically, to a thinking of exception without sovereignty, a thinking that may well be the task of our new millennium. It is my contention that the Schellingian political-theological idea of "actuality without potentiality" is Pauline in spirit and inspiration;[2] it draws, more implicitly than explicitly on the Pauline idea of *kenosis* that Paul develops in his letter to the Philippians (2:7). Schelling thinks of the event of actuality as emptying out of potentialities that constitute the nomothetic order of worldly hegemonies. The world order of history is seen to be the order of passing-away—as Paul speaks of nature—that groans for redemption.[3]

The Schellingian deconstructive phenomenology or phenomenological deconstruction—the task of which is that of making manifest the epochal closure of the constituted phenomenality (a paradoxical phenomenology it is, for it makes manifest what is foreclosed in the constituted order of phenomenality)—can be said to have a two-fold task:

a. To decisively put into question the fundamental metaphysical principle of Hegelian theodicy of history, namely, the immanence of potentiality, for it is in Hegelian theodicy of history, so contends Schelling, the Occidental metaphysics comes to realize itself in its utmost possibility. This demands rethinking of potentiality, or radicalizing potentiality, without abandoning it, and yet, without making potentiality "the sovereign referent" or the "hegemonic fantasm" of the epoch of modernity,[4] without having to make potentiality the legitimating *arché* of the epoch of modernity.

b. This demands—in a reversal to the former, and yet transcending the gesture of mere reversal—that we think "actuality without potentiality"; actuality in which there is no potentiality: a radical transcendence, infinity itself, an exception (like the Platonic "Good beyond being") that does not become in turn rule. This exception, which does not serve as the legitimating principle of hegemonies, or of the order of constituted phenomenality, cannot be understood as "onto" and "theological" ground of beings, whether as nature, as reason, or as Subject: an exceptional and "unprethinkable" (*Unvordenkliche*) exuberance of beyond or "over-being" (*Überseyn*). If this is so, then the beyond or "over-being" cannot be an ontological principle; it cannot even be thought as principle: the actuality exposes all the potentialities of being—and the very potentiality of being, and the being of potentiality—to the groundlessness of inscrutable, sublime freedom.

This double task, to be carried out at the same instance, comes to introduce, in the wake of Schelling, the decisive caesura into the fundamental ground of the Occidental metaphysics, that is: the caesura into the univocity of Being. This has led Schelling—foreshadowing Karl Marx, Friedrich Nietzsche, Heidegger, and Søren Kierkegaard—to make the gesture of (what we can say, borrowing the word from Marx) the exit (*Ausgang*) from/of philosophy:[5] philosophy (as a system or as an ontology) cannot think actuality as actuality, that is, actuality without potentiality (which is neither mere potential actuality nor mere representation of actuality).

In fact, Schelling makes not just one gesture but multiple gestures, often in unforeseeable and unprethinkable manner, given the complexity and immensity of the task. All throughout his long career Schelling seems to have been involved in this gigantic and raging discordance—as Heidegger (1985) beautifully brings out—between the undeniable claim of an abyssal freedom and the undeniable attraction toward a system, and the result is, so Heidegger contends, a failure. But it is this failure, rather than (Hegelian) success (that Hegel could create a system in the most rigorous sense of the term), that seems to have far more profound consequences for us: in so many different and subterranean ways this failure has never ceased to haunt the destiny of thinking to come, opening the closure of metaphysics to its outside which will never be recuperated once more (think of Kierkegaard, Heidegger, Ernst Bloch, and Franz Rosenzweig).

Schmitt's *Political Theology: Four Chapters on the Concept of Sovereignty* stands against the immanent metaphysics of history on which Hegel grounds his philosophical discourse of modernity.[6] Schmitt argues that many fundamental concepts that the metaphysical-political discourse of modernity deploys—and Hegel is the best example—are but secularized versions of what are primarily theological concepts. By secularizing the theological concepts, and thereby immanentizing them, the Hegelian metaphysics of history has neutralized the apocalyptic sting of transcendence[7]: the result is the loss of *auctoritas*—the very place of sovereignty—and, thus, of the political itself, that is, of the very possibility of distinction between friend and enemy; and the result is the emergence of the whole technological apparatus of politics where decision-making (which must be the prerogative of the sovereign power) becomes impossible. It is against this technology of politics, or rather, the technological neutralization of the political (of which the secular-liberal-parliamentary democracy is the best example for Schmitt) that Schmitt introduces his political-theological concept of sovereignty which exceptionally (the exception of decision, or the decision of exception), by suspending the constituted order of the law, brings a new legal order into being and bestows on it the legitimacy that it demands. The logic of sovereignty is, then, something of a paradoxical logic: the sovereign legally (by using a certain specific article in the constitution) suspends the order of the law in a sovereign decision on a state of exceptions. Such paradox can only have, according to Schmitt, a theological analogy (the miracle). Schmitt, then, grounds his political concept of sovereignty—the sovereign being the figure of the *katechon* who restrains the anarchy erupting from below[8]—in his own interpretation of the Catholic theological principle of *analogia entis* (an interpretation that is, however, contested by many Catholic theologians): the analogy between the divine sovereign above and the earthly sovereign in the profane order. The Schmittian political theology, thus, introduces the theological notion of transcendence (through a critique of the Hegelian immanent metaphysics of history) only to legitimate the earthly, political sovereign figure on a theological foundation, and only to reintroduce the legitimating political order based on myth (*arcanum*): "to great politics belongs the *arcanum*."[9] In this way, Schmitt grounds his political theology on a mythic foundation (thereby confounding the theological with the mythic); Walter Benjamin (followed by Gershom Scholem and Jacob Taubes), in contrast, thinks of the theological as the radical ungrounding of any mythic foundation.

The double gesture of Schellingian "deconstruction" radically not only puts into question the immanence of Hegelian theodicy of history (and Schmitt does it, in his own political-theological manner) but also thinks of an exception which is, nevertheless, without sovereignty. Following

Taubes, I have called this "negative political theology," as distinct from Schmittian political theology.[10] The actuality without potentiality that Schelling thinks is neither the actuality of the concrete political order nor is it tied to the *nomos* of the earth; it does not have any analogy with any order of potentiality. Like the Pauline idea of *kenosis*, the exceptional actuality of *Überseyn* in all its exuberance empties out all the attributes of potentiality that fascinate our gaze with its "hegemonic fantasm." It opens up, by radically suspending the order of worldly *nomos*, to what Reiner Schürmann calls "the singularization to come" where the hegemonic principle withers away, uncoupled from the law of the common and binding (*koinon*).[11] This mode of thinking, which comes to Schelling via Meister Eckhart, consists of, on the one hand, a distinction made between God as the principle or *arché* of beings (as *hegemonikon*: the sovereign principle, or the principle of sovereignty that founds the order of creation) and, on the other hand, the idea of a Godhead without sovereignty (without principle and without *arché*). We must learn to exist without principle and without *arché*.

Between Godhead (whose exuberance, un-pre-thinkable, is beyond being) and God (the nature of God, or the God of nature, God as the governing principle of the world) is neither analogy nor any (Neo-Platonic) emanation but an irreducible abyss: the political-theological principle of *analogia entis* cannot explain the abyss of the difference in God himself, not to speak of any possible analogia at all between the exception of the divine and any earthly sovereignty. Only by rigorous mortification of our will and all forms of egotism is it possible to participate, by a gratuitous grace, in the *beatitude to come* which is, for Schelling, the eschatological event par excellence.[12] Schelling thinks the Christian idea of *beatitude* eschatologically, that is, in its futurity. The interesting part of Schellingian eschatology lies in thinking the "always already" in relation to "to come": the past is never done with once and for all, and is never a passed past; the true past is that which remains—as an irreducible remainder—as the opening to what is always "to come." In that sense, the "always already" is not incommensurable with "to come" but is the promise of all that is *to come*, not as a determinate condition but as the event of *spacing*-open. The essence of religion (understood in all its eschatological radicality) and the fundamental vocation for philosophy lies in this infinite task of mortification of any earthly claims to sovereignty: Schelling here translates, in his own thinking and in his own manner, the Eckhartian *kenotic* idea of abandonment (*Gelassenheit*): "Only he has come to the ground of himself and has known the whole depth of life who has once abandoned everything and has himself been abandoned by everything."[13]

The crucial word here is *abandonment* (*Gelassenheit*) that even Heidegger, following Eckhart and Schelling, makes a decisive word in his later thinking: we must abandon not only the world and empty out all the worldly attributes but even God (God insofar as he is mere nature, and as the mere ground of beings, God as no more than the nomothetic and monothetic ground of worldly existence): the glory of the lord is *kenosis*. This infinite paradox—which is the paralysis of worldly potentialities and vertigo of thought—is the essence of religion and also of philosophy. In two ways they are oriented toward the event *to come*, namely, the infinite and gratuitous gift of beatitude. What arrives as an eschatological event and as pure generosity infinitely exceeds not only the totality of beings but being itself. Hence, there is not only no possible *analogia entis* between the two orders, the Godhead is not even *ens* at all: the ontotheological constitution of metaphysics has come here to a decisive failure.

Understanding religion eschatologically in this way, Schelling carefully distinguishes it, as early as his lectures on the philosophy of art of 1804, from myth: religion, or the eschatological event *to come*, interrupts the mythic-political foundation of the worldly order, and empties out, *kenotically*, any sovereign claims of worldly potentialities. This subtraction (emptying out) is also an infinite excess—over potentiality as such, which, unlike the worldly order of the mythic-political, is not an auto-constitutional origin of the *nomos* but is Love: Love does not rule over life by violently imprisoning us in the cages of necessity but places us in radical freedom. The political-theological apparatus of the worldly order, mythically founded, is eschatologically burst open and is rendered nonautochthonous and non-sovereign and exposed to the *that* which exists, ecstatically, without *potestas*: namely, to the actuality without potentiality, to the exception which is without sovereignty.

As early as 1804 Schelling decisively puts into question the political-theological consequences that arise from the Neo-Platonic idea of emanation as the generative principle of the world. Plotinus explicates the generation of the phenomenal order and its relation to its origin as the continuous diminishing of the absolute light. This way of understanding the eternal birth of the phenomenal order and its relation to the absolute does not serve to explain satisfactorily the very possibility of radical evil, because: "In the absolute world there are no confines anywhere, and just as God can only bring forth the real-per-se and absolute, so any ensuing effulgence is again absolute and can itself only bring forth something akin to it. There can be no continuous passage into the exact opposite, the absolute privation of all reality, nor can the finite arise from the infinite by decrements."[14]

Only the idea of an irreducible distance or remove (*Abfall*, which also means apostasy or falling away) can serve as the explicative principle of not only the coming into being of the phenomenal order but also the very possibility (and actuality) of radical evil. Gnostic-Kabbalistic in inspiration, which is farther intensified through his reading of Jacob Böhme,[15] the idea of falling away makes impossible any attempt to embody the divine on the immanent plane of world-historical politics, for it undoes in advance any possible analogy between the absolute and the phenomenal order: not only the Hegelian immanent theodicy of history but also the Schmittian political theology of transcendence receives here a decisive undoing.

Schelling elaborates this antinomic idea in much more detail in his 1810 private lectures in Stuttgart. The emergence of the world is not explained by the generative principle of continuity but by a divine un-pre-thinkable decision: by a fundamental (de)cision or separation the world comes into being that sets apart being (*das Seyende*) from Being (*Seyn*). The emergence of the world is *set apart* from the groundless foundation: such must be the divine freedom which, by a constriction or withdrawal of itself—more out of an abyss of Love than out of divine *potestas*—lets the world come into being. That is to say: divine abandonment of sovereign power and abounding Love, given in pure donation, is the origin of the phenomenal order. The coming into being of the world which, in a sense, is nondivine (although without God there is no *is*)—where any *is* is also, in a sense, nonbeing—lies less in the overwhelming and majestic divine power but in an un-pre-thinkable (*Unvordenkliche*) renunciation of divine force so that the creaturely being *be*: the divine empties itself and subtracts its own sovereignty, so that the phenomenal order, which in a way is outside divinity, may come into being at all. In other words, to say: God(head) im-potentiates himself and reduces himself to non-sovereignty—by rendering himself weak—so that something outside himself may *be* and that *something*—whose being is, in a way, *nonbeing*—*is* such that its very being is *loaned*. As such, no being in the worldly order can claim for itself autochthony and an aboriginal existence. As loaned being (whose very being is loaned, and to that extent is nonbeing), any being in the worldly order—even the earthly sovereign figure—is that whose possibility is never actualizable: hence it is the infinite veil of melancholy of all earthly creature.[16] Actuality where no potentiality is left, does not belong as capacity or possession to any worldly being: it is the consummate fire where any sovereign claim of the worldly power is burnt and annihilated, not by the violence of divine *potestas* but by the divine violence of Love, which, while annihilating it, also redeems it. Here is at work not only the Heraclitean fire but also the Pauline opposition between the spirit and the letter and *pistis* and *nomos*.

The event of the Fall marks—so Schelling continues in his 1810 private lectures—the breakage or fissure into the nexus of beings (God, man, nature): the jointure of beings is disjoined. This disjointure is the origin of the historical order, the unredeemed state of destitution and evil which has its analogy, in the realm of nature, its sickness. What sickness is in the realm of nature, evil is in the order of history. As Stanislas Breton rightly points out, Schellingian phenomenology of nature here is Pauline in inspiration: nature as the order of passing away, in its fallen and unredeemed state, is groaning and crying for redemption.[17] As the order that cannot ground itself on its immanent foundation, the apostate state of history is the realm of mere passing away and transiency. It is what must, by the very logic of its origin, pass away, and is passing away; no figure in the apostate order of world-historical existence can claim sovereignty without, ultimately, having to pass away. It is here we see the Schellingian political-theological deduction of the state and the church.

The state is the mortal being's impoverished attempt to supplement an absolute impoverishment, namely, the link or the jointure that is broken among beings as consequence of the Fall. As such, the state is, like anything in the profane order, transient: it is this supplement that forcefully tries to affect the lost unity by always making legitimate use of power, which is the source of violence. Far from seeing the state as the figure of the absolute, the state is thought here as precarious and fragile (the order of nonbeing), and thereby being dangerous and tyrannical: the evil of the state lies not in the power of its being but in its malicious, devouring hunger for being. This totalizing tendency is the intrinsic logic of its very (non)being; the state is necessarily and potentially—because it is ruled by power alone—unjust and tyrannical. That means that any worldly regime, ruled by any earthly sovereign power, is always wrong and is always bad.

What the state is in the external realm the church is in the internal realm: an attempt to supplement the lost nexus among beings. The insufficient and precarious character of the state, instituted as supplement of the lost nexus of beings, demands the second revelation to restore the lost unity: here Christ is the mediator between God and man, himself God-man, dying the most ignoble death on the cross and bearing the intolerable suffering and evil only to redeem the unredeemed condition of the fallen state. The church is the immediate consequence of the second revelation. But insofar as the church, in the process of its historical evolution as institution, takes part in negotiations with worldly *potestas* and allies itself with the state, it forgets its initial eschatological impulse—that burning desire for the end of the unjust world and for the freedom from the earthly ties (both ties with the sovereign power of the Roman empire and the family ties of *oikonomia*)—and becomes just like any other worldly institution: the church here becomes the very theological foundation of worldly sovereignties. Schellingian deconstruction of the political-theological legitimation of worldly sovereignty is nowhere as explicit as here. Far from deifying the profane order of the world-historical becoming, and far from seeing the modern state of Prussia as embodiment of divine reason, Schelling here argues for separation of the theological from the political realm. This separation alone can redress the political tyranny and the horror of universal domination:

> In surveying more recent history, which with good reason is said to begin with the arrival of Christianity in Europe, we note that humanity had to pass through two stages in its attempt to discover or produce a unity; first that of producing an internal unity through the Church, which had to fail because the Church simultaneously sought to become the external unity and eventually attempted to produce external unity by means of the state. Only with the demise of hierarchical [systems] has the state attained this importance, and it is manifest that the pressure of political tyranny has increased ever since in exact proportion to the belief that an inner unity seemed dispensable; indeed it is bound to increase to a maximum intensity until, perhaps, upon the collapse of these one-dimensional attempts humanity will discover the right way.[18]

And therefore,

> God, however, as identity of the highest order, remains above all reality and eternally has merely an indirect relationship. If then in the higher moral order the State represents a *second nature*, then the divine can never have anything other than an indirect relationship to it; never can it bear any real relationship to it, and religion, if it seeks to preserve itself in unscathed pure ideality, can therefore never exist—even in the most perfect State—other than esoterically in the form of *mystery cults*.[19]

In contrast to Hegel's philosophical discourse of modernity that formulates the immanence of world history as theodicy, Schelling eschatologically thinks religion as the promised religion—the religion to come—which refuses to be embodied in any given order of worldly hegemonies:

> Whatever the ultimate goal may turn out to be, this much is certain, namely, that true unity can be attained only *via* the path of religion; only the supreme and most diverse culture of religious knowledge will enable humanity, if not to abolish the state outright, then at least to

ensure that the state will progressively divest itself of the blind force that governs it and to transfigure this force into intelligence. It is not that the Church ought to dominate the state or vice versa but that the state ought to cultivate the religious principles within itself and that the community of all peoples ought to be founded on religious convictions that, themselves, ought to become universal.[20]

This is not a conventional, conservative project to recuperate a premodern political theology. Schelling's negative political theology can rather be understood as that which seeks to radically keep open any immanent theodicy to the untotalizable event of redemption to come.

The caesura that Schelling explicitly introduces between the negative and the positive philosophy in his Berlin lectures (1841–1854)—although the germ of this distinction can be traced back to his incomplete magnum opus, *Die Weltalter*—is based upon the distinction that he makes between *quid sit* (what a being is) and *quod sit* (that it is): while *quid sit*, in its infinite potentiality or capacity to be, can be "grasped" (*greifen*) by the power of the "concept" (*Begriff*, which means grasping or seizing: the concept seizes and grasps), *quod sit* refuses the potentiality of the concept's self-grasping. Here is Schelling's decisive confrontation with Hegelian onto-theological foundation of metaphysics. The Hegelian concept of the concept—the absolute concept, the absolute concept as infinite negativity (where the negation arrives at the absolute by a dialectical self-cancelation)—can grasp, in its auto-grasping, only the *dunamis* (that is, the immanent auto-movement) of being-in-its-infinite-potentiality-to-be: the metaphysical violence of the (Hegelian) concept (grasping, seizing, appropriating) can measure up to being only insofar as being is being-in-its-power (being as potentiality), that is, the whatness (*quid sit*) of being. The concept determines—by negating the negation, in an immanent movement of self-cancelation of the negative—only the essence, the whatness, of being. But the immeasurable actuality of being, the *that* (*Daß*), in all its exuberance, refuses the measure of the concept, for it does not need any potentiality to be: "The former—the answer to the question *what* it is—accords me into the *essence* of the thing, or it provides that I understand the thing, that I have an understanding or a concept of it, or have it *itself* within the concept. The other insight however, *that* it is, does not accord me just the concept, but rather something that goes beyond just the concept, which is existence."[21] This actuality of existence which is neither the telos of an immanent movement of the negative nor the conditioned-hypothetic ("if being were to exist") being, "is," rigorously speaking, not even being but "beyond-being" (*Überseyn*): a pure and unconditional generosity that exists prior to any potentiality (to be), and that groundlessly keeps the very order of being open to transcendence. This transcendence of actuality cannot be determined to have resulted from the immanent movement of auto-generative negation (this was Hegel's confusion who thought in an inverted manner), for one cannot conceive the radically positive as arising out of the self-cancelation of the negation. What Hegel's *Logic* can achieve, at the end of the auto-generative movement of the negation, is only the conceptual-logical actuality, which is still only "conceptual," while the radical actuality without potentiality is still outside of the telos, because it is always already (that is, immemorially), at the very beginning of the movement, excluded from the immanence of potentiality: this is why Schelling calls it "exuberance" and "unprethinkable" (*Unvordenkliche*). There is no radical futurity to come if the thought of the past is not radicalized and released at the same time. This "always already" is not an available fact of the world already accomplished; the "always already" has not come to pass by, and that is why this "always already" is the event future anterior par excellence: it is still living, and still to come. Neither a dead past nor an accomplished reality, it is the structural opening of the world to come. What Hegel's system can achieve at best—given that even the concept can have movement, but only a conceptual movement (while Hegel thought that it is actual-real movement)—is what results from the self-cancelation of "not-not": that is, what is still a "not-not," although at a higher degree of making explicit of what is an immanent potentiality; if it is positive, it is still a potentially positive, which Aristotle grasped much more profoundly than Hegel. Thus, he (Aristotle) renounced the *Daß* from the purest fire of his rigorous analysis (without pretending to have grasped it). What returns in the Hegelian self-canceling movement of "not-not" is the circular return of potentialities, while the exuberant excess of the immeasurable actuality disrupts or interrupts this circular return of potentiality and exposes it to what exceeds its closure: to the actuality without potentiality. The mythic violence of potentiality that returns, in ever new modes, to the same, is radically interrupted and is burst open, apocalyptically, to its radical outside. The horror of the eternal return of the same in its vicious circling and recircling can only be redeemed by an arrival of that which is absolutely heterogeneous, which does not need any potentiality to exist: it must radically suspend the mythic foundation of potentiality that constitutes the law.

From Walter Benjamin's famous essay "Critique of Violence," we know that the law has mythic foundation;[22] this is why Benjamin calls the violence that erupts from the force of the law—which serves the sovereign power—a "mythic violence," against which Benjamin welcomes the "divine violence" that alone redeems us from violence without bloodshed. This divine violence—which paradoxically is without violence—is messianic religiosity, to be distinguished from the mythic constitution of worldly sovereignties.[23] This messianic has to do with the exception—and here Benjamin confronts Schmitt without naming him—that does not become rule in turn, and is, thus, an exception without sovereignty: "The tradition of the oppressed teaches us that 'the state of emergency' in which we live is not the exception but the rule. We must attain to a conception of history that is in keeping with this insight. Then we shall clearly realize that it is our task to bring about a real state of emergency, and this will improve our position in the struggle against fascism."[24] Anticipating Benjamin, Schelling distinguishes religion—eschatologically thought—from myth: when religion (Christianity) appears, there occurs the withering away of myth: "mythology concludes as soon as allegory begins."[25] Religion, according to Schelling, "necessarily assumes the character of a revealed religion and is for that reason historical at its very foundation," unlike the mythic consciousness of the Greeks for which "the manifestations and figures of the Gods here were eternal."[26] Religion here is a negation or, better, a replacement of mythology. By suspending the mythic constitution of the law, the eschatological event releases us from the realm of necessity (which moves in the circular return of potencies) to freedom.[27] We know that Schelling makes the thought of freedom into the alpha and omega of his philosophy: freedom here is the eschatological principle which he thinks in a Gnostic-Kabbalistic manner. Ernst Bloch, whom Jürgen Habermas describes as "Marxist Schelling,"[28] takes it up and transforms it in his own political-theological critique.[29] The event of *eschaton* is the innermost axis around which the historical moves (as distinguished from the mythic): this eschatology of history, predicated upon freedom, is qualitatively a different vision of history than the vision that constitutes the Hegelian theodicy of history. Later in the Kierkegaardian eschatological "Christianity without Christendom" (Kierkegaard who wants, in a quantum leap, to bypass eighteen hundred years of Christendom so as to be contemporary with the Christ-event) this Schellingian deconstruction of theodicy finds a much sharper tone: the fundamental *arché* of modernity—modernity whose fundamental concepts are secularized versions of theological concepts—is decisively put into question by Kierkegaard. In still another manner, following Schelling, Franz Rosenzweig in his monumental *The Star of Redemption* messianically puts into question the whole political-theological principle that moves the Hegelian world-historical politics. In all these instances we see at work the Schellingian attempt to think the exception—which he calls "actuality without potentiality"—that is without sovereignty: the exception of actuality suspends the mythic constitution of the law, thereby delegitimating any attempt on the part of earthly sovereignty to legitimate itself on a theological foundation. True to the spirit of Meister Eckhart whom he follows, the Schellingian distinction between God and Godhead—a distinction dubbed heretica by the official Christendom—preempted any political-theological analogy between the worldly realm of *nomos* and the divine exception. One cannot fail to mark here the Pauline inspiration again: this withdrawing of stake from the whole worldly order of *nomos* because it is only the order of "passing away." And we remember that Walter Benjamin, in a similar spirit, calls this kenotic eschatology the world politics of nihilism.[30]

As Heidegger rightly remarked, Schelling has remained and will remain the unique and the singular thinker of the West. If the *arché* of Reason constitutes the hegemonic phantasm of the epochal condition of modernity, then by opening the principle of Reason to that which exists, ecstatically, without a "why," Schelling impoverishes the hegemony of modernity: actuality without potentiality cannot be grasped, unlike the essences of entities, by the principle of Reason. And we have seen how Schelling, in the opposite front, equally impoverishes the political-theological exception of legitimacy that threatens to become the rule. Irreducible to worldly potentialities, the sovereignty of divine actuality is at once a *kenosis*, that is, non-sovereign: without this, even the emergence of the phenomenal order cannot be explicated. Only by abandonment—of all worldly *potestas*—and by rigorous mortification of the will can a mortal participate in beatitude, which is the highest vocation and the highest gift for the mortals. This mortification is the fire that does not annihilate us, but it redeems us through its work of purification and releases us from the cages of the world. The fire of exuberance beyond being is the Good which precedes even the distinction between good and evil: already in his 1809 essay on human freedom, Schelling elaborates this fundamental and unique thought of his. To participate in the highest gift possible for the mortal—which, as gift, exceeds any economy of the worldly order—it is necessary that all the worldly attributes must enter destitution. As Eckhart says, so does Schelling in the following, that one must abandon even God: "He who wishes to place himself in the beginning of a truly free philosophy must abandon even God. Here we say: who wishes to maintain it, he will lose it; and who gives up, he will find it. Only he has come to the ground of himself and has known the whole depth of life who has once abandoned everything and has himself been abandoned by everything. He for whom everything disappeared and who saw himself alone with the infinite: a great step which Plato compared to death."[31]

The philosophy of Schelling, especially his later philosophy, inaugurates a new political-theological thinking outside Occidental metaphysics; he thus prepares the way for the postmetaphysical philosophy of, among others, Martin Heidegger, Franz Rosenzweig, and Jacques Derrida. Rising against the Hegelian immanent theodicy of history which constitutes the philosophical discourse of modernity, Schelling eschatologically opens up the thought of an exception that interrupts the historical continuum and exposes it to the untotalizable surprise of the event (to come). In this manner, Schelling has helped us rethink our common being with for our contemporary time.

Notes

1. See Saitya Brata Das, *The Political Theology of Schelling* (Edinburgh: Edinburgh University Press, 2016), 154–155. The fundamental project of modernity can be understood as *immanence* or *autonomy*. Without grounding itself upon any transcendence—God or Nature—the human Subject gives itself its own *nomos*: this is the meaning of *auto-nomos*. It is this principle or *arché* of modernity—the self-constituting, immanent Subject—that now comes to a closure.

2. See also Stanislas Breton, *A Radical Philosophy of Saint Paul*, trans. Joseph N. Ballan with an introduction by Ward Blanton (New York: Columbia University Press, 2011).

3. Some of the following paragraphs are taken from the introduction to my *The Political Theology of Schelling*.

4. Reiner Schürmann, *Broken Hegemonies*, trans. Reginald Lilly (Bloomington: Indiana University Press, 2003).

5. Gerard Bensussan, *Marx le Sortant* (Paris: Hermann, 2007).

6. Carl Schmitt, *Political Theology: Four Chapters on the Concept of Sovereignty*, trans. George Schwab with a foreword by Tracy B. Strong (Chicago: Chicago University Press, 2005).

7. Jacob Taubes understands—and I accept Taubes's argument—the Schmittian position as "apocalypse of the counter-revolution": Schmitt is an apocalyptic thinker, insofar as he envisions the chaos coming from below, and yet, he is counterrevolutionary, insofar as he thinks the apocalypse must be restrained. Taubes, *To Carl Schmitt: Letters and Reflections*, trans. Keith Tribe (New York: Columbia University Press, 2013), 1–18.

8. Carl Schmitt, *The Nomos of the Earth in the International Law of Jus Publicum Europaeum*, trans. G. L. Ulmen (New York: Telos Press, 2006).

9. Carl Schmitt, *Roman Catholicism and Political Form*, trans. G. L. Ulmen (New York: Greenwood Press, 1996), 34.

10. See Jacob Taubes, *The Political Theology of Paul*, trans. Dana Hollander (Stanford, CA: Stanford University Press, 2003) and *Occidental Eschatology*, trans. David Ratmoko (Stanford, CA: Stanford University Press, 2009).

11. Schürmann, *Broken Hegemonies*, 14 and *passim*.

12. F. W. J. Schelling, *Philosophy and Religion*, trans. Klaus Ottmann (Putnam: Spring Publications, 2010).

13. Quoted in Martin Heidegger, *Schelling's Treatise on the Essence of Human Freedom*, trans. Joan Stambaugh (Athens: Ohio University Press, 1985), 6–7.

14. Schelling, *Philosophy and Religion*, 24.

15. See Gershom Scholem, *Major Trends in Jewish Mysticism*, foreword by Robert Alter (New York: Schocken Books, 1995), 412. The importance of Jacob Böhme for the middle and later Schelling is well-known and well-discussed. See Dale Snow, *Schelling and the End of Idealism* (Albany: State University of New York Press, 1996) and Robert Brown, *The Later Philosophy of Schelling: The Influence of Boehme on the Works of 1809–1815* (Lewisburg, PA: Bucknell University Press, 1977). On the questions of "life" in God himself, of evil and of human freedom, and above all, of the abyss (*Abgrund*) as the very ground of human and divine being, his reading of Böhme was crucial for Schelling's middle works, especially his essay on human freedom and his *Ages of the World*.

16. F. W. J. Schelling, *Philosophical Inquiries into the Nature of Human Freedom*, trans. James Gutmann (La Salle, IL: Open Court, 1936), 79.

17. Breton, *Radical Philosophy*, 124.

18. F. W. J. Schelling, *Idealism and the Endgame of Theory*, trans. Thomas Pfau (Albany: State University of New York Press, 1994), 229.

19. Schelling, *Philosophy and Religion*, 51.

20. Schelling, *Idealism*, 229.

21. F. W. J. Schelling, *The Grounding of Positive Philosophy*, trans. Bruce Matthews (Albany: State University of New York Press, 2007), 129.

22. Walter Benjamin, "Critique of Violence," in *Reflections*, ed. Peter Demetz (New York: Schocken Press, 1986), 277–300.

23. Maria Joao Cantinho, "The Necessity for Clean Air and Space Is Stronger than Any Kind of Hatred: An Essay on the Concept of Violence and Religion in Walter Benjamin," in *The Weight of Violence: Religion, Language, Politics*, ed. Saitya Brata Das and Soumyabrata Choudhury (New Delhi: Oxford University Press, 2015), 75–90.

24. Walter Benjamin, "Theses on the Philosophy of History," in *Illuminations*, ed. with an introduction by Hannah Arendt, trans. Harry Zohn (New York: Schocken Books, 1969), 257.

25. F. W. J. von Schelling, *The Philosophy of Art*, trans. Douglas W. Stott (Minneapolis: University of Minnesota Press, 1989), 48. See also Das, *Political Theology*, 182–210.

26. Schelling, *Philosophy of Art*, 69.

27. Paul Tillich, *The Construction of the History of Religion in Schelling's Positive Philosophy: Its Presuppositions and Principles* (London: Associated University Press, 1975).

28. Jürgen Habermas, "Ernst Bloch: A Marxist Schelling," in *Philosophical-Political Profiles*, trans. Frederick G. Lawrence (Cambridge, MA: MIT Press, 1985), 61–78.

29. Ernst Bloch, *Atheism in Christianity: The Religion of the Exodus and the Kingdom*, trans. Peter Thomson (London: Verso, 2009).

30. Walter Benjamin, "Theologico-Political Fragment," in *Reflections*, ed. Peter Demetz (New York: Schocken Press, 1986), 312–313.

31. Quoted in Heidegger, *Schelling's Treatise*, 6–7.

12

Once More, from Below
The Concept of Reduplication and the Immanence of Political Theology

STEVEN SHAKESPEARE

This essay will fall apart at the seams. It will attempt to articulate a threefold typology of subjectivities (broadly derived from Immanuel Kant, Friedrich Wilhelm Joseph von Schelling, and Søren Kierkegaard) and their relevance to political theology. The risk of adopting such an obviously Hegelian form is that it dictates the result in advance: the promise is that the one-sided extremes of Kant and absolute idealism are overcome and sublimated in a Kierkegaardian resolution. Such a risk persists, even if Kierkegaard's language of absurdity, indirection, and paradox is retained. Hegel, after all, was no stranger to the "labor of the negative," the surplus which could be extracted when tropes of dereliction, contradiction, and death were allowed to do their work to the utmost. Even paradox can be the mask worn by an ultimate resolution of opposites held in harmonious tension.

Nevertheless, the hazard is worthwhile if something other than a redemption of the subject or its world can result. Therefore, I am not aiming at a representation of the real nor at a reconciliation of its represented contradictions. Instead, my intention is to perform a reduplication of the failure and exhaustion of attempts to construct a world and a subject of that world. Political theology is busy with the construction of worlds or the hope that other worlds are possible; simultaneously, it is busy recruiting subjects for itself. Perhaps it is time for political theology to be deprived of its self-given authorization to issue such fiats.

My claim is that the futility of such projects is itself an index of the insistence of a real which is, to borrow François Laruelle's terminology, "foreclosed to thought." In other words, the real is not an object given to perception or thought. It is that from which perception and thought proceeds. However, neither is it the presupposed, transcendental structure of a thinking and perceiving subject, since the analysis of such a structure itself presupposes the validity of a real divided between subject and object, experience and understanding, the transcendental and the empirical. The real is not subject to or object of any procedure of division (any philosophical decision, as Laruelle puts it). Such a division is only possible if it assumes the ultimately transcendent position of a critique. Seen from the real, however, such transcendences are only occasional modes of thinking which cannot determine their own, ultimately immanent identity.[1]

This is not a new problem. It is endemic to what Rodolph Gasché dubbed the "philosophy of reflection," the post-Cartesian attempt to secure the grounds of self and world via an introspective turn.[2] The problem is that such a turn entails the self reflecting upon—and therefore divided against—itself. One of the aims of idealist philosophy, it could be argued, is the attempt to thematize this split within the self (and, correlatively, between self and world) and explore strategies for overcoming it.

In these projects, however, what remains to be thought is precisely the *gap*: between the self and its reflected counterpart, between the self and its world. The correlation between subject and object is predicated upon a distinction between them. However, to think this distinction is to turn it once more into an object of a subject's thought, thus begging the question by building the subject-object gap into its own analysis of itself. This opens the door to an infinite regress, in which the project of thinking the possibility of thought disappears down the rabbit hole.

Kant, Schelling, and Kierkegaard, each in their own way, register the split within the subject and the subject-world distinction without trying to resolve the split in the terms provided by a subject-object structure of thinking itself. Thus, they do *not* attempt a dialectical unification of self and world.[3]

For the purposes of consistency in this essay, the three proper names (Kant, Schelling, and Kierkegaard) are not hierarchically arranged moments in a dialectic, nor even a trinity of "stages of existence" in Kierkegaard's sense. They are used to index three ways of philosophically constituting a world and a subject and, implicitly, a politics. Each renders the gap between subject and object-world in order to suture it or to stretch a skin across the wound. It will be argued that each of them is insufficient, in that they assume a transcendence for which they cannot account. However, rather than this opening the door to a political theology able to refer to and deploy such a transcendence, the essay identifies the corresponding insufficiency of theology and politics.

The term I shall adopt for the way in which that difference or gap in the real is overcome is *reduplication*. Although this term is most readily associated with Kierkegaard, I will argue that analogous reduplications are at work in the other two positions as well. The key commonality between these otherwise divergent positions is that they all avoid a certain way of appealing to transcendent authority to close the gap in the real. The gap is not healed by an operation of grace. Grace, in the sense I am using it here, whatever its intimate and inward force, is ultimately given from outside the world and the subject. The positions I am exploring do not avail themselves of this gracious healing of the gap in the real but operate by a re-doubling, a reintensification and refiguring *of the gap itself*.

Reduplicating the Gap

In his *Concluding Unscientific Postscript*, Kierkegaard writes: "When for the existing spirit *qua* existing there is a question about truth, that abstract reduplication [*Reduplikation*] of truth recurs; but existence itself, existence in the questioner, who does indeed exist, holds the two factors apart, one from the other, and reflection shows two relations."[4]

The concept of reduplication appears at key points in a number of Kierkegaard's texts. Depending on the context, it overlaps, or is even identified with the notion of "redoubling" (*Fordobelse*).[5] It indicates aspects of an existing individual's relation to truth which no objective analysis can capture. Specifically, it concerns the way in which a person exists in the truth or expresses it in their life; and this in turn reflects Kierkegaard's understanding of the human self as spirit. This means that the self does not merely know truths but knows itself in knowing truths. When it comes to irreducibly subjective truths—meaning those in which the existing person has a decisive interest, but which admit of no objective determination—this reduplication encompasses both the appropriation of the truth and its existential expression. In turn, that expression to communication cannot be direct: the subjectivity of truth could only be betrayed if it were reduced to a result, a directly appropriable piece of objective knowledge. Communication, therefore, must consist in awakening of the capability of the other to reduplicate the truth in their own existence. Such an awakening cannot be forced.

Implicit in the notion of reduplication, then, is an account of subjectivity, existence, truth, and communication. However, what is often missed in analyses of this concept is its root in logical investigations which go back to Aristotle. The logical form of reduplication, I argue, not only sheds a new light on Kierkegaard's use of the concept, it also connects him in significant ways to wider conceptual innovations in Kantian and post-Kantian thought, where reduplication implicitly or (in the case of Schelling) explicitly structures attempts to conceive the relationship between thought and reality without grounding that relationship on a transcendence: a source or a goal that exceeds and donates to thought and reality their being within an ultimately harmonious creation.

By extension, innovations centered on reduplication—at once logical and ontological—have implications for a political theology which turns on the power of subjects immanent to their world. On the one hand, reduplication challenges decisionistic or ontotheological models of political theology by situating the subject as the reduplication of the *ontological gap*, the minimal difference necessary for immanence to express itself. In other words, the redoubled subject embodies the structurally necessary but existentially contingent failure of the world to be wholly at one with itself and thus opens the possibility for the world to be deranged and disturbed from within its immanent heart. Examples of such moves are contained in thinkers as disparate as Slavoj Žižek and Judith Butler.[6]

The stakes of this dilemma will be sketched by linking the philosophical application of reduplication, the concept of life and the persistence of Christian supersessionism. Kant, Kierkegaard, and Schelling resolve the ontological gap by appealing to life. Life is posited as an overcoming of death, not by means of transcendent escape but by refiguring the lack that is death into the engine of life itself: life is a redoubling of this lack. The ability of the living to relate to itself and to move into a future is underwritten by this recuperation of a lack internal to life: a living (beyond) death. Christian supersessionism determines this life-death dynamic through characterizing Judaism as the epitome of unlife, to be swallowed up in Christian life. I will suggest that such anti-Judaism also represents an attempted disavowal of the political per se, one which occludes its own transcendent political structure.

The Logic of Reduplication

In the Western philosophical tradition, *reduplicatio* comes to name a proposition that "qualifies the relation of the predicate to the subject in the way in which a connective such as '*qua*' does."[7] The qualification of the predicate specifies an aspect under which the subject is being considered. For example: water *qua* chemical substance is composed of hydrogen and oxygen; a human being *qua* physical object has mass. Such qualifications do not exclude others which may present the subject in a very different light (water *qua* cultural symbol connotes life; or consider the possible implications of the qualifications, a human being *qua* conscious or *qua* moral agent).

Reduplication can take a variety of forms, but for our limited purposes, those identified by Roberto Poli as the locative and the reflexive are most relevant.[8]

In its locative form, the whole is reduplicated via a specific conceptually distinguishable part or aspect. The form of this reduplication is "A *qua* B is C" (this is the form used in the examples given earlier; Aristotle's example is "every man *qua* rational is risible"). This form allows the consideration of a subject under various aspects, such that predicates which might appear contradictory are nevertheless shown to be compatible, since reduplication distinguishes the distinctive quality under which they are applied.

The reflexive form of reduplication is when the whole is reduplicated through itself. Its form is "A *qua* A is B." This form can play a variety of roles. As Poli shows, it can, for example, distinguish between a predicate belonging inherently to a subject and one that belongs to a subject only by virtue of a role they assume (compare "Jones *qua* Jones is helpful and polite" to "Jones *qua* waiter is helpful and polite"—the second proposition would be compatible with Jones acting like a jerk in their off-duty time). An example with deeper moral connotations might be "a human being, simply considered as human, bears inalienable rights." This statement seems to identify what belongs to the essence of the human as human, and not under any more restrictive qualification, or as the bearer of any specific role or status.

It is because the reflexive form pertains to the essence of its subject that it plays a key role in Aristotle's metaphysics, defined as the study of being *qua* being. Without attempting to delve into the scholarly discussion of this phrase in any detail, its appearance, without even a predicate, suggests that Aristotle's concern is not the study of being in its ontic diversity but in itself: according to its most universal and abstract quality.

As Bäck makes clear, Aristotle's analysis, in this area of logic as in others, was only the start of a long tradition of investigation of how reduplication worked and what fallacies it needed to avoid. My concern is not with the specifics of this history but with the way that the use of reduplication as logical form gets caught up in ontological issues.[9] The reason for this seems to be that reduplication implies that the determination of an essence is inseparable from the aspect under which something is regarded; and that such determination under an aspect need imply no fundamental ontological splitting of the essence. This makes it fertile ground for thinkers concerned to emphasize irreducibly distinct aspects of reality, without committing to dualism, as was the case in the idealist era.

Kant: Regulative Ideas and Their Ontological Gap

Nineteenth-century idealism and anti-idealism share a Kantian legacy. Kant attempted to overcome the skeptical legacy of empiricism, without reverting to ungrounded metaphysical speculation. The matter of experience and the formative power of the understanding were both integral to the creation of an objectively (i.e., universally) intelligible world.

For Kant, as is well known, we conceive the world via the categories of the understanding as they are applied to experience. Consequently, no claim to metaphysical knowledge which transcends the realm of possible experience can be justified. However, Kant believes it is perfectly natural for the rational desire for such knowledge to arise. Reason—as distinct from understanding—aims at the unconditioned basis for our representations, knowledge and moral agency. It cannot deliver us cognitive access to any unconditioned ground but regulates—gives the rule and direction to—our intellectual and moral striving.

Notoriously, Kant is left with the problem of how to reconcile the parts of his philosophical system which seem to be in tension or even contradictory. This works on at least two levels. First, there is the contrast between the understanding and reason. The understanding renders conditioned things knowable; reason regulates, guides, and inspires the understanding by creating an idea of the unconditioned. The issue here is that the rational idea, which works to inspire and complete the work of the understanding, depends on a claim to access the unconditioned, which the understanding rules out. The second level on which Kant's thought appears to be riven by opposition is of course between nature and freedom. As known by the understanding, nature is a closed and determined system. However, as the arena for moral action, it must be a realm in which freedom is possible and effective.

Kant's detailed attempts to address these gaps, including his third critique, are beyond the scope of this essay. The claim I would like to make, however, is that key to these attempts is a kind of reduplication. This is perhaps most clearly stated in the *Critique of Pure Reason*, where Kant draws our attention to the *as if* structure which governs (and limits) metaphysical claims. For example, Kant argues that "in the domain of theology, we must view everything that can belong to the context of possible experience *as if* this experience formed an absolute but at the same time completely dependent and *sensibly* conditioned unity, and yet also at the same time *as if* the sum of all appearances (the sensible world itself) had a single, highest and all-sufficient ground beyond itself, namely, a self-subsistent, original, creative reason."[10] Similarly, we can only cognize the world as determined; but our practical reason requires us to live in the world *as if* it were susceptible to the influence of free action.

The world is thus reduplicated: one and the same reality (or so our reason posits) is not only *viewed* under irreducibly different aspects; these different aspects—the world *qua* theoretically cognizable/the world *qua* arena of moral action—legitimate fundamentally different modes of being and activity. As Kirill Chepurin puts it: "There is nowhere to begin within the dogmatic status quo of the real, which is why we must begin, positively, necessarily and immanently, from a utopian point of the ideal's own facticity, out of which it then immanently unfolds—via two causalities, that of experience (ideas of reason) and that of morality (the same ideas as postulates). The theoretical origin-as-if and the practical origin thus coincide or are reduplicated."[11] It is possible to discern a similar move in *Religion within the Limits of Mere Reason*. Here, Kant affirms both that morality has no need of religion and that morality inevitably leads to religion. Moral law, as autonomous, needs no external authority or guarantor. However, morality also leads us to will the highest good, which Kant characterizes as a world in which there is the coincidence of perfect virtue and perfect happiness. Since this is an appropriate object of our moral will, the highest good must be possible (since it is incoherent to say a person is morally obliged to will what is not possible). And it is only possible, Kant argues, if we posit the existence of an almighty and perfectly good being who is able to bring it about.

Practical reason thus leads us to religion; but this is quite different from any theoretical attempt to prove the existence of God. We are required to believe in God as a regulative principle of our moral striving but can claim no theoretical knowledge of that God's existence. Again, all hangs on a reduplication: seeing the world *as* cognizable (and so always conditioned and determined) or *as* the theatre of an unconditional free moral vocation.

The reduplication of the world allows for a nonreductive synthesis of what is machinic and what is free. The synthesis itself, however, is not cognized but postulated as a rule. There is no totalizing attempt to comprehend the ontological gap between the conditioned and the unconditioned. Kant's reduplications are, in a sense, the reduplication of this gap (the irreducible opposition of the determined and the free *qua* grounded in the supersensible). Such a structure is arguably key to understanding the various ways in which post-Kantian thought seeks to respond to difference: otherness is construed as unconditionally constitutive of (or prior to) thinking and cannot be wholly reduced to a vanishing moment which thought comprehends.

Such a reduplication thus forms the possibility of a utopian political theology, one at odds with the Schmittian version. The world is non-totalizable as a field of both theoretical investigation and moral action. Politics proceeds theologically, not because it is founded on theological claims about authority and revelation of the unconditioned, but because it freely sets before it the unconditioned as an idea of reason. This idea relativizes all established authorities and opens the horizon to endless possible approximations to a democratic and cosmopolitan future.

There is, however, a way in which this utopian rendering of the ontological gap takes on a more disturbing form in Kant's work and beyond. In *Religion*, Kant narrates the emergence of Jesus and Christianity from Judaism. This emergence cannot be one of continuity, since Judaism, for Kant, is a religion of dogmatic subservience to law rather than true moral autonomy. In fact, given that Kant argues for "true religion" being wholly centered on moral autonomy, Judaism is "not a religion at all, but simply the union of a number of individuals, who since they belonged to a particular stock, established themselves into a community under purely political laws, hence not into a church."[12] Judaism contributes nothing to Christianity beyond being its mere "physical occasion."[13] In essence, it is secular and political in the sense of being bound by external coercive laws, with no authentic religious dimension. It is ethnically limited, this-worldly, materialistic, and dedicated to a "mechanical cult."[14] The consequence is that Christianity arises as the "total abandonment" of Judaism.[15] Kant immediately nuances this a little to say that the Judaism of Jesus's day prepared the ground for Christianity, but only to the extent that it had already been mingled with Greek ideas.

Judaism thus provides us with not *a* figure, but *the* figure of what is mechanical; and the mechanical must be wholly abandoned by the moral religion of Christianity. The old supersession of letter by Spirit, old Israel by new is played out, in a way which gives a specific character to the machine/freedom split. Rather than being seen as irreducible aspects of one reduplicated world, they are entirely at odds.

This is no mere contingency. The call to be universal citizens is defined by—is made possible by—the indelible rejection of Judaism, and of a certain kind of flesh and blood political community. In a sense, Kant's Christianity comes from nowhere, hence its utopian character. It is itself the expression of the ontological gap which makes moral hope possible, but this utopian "reduplication of the non-place" establishes itself in this text at least by weaponizing that gap against the Jews, who represent the stubborn refusal to abandon particularity.[16] Reduplication renders the gap irreducible, without abandoning either the scientific cognition of the conditioned world or moral striving for a cosmopolitan future; but it *also* feeds off the abandoned body of the Jew, whose inert form is the stepping stone toward a future freed from the merely "political." There is no Jew *qua* free or *qua* religious.

Schelling: Reduplication in the Organic Body

Kant circumscribes ontology in order to cure reason of its metaphysical pretenses. Ideas of reason—among which we can plausibly count that of a political utopia or perfect commonwealth—do not give us constitutive access to what there is but function regulatively to guide action and thought.

As Markus Gabriel has argued, it is this ontological modesty which German Idealism finds problematic. Kant is forced to assume the being of the knowing subject but cannot integrate this subjectivity into what it is possible to know. Knowing must take its own possibility for granted, which arguably presents an arbitrary and vicious circle for a philosophy with systematic ambitions. The idealists therefore argued that the existence of the subject cannot simply be treated as a brute fact or a given, somehow denuded of its worldliness. Some account must be made of how it is that the world *qua* subject can refer to and know itself.[17]

In other words, reduplication is not abandoned but radicalized, or turned back upon itself. What does it mean that the world is subject to reduplication, that the world appears *qua* world but also *qua* subject of that world? In the light of our previous section, this raises a further question: Does the radicalization and reflexivity of reduplication help us avoid the way it is subjected to a philosophical decision about who and what falls on either side of the mechanical/free boundary? Can it suspend the predetermined decision of who is friend and who is enemy? Or even: Who is human and who is not?

Clearly, all we can do is offer a brief foray into the vastness of German Idealism here. I choose Schelling's philosophy of identity, along with his later reflections upon it, for two reasons.

The first is Schelling's approach to determination. Previously, Spinoza's formula that all determination occurs through negation had been hugely influential on philosophy. Something is defined as the specific thing it is only because it is a limitation or negation of the infinite. Particular things are always characterized by lack: they are what they are because they are not this or that (and, ultimately, because they lack the fullness of infinity).

However, Schelling reverses the formula. For him, determination proceeds via affirmation, not negation. The finite is the positive expression of the absolute. The figure which delineates a finite being is not therefore merely negative but expressive, in a particular way, of the fullness of the infinite. In every finite reality, the infinite is exhibited.[18]

The significance for us is that a more thoroughgoing reduplication becomes possible: there is no opposition between the world *qua* finite conditions and the world *qua* absolute and unconditioned, since every finite being expresses the infinite, and infinite does not negate the finite.

This leads to the second reason for turning to Schelling's philosophy of identity: as Manfred Frank shows in some detail, Schelling explicitly drew on the tradition of logical reduplication to set out his position. The formula for identity is $A=A$. Frank argues that Schelling follows Kant's distinction between identity understood merely logically as an empty tautology and an *ontological* principle of identity which "forms *a genuine relation between two things* that are not obviously one."[19]

Schelling uses this notion to push further Kant's reduplicative project. Frank shows how Schelling cites the notion of "reduplicative positing" in order to clarify the sense in which identity and nonidentity are one. If $a=b$, it is because "*a* steps out from the implicit ability to be *b*, and then *a* consequently is *a* multiplied with itself."[20] In a later Munich lecture course, Schelling relates this more closely to the $A=A$ formula in which "the A posited as A is no longer the simple A, but A, which is A, not—is and is not, but rather is decided."[21] Explicitly invoking the "older logic" of *reduplicatio*, Schelling uses this logic to structure an ontology which is neither rationalist, empiricist nor even transcendental. The finite is an expression, an intensive particularization of the infinite, in which the infinite becomes "decided," an aspect of it becomes affirmed and manifest. Commenting on Schelling's claim that "the absolute is that which is *of itself* the affirming and the affirmed," Frank argues that "the formula 'of itself' is meant reduplicatively . . . each, the affirming and the affirmed . . . is the *entire* absolute."[22]

Important consequences follow from this model, if it is successful. First, it means that identity is not a relative byproduct of the dialectic, but its encompassing reality. Furthermore, that encompassing reality is not to be primarily identified with mind rather than nature. Mind is a manifestation of identity, an aspect under which it is reduplicated; but so, equally is nature. The absolute remains "unprethinkable": it cannot be subject in advance to any predicate, let alone that of consciousness or sovereign intention.[23]

The gap between subject and object is not nullified by this move, nor is it—in Hegelian mode—the engine that drives the philosophical project. As Frank puts it, referring to Schelling's early philosophy of identity, "absolute identity is radically and completely independent of its *relata* and cannot be explained as a 'product' of their interaction."[24] Representation and dialectic are relativized as philosophical attempts to determine the absolute by operating upon it from a transcendent perspective, above the fray; rather, in absolute identity's reduplication, the absolute affirms and decides itself immanently, while remaining foreclosed to philosophical decision.

However, a caveat remains. A great influence upon Schelling's approach is the Kantian model of the organism as cause and effect of itself. The organism provides a manifestation of the absolute, which, to some degree, is able to express differentiation and identity in a single body. In his early philosophy of nature, Schelling notes the original duplicity of the organism along these lines. On the one hand, the organism's identity remains inviolate and unreachable; nevertheless, it is clearly "excited," seemingly affected by its environment. Schelling's resolution of this tension is to claim that the organism is itself the medium through which the external acts upon it.[25]

The concern here is that in his efforts to avoid explaining change by reference to what is a merely external (and so transcendent to the immanent organic body), Schelling elevates a principle of self-affecting life to a controlling position. However fruitful such a shift may be, the prioritization of life, especially organized life, cannot but subjugate all that is unliving or placed lower on the hierarchy of life.[26]

If this concern seems overblown, it is worth considering the way in which Christianity is understood in *The Philosophy of Art*, a key part of the early philosophy of identity. There is no mistaking the imprint of critical approaches to scripture and doctrine in this text, but the way Christianity is presented sustains older motifs. Christ plants the seed of a "higher morality" within Judaism, which itself needs the influence of foreign peoples in order to be purified of its merely national character. For Christianity, by contrast, the theater of salvation is that of universal history, conceived as an arena of moral action. This is achieved through the implantation of Oriental ideas into Occidental soil, since only this combination of opposites can "generate life."[27]

The manifestation of the infinite in the finite offers an opening to universal, democratic politics; but it does so through the geographical movement which dissolves Jewish territory in order to root spirit in European soil. Rome nurtures the seed, drawing all peoples to itself—and it is the "Germanic migrations" which take on the character of universal natural law and the true beginning of universal history.[28]

Schelling's ontological commitments, although shaped in a Kantian milieu, are nevertheless very different from Kant's. However, while the shift toward a more fundamentally ontological understanding of reduplication helps to resolve the lingering dualism of Kant's system, the residue of supersessionist politics persists: life—understood as European Christian life—is what ultimately must find a way beyond its Jewish (and other) material roots. Spirit must trump the flesh, undermining the radical potential of reduplication.

Kierkegaard: Reopening the Wound—Subjectivity and Reduplication

Kierkegaard was clearly concerned that the idealist response to the legacy of Kant nullified individually existing subjectivity, subordinating it to a quantitative conception of being. Insisting on the gap between thought and being, he nevertheless offers an innovative way beyond Kant. Drawing on the notion of reduplication, Kierkegaard seeks to articulate a notion of the subject which avoids either quantifying it or mystifying it. As discussed earlier, he uses the logical form of the *qua* statement in articulating his own existential sense of reduplication.

Reduplication is required for the existing subject, because she does not stand in a direct relation to truth. The later work, *Practice in Christianity*, spells this out more clearly:

> The being of truth is not the direct redoubling of being in relation to thinking, which gives only thought-being, safeguards thinking only against being a brain-figment that is not, guarantees validity to thinking, that what is thought is—that is, has validity. No, the being of truth is the redoubling of truth within yourself, within me, within him, that your life, my life, his life expresses the truth approximately in the striving for it, that your life, my life, his life is approximately the being of the truth in the striving for it, just as the truth was in Christ a *life* for he was the truth.[29]

Kierkegaard describes two levels of reduplication. The first is an abstract one: truth is a redoubling of being, in that one can consider truth itself as something that *is*: "Truth *is*—that is, truth is a redoubling [*Fordobelse*]. Truth is the first, but truth's other, that it *is* is the same as the first; this, its being, is the abstract form of truth. In this way it is expressed that truth is not something simple but in an entirely abstract sense a redoubling, which is nevertheless cancelled at the very same moment."[30] This reduplication—truth, insofar as it is, or truth *qua* being—does not, for Kierkegaard take us beyond abstraction. That only occurs when truth is redoubled in existence, when the truth is of a kind that can be and is expressed in a life. In its Christian form (at least as set out in *Practice*), this involves the individual in struggle with the world and in particular with any established order (secular or religious) which appropriates sacred power to itself.

Reduplication is thus a question of form. Truth *qua* abstract form has the being of thought; truth *qua* subjective form has the being of life. Objective truth concerns the *what*; subjective truth the *how* of existence. Kierkegaard wants to separate thought from lived being, or existence, so that we do not make the mistake of trying to resolve issues of subjective interest and commitment by means suited only to abstract and objective problems. And this gives to individual existence its radical, anti-systematic and potentially politically subversive edge. The living individual is not be subsumed into the world (understood as an organized system of distributed meaning).[31]

It seems we have reached a point of separation from both Kant and Schelling here. In different ways, their use of reduplication seeks to suture the ontological gap between nature and freedom, or the real and the ideal. Kierkegaard's approach appears to reject such systematic ontological concerns, even in their regulative Kantian form, in order to put the whole emphasis on the existential striving of the individual and the rupture of existence from thought.

However, this appearance is partly deceptive. Kierkegaard is not simply rejecting ontology, but only certain forms which make existential, temporal subjectivity and its passion into a secondary, vanishing moment. Indeed, the disjunction between abstract and existential reduplication only appears against the backdrop of a continuity: the reexpression of being in truth and truth in being, potentiates both abstract and existential forms of reduplication. Existential striving is possible *because* being and truth are redoubled in this way, and therefore not reducible to a single, consistent, and homogenous set of predicates.

The other side of this continuity concerns that little term *life*. In his own way, Kierkegaard prioritizes life over unlife. And the supersessionist undertones of how this priority is constructed return.

It is in a "life" that this redoubling finds expression. However, it is first and foremost a *Christian* life that is meant. The contrast with Judaism can be traced in *Works of Love*, where we read that a human being is considered as irreducibly temporal and eternal, that "this eternal redoubles in him."[32] The eternal—like love—goes out of itself but remains in relation with itself. The relation or communication and the inwardness are one and the same; and it is easy to see how the logical tradition of reduplication stands in the background to this articulation of the human qua temporal/eternal or qua outward/inward, without the human self being irretrievably split by these distinct aspects.

Kierkegaard takes up this theme in the conclusion to the book. He talks of the Christian "like for like," in which one's actuality—even one's God—is a "rendition" (*Gjengivelse*) of one's inward attitude. In other words, if one lives in vengeance and enmity, or if one lives in love, then one's actuality and one's God will take on that aspect. Indeed, "God is actually himself this pure like for like, the pure rendition of how you yourself are."[33] God is the possibility of this reduplication, such that God is the ontological ground of the rendition, not merely one of its objects. Granted, the precise terminology of reduplication is lacking here, but the sense is surely the same.

Notably, this pure rendition of actuality via inwardness is starkly contrasted with Judaism. The Jewish like for like—"an eye for an eye"—is external, equated with "the worldly and the bustling."[34] It is "abolished" and replaced by the Christian version.[35] By implication, Judaism is a merely temporal phenomenon, lacking eternity and inwardness. Reduplication, here at least, wears a Christian mask.

My intent here is not the simplistic one of discrediting authors *in toto* where some evidence of anti-Jewishness appears in their thought. Reduplication in fact offers an alternative to models of truth and allied models of sovereignty, in which the meaning of the world is dictated to it from above. The problem is that this is often still overcoded with the structure of previous emergence: that of Christianity from Judaism. And that emergence is turned into a rupture, an abolition of the Jewish worldly political theology in favor of a hallucinated release into pure spirit. Unable to detect the political grounds of its own decision, Christian supersessionism raises itself above politics and so reinscribes a malevolent transcendence at the heart of the definition of the world.

The Different Registers of Reduplication

The critical question to be faced here is: to what extent is reduplication also a recuperation? Thought's domination of the real is resisted in the name of life; but life in this context is itself a dialectical conception, in which tensions are resolved or existentially held in a coincidence of opposites. The reduplicated real is inevitably figured as organic, holistic, and subject to decision. Even when, as for Kierkegaard, the real is the actuality of finite existence.

According to Laruelle, "Every notion of a philosophical spirit is surreptitiously assumed sufficient for itself and for the real that is being thought. For this the philosophical spirit is redoubled or reflected in itself, forming a double with itself, assertion and reassertion; in this way the philosophical assures itself of itself against the hazards of the real."[36] The spirit of philosophy, in the complexity of reduplication, I am suggesting, remains a spirit defined over and against the letter and the body of Judaism, and all that Judaism represents in this tradition: slavery, externality, mechanism, animality, diabolical opposition—and politics.

Is another reduplication possible? I suggest there is: but it would have to be one that explicitly foregrounds its own failure to recuperate and resolve the real. This is the subtext of the positions we have been exploring so far, because each of them deflates the sovereign claim of Christian revelation. Each treats the Christian *qua* something else: *qua* rational, *qua* natural, *qua* existential. Reduplication therefore renders the Christian *generic*. And while this might be a basis on which to reassert Christian dominance over the world, it need not be.

Reduplication would not posit the ontological gap in order to suture it, but in order *to express it again*—keeping, as Kierkegaard would say, the wound of the negative open. It is the irreducibility of this gap to which reduplication lends itself: to recall our earlier analysis, reduplication allows the determination of the essence of something under a particular aspect *without* thereby splitting that essence. The identity of the real resists conceptual capture while grounding specific determinations.

This is both an immanent structure, since it does not elevate any immanent principle (such as life) to quasi-transcendent status. It is also a potentially fruitful one for political theology, because it facilitates thinking about the indelible wounds and subjugations forged in and through the subjects of political worlds, without evacuating subjects of their worldless identity and resistance. Reduplication, as logical, ontological, and existential intervention, expresses the subject *qua* the inconsistency of the world. It could be an important tool in articulating theories of political subjectivity and resistance outside the parameters set by the discourse of sovereignty.

Notes

1. See François Laruelle, *Philosophies of Difference: A Critical Introduction to Non-Philosophy*, trans. Rocco Gangle (London: Continuum, 2010).

2. Rodolph Gasché, *The Tain of the Mirror: Derrida and the Philosophy of Reflection* (Cambridge, MA: Harvard University Press, 1986).

3. For an exploration of the political significance of Kierkegaard's ontology and "fractured dialectic" in relation to idealism, see Michael O'Neill Burns, *Kierkegaard and the Matter of Philosophy: A Fractured Dialectic* (London: Rowman and Littlefield, 2015).

4. Søren Kierkegaard, *Concluding Unscientific Postscript to the Philosophical Fragments*, vol. 1, trans. Howard and Edna Hong (Princeton, NJ: Princeton University Press, 1992), 191–192.

5. See Wojciech Kaftanski, "Redoubling/Reduplication," in *Kierkegaard's Concepts*, Tome 5, *Objectivity to Sacrifice*, ed. Steven M. Emmanuel, William McDonald, and Jon Stewart (Abingdon and New York: Routledge, 2016), 205–212. In a discussion focused on Kierkegaard's *Works of Love*, Martin Andic argues that "redoubling" concerns the way a person understands herself as living the truth; reduplication focuses on the need to communicate that truth. He also argues that the primary act of redoubling comes from God. See Martin Andic, "Love's Redoubling and the Eternal Like for Like," in *International Kierkegaard Commentary*, vol. 16, *Works of Love*, ed. Robert Perkins (Macon, GA: Mercer University Press, 1999), 9–38. I am not convinced such a strict division holds throughout Kierkegaard's use of these terms, or by the necessary reference to a transcendent operation of grace. For my general understanding of transcendence and immanence in Kierkegaard, see Steven Shakespeare, *Kierkegaard and the Refusal of Transcendence* (Basingstoke and New York: Palgrave Macmillan, 2015).

6. See, inter alia, Slavoj Žižek, *The Fragile Absolute: Or, why is the Christian Legacy Worth Fighting For?* (London: Verso, 2000), and Judith Butler, "Critique, Coercion and Sacred Life in Benjamin's 'Critique of Violence,'" in *Political Theologies: Public Religions in a Post-Secular World*, Hent de Vries and Lawrence E. Sullivan (New York: Fordham University Press, 2006), 201–219.

7. Allan Bäck, *On Reduplication: Logical Theories of Qualification* (Brill: Leiden, 1996), 1.

8. Roberto Poli, "Formal Aspects of Reduplication," in *Logic and Logical Philosophy* 2 (1994): 91–92.

9. For a discussion of the role of reduplication in debates about nominalism and the incarnation, see Bäck, *On Reduplication*, 319–352.

10. Immanuel Kant, *Critique of Pure Reason*, trans. Norman Kemp Smith (Basingstoke: Macmillam, 1933), 551; A672/B700.

11. Kirill Chepurin, "Beginning with Kant: Utopia, Immanence, and the Origin of German Idealism," *Russian Journal of Philosophy and Humanities* 1, no. 2 (2017): 83.

12. Immanuel Kant, *Religion Within the Boundaries of Mere Reason and Other Writings*, ed. and trans. Allen Wood and George di Giovanni (Cambridge: Cambridge University Press, 1998), 130.

13. Kant, 130.

14. Kant, 132.

15. Kant, 132.

16. Chepurin, "Beginning with Kant," 89.

17. Markus Gabriel, *Transcendental Ontology: Essays in German Idealism* (London: Bloomsbury, 2011).

18. For a full analysis of the philosophy of identity, see Daniel Whistler, *Schelling's Theory of Symbolic Language: Forming the System of Identity* (Oxford: Oxford University Press, 2013).

19. Manfred Frank, "'Identity of identity and non-identity': Schelling's path to the 'absolute system of identity,'" in *Interpreting Schelling: Critical Essays*, Lara Ostaric (Cambridge: Cambridge University Press, 2014), 123.

20. Schelling, quoted in Frank, 130.

21. Schelling, quoted in Frank, 131.

22. Frank, 137.

23. On the relation of logic to *Naturphilosophie* in Schelling, see Iain Hamilton Grant, "Everything Is Primal Germ or Nothing Is: The Deep Field Logic of Nature," in *Symposium: Canadian Journal of Continental Philosophy* 19, no. 1 (2015): 106–124.

24. Frank, "Identity of identity and non-identity," 143.

25. See F. W. J. Schelling, *First Outline of a System of the Philosophy of Nature*, trans. Keith R. Peterson (New York: State University of New York Press, 2004), 107.

26. This lays the basis for Schelling's later racial theory, in which less developed races must disappear following contact with more developed ones. See K. F. A. Schelling, ed., *Schellings Werke* (Stuttgart: Cotta, 1856–1861), 2.1:490–515.

27. F. W. J. Schelling, *The Philosophy of Art*, trans. Douglas W. Stott (Minneapolis: University of Minnesota Press, 1989), 58–59.

28. Schelling, *Philosophy of Art*, 60.

29. Søren Kierkegaard, *Practice in Christianity*, trans. Howard and Edna Hong (Princeton, NJ: Princeton University Press, 1991), 205.

30. Kierkegaard, *Concluding Unscientific Postscript*, 190.

31. Schelling's work after his identity philosophy is of course much closer to Kierkegaard, at least on the need to recognize an irruption of subjective freedom which is not necessitated by any abstract philosophical system. However, for the purposes of the contrasting exposition in this essay, I have opted for Kierkegaard's more decisive break with the idealist logics.

32. Søren Kierkegaard, *Works of Love*, trans. Howard and Edna Hong (Princeton, NJ: Princeton University Press, 1998), 280.

33. Kierkegaard, 385.

34. Kierkegaard, 383.

35. Kierkegaard, 376.

36. François Laruelle, foreword to Katerina Kolozova, *Cut of the Real: Subjectivity in Poststructuralist Philosophy* (New York: Columbia University Press, 2014), x.

On the General Secular Contradiction
Secularization, Christianity, and Political Theology

ALEX DUBILET

The general omission of Karl Marx from contemporary discussions of political theology is surprising given that "On the Jewish Question" not only offers one of the first frontal critiques of the modern state, it does so through a resolutely political-theological prism. Significantly, the essay does not critique a particular form of the state in order to reconstruct it on some supposedly more legitimate basis. It seeks instead to delineate the presence of the theological within the political form and operations of the state as such. Marx does not confuse political theology with the question of the theological legitimation of politics, as though theology was merely a name for an external surplus; rather, he diagnoses the structural and historical interrelatedness of the two fields and their operations. In his elaboration of the essential analogies of theological and political concepts and operations, Marx partakes in political theology—but he does so by deforming its accepted coordinates, rejecting at once the liberal statist visions of modernity *and* any theological or quasi-theological critiques of that modernity that emerge from a bolstering of the structures (and strictures) of transcendence, in order to think outside the field structured by this duality across its various articulations. It is the danger of the resulting realignment, which has the power to redraw the entire problematic as well as the status, morphology, and significance of its central concepts, that renders Marx's exclusion understandable but also engenders the exigency to challenge it. What follows seeks to rectify this genealogical lacuna through an exploration of the transformations entailed by "On the Jewish Question" for political theology as a discourse—an exploration that will reassess some of the discourse's foundational conceptual contours, including the significance of immanence and transcendence, the relation of Christianity to the secular state, and the link between mediation and sovereignty. Resisting the persistent counterposing of the Christian to the secular, it will instead reorient political theology around the drive for delegitimation and the abolition of the order of the world.

From certain perspectives, often liberal in inclination, the insights of political theology are reducible to the cunning deployments of theological supplements within the political, as in, for example, the state appealing to transcendent authority for its legitimation, sanctification, or grounding.[1] To follow such a definition would, in turn, imply the critical necessity of displacing or exiting political theology by freeing the political from its contamination by religion and theology. The theological supplement would be merely a foreign element to be subtracted—or overcome with time—in order to perfect the freedom of the political. Were the question as simple as that, were it a question of a supplement, a transcendent theological legitimation, then Bruno Bauer, the target of Marx's critique, would be right: all that would be required to perfect the state would be to free it from its theological sanctifications. In fact, however, it is precisely at the moment of such subtraction that the power of the political-theological critique becomes truly necessary and operative.

Exiting from political theology is not nearly so easy to accomplish, because the logic of political theology—formulated by Carl Schmitt and earlier (and with a distinctly different aim) by Marx—is not that of the supplement but that of structural systematic analogy and historical transfer. The import of political theology lies in the diagnosis of a theological grammar operating at the heart of the secular state and of a more general transference of theological concepts into political ones.[2] It is not a question of use or of legitimation, as much as of the secularized persistence of theological concepts and operations within the putatively secular state. Hence Schmitt's famous dictum: "All significant concepts of the modern theory of the state are secularized theological concepts not only because of their historical development . . . but also because of their systematic structure."[3] Or, one might call to mind Jan Assmann's broader definition of political theology as encompassing not merely the secularization of theological concepts, but the more complex set of movements of secularization and theologization that inflect most of the fundamental concepts of Western modernity.[4] Either way, the theological element is not external to the political, but internal to its operation of power. It marks not its contingent failure or incompletion, but the nature of its operation according to its concept and, as such, cannot be purified through subtraction or evolution. In other words, political theology is important as a problematic and a discourse not because it legitimates power transcendently, thereby necessitating secular critique—allowing for the self-satisfied restaging of Enlightenment's critique of religion—but precisely because it undercuts the triumphalist narrative of secularized modernity, disallowing its desires to dissociate and wash its hands of Christianity and enter into a world of secular self-legitimation.[5]

This is at the heart of Marx's response to Bauer's critique of the limitations inherent to the so-called Christian state, which for Marx is precisely "the *imperfect* state and Christianity serves as *supplement* and *sanctification* of this imperfection."[6] The critical task that Marx bequeaths is more complicated than simply the affirmation of a secular politics of the modern state against its theological distortions. Hence Marx's dialectical formula: "The perfected Christian state is not the so-called *Christian* state which recognizes Christianity as its foundation, as the state religion, and which therefore excludes other religions. The perfected Christian state is rather the *atheist* state, the *democratic* state, the state which relegates religion to the level of other elements of civil society" (222). In other words, it is the state as such, one that is no longer grounded through a theological supplement, that is the ultimately Christian one, in the sense that it fundamentally operates, as I will show shortly, according to the diremptive logic of Christianity. The conceptual operations of Christianity are not overcome into the neutrality of the state, rather the power of Christianity is exercised in and by the secular state when it operates according to its very concept and power.[7]

Exiting from the apparatus of political theology, according to this diagnosis, entails not merely moving beyond theology into the brave new world of pure politics, into the secular human order freed of all illusions, but the subversion of the conceptual analogy and transference of operations that structures and co-imbricates the theological and the political. The fundamental question is neither a theological legitimation of politics nor the formation of purely secular political realm, but the critical tracing of a complex morphology and the interleafing exchange of concepts that prevents theology and secular thought from being separated out into distinct containers and played off each other. This is the power of Marx's insistence that "The so-called Christian state is the Christian negation of the state, but is certainly not the political realization of Christianity" (222). The political realization of Christianity, by contrast, is found in the purely secular state: Christianity operates as religion *as well as* the name for the political form of modernity itself. In his own way, Marx here prefigures a claim articulated recently by Gil Anidjar, that secularism is the name Christianity gives itself in modernity, one of the ways "by which Christianity *forgot and forgave* itself" and rendered itself invisible and neutral.⁸

As has been frequently explored, the critique of the limits of political emancipation—the attainment of the equal rights and equal standing before the state—is at the heart of Marx's essay.⁹ Marx suggest that we examine political emancipation critically, since it always and necessarily remains *merely* political and ideal; but he does so also for another reason. Political emancipation marks also the emancipation of the political itself—a process through which the political separates itself from and disburdens itself of material life, establishing itself as an autonomous realm, coinciding with the state. The state creates its subject-citizens in the very same gesture in which it emancipates itself from the material elements that make up the life of those individuals, elements that now become permanently consigned to civil society. It is rendered an autonomous and pure sphere by making everything else count as merely "non-political distinctions" of civil society (219). The autonomy of the political and its concentration in the state is an act of purification that allows it to stand above the now-depoliticized material life, which is not abolished in the process but is instead rendered a presupposition for the state. The result is a universality of "the standpoint of the state" (*Staatsgesichtspunkt*) standing above all the spheres of material life that it has relegated to civil society as apolitical, of merely private concern (219).

This critique of the political, of its purification and genesis, is revealed as a political-theological critique at the moment when the structure so enacted is shown to be a secularization—and a fulfillment—of Christianity. The very relation of state to civil society carries a genetic and structural analogy within it: "Where the political state has attained its full degree of development man leads a double life, a life in heaven and a life on earth, not only in his mind, in his consciousness, but in *reality*" (220). As secular, the state in fact enacts a double life, whose diremption carries a direct trace of secularization. The theological grammar of the celestial and the terrestrial, "a life in heaven and a life on earth" (220), is secularized and materialized into the grammar of the state and civil society. This secularization preserves the form and logic while enacting a displacement of site and register, by means of which the theological is divested of the substantive need to justify and defend itself. For Marx, this secularization marks not the decline but rather the genuine realization of Christianity, by which the theological diremption is rendered into one that actually structures real lived experience. The modern state is the worldly truth of Christianity and not its radical overcoming. It materializes a theological transcendence in the secular, or as Marx formulates it: "The so-called Christian state needs the Christian religion to complete itself as a *state*. The democratic state, the true state, does not need religion for its completion. On the contrary, it can discard religion [*von der Religion abstrahiren*] because in it the human foundation of religion is realized in a secular [*weltliche*] way" (223).

To say that the secular state realizes Christianity is not to embrace the West by taking up secularization as a uniting thread that constitutes it.[10] Rather, it is to insist that it is not enough to affirm secularism to break with Christianity, just as, in contrast, it is insufficient to reaffirm Christianity to break with secularism. In other words, Marx's move is to avow that the central operation of secular power is not purely secular but, through a set of complex transferences and mutations, a secularized Christian one: "The final form of the Christian state is one which recognizes itself as state and disregards the religion of its members" (226). The modern state is not a break with Christianity, but a transmutation of Christianity—its very political realization—into a purely political and self-declared neutral and impartial space. It is precisely through the production of this neutral space, which insofar as it is neutral is also unmarked and invisible, that the secular state is, paradoxically, "the *practical* expression of [Christianity's] universal religious significance" (226).

Is there not, however, something fundamentally mistaken in such a political theological approach to Marx? After all, Marx's methodological insistence seems clear enough: "We do no turn secular questions into theological questions. We turn theological questions into secular questions" (217). Despite appearances, this is hardly a call for a worldly, secular criticism. Rather than rendering theology immaterial, what Marx suggests is that theological questions in modernity always have to be analyzed within the ambit of secular power. We fundamentally mistake the way secular power works if we take "religion" in modernity as offering the appropriate or sufficient object of polemic, rather than indicating something that is repeatedly produced and reproduced as an object and a problem by the state, its powers of sovereignty and mediation, its morphological relation to the life of civil society. In other words, all theoretical investments in or cathexes on religion are cases of mistaken displacement that render invisible the more foundational dialectics of secular state power in which they materially participate. "The contradiction in which the adherent of a particular religion finds himself in relation to his citizenship is only *one aspect* of the general *secular contradiction between the political state and civil society*" (226). The Jewish question—as other questions of religious difference—is produced as a question, as a problem, by the dominant epistemic regime of secular state power that incessantly engenders a depoliticized private sphere of civil society, while seeing it as a problem requiring regulation and management.[11] To fixate on religion, or religious difference, as an obstacle to freedom, as Bauer or contemporary defenders of secularism do, is to fall into a fundamental inversion, mistaking an effect for a cause and failing to grapple with the general secular contradiction. For religion as a distinct object and problem is produced and reproduced in modernity by the secular state apparatus: being relegated to civil society by the state, it is forced to fit into the criteria of the normative category of religion entailed by the modern regime of secular power—relegated to the private sphere, depoliticized, centered on belief, lodged into the interiority of the subject, and so on.[12] In insisting that critique remains theological when it fails to be posed correctly, Marx was the first to insist on the primacy of the secular state as the dominant politico-epistemic framework in which religion and religious difference become formulated, managed, and reproduced. This is what is entailed in turning theological questions into secular ones.

As Marx notes, using the case of the United States, complete political emancipation leads not to the abolition of religion, but to its vigorous flourishing, which occurs as religion is "relegated to the level of private interest" and becomes "a private whim, a caprice" (221–222). Insofar as political emancipation entails the elevation of the state above material life—rendering it apolitical, something presupposed and to be managed—it also produces the modern concept of religion and its lived, materialized reality. Marx was one of the first to arrive at the truth that religion as a privatized phenomenon centered on belief is an effect of secular political modernity, one of the byproducts of the formation of the modern state.[13] As such, rather than subscribing to the modern concept of religion, Marx should be seen as critically delineating its logic and elaborating a genealogy of its formation.[14] Indeed, turning theological questions into secular ones requires inserting them into broader analytics of secular power and exploring the ways in which secular power produces religion and allows it to flourish—offering it up as a reified target for polemic and critique, while dissimulating its own primacy and productivity. This is the power of Marx's insistence to "no longer see religion as the *basis* but simply as a *phenomenon* of secular narrowness" (217).

According to Talal Asad's definition of secularism as a political doctrine and the secular as an epistemic category that undergirds its assumptions and sensibilities,[15] not only is Marx not a secular thinker, it is the position of secularism that he fundamentally targets in his polemic with Bauer, who poses the conceptual logic of secularism as the ideal horizon. For Bauer, the religious opposition between Jews and Christians is a problem that is to be overcome through recourse to a properly secular state: religious difference is a material difference that must be overcome into the universality of citizenship. This proposal is precisely the project of secularism, the restructuring of the subject and its allegiances within a nation-state paradigm. It declares that it is necessary to renounce religion as a special marker, as a marker of substantial difference, in order to be emancipated as citizens and members of civil society, of the civil life of the world, and to inhabit the liberal secular dream of a neutral space. By contrast, Marx's political theological reflections reject such a secularist distribution of concepts in order to confront Christianity's mutations through which it persists and is fully realized in the putatively secular life of the state. One might say that if theological criticism has to become secular criticism, then secular criticism has to be apprehended as political theological criticism, otherwise it fails to trace the transmuted persistence of Christianity in the political form of the state. In other words, because Christianity spans across the theologico-political morphological divide, it cannot be posed as exclusively a theological question, but must be posed as a political theological one—thereby disallowing all narration that would affirm the purified life of the secular freed from its links with Christianity.[16]

Therefore, Marx's quip that when "the question ceases to be *theological*, Bauer's criticism ceases to be critical" is hardly a call for a worldly, secular criticism (217). This would be to underestimate and misjudge the nature, scope, ontology, and operation of secular power. Indeed, the secularist argument morphologically reenacts the Christian operation that requires the conversion of the other toward a true religion: in both cases a (Jewish) remainder is seen as a culprit for unattained and incomplete universality. The state project of a universality that abstracts from difference is a mutation and persistence of a Christian project, wherein the material difference deemed religious is seen as a resistant remainder that must be overcome. In this schema, religious difference always doubles as historical difference, which, in this case, positions the Jews in particular as the backward remainder to a universalized history of mankind. In short, secular modernity retains the Christian structure of supersessionism. Indeed, the concrete power, persistent to this day, of Marx's question becomes obvious if this demand is seen as a broader instigation: "If you [Jews, but also Muslims] want to be politically emancipated without emancipating yourselves as humans, the incompleteness and the contradiction lies not in you but in the *nature* and the *category* of political emancipation" (226).[17]

For Marx, secular power works as a multifaceted apparatus of transcendent mediation generated by the general secular contradiction between civil society and the state.[18] But this secular contradiction enacts and materializes a structure of diremption, of the double life, originally articulated in a theological form in Christianity. With this diagnosis, Marx places the operation of mediation at the heart of the political theological problematic. "The state is the mediator [*Mittler*] between man and man's freedom. Just as Christ is the mediator to whom man attributes all his divinity, all his *religious bonds*, so the state is the mediator to which man transfers all his non-divinity, all his *human freedom*" (219; trans. modified). Here, Marx is concerned not with the way religion is constituted as a merely private affair under secular power but rather with the way religion—less as a generic category than as a second name for Christianity—operates as an apparatus of transcendence, diremption, and mediation that is secularized and persists in the form of the secular state. Religion in this case names not merely what is delimited and lodged within one side of the general secular contradiction (i.e., within civil society) but rather, in a way, the entire diremptive logic underlying the general secular contradiction.

At the heart of mediation for Marx is the exception—not the sovereign state of exception that suspends the law as a way to uphold it against the perceived threat of antinomian chaos but the exceptional apparatus of secularized eucharistic mediation. To understand how the exception operates, it is useful to turn to another of Marx's judgments: "Man in his *immediate* reality, in civil society, is a profane being" (220). Despite all its apparent immediacy, this figure of man is not a natural being but an "illusory phenomenon," a product of the secularized structure of diremption. It indicates the materialized terrestrial life severed not only from the celestial heavenly life but also from all that is not private, individuated, or appropriated, from all that is common, from what Marx terms species being. In fact, we might say that if the secular is the entire structure of diremption, the immediate reality, the earthly part of the secular contradiction is the profane. But this profane life does participate in the common life, in the secularized celestial life in the state: for the member of civil society, for the bourgeois, as Marx writes, "life in the state is nothing more than an appearance or a momentary exception" (220). Marx is here redeploying Bauer's words, but does so while replacing the subject—it is no longer the figure of the Jew, as the remainder to the universal, that lives or participates as an exception, but the figure of the bourgeois, the generic member of civil society (220). In other words, the exception is political life itself, which temporarily suspends the primacy of private (and privative) life, a kind of communion with the communal in excess of the "profane being" that makes up its (illusory, but actual) existence in civil society.

This secularized model of exceptional participation in the celestial community ultimately upholds life as fundamentally dirempted. "The sovereignty of man—but of man as an alien being distinct from actual man—is the fantasy, the dream, the postulate of Christianity, whereas in democracy it is a present and material reality, a secular maxim" (226). The Christian dream, along with the apparatus of external mediation that binds the earthly and the transcendent aspects of life, is secularized and actualized in the structure of modernity. But of course, the sovereignty this exception generates is a "fictitious sovereignty," as Marx writes, "divested of his real individual life and filled with an unreal universality" (220). So, the structure of mediational exception suspends the profane being, but does not abolish it, does not dissolve the structure that generates it. Rather, it temporarily suspends it only in order to perpetuate what it suspends all the more.

Mediational exception justifies itself by posing profane being and the state of diremption as natural and ineluctable—and then makes them livable, makes them meaningful. It provides an idealistic cadence, a taste of secularized heaven, of communal life, but it never challenges the naturalization of the unpolitical man "der *unpolitische* Mensch," the figure of the bourgeois, which appears as natural only as the result of the constitution of civil society as a realm severed from the state (233). More fundamentally, what Marx is diagnosing is a theologico-political apparatus of power that perpetuates itself by posing itself as necessary, naturalizing the general secular contradiction as an unsurpassable horizon of life itself. The function of mediation and the mediator is to stabilize external relations, rather than pushing the grammar toward dissolution. It offers a constrained participation, the necessary mechanism for the continual reproduction of the dirempted life. We might say that mediation is the modality in which transcendence is made livable and is lived.

This exceptional mediation arises not as a result of some anthropological givens but insofar as the secular state (the atheistic, democratic state in Marx's parlance) produces and maintains in its pure form what it presupposes—the existence of civil society and in it the "restricted individual, restricted to himself [*auf sich beschränkten Individuums*]" (229). It is not that depoliticized life has absconded from its existential duties (as Schmitt might have it), or that it has to be overcome and secured by sovereignty (as in Hobbes), but rather that civil society, "the sphere of egoism and of the *bellum omnium contra omnes*," is produced as such through a depoliticization that arises as the obverse side of the becoming autonomous of the state[19]—a materialization of the Christian division of the terrestrial and the celestial into "the secular division" (220–221).

So, the figure of the bourgeois is hardly a natural figure.[20] Its structure suggests something more. Parallel to Kantorowicz's thesis on the two bodies of the king, the figure or the bourgeois, despite all appearances, is itself not purely a secular figure but a political theological double: a profane and private individual that participates in the celestial species life as an exception, and only as an exception. That is, if with "the regicide, the gap closes between the king's two bodies,"[21] then perhaps a gap opens anew—less spectacularly, but no less tenaciously—in the unitary doublet of the egoistic individual/citizen.[22] The task, Marx's essay suggests, is not to mistake this structure for freedom, and instead to see in it a secularization of Christian life in order to open the path to its abolition.

On this account, the modern secular state marks not the inauguration of political theology of immanence but rather reveals itself as a mechanism of transcendent mediation. The significance of this comes to light if we recall that in formulating the problematic of political theology, Schmitt diagnosed the nineteenth century as the moment of the shift into a metaphysics of immanence, against which his particular orientation of political theology of the sovereign exception that suspends the law is formulated. Schmitt formulates this transition as follows: "To the conception of God in the seventeenth and eighteenth centuries belongs the idea of his transcendence vis-à-vis the world, just as to that period's philosophy of state belongs the notion of the transcendence of the sovereign vis-a-vis the state. Everything in the nineteenth century was increasingly governed by conceptions of immanence. All the identities that recur in the political ideas and in the state doctrines of the nineteenth century rest on such conceptions of immanence."[23] Marx's account disturbs this genealogical narration by demonstrating that what Schmitt will call immanence is itself a transcendent apparatus of mediation. There has *never been* immanence, but only a polemical conflation of mediation with immanence perpetrated from the perspective of sovereign transcendence. Indeed, reading Marx alongside but against Schmitt, we might say that uncovering the operation of the secular state as one of transcendent mediation allows Marx to shed light on one half of a single *katechonic* mechanism, the other side of which is the sovereign exception.[24] Transcendence as mediation and transcendence as sovereignty together form a single mechanism that prevents real immanence from irrupting, an immanence that would not be within the prevailing "order of the world [*Weltordnung*]."[25] What Schmitt, whose position begins to appear as a kind of rearguard action, diagnoses as the indecisive hesitancy of a flailing liberalism and its apolitical bourgeois subjects, becomes, on this account, the internal counterpart to his theory of sovereign dictatorial exception. Immediate transcendence might see itself as radically distinct from its meditational counterpart, but in relation to real immanence, the two operate as an ensemble.

Political theology can be used as a way to delegitimate the secular in the direction of the Christian, or it can be rejected to uphold the legitimacy of the secular—both of these maneuvers, however, render invisible (if not actively dissimulate) the single mechanism that unites Christianity and secularism into one theologico-political space.[26] In contrast to these prevailing positions, Marx diagnoses an apparatus of diremption, transcendence, and mediation operative in Christianity and, subsequently, materialized and secularized in the operations of the secular state. Mediation and transcendence do not belong exclusively on either side of the polemical divide between the Christian and the secular but are rather operative across it. Indeed, when Marx calls the existence of religion "a defect," religion in this instance should be understood as a name for a mechanism—like the state itself—of recognition by means of an intermediary, an inhabitation of a specular relation with transcendence (217–218). Moreover, the solution to this so-called defect is not found in the secular state (which is why Marx is no secularist), but in the abolition of the very binary between the secular and the religious, in the abolition of the general secular contradiction that constitutes modernity.[27] If Marx seeks the abolition of religion, he does so only as part of a more general abolition of secular power, the abolition of the order of the world in which the distinction between the secular and the religious is operative and dominant.[28]

What we have traced is a political theological diagnosis that undermines secular modernity's own self-authorizing and self-legitimating conceptual operations, without asserting either theological sources of legitimation and authority or sovereign-dictatorial ones. Marx's essay inaugurates a trajectory of thought that critiques the secular modern, by identifying its morphological and genetic entanglements with Christianity, disallowing them to claim each other as enemies, but without appealing to preexistent traditions—be they discursive, religious, or otherwise—as levers of critique.[29] We are faced with the question of what it might mean to challenge the secular frame without having recourse to a tradition or stable identity that might somehow be recovered from the violent impositions of political modernity. Indeed, by outlining the political theology of mediated transcendence, Marx asserts a structural analogy neither as a form of legitimation nor as a tragic impossibility but as an apparatus requiring delegitimation. For, it is the desire and drive for legitimation—of the modern age, the secular state, or a certain theological imaginary—that remains itself the problem. The drive to delegitimate the order of the world—along with its *katechonic* mechanisms of temporal distension, the temporalization and deferral that sustain the world across the political-theological domain—suggests a political-theological orientation toward dissolution and abolition rather than toward sovereignty or recovery. At hand is not preservation, recuperation, or reconstitution but the end of world and its determinate order. Rather than fearing lawlessness or *anomia*—as thinkers of order, Schmitt included, have always done—what must be challenged is the Christian-secular apparatus of the profanation and individuation of life and its ontological declaration that there is nothing but the self-enclosed individual, a position that legitimates, as Schmitt correctly pointed out, all of the punitive and salvific undertakings of theologians and politicians.[30]

Let me conclude with the conceptual element obviously kept in abeyance up to this point: human emancipation—the full emancipation Marx opposes to political emancipation—which would subvert rather than perpetuate the alienated, secularized structure of "a double life, a life in heaven and a life on earth" (220). For it is full human emancipation that indexes the breakdown of the general secular contradiction and the collapse of the order of the world—as opposed to political emancipation, which is "the last form of human emancipation *within* the prevailing *Weltordnung*" (221). In Marx's essay, the immanence that emerges with the collapse of the apparatus of mediated transcendence is correlated with the name of the human. But what assures us that what arises at the breakdown of the order of the world is the human, if not the dogmatic kernel of the specific secularization thesis that declares that at the end history stands the human in adequation of itself? If emancipation necessitates the dissolution of the world and its order, then how does the human remain, as it does in Marx's discourse, an obvious indexical and name? Perhaps, a genuine disruption of the political theological mechanism of dual transcendence, of mediation and sovereignty, might disclose a real immanence that no longer is allowed to carry the name of the human.

Much points toward the equivalence of immanence and the human in early Marx, and yet, there is a moment that points, however briefly, in a different direction. For, the necessity behind the breakdown of the order of the world, the delegitimation of the world as it is, arises not only because of the division between the state and the civil society but also because of an excess of dehumanization that occurs as the result of that structure. If, as Marx notes, "the rights of man" are nothing but those of civil society, there still remains the question of what is excluded even from this figure of "the restricted individual." The question of the human and political theology begins to be altered when we note that the figure of the proletariat emerges in the same issue of the *Deutsch-Französische Jahrbücher*, in the final passages of Marx's "Contribution to the Critique of Hegel's *Philosophy of Right*." There, it is presented as "a class of civil society which is not a class of civil society, a class which is the dissolution of all classes"—and, more fundamentally, "the *total loss* of humanity." This an immanent dissolution since it arises not from an ideal or a norm, but immediately from the truth of being: "When the proletariat proclaims the *dissolution of the existing world order*, it is only declaring the secret of its own existence, for it *is* the *actual* [*faktische*] dissolution of that order." The question is, then, if it is indeed a total loss of the world, its order, and the state-civil society divide that structures it, then on what grounds can that name, the name of the human, be retained? There is a movement from dehumanization that renders the human a profane being, to a further, total dehumanization of the wretched being. The split between the profane and the celestial is here complicated by this irrecuperable third. And if the secular is the worldly, then what undermines its coherence also might have to lie outside of the grammar of the human, which it has incessantly produced and reproduced. Yet Marx closes this trajectory as soon as he opens it, for the total loss of humanity is reinscribed into the normative horizon of the human: total loss leads to "the *total redemption of humanity*" and even more, it marks the proper opening onto the human, because this figure "can no longer lay claim to a *historical* title, but merely to a *human* one" (256). In light of the incorporation of the proletariat over the course of subsequent history into the fibers of civil society, a process that shows that one cannot retain the human while affirming total loss and deracination, it may be necessary to reopen the question of a radical immanence without the human. What would it mean to affirm the abolition of the prevailing order of the world from the perspective of that which is without tradition, from the position that does not belong except by and for delegitimation?

Notes

1. One of the more creative and original accounts that nevertheless positions political theology in this way is Victoria Kahn, *The Future of Illusion: Political Theology and Early Modern Texts* (Chicago: Chicago University Press, 2014).

2. For a general overview, see Yannik Thiem, "Schmittian Shadows and Contemporary Theological-Political Constellations," *Social Research: An International Quarterly* 80, no. 1 (2013): 1–32. Thiem does include Marx in the prehistory of political theology, albeit only cursorily.

3. Carl Schmitt, *Political Theology: Four Chapters on the Concept of Sovereignty* (Chicago: University of Chicago, 2005), 36.

4. Jan Assmann, *Herrschaft und Heil: Politische Theologie in Altägypten, Israel und Europa* (München: Carl Hanser Verlag, 2000). To draw on this definition does not require subscribing to Assmann's specific theses on the price of monotheism, *religio duplex*, or the Mosaic distinction.

5. The most powerful critique of the legitimation of modernity in relation to the question of secularization is found in Kathleen Davis, *Periodization and Sovereignty: How the Ideas of Feudalism and Secularization Govern the Politics of Time* (Philadelphia: University of Pennsylvania Press, 2008), 1–20 and 77–102.

6. Karl Marx, *Early Writings*, trans. Rodney Livingstone and Gregor Benton (London: Penguin Books, 1992), 223. Hereafter cited in text by page number in parentheses. For the German version, see *Karl Marx / Friedrich Engels Gesamtausgabe*, Bd. 1.2, *Werke, Artikel, Entwürfe: März 1843 bis August 1844* (Berlin: Dietz Verlag, 1982).

7. Roland Boer's multivolume work *On Marxism and Theology* offers a magisterial synthetic account of Marx's (and Marxism's) relation to theology. For elements that are especially relevant to this essay, see Roland Boer, *Criticism of Earth: On Marxism and Theology IV* (Chicago: Haymarket Books, 2012), 69–125.

8. Gil Anidjar, "Secularism," *Critical Inquiry* 33, no. 1 (2006): 52–77.

9. For a powerful political-theoretical reconstruction of Marx's discussion on rights, recognition, and the ruses of political or ideal emancipation as it relates to the liberal state, see Wendy Brown, *States of Injury: Power and Freedom in Late Modernity* (Princeton, NJ: Princeton University Press, 1995), 100–114.

10. For one example of such a position, see Jürgen Habermas, *An Awareness of What is Missing: Faith and Reason in a Post-secular Age* (Cambridge: Polity, 2010); for a critical diagnosis of this gesture see Joan Wallach Scott, *Sex and Secularism* (Princeton, NJ: Princeton University Press, 2018).

11. On secularism not only as a normative power but also as a questioning power, one that repeatedly invests with significance the very boundary dividing the religious from the secular, see Hussein Ali Agrama, *Questioning Secularism: Islam, Sovereignty, and the Rule of Law in Modern Egypt* (Chicago: University of Chicago, 2012).

12. See, for example, Talal Asad, *Genealogies of Religion: Discipline and Reasons of Power in Christianity and Islam* (Baltimore, MD: Johns Hopkins University Press, 1993); Talal Asad, *Formations of the Secular: Christianity, Islam, Modernity* (Stanford, CA: Stanford University Press, 2003).

13. In this, I take Marx's claim to be fully in line with, for example, Asad's assessment that "the constitution of the modern state required the forcible redefinition of religion as belief, and of religious belief, sentiment, and identity as personal matters that belong to the new emerging space of private (as opposed to public) life" (*Genealogies of Religion*, 205).

14. Taking this into account, I do not think it is quite fair to say, as Saba Mahmood does, that Marx carries a "conception of religion as distorted belief." *Religious Difference in a Secular Age: A Minority Report* (Princeton, NJ: Princeton

University Press, 2015), 15. On the one hand, Marx offers a critical analysis of the modern concept of religion as it is imbricated in the general secular contradiction, while on the other hand, as will be explored more fully in what follows, he elaborates a complex understanding of the relation between Christianity and the state centered on the interplay of transcendence and mediation.

15. Asad, *Formations of the Secular*, 1–17.

16. A version of this narration is recounted by Tomoko Masuzawa, *The Invention of World Religions: Or, How European Universalism Was Preserved in the Language of Pluralism* (Chicago: Chicago University Press, 2005).

17. For a complex analysis in which the position of the Muslim is produced as a problem by secular power in the contemporary moment, see Mayanthi L. Fernando, *The Republic Unsettled: Muslim French and the Contradictions of Secularism* (Durham, NC: Duke University Press, 2014). Fernando's book enacts in the contemporary moment for the Muslim French what Marx suggests doing in the case of nineteenth-century Jews: "Only the critique of *political emancipation itself* would constitute a definitive critique of the Jewish question itself and its true resolution into 'the general question of the age'" (215). For a more complex genealogical history that complicates this point of convergence, see Gil Anidjar, *The Jew, the Arab: A History of the Enemy* (Stanford, CA: Stanford University Press, 2003).

18. Asad also formulates secularism as an apparatus of transcendent mediation (and not of immanence): "In an important sense, this transcendent mediation *is* secularism. Secularism . . . is an enactment by which a *political medium* (representation of citizenship) redefines and transcends particular and differentiating practices of the self that are articulated through class, gender, and religion" (*Formations of the Secular*, 5).

19. For an astute exploration of the way in which Marx's elaboration of the state as productive of civil society undermines the claim that civil society is the theater of all history, see Wendy Brown, *Politics Out of History* (Princeton, NJ: Princeton University Press, 2001), 88.

20. Wendy Brown notes that Marx is here offering "a political genealogy of the sovereign individual" (*Politics*, 112).

21. Rebecca Comay, *Mourning Sickness: Hegel and the French Revolution* (Stanford, CA: Stanford University Press, 2011), 39.

22. This then implies a different political theological trajectory of royal remains than the one centered on the flesh elaborated in Eric Santner, *The Royal Remains: The People's Two Bodies and the Endgames of Sovereignty* (Chicago: University of Chicago Press, 2011).

23. Schmitt, *Political Theology*, 49.

24. For a polemical analysis of Schmitt's deployment of the *katechon*, see Jacob Taubes, *The Political Theology of Paul*, trans. Dana Hollander (Stanford, CA: Stanford University Press, 2004), 97–113.

25. That Marx speaks of the order of the world is rendered invisible in the English rendering of *Weltordnung* as "scheme of things" (221).

26. There is also, of course, the position, espoused first by Erik Peterson, that there is no possible Christian political theology; however, as Nicholas Heron makes clear, this is because it entails an explicitly Christian modality of power—liturgical power—and defends an altogether different (Christian) vision of politics. Nicholas Heron, *Liturgical Power: Between Economic and Political Theology* (New York: Fordham University Press, 2017).

27. For the way the secular and the religious are played off each other by philosophers and theologians, see Alex Dubilet, *The Self-Emptying Subject: Kenosis and Immanence, Medieval to Modern* (New York: Fordham University Press, 2018). On the way that this polemical divide is produced by secular power, see Agrama, *Questioning Secularism*.

28. It is worth noting that Marx states that this *cannot* be accomplished through a forceful abolition of religion by the state, through the kind of revolutionary secularism that is frequently attributed to Marx and the Marxist tradition. This is clear from his discussion of revolutionary moments, such as the French Revolution, in which "the state can and must proceed to the *abolition of religion*, to the *destruction* of religion" as part of a broader process in which "political life attempts to suppress its presupposition, civil society and its elements" (222). Yet, such attempts are self-subverting—for civil society is presupposed by the state as part of the general secular contradiction—leading first to an impossible permanent revolution against the state's own presuppositions, and then, in the end, in the restoration of all elements of civil society (222). This is the logic of the state *in extremis*, of the general secular contradiction taken to its political crescendo—but it does not inaugurate the dissolution of the order of the world. Marx's analysis here is another argument against understanding him as a radical secularist: for Marx, the task is neither for the state to manage religion as something privatized, nor for the state to abolish it by force. Rather, the task is the subversion of the entire foundational secular division between the state and civil society.

29. Recent critiques of the secular have frequently been imbricated with theorizations of alternative traditions. For Islam as discursive tradition in this line of thought, see Talal Asad, "The Idea of an Anthropology of Islam," *Qui Parle* 17, no. 2 (2000): 1–30; and Saba Mahmood, *Politics of Piety: The Islamic Revival and the Feminist Subject* (Princeton, NJ: Princeton University Press, 2005), 113–117.

30. See Carl Schmitt, *The Concept of the Political*, trans. George Schwab (Chicago: Chicago University Press, 1996), 64–65.

Contributors

Joseph Albernaz is assistant professor of English and comparative literature at Columbia University. He is currently working on a book about conceptions of community in Romanticism, tentatively entitled *All Things Common*.

Daniel C. Barber is assistant professor of philosophy and religious studies at Pace University. He is the author of *On Diaspora: Christianity, Religion, and Secularity* (Cascade, 2011) and *Deleuze and the Naming of God: Post-Secularism and the Future of Immanence* (Edinburgh University Press, 2014).

Agata Bielik-Robson is professor of Jewish studies in the Department of Theology and Religious Studies at the University of Nottingham. She is the author of *The Saving Lie: Harold Bloom and Deconstruction* (Northwestern University Press, 2011), *Jewish Cryptotheologies of Late Modernity: Philosophical Marranos* (Routledge, 2014), and *Another Finitude: Messianic Vitalism and Philosophy* (Bloomsbury, 2019).

Kirill Chepurin is senior lecturer in philosophy at HSE University, Moscow. He is the author of *Filosofskaya Antropologiya Gegelya* (Философская антропология Гегеля; SGT Press, 2012).

S. D. Chrostowska is professor of humanities at York University, Toronto. She is the author of *Literature on Trial: The Emergence of Critical Discourse* *in Germany, Poland, and Russia, 1700–1800* (University of Toronto Press, 2012) and *Matches: A Light Book* (Punctum, 2015, 2nd enl. ed. 2019), and coeditor of *Political Uses of Utopia: New Marxist, Anarchist, and Radical Democratic Perspectives* (Columbia University Press, 2017).

Saitya Brata Das is associate professor in the School of Language, Literature, and Culture Studies at Jawaharlal Nehru University, New Delhi. He is the author of *The Political Theology of Schelling* (Edinburgh University Press, 2016) and coeditor of *The Weight of Violence: Religion, Language, Politics* (Oxford University Press, 2015).

Alex Dubilet is assistant professor of English at Vanderbilt University. He is the author of *The Self-Emptying Subject: Kenosis and Immanence, Medieval to Modern* (Fordham University Press, 2018) and cotranslator (with Jessie Hock) of François Laruelle's *General Theory of Victims* (Polity, 2015) and *A Biography of Ordinary Man: On Authorities and Minorities* (Polity, 2018).

Vincent Lloyd is associate professor of theology and religious studies at Villanova University. He is the author of *The Problem with Grace: Reconfiguring Political Theology* (Stanford University Press, 2011), *Black Natural Law* (Oxford University Press, 2016), *Religion of the Field Negro: On Black Secularism and Black Theology* (Fordham University Press, 2017), and *In Defense of Charisma* (Columbia University Press, 2018).

Thomas Lynch is senior lecturer in philosophy of religion at the University of Chichester. He is the author of *Apocalyptic Political Theology: Hegel, Taubes and Malabou* (Bloomsbury, 2019).

James Martel is professor of political science at San Francisco State University. He is the author of *Divine Violence: Walter Benjamin and the Eschatology of Sovereignty* (Routledge, 2011), *The One and Only Law: Walter Benjamin and the Second Commandment* (University of Michigan Press, 2014), and *The Misinterpellated Subject* (Duke University Press, 2017).

Steven Shakespeare is associate professor of philosophy at Liverpool Hope University. He is the author of *Kierkegaard, Language and the Reality of God* (Ashgate, 2001), *Derrida and Theology* (T&T Clark, 2009), and *Kierkegaard and the Refusal of Transcendence* (Palgrave Macmillan, 2015).

Oxana Timofeeva is professor of philosophy at the European University at St. Petersburg. She is the author of *History of Animals: An Essay on Negativity, Immanence and Freedom* (Bloomsbury, 2018).

Daniel Whistler is reader in modern European philosophy at Royal Holloway, University of London. He is coauthor of *The Schelling-Eschenmayer Controversy, 1801: Nature and Identity* (Edinburgh University Press, 2020) and the author of *Schelling's Theory of Symbolic Language: Forming the System of Identity* (Oxford University Press, 2013), as well as coeditor of *The Schelling Reader* (Bloomsbury, 2020).

Index

abolition, 22, 59–60, 236, 241, 245, 249–252
absolute, 14, 18–20, 26, 37–44, 62–64, 91, 135–136, 147, 156, 161, 183, 190–191, 198, 201, 212–214, 216, 232–233. *See also* God; infinite
abstraction, 23, 58 87–103, 115, 148, 178–179, 234–235, 246
actuality, actual, 13, 20, 24, 38, 48, 150, 180, 209, 216, 236–237, 252; actuality without potentiality, 207–213, 217–219
actualization, 7, 13, 24, 27–28, 43, 46, 49, 162, 169, 248
Adorno, Theodor, 65, 92
aesthetic, aesthetics, 56–58, 61, 64, 110, 168, 198
Africa, 162; in Hegel, 25–26, 176–185; in Schelling, 27
Afropessimism, 35–36
Agamben, Giorgio, 4, 128
Agrama, Hussein Ali, 6
a-Hegelian, 88–90
alienation, 2, 13–14, 16, 20, 37, 42, 195, 204n13, 205n31
analogy, 2, 66, 109, 130, 210–214, 219, 241–243, 250

anarchy, an-archy, anarchic, 17, 58–59, 63–64, 106, 120–121, 145–147, 210
Angelus Silesius, 197–199
Anidjar, Gil, 32n30, 243
annihilation, annihilate, 18–22, 26, 35–51, 93, 112, 119, 121, 154, 194, 213, 219. *See also* nothingness; nullity; void
annulment. *See* nullity
anomia, 251
Anthropocene, 44, 126, 138
antinomian, 188, 213, 247
apocalyptic, apocalypticism, apocalyptics, 2, 5, 9–10, 19, 22, 35, 62, 73–86, 148–149, 194, 210, 217
appropriation, 17, 124–132, 137, 216, 225, 247. *See also* enclosure
arché, 207–208, 211, 218–219
Aristotle, 217, 226–227
Armstrong, Amaryah, 168
Asad, Talal, 6, 89, 161, 245, 253n13, 254n18
Assmann, Jan, 241
atemporality, 38, 43
atheism, atheistic, 15, 32n33, 88–90, 93, 97, 99–100, 188–190, 193–194, 202, 242, 248. *See also* secular; secularity
atheization, 188–200

261

a/theologization, 189–191
Aufhebung. See sublation

Badiou, Alain, 5, 88, 94, 154, 168–170
Bauer, Bruno, 241–242, 245–247
beatitude, 24, 211–212, 219. *See also* bliss
beauty, beautiful, 43, 47, 56–57, 64, 114, 118, 147
Benjamin, Walter, 2, 5, 17, 56, 65–68, 119–121, 189, 201, 210, 217–219
blackness, 8, 26, 31n17, 35, 69n3, 86n18, 126, 140n9, 168, 174, 174–187
Blanchot, Maurice, 88, 91–92
bliss, 14, 17, 19–21, 26–8, 38–43, 50.
    See also beatitude; heaven
Bloch, Ernst, 56, 65, 68, 188, 209, 218
Blumenberg, Hans, 2–6, 9, 11, 24, 188
de Boer, Karin, 165
Böhme, Jacob, 199, 213, 221n15
bourgeois, 60, 66, 68, 156, 247–250.
    See also individual
Bouteldja, Houria, 169
Breton, Stanislas, 214
Brown, Wendy, 253n9

capital, 90–91, 94, 100
catastrophe, catastrophic event, 143n44, 148, 193, 202
causa sui, 197, 199
chaos, chaotic, 17, 19–20, 26, 35, 46–50, 75–76, 220n7, 247. *See also* collapse; disorder
Chiesa, Lorenzo, 153
Christ, Christology, 17, 79–80, 148, 168, 214, 218–219, 234, 247
Christianity, Christian, 2–33, 64–66, 79, 85n10, 86n11, 93, 98, 117–119, 125–126, 139n8, 147, 181–184, 189–191, 230, 233, 236–237, 242–250; deconstruction of, 191–193; Epimetheus, 56, 66–68; and Europe, 26–28, 125, 215, 234, 244; faith, 14, 57, 64; and Hegel, 12–13, 23, 88, 160–165, 181, 194–197, 201; and modernity/modern world, 2–5, 9, 12–17, 23–28, 36, 51; political theology, 79, 182, 246–250; and the secular, 3–4, 11, 22, 26, 241–242, 249–251,

254n14; and the state, 22, 242–249; and universality, 22, 167–170, 244.
    See also *kenosis*; supersessionism
citizen, citizen-subject, citizenship, 6, 22, 60, 89, 160, 162, 166–167, 230, 243–244, 246, 249, 254n18
civil society, 22, 242, 243–252. *See also* general secular contradiction
coherence, 8–9, 129, 252
collapse, 17, 20, 22–23, 39, 47, 49, 76–80, 83–84, 137, 141n21, 181, 215, 251.
    See also chaos; destitution; ruin
colonial, coloniality, colonialism, 7–8, 12–13, 17, 27, 44, 89, 126, 138, 139n4, 142n44, 168
colonization, 125, 137
Comay, Rebecca, 87, 149, 153, 156, 249
common, commons, 10, 17, 41–42, 124, 129–139, 142n37, 143n46, 211, 247
communion, 247
communism, 139
community, 5, 12, 14, 59, 63–64, 115, 145, 157, 160, 162–167, 175–176, 180–184, 191, 216, 225, 230, 236, 248; "concrete order and community," 125, 131
conditioned and unconditioned, 19, 96, 100, 154, 211, 228–232
conditions of possibility, 7, 21, 36, 42, 44–46, 49–50, 89, 95–100, 124
construction, 9, 19, 21, 26, 35–51
contingency, contingent, 2, 26, 35–37, 42–43, 125, 177–178, 185, 230
creation, 2, 66, 136, 149, 192, 196–201, 211, 226; and decreation, 19, 48; out of nothing, 48, 190–191
criticism, 49, 63, 244, 246. *See also* critique
critique, critical, 74–75, 81, 224, 240–245, 251; and German Idealism, 13–16, 48, 210; and political theology, 3–4, 218, 241–245; postsecular, 89, 100; of secularism, 98, 161; and utopia, 54–64, 68
cross, 98, 145–150, 195, 197, 201–203, 214
Crowther, Paul, 107–111, 114, 118

da Silva, Denise Ferreira, 10, 138
dance, 144, 147, 150, 157

death, 87–88, 94, 98, 144, 147, 156–157, 176, 179, 181, 198–199, 223, 226
death drive, 151, 194
death of God, 19, 24, 32n33, 144–157, 188–206, 214. *See also* sacrifice
debt, 25, 66, 192–194, 198–202. *See also* gift; guilt; sacrifice
decision, 9, 21, 74–77, 81, 83, 91, 128, 184, 189, 208, 210, 213, 224, 226, 231, 233, 236–237
decolonial, 7, 142n44
deconstruction, deconstructive, 28, 50–51, 189, 200–201, 208, 215, 218; of Christianity, 193, 197; of the world, 28, 37, 48
decreation, 19, 48
deferral, 11, 15, 68, 180, 248, 251. *See also* not-yet; postponement
delegitimation, 2–6, 16, 24, 208, 219, 241, 250–252. *See also* justification; legitimation
Deleuze, Gilles, 88, 91
deracination, 252
Derrida, Jacques, 24, 90, 93, 184, 188–206, 220
desire, 9, 35, 154–155, 174–84, 214, 228, 242; utopian, 54–55, 58–62
despotism, despotic, 26, 60, 151, 155, 181
destitution, destitute, 10, 17, 23, 50, 95, 100, 130–133, 137, 139, 214, 219. *See also* annihilation; collapse; ruin
determination, 37–38, 108, 115, 119, 161, 225–228, 237, 251; and Schelling, 231–232
deus absconditus, 189
dialectic, dialectical, 13, 25, 55–56, 59–62, 64–66, 82, 87, 90, 93, 96, 148, 157, 160, 165–167, 174–5, 184–185, 192, 216, 224, 232–233, 236, 242, 244; the nondialectical and the refusal of the dialectic, 14, 24–26, 87–100, 176. *See also* Hegel; mediation
difference, 19, 25, 42, 88, 93–94, 126, 168–170, 175, 178, 182, 195, 211, 225–226, 246; religious, 22–23, 167–170, 245–246
diremption, dirempted life, 16, 22, 126, 130, 196, 242–243, 247–248, 250
dis-enclosure, 137, 191. *See also* common

disorder, disorganization, 47, 127, 131, 133, 140n18, 152, 161. *See also* catastrophe; chaos; collapse; ruin
dispossession, 10, 37
dissolution, 18, 22, 27, 64, 127, 131, 134, 135, 137, 247, 251–252, 255n28
divestment, 80, 84, 86n18, 216, 243, 248
divine, divinity. *See* God
division, divide, 8–9, 17–22, 27, 36–44, 47–49, 79–80, 84, 86n19, 104, 124–143, 224, 249, 251, 252, 255n28; Christian-secular, 11, 169, 246, 250; subject-object, 20, 37, 224. *See also* diremption; enclosure; separation
Dolar, Mladen, 148–151
domination, 8–10, 14, 16, 26–28, 61–63, 116, 152, 185, 215–216, 236
Dussel, Enrique, 176

earth, 8, 10–11, 17, 26, 106, 112–113, 124–143, 146, 211–214, 248; heaven and, 22, 243, 247, 251
Eckhart, Meister, 10, 211–212, 219
ecological crisis, ecology, 126, 132–133, 137–138
Eden. *See* paradise
Ein-Sof, 190, 186
emancipation, emancipatory, 25, 54, 58–68; human, 251; political, 243–246, 254n17
emptying out, emptiness, 24, 156, 204n16, 205n17, 208, 212. See also *kenosis*
enclosure, 7, 17, 124–139. *See also* common
enjoyment, 19, 116, 144–156, 191
Enlightenment, 1–2, 4, 10, 12, 15–16, 28, 30n15, 58, 64–66, 89, 119, 145, 153–156; critique of religion, 4, 142
enthusiasm, 113–115, 199
Epimetheus, Epimethean, 55–56, 65–68
equality, 57, 60–61, 167
Esposito, Roberto, 4–5
eschatological, eschatology, *eschaton*, 2–3, 13, 46, 54, 56–59, 64–66, 68, 72, 86n19, 91–92, 120, 207–220; and beatitude, 211; and delegitimation, 208; event, 211–212, 218; Kierkegaardian, 218; paralysis, 68; secularization of, 2, 63

Index ■ 263

ethics, ethical, 9, 13–14, 35, 57, 98, 144–145, 151–152, 176, 184; ethical life, 13, 157, 162, 165
event, 42, 64, 66, 125, 148, 157, 202–203, 208, 211–212, 216–220; of the gift, 192–195
exclusion, excluded, 7–9, 28, 35–36, 96, 166–169, 180, 242, 251
exception, 22, 128, 183–184, 219–220, 247–250; and mediation, 247–248; without sovereignty, 207–212, 218; state of, 4, 60, 247
excess, 114, 124, 212, 217, 247, 251
exhaustion, 27, 223
expression, abstract, 90–92
exteriority, 5, 26, 176–178, 184–185, 207

faith, 3, 13–15, 18, 20, 30n15, 57, 62–64, 92, 98
fall, fallen, 126, 198, 213–215
Fernando, Mayanthi, 166, 254n17
Fichte, J. G., 13–15, 18–21, 26–27, 45–49, 88, 128–129; on abstraction and negation, 92–97; on God, 45; on modernity and Christianity, 13–14; on the *ought* of the world, 45–46
finitude, 19, 24, 37, 41, 189, 191, 196, 202; refusal of, 20–21
fire, 44, 182, 192–197, 213, 219
foreclosure, 5, 8–10, 14–17, 22, 25–28, 35, 39, 45–46, 50, 153–154, 156, 208, 224, 233
Foucault, Michel, 5
Frank, Manfred, 232–233
freedom, 218, 7–8, 12–14, 56–57, 61–64, 106, 115, 146, 150, 162–163, 169, 183–185, 201, 213–214, 218–219, 228, 235, 241, 247, 249; absolute, 37–40, 59, 144, 156–157; of religion, 95, 160, 245; sublime, 209
French Revolution. *See* revolution
future, futurity, 7–8, 11, 14, 21, 38–41, 44, 54–69, 76, 120, 180, 184, 204n16, 211, 217, 226, 231; of political theology, 28, 36, 137, 139, 202–203; and transcendence, 7, 17, 19. *See also* not-yet

Gabriel, Markus, 231
gap, 19, 25, 39, 41, 46, 153, 224–237, 249
Geist. *See* spirit
Gelassenheit, 199–200, 211–212
genealogy, 1, 11–16, 28, 202, 240, 245, 249
general secular contradiction, 22, 244–248, 250–251, 255n28
German Romanticism. *See* Romanticism
gift, 191–195, 197–201, 212, 219; gift without sacrifice, 24, 192, 193. *See also* debt; sacrifice; *tsimtsum*
Gilroy, Paul, 186n7
globe, global, 8, 125, 126, 130, 139, 182
Gnosticism, Gnostic, Gnosis, 9–10, 80, 133, 136, 146, 213, 218
goal, 7, 27, 37–41, 206n31, 226. *See also* telos
God, 2, 10, 14–15, 18, 27, 41, 45, 51, 51n4, 79–81, 98, 126–128, 135–137, 181–185, 197–199, 211–215, 219, 229, 236, 247, 249; as contingent, 42–44; death of, 19, 24, 32n33, 93–94, 144–157, 188–206, 214; departure of, 127, 131–132, 137; Hegel's conception of, 13, 55, 162, 178–179, 189–190, 199; and love, 44, 63, 213; naming of, 78–81; and world, 22, 78–82. *See also* death of God; *kenosis*; Kingdom of God; *tsimtsum*
Godhead, 63, 190, 211–212, 219
good, goodness, 56, 128, 160, 200, 229; abstract, 155; and evil, 180, 219
grace, 5, 118, 211, 225
graven image. *See* idolatry
groundless, groundlessness, 19, 78, 131–132, 138, 209, 213, 217. *See also* ungrounding
guilt, 14, 191–192, 198–202. *See also* debt; gift; sacrifice
Günderrode, Karoline von, 17, 126–127, 133–139

Hallward, Peter, 94
happiness, 19, 56, 61, 149, 229. *See also* bliss; morality
Harnack, Adolf von, 9
Harney, Stefano, 32n29, 124, 135, 138

haunting, 35, 42, 49, 114–115, 117, 169, 209
heaven, 22, 57, 111, 180–181, 243, 247–248, 251. *See also* bliss; earth; paradise
Hegel, G. W. F., 12–13, 17, 19, 21–26, 32–34, 49, 51–52, 55, 58–65, 69n3, 70n16, 73–74, 81–83, 87–88, 93, 95, 99–100, 125–130, 140nn9,17, 144–157, 160–170, 174–203, 208–220, 223, 233; on abstraction, 87, 92–93, 95, 103n39, 161, 165, 168–169, 178–179, 186–187; on Africa, 25–6, 176–185; on conversion, 165, 181; critique of irony, 49; on freedom, religion, and the state, 63, 161–166; on French Revolution, 87–88, 144–146, 155–156; Hegel's philosophy as Christian, 13, 23–24, 88, 160–170, 189–197, 201, 203; on joy at the end of the world, 19, 147–148, 157; on modernity and Christianity, 13, 126; *Phenomenology of Spirit*, 30n14, 52n32, 81, 87–88, 147, 149, 154–156, 162, 173n43, 174, 186n7, 191, 194; *Philosophy of Right*, 65, 144–147, 160–162, 167, 252; rejection of, 22–24, 82, 89–90, 175–176; on "religion of flowers," 24, 197–201; on the tragic, 165; on world-history, 13, 24–26, 169, 176–178, 184. *See also* dialectic; mediation
hegemony, hegemonic, 83, 86n19, 88, 207–208, 211, 215, 219
Heidegger, Martin, 193, 199, 209, 212, 219–220
Hickman, Jared, 31n16, 69n3, 176–177, 182–184, 187n30
hierarchy, 7, 13, 27, 30n16, 57, 106, 125, 137, 162, 168, 170, 179, 199, 224, 233
Hinduism, 134, 169
history, 27–28, 55–69, 98–100, 201–202; end of, 24, 27, 54–59, 149, 191, 251–252; in Hegel, 160–162, 169, 174–185, 194–195, 198, 209–210; historical transfer of concepts, 2, 240–241; philosophy of, 12–14, 21, 26, 62–65; and political theology, 11; and theodicy, 207–208, 213, 218–219; universal, 59, 65, 68, 233–234, 246; world-history, 12–13, 24–27, 49, 51n4, 125, 213–215, 218. *See also* genealogy; progress; spiral; theodicy
Hobbes, Thomas, 6, 11, 28n1, 248
Hölderlin, Friedrich, 17, 88, 91, 126–139, 145
holy man, holy, 43, 49, 128, 191
human, humanity, 7–8, 23, 27, 30n16, 42, 56–69, 79, 93, 104, 106, 116, 121, 128, 162–163, 175, 178–183, 225, 227, 231, 235–236, 244, 246–247, 251–252
humiliation, 107–108, 116
Hyppolite, Jean, 7

idolatry, idol, 113, 115, 132
illusion, illusory, 8, 41–42, 109, 242, 247–252; world as, 8, 35–39, 43–44, 46
imagination, 51, 54, 57, 62, 79, 107, 113–116; apocalyptic, 73, 76–77, 80–83, 85n12
immanence, 5–11, 14, 16–31, 38, 41–43, 48, 241, 249–252; atheistic and worldly, 190, 202; of the common, 130; and earth, 134–136; and expression, 226, 237; Hegelian, 183–184, 207–210, 215–217, 220; plane of, 179, 213; political theology, 5–11, 249–251; radical, 9–10, 17, 28, 38
immediacy, immediate, 26, 22, 23, 88, 94–95, 99, 128, 178–179, 182–183, 202, 247, 250
imperative, 40, 63, 77, 81–84, 136, 144, 149–153, 174, 200. *See also* moral
incarnation, incarnational, 57, 67, 79, 196. *See also* Christ; *kenosis*
indifference, indifferent, 10–11, 19–20, 23, 43–44, 47–48, 81, 88–100, 109, 130, 149, 161, 167–170, 194, 198, 200. *See also* neutral; Schelling
individual, individuality, individuation, 13, 57, 90, 134, 236, 155–157, 162–163, 181, 196, 198, 234–235, 243, 247–249, 251
infinite, 20, 47, 109–115, 209, 212–213, 216, 232–233; relation to the finite, 189–201, 212

injustice, 61, 136
innocence, 180, 193, 198, 199, 201
inseparability, 85n10, 129, 133, 135, 155
irony, 47, 49–50
Islam, 79, 113, 134, 166–169, 246

Jacobi, Friedrich, 15, 18–20
Jacobin. *See* Reign of Terror
Jean Paul, 18, 20
Jewish: apocalypticism, 2, 80; apocalypticism and Christianity, 234, 236, 246; law, 63, 113; messianism, 189; modernity, 190; mysticism, 68, 206n31; people, 113, 233; question, 245, 254n17; tradition, 24. *See also* Judaism; Marx: "On the Jewish Question"; supersessionism
Joachim of Fiore, 13
Judaism, 25, 66, 79, 162, 196, 226, 230, 233, 235–237. *See also* Jewish
judgment, 17, 93, 107, 110, 128–130; reflective, 107–108, 114
justification, 8–9, 11, 13, 35–51, 63, 77, 125, 162, 197. *See also* delegitimation; legitimation; theodicy

kabbalah, kabbalistic, 189–190, 199, 206n31, 213, 218
Kahn, Victoria, 3, 252n1
Kant, Immanuel, 15–20, 25, 36, 46–47, 56, 60–61, 63, 104–121, 125, 144, 150–157, 223–226, 228–235. *See also* transcendental
Kantorowicz, Ernst, 249
katechon, katechontic, 66–68, 210, 249, 251
kenosis, 11, 13, 24, 191–197, 201, 204nn13,16, 206n31, 208, 211, 211, 219. *See also* emptying out; gift; sacrifice
Kierkegaard, Søren, 25, 209, 218, 223–226, 234–237
Kingdom of God, 64, 72n47
Koselleck, Reinhart, 58
Kuiken, Kir, 131, 141n21

Lacan, Jacques, 32n33, 144, 151–154
laïcité, 93

Laruelle, François, 8–11, 32n29, 36–37, 44, 224, 237
Lautsi v. Italy, 95–99
law, 63–65, 132, 142n37, 161, 165, 183–184, 208–211, 217–219, 230–231, 247, 249, 251; moral, 40, 105–108, 111–115, 119, 144, 150–156, 229; in contrast to *nomos*, 127. *See also nomos*
legitimation, legitimacy, 2–11, 14, 21–24, 35, 42–43, 67–68, 128, 131, 162–166, 207 210, 214–215, 219, 240–242, 250–252. *See also* delegitimation; justification; theodicy
Levinas, Emmanuel, 176, 184
liberal, liberalism, 3–4, 22, 160–166, 170, 240–241, 246, 250
life, 4–5, 7, 10, 25–26, 63–65, 112, 134, 178–179, 212, 233–237, 248; as Christian, 234–235, 247–249; common, 135–137; and death, 147–148, 198–199, 226; dirempted, 22, 243, 248; divine, 27, 136; double, 243, 247, 251; earthly, 146, 243, 247, 251; ethical, 13, 157, 162, 165; finite, 201–202; form of, 89; material, 243–247; in relation to unlife, 25, 226, 233–235; in Schelling, 233; secular, 164. *See also* unlife
Lilla, Mark, 3, 68
locality, 126–127, 131, 133
longing, 14, 38, 61, 134–137
loop, 39, 54–57, 62, 65–66. *See also* spiral
love, 44, 63–64, 136, 179, 181, 196, 212–213, 236
Löwith, Karl, 2, 59, 63, 66, 145, 147, 188
Luria, Isaac, 24, 189–193, 196, 199, 201, 203n5. *See also tsimtsum*
Luther, Lutheran, 13, 190, 201, 204n13

magic, magician, 179, 182, 186n18
Mahmood, Saba, 89, 97, 161, 164, 253n14
Malabou, Catherine, 5, 149, 204n16
Marin, Louis, 88–90, 93
Marquard, Odo, 51n4
Marx, Karl, 12, 21–22, 49, 56, 61–62, 65–66, 68, 195, 202, 240–255; and political theology, 240–247; "On the Jewish Question," 22, 61, 240, 245

materialism, materialist, 26, 55–56, 66–68, 92, 104–107, 108–111, 117–120, 230
materiality, material, 11, 17, 19, 46, 48, 111–121, 243–248
measure, 38, 75, 79, 83, 125, 133, 146, 216
mediation, mediator, 11, 14, 20–23, 26, 36–41, 43, 46–8, 85n11, 91, 127–135, 145, 162, 179, 241, 244, 247–249; transcendent, 6–7, 22, 26, 247–251, 254n18. *See also* dialectic
Meillassoux, Quentin, 35–36, 42
melancholia, 149, 154, 156, 213
Menon, Madhavi, 168–170
messianicity, messiah, messianism, 5, 17, 25, 35, 54–68, 106–107, 119–121, 189, 199–202, 218
Milbank, John, 104–105, 118
modernity, modern world, 2–17, 21–24, 26–31, 36, 42, 48, 55, 58, 68, 188–193, 197–200, 207–210, 218–220, 240–246, 250; the Christian-modern, 9, 11–17, 22–24, 26–28, 33, 36; modern state, 59, 62, 64, 162, 240–245, 249, 253n13. *See also* secular
monotheism, 57–58, 80, 138, 212
moral, morality, 19, 37, 41, 63, 68, 109–110, 193, 196, 215, 229–233; agent/agency, 43, 56, 227–228; law, 40, 105–108, 111–115, 119, 144, 150–156, 229. *See also* happiness
Moten, Fred, 10, 32n29, 124, 135, 138
mourning, 148, 189, 201
Muslims: *see* Islam
myth, mythic, mythology, 54–58, 61, 64, 67, 136, 142n36, 181–182, 201, 208, 210–212, 217–219

Nancy, Jean-Luc, 35, 133, 189, 191, 193
negation, 14, 23, 38–40, 45, 61, 63, 88–99, 169, 180, 188, 216–218, 231–232, 242; double, 87, 147, 194, 204n16
negativity, 10, 14–15, 19, 22, 36–40, 48, 51, 65, 80, 85n18, 87, 115, 148, 174, 191, 216
Negri, Antonio, 5, 205n19
Nesbitt, Nick, 169

neutral, neutrality, 1, 48, 89–100, 161, 164–167, 170, 242–246. *See also* indifference
new, newness, novelty, 6, 19, 54, 57, 131, 138, 157, 169, 175, 189–190
Neyrat, Frédéric, 138, 141n21, 143n46
Nietzsche, Friedrich, 104–106, 118–121, 188, 193, 200, 209
nihilism, 15, 17–19, 104–107, 118, 219
nomos, 124–138, 211–213, 219. *See also* law
nonbeing, 130, 148, 213–214. *See also* nothingness; void
noneschatological, 91
nonplace, no-place, 38, 45, 52n22, 58, 91, 100, 125, 231. *See also* utopia
nonproductivity, 19, 27
non-will, 18
nothingness, 11, 16, 18–20, 28, 35–51, 77, 113, 115, 121, 133, 149, 190, 193; affirmation of, 8, 18, 20, 50; blackness and, 8, 31n17; dispossessed, 10; immanent, 20, 27; and the world, 14, 18–20, 26, 35, 50. *See also* annihilation; chaos; nonbeing; nullity; void
not-yet, 2, 7, 14, 16, 26, 28, 41, 43–46, 49, 76. *See also* deferral; postponement
noumenal, 104–105, 111
now, 15, 17, 22, 38–41, 82–83, 100, 147, 202; now-time, 66
nullity, nullification, 23, 63, 93, 192, 194, 200, 202, 233–234

ontotheology, 191, 212, 216, 226
operativity, 43, 241, 250; and inoperativity, 28
ordinary, 17, 106–107, 111, 113, 119–121, 146
organism, 135, 233
other, otherness, 7, 38, 45, 82, 151–154, 156–157, 166, 176, 190, 195–196, 202, 230
ought, 45–46, 155
Owl of Minerva, 13, 19, 145–146, 148

paradise, 54, 180–184. *See also* bliss; heaven
Paul, Pauline, 5, 11, 14, 94, 136, 168, 170, 208, 211, 213–214, 219
personality, 95, 111–112

phenomenal, phenomenalization, 104–110, 115–118, 121, 151, 154, 207–209, 212–213, 219, 245, 247
Pindar, 127–128
Plato, Platonic, 15, 54, 56, 69n3, 71n28, 190, 209, 211–212, 220
pleasure, pleasure principle, 63, 104, 107–108, 116, 118, 149, 151, 154–155
Plotinus, 212
poetry, poetic, poet, 48–50, 56–58, 64, 131–134
political, 2–6, 65, 78, 106, 136, 211, 226, 240–243. *See also* state
political theology, 1–5, 9–28, 36–37, 50, 63, 68, 73–83, 126, 132, 181–185, 188–191, 200–202, 210–220, 223, 236–237, 240–252; of earth, 131, 137–138; future of, 28, 36, 137, 139, 202–203; Gnostic, 9–10; and Hegel, 160–162, 165, 167, 177, 182; negative, 208, 211; utopian, 55–8, 68, 72, 230
polytheism, 57–58
possibility, possible, 2, 7–8, 11, 14, 16–24, 27–28, 35–51, 77–84, 89, 95–100, 202, 208, 213, 236. *See also* conditions of possibility
postapocalyptic, 19, 35, 145, 149
postponement, 2, 19, 36–41. *See also* deferral; not-yet
potentiality, 24, 45, 49, 76–77, 207–219
potestas, 212–214, 219
private, 162, 243, 245, 247, 249, 253n13
production, productivity, 7, 18, 43, 48, 75, 244–245. *See also* nonproductivity
profanation, profane, 165, 210, 214–215, 247–252
progress, 7, 16, 27–28, 41, 43, 58–59, 62, 66–68, 177, 198. *See also* history
proletariat, 65, 252
Prometheus, Promethean, 55, 65, 67–68, 69n3, 71n28, 182–183
providence, providential, 4, 30n15, 59. *See also* theodicy
psychosis, 144, 152–154, 157
pure means, 120–121

race, racialization, 8, 27, 137, 140n9
radical evil, 212–213

Real, 8–11, 17, 19, 21 36–42, 44, 46–7, 50, 144, 153–154, 212, 223–225, 229, 235–237
reason, 2, 54, 58, 64–65, 89, 104–105, 114–115, 119, 144–157, 178–179, 228–231; principle of, 200, 219; speculative, 56, 193, 201; without, 199–200. *See also* groundlessness; without a why
reconciliation, 14, 15, 142n36, 144–147, 149–150, 175–178, 223
recuperation, 25–26, 57, 226, 236–237, 251
redemption, 2, 8, 59, 67–68, 107, 193, 198, 200, 202, 204n16, 208, 214, 216, 223, 252
redoubling, 45, 225–226, 234–238. *See also* reduplication
reduplication, 25, 223–238. *See also* gap
reflection, reflexivity, 25, 28, 41, 44, 63–65, 192–193, 224–227, 237; reflective judgement, 107–108
refusal. *See* world: refusal of
regulative, 61, 228–230, 235
Reign of Terror, 60, 87–88, 95, 100, 144–145, 153, 155–156
relation, relationality, 18–21, 36–43, 73–86, 89, 94, 188, 195, 225–226, 243–243, 250
religion: abolition of, 250, 255n28; to come, 215–216; critique of, 4, 242; death of God, 189–195, 200; and eschatology, 211–212; religious difference, 94, 167–170, 245–246; on Hegel, Africa, and, 174–175, 179; legitimate and illegitimate, 22–23, 161–163; and modernist secular, 89–98; modernity and, 12, 244–247, 254n14; and morality, 229–230; new, 54, 57–58, 62–64; philosophy of, 12, 88, 194–195; and politics, 60, 144; return of, 15; revealed, 148, 218; and the state, 161–167, 241–247, 250. *See also* Christianity; Judaism; secular; secularism
"religion of flowers," 24, 197–198, 200–201
religious minorities, 160–167
remediation, 13, 21, 23, 40–41. *See also* mediation

268 ▪ Index

respect, 98, 107–108
restlessness, 189–190, 197, 199
resurrection, resurrective, 76, 147–148, 195, 202, 205n17
retroactivity, 148–149
revelation, revealed, 13, 214, 218, 230, 237
revolution, revolutionary, 12, 19, 25, 48, 55–57, 60–68, 87–88, 131, 144–147, 153, 155–156, 168, 255n28
Robertson, Lisa, 49
Romanticism, Romantic, 17–18, 25, 46, 48–50, 52n32, 64–65, 68, 69n7, 127, 131, 133, 136
rose, 146–147, 150, 197–198
Rosenzweig, Franz, 56, 65, 209, 218, 220
Ruda, Frank, 53n32, 149
ruin, ruination, 17–19, 127, 131–134, 137, 148–149, 156

sacrifice, 24, 189, 191–202. *See also* death of God; debt; gift; guilt
Sade, Marquis de, 144, 151–157
salvation, salvific, 5, 17, 21, 30n15, 38, 66, 106–107, 119, 233, 251
Schein. See illusion
Schelling, F. W. J., 13–27, 33nn34,37, 37–45, 49, 58, 65, 69n1, 88, 96–100, 128–129, 133, 137, 140nn17,20, 145, 203n5, 207–220, 223–224, 226, 231–235, 239n31; on the absolute, 14, 18–20, 38–40, 212–213, 232–233; on absolute freedom and beatitude or bliss, 37–39, 41–43, 211–212, 219; on abstraction, 58, 96–97; against Hegel, 23–24, 87–88, 95, 100, 208–220; on identity, 38–40, 215, 232–233; identity philosophy, Schelling's, and 1801 *Presentation of My System*, 41, 58, 96, 231–233; indifference (Schellingian), 23, 43, 88, 96–100; *kenosis* (Schellingian), 24, 208, 211–212, 219; on modernity, 14–15, 208, 219; on morality, 37, 40–41, 43, 215, 233; on nothingness, 19–20, 37–41; on the organism, 233; positive and negative philosophy, Schelling's, 207, 216; secular (Schellingian), 97–98; on *thatness* and *whatness*, 216; on the utopic, 23, 39, 58; on the will that wills nothing, 18; on world-history, racialization, and supersession, 27, 233–234, 239n26. *See also* bliss; indifference; unprethinkable
Schlegel, Friedrich, 19, 21, 46–50; on chaos and nothingness, 47–49; on poetry, 48–49; on revolution, 48. *See also* chaos; irony
Schleiermacher, Friedrich, 13, 15
Schmitt, Carl, 1–6, 9, 11, 17, 21–22, 25, 28n1, 56, 65–68, 68, 73–85, 183–184, 188–189, 191, 201, 208–213, 218, 230, 241, 248–251; *The* Nomos *of the Earth*, 124–133, 138
Scholem, Gershom, 189–190, 196, 200, 203n5, 210
Schürmann, Reiner, 207, 211
secular, 2–6, 9–11, 14–15, 22–23, 161–170, 241–255; modernist, 87–101; and religious binary, 4, 9–11, 14–16, 25–26, 169, 246–250
secularity, 4–6, 11–12, 88–100
secularism, 6–7, 11, 15, 16, 23, 88, 95–98, 160–166, 243–246, 250, 254n18, 255n28
secularization, 2–4, 8, 15, 22–23, 55, 62, 68, 87–88, 100, 164–167, 210, 240–244, 247–251; thesis, 2, 15, 99–100, 188–189, 251
segregation, 17, 124–139. *See also* division; separation
Sehnsucht. See longing
self-assertion, 2, 7, 24, 29n3, 30n16, 38, 182–183, 187n19. *See also* Blumenberg, Hans
self-organization, 30n15
separation, 6–8, 20, 36, 115, 124, 127–138, 182, 196, 213, 215, 243
Sexton, Jared, 35, 138
slave, slavery, enslaved, 7–8, 27, 60, 86n18, 138, 142n41, 166, 183–184, 237; dialectics of master and, 155, 186n7
socialism, socialist, 58, 66, 72n47
solitude, 19, 92, 145, 156–157
soul, 39–40, 43, 113–114, 147, 150, 175

Index ▪ *269*

sovereignty, sovereign, 1–11, 17–18, 21–28, 37, 60, 73–86, 128, 177, 181–185, 188–193, 200–201, 208–219, 236–237, 240–241, 244, 247–251. *See also* Schmitt, Carl; transcendence
species being, species life, 247–249
speculation, speculative thought, 10–15, 21, 38–40, 50, 55–56, 61, 104, 193, 195, 201, 206n31
Spinoza, Spinozism, 5, 11, 18, 20, 149, 231
spiral, 25, 55–56, 59–68. *See also* loop
spirit, 56–64, 117, 134, 139n6, 162; and flesh, 126, 234–237; Hegelian, 24, 26, 30n14, 49, 55, 145–147, 155–157, 164, 178–185, 191, 195–198, 201; and letter, 213, 230, 233, 237; no spiritual investment, 5, 73, 76, 83–86
state: and Christianity, 12, 22–23, 162–165, 242–250; modern, 2, 6–7, 12–14, 22–23, 27, 55–56, 59, 60–64, 68, 97, 240–255; and religion, 160–167, 244–252; and Schelling, 214–216. *See also* political; political theology
striving, 14, 18, 27, 36, 39–43, 228–231, 234–235. *See also* longing
subject, subjectivity, 4, 7–8, 10, 16–21, 23–26, 32n29, 36–42, 46–47, 50, 56, 91–92, 96, 99, 107, 114, 120–121, 129, 148–154, 156, 158n15, 161, 178, 182, 184–185, 192, 194, 196–197, 200, 207, 209, 220n1, 223–227, 231–237, 245–246; autonomy of, 156; in bliss, 38; bourgeois, 250; collective, 84; divine, 197; modern, 7–8, 12–14, 16, 24, 28, 31n17, 36, 42, 99; and predicate, 96, 226–227, 232–233; redoubled or reduplicated, 226, 231, 234, 237; secular, 99; spectral, 196; of striving, 38; and subjection, 7, 11, 18, 202, 237; from substance to subject, 148–149, 192, 194, 196; transcendental, 23, 38, 152, 224. *See also* citizen-subject; division; self-assertion; subject-object; world: and subject
sublation, 13, 21, 23, 58, 155, 194
sublime, 104–123, 189, 198, 201, 209
submission, 63, 105, 150

subtraction; subtract, 212–213, 241–242
supersensible, 104–121, 229
supersessionism, 25, 63, 120, 226, 230, 234–236, 246
suspension, 20, 39, 45, 47–49, 75, 92–93, 96, 109, 183, 210–211, 217–219, 231, 247–249
synthesis, 15–16, 19–20 36–37, 54, 62, 64
system, 39, 45–46, 56–57, 108, 111, 174–178, 181, 184, 209, 217, 228, 234–235; "system of the world," 39
Szondi, Peter, 165–166

Taubes, Jacob, 2, 5, 9, 11, 22, 63, 68, 73–77, 83–86, 188, 208, 210–211, 220n7
Taylor, Charles, 6, 99–100, 188
telos, telic, 7, 24, 28, 38, 41, 44, 46, 49, 55, 59, 63–66, 97, 180, 217. *See also* goal
temporality, temporalization, 7, 15, 39, 41, 43, 58, 62, 67, 76, 91, 251
Terror. *See* Reign of Terror
theodicy, theodical, 9, 24, 27, 36, 49, 51n4, 207–210, 213, 215–220. *See also* justification; legitimation; world: justification of
theology. *See* Christianity
tolerance, toleration, 22, 89, 90, 94, 98, 110, 160–170
topos, 2, 48, 125, 139n2; and atopos, 151–152
totality, 24, 26–27, 35, 37, 45, 74, 129, 134–138, 178, 212
tragedy, tragic, 132, 165, 172n32, 195, 201
transcendence, transcendent, 2–10, 14–22, 25, 30n15, 31n16, 38, 44, 57–58, 63, 93, 104, 106, 153, 183–184, 207–220, 224–226, 233, 236–237, 238n5, 240–242, 244, 247–251; divine or theological, 14, 44, 118, 128, 210, 241, 244; future, transcendent, 7, 19; horizontal, 7; interplay of secular and religious, 5–6, 10, 58, 240–252; pure or radical, 9, 23–4, 207, 209–210, 217; self-transcending, process of, 7; and world, 6–10

transcendental, 17, 35–51, 99–100, 106, 117, 119, 152, 156, 187n20, 202, 224, 232; destitution or ungrounding of, 23, 42, 46, 95–100; illusion, 8; imagination, 80; immune, 95–97; knot, 21, 35–51
tsimtsum, 11, 24, 190–201, 206n31

unconditioned. *See* conditioned and unconditioned
undercommons, 10, 32n29
ungrounding, unground, 5, 10–11, 14, 17, 19–20, 26, 28, 36, 42, 45–47, 79, 210. *See also* delegitimation; groundless
understanding (*Verstand*), 46, 93, 107, 224, 228
universal, universality, 11–13, 17, 20–23, 25, 28, 42, 58, 89, 94, 99, 108, 124–139, 155, 160–170, 182, 244, 246–248; concrete and abstract universal, 93–96, 129–130, 161–170; universal history, 65, 68, 233–234, 246
universalism, 160–173; indifferent, 168; negative, 167–170
univocity, *univocatio entis*, 190–192, 197, 199, 207, 209
unlife, 25, 226, 235
unprethinkable (*Unvordenkliche*), 208–209, 211, 213, 217, 232. *See also* Schelling
utopia, utopian, utopic, 7, 11, 19, 23, 25, 27, 32n32, 36, 39, 46, 52n22, 54–72, 87–100, 145, 151, 157, 202, 229–231; desire, 55, 58, 60–61; futurity, 7, 62; immanence, 11, 27, 32n32; loop, 39; space and time, 100; *we*, 157. *See also* nonplace; political theology, utopian
Urteil. *See* judgment

vanishing: corpses, 87; moment, 230, 235; object, 111; reality, 149; truth, 82
Vico, Giambattista, 59, 70n11
violence, 23, 27, 43–44, 89, 96, 116, 171n20, 214, 216–218; appropriative, 132, 137, 216; divine, 5, 44, 213, 218; mythic, 217–218; secular, 88–89, 95
virtue, 43, 64, 136, 155, 160, 229
voice, 92, 144, 146, 149–154, 156–157
void, 18–21, 48, 190. *See also* annihilation; nothingness; nullity

without a why (*ohne warum*), 10, 197, 200
world, 2–11, 14, 16–28, 35–51, 57–58, 61, 73–86, 91–92, 105, 111–112, 117–121, 126–139, 146, 148–149, 155–156, 174, 176, 178–181, 183–184, 189–192, 197–199, 208, 212–215, 217–219, 226, 229–230, 232, 237, 246, 251–252; annihilation of, 18–22, 26, 28, 33n36, 35–52, 86n18, 213; as colonial settlement, 44; construction of, 9, 19, 21, 26, 28, 35–51, 223–224; end of, 2, 35, 37, 40–41, 45–46, 49, 80, 86n18, 145, 148–149, 214, 251; faith or spiritual investment in, 14, 18–20, 30n15, 49, 73, 76, 80, 83–84; justification, legitimation, or delegitimation of, 2, 5, 8–10, 13, 19, 24, 26–28, 36–37, 41–43, 45–46, 49–50, 77–78, 215, 224, 242, 251; "night of the world," 190; order of, 22, 74, 208, 211–213, 219, 241, 249–252, 254n25, 255n28; refusal of, 10, 18–20, 22, 24, 28, 37, 41–43, 73–76, 81, 215; reproduction of, 7, 16, 18–19, 41, 43, 47, 50, 129; and sovereignty, 9, 73–83, 236; and subject, 7–8, 10, 16, 18–21, 24–25, 36–42, 50, 129, 223–237; as transcendent, 6–10; *Why must the world be?*, 36, 39, 40, 77, 80–83; worldly and spiritual, 64, 83–84, 86n19
world, modern. *See* modernity
Wynter, Sylvia, 7, 126, 140n9

zero, zero degree, zero point, 8, 26, 28, 38, 48, 50, 90, 149. *See also* nullity; void
Žižek, Slavoj, 5, 32n33, 189, 226

Perspectives in Continental Philosophy
John D. Caputo, series editor

Recent titles:

Kirill Chepurin and Alex Dubilet, eds., *Nothing Absolute: German Idealism and the Question of Political Theology*

John D. Caputo, *In Search of Radical Theology: Expositions, Explorations, Exhortations*

Galen A. Johnson, Mauro Carbone, and Emmanuel de Saint Aubert, *Merleau-Ponty's Poetics: Figurations of Literature and Philosophy*

Ole Jakob Løland, *Pauline Ugliness: Jacob Taubes and the Turn to Paul.*

Marika Rose, *A Theology of Failure: Žižek against Christian Innocence.*

Marc Crépon, *Murderous Consent: On the Accommodation of Violent Death.* Translated by Michael Loriaux and Jacob Levi, Foreword by James Martel

Emmanuel Falque, *The Guide to Gethsemane: Anxiety, Suffering, and Death.* Translated by George Hughes.

Emmanuel Alloa, *Resistance of the Sensible World: An Introduction to Merleau-Ponty.* Translated by Jane Marie Todd. Foreword by Renaud Barbaras.

Françoise Dastur, *Questions of Phenomenology: Language, Alterity, Temporality, Finitude.* Translated by Robert Vallier.

Jean-Luc Marion, *Believing in Order to See: On the Rationality of Revelation and the Irrationality of Some Believers.* Translated by Christina M. Gschwandtner.

Adam Y. Wells, ed., *Phenomenologies of Scripture.*

An Yountae, *The Decolonial Abyss: Mysticism and Cosmopolitics from the Ruins.*

Jean Wahl, *Transcendence and the Concrete: Selected Writings.* Edited and with an Introduction by Alan D. Schrift and Ian Alexander Moore.

Colby Dickinson, *Words Fail: Theology, Poetry, and the Challenge of Representation.*

Emmanuel Falque, *The Wedding Feast of the Lamb: Eros, the Body, and the Eucharist.* Translated by George Hughes.

Emmanuel Falque, *Crossing the Rubicon: The Borderlands of Philosophy and Theology.* Translated by Reuben Shank. Introduction by Matthew Farley.

Colby Dickinson and Stéphane Symons (eds.), *Walter Benjamin and Theology.*

Don Ihde, *Husserl's Missing Technologies.*

William S. Allen, *Aesthetics of Negativity: Blanchot, Adorno, and Autonomy.*

Jeremy Biles and Kent L. Brintnall, eds., *Georges Bataille and the Study of Religion.*

Tarek R. Dika and W. Chris Hackett, *Quiet Powers of the Possible: Interviews in Contemporary French Phenomenology.* Foreword by Richard Kearney.

Richard Kearney and Brian Treanor, eds., *Carnal Hermeneutics.*

A complete list of titles is available at http://fordhampress.com.

www.ingramcontent.com/pod-product-compliance
Lightning Source LLC
Chambersburg PA
CBHW030436300426
44112CB00009B/1029